A Humanistic Approach to Teaching Secondary School English

HELEN C. LEE
Associate Professor of Education
Indiana University at Fort Wayne

CHARLES E. MERRILL PUBLISHING COMPANY
A Bell & Howell Company   Columbus, Ohio

Published by
Charles E. Merrill Publishing Company
A Bell & Howell Company
Columbus, Ohio 43216

Library of Congress Catalog Card Number: 73-75506
International Standard Book Number: 0-675-08942-5

1 2 3 4 5 6 7 8 9 10—77 76 75 74 73

Preface

The methods course builds a bridge between what the prospective teacher has learned from courses in literature, language and writing and what he must do in his own classes when he becomes a teacher of English. A methods course cannot afford to spend the limited time available to reteach these aspects of English. In this book the activities at the end of each section of the chapter on reading, for instance, provide examples of ways to build these bridges for each genre. Rather than dictating directions for teaching genre, echoing college courses in literature, the text indicates the questions that must be resolved by each teacher who teaches each genre and suggests ways the prospective teacher may begin a search for his own philosophy of answers.

Paradoxes that exist are admitted to exist, and there is no attempt to make easy resolutions of these questions, resolutions which might disillusion the teacher who tries to use them. Most important questions have answers which vary with each teacher and which he must spend a professional lifetime, amid many fads and phases of literary fashion, resolving and developing. The book does not try to find for the teacher what he can find only by his own search, but it tries to indicate fruitful lines of inquiry and ways to be comfortable in that search.

Units of material are well-arranged in texts available to most teachers of English. Well-stocked libraries and class sets of paperbacks are found in more and more schools. But this growing abundance of materials has not helped great numbers of high school students who do not grow satisfactorily in their language proficiency and their love for the things they can do with language.

Nor can the methods student be greatly concerned with an extensive paraphernalia of scholarly references to research and bibliographies, few of which he has time to read or use. Or if he does absorb himself in these materials, he is probably doing the kind of learning that only minimally helps him to be effective in the classroom—just accumulating information. A torrent of research in the last two decades and a proliferation of methods courses based on it have changed teaching in English classrooms surprisingly little.

An effective methods course must deal primarily with what the teacher is to do with materials, how he can exhibit the kinds of teacher behavior learning theory tells him he should exhibit, and how he can elicit from students the kind of behavior learning theorists have said constitutes learning. The beginning teacher who does less well in his early years of teaching than he and his employers hope he will do is not usually handicapped as much by his lack of information about subject matter or by his lack of materials as by his lack of ability to do what he has to do and be what he has to be to be effective.

The humanistic activities described in this book are designed to improve what the methods student will do in his classes, to give him insight into the results of his own behavior. He must by guided to design for himself and his students kinds of behavior that will lead him to the results he wants. The humanistic curriculum manifests a primary concern, not with materials or content, but with those who will use ideas and content, the students of the prospective teacher. The humanistic teacher is committed to the belief that his primary materials come walking in the classroom door and sit in the seats of his classroom. His students' own use of language as they read, listen, write and speak constitute his materials for the teaching of English. The teacher's means of eliciting this language is the way he "handles materials" in his class.

The methods teacher is here invited to engage in his own research and adduce his own proofs about the way language learning is achieved. Each activity helps the prospective teacher see how a particular aspect of the teaching of English fits into the humanistic approach. It accustoms the methods student who has focused four years of academic preparation on materials to think first of what the materials will do for the student and only second what the student will do with the materials. The learning the student actually achieves, the changing of his behavior, not for the teacher or the present, but for himself and forever, is the aim of the experience. Through reading the activities and performing whatever of them they have time to do, methods students become accustomed to this approach, which differs from the way many of them will, themselves, have been taught in high school and college courses. As a pattern of multiple designs for learning, the activities key the way the prospective teacher can translate the understandings he has gained in his subject matter courses into ways to teach his own students.

It would be inconsistent to write a humanistic text whose intent is to persuade the reader to follow humanistic patterns which pay respect to the ideas and feelings of all involved in the teaching-learning experience and make the major part of the presentation in a form which the text opposes. Hence, this book indicates briefly the theorectical constructs of humanistic approaches to each aspect of English, but, more importantly, it illustrates practical designs for humanistic learning, which teach each aspect of the language arts and which draw the student, through reading or actual performance, into participation in those methods. The heart of the program for the prospective teacher is the activities which he will gain confidence in as he reads and performs them. The experiences and the debriefing questions cause him to practice the behavior and the methodology he needs to learn to be a humanistic teacher within the content area of English. Learning is not expected to happen because of information given but from involvement of the student with activities.

Beginning teachers teach, not as they have been told and trained to teach, but as they have been taught. Are they to believe what methods teachers tell them about teaching or what methods teachers themselves obviously have faith in, as evidenced by the way those methods teachers themselves teach their students? A methods course must model the methods it advocates. If methods students are to become teacher humanists, with a large repertoire of learning designs at their command, they themselves must be taught humanistically, with a wide variety of learning designs. This book provides an abundance of such designs for learning English, humanistically planned, which prospective teachers can choose to do and see their classmates do and which they can easily translate into learning designs for their students.

Of course, not every student can do every activity, nor can he see every activity being done, except in a very large methods class, but each methods student should read every activity design. These should be considered, not as exercises at the end of a chapter, but as part of the text, since they give insight into a wide variety of approaches. In these activities, information is presented in the interrogative mode, to engage students in developing their own questioning strategies that will improve the language proficiency of their students.

By questions, the activities in the learning designs are debriefed. Directive and explanatory statements should be minimized in humanistic teaching, since they pay insufficient respect to the ideas of the reader. The interrogative mode, on the other hand, continually and actively involves the reader in producing his own ideas and in judging them. Even when activities are read rather than performed, they draw the reader into a dialogue. They stimulate him to arrive at his own generalizations, his own explicatory statements, appropriate to his own level of insight and growth, statements which often lead him to ask new questions of himself and lead to new learnings. Methods students become accustomed to the vocabulary and rhetoric they will need to use with students when they make their own learning designs. Kinds of teacher and student talk are investigated and explored in many of the contexts teachers use in their own classes. By experiencing these activities prospective teachers learn to have faith in methods that may differ greatly from ways they themselves have been taught.

Because each activity in the book is a learning mini-package, containing behavioral objectives in promise and product, these activities help teachers who have to develop learning packages in their first years of teaching. Other parts of learning packages, generating student involvement in activities and debriefing that involvement with a variety of questioning strategies is also provided. Experienced teachers also can start their "open classroom" patterns with the activities as springboards for creating a variety of learning designs. Consultants and graduate programs concerned with this kind of teacher activity might well use this text for in-service programs for teachers who want to make practical change without excessive expense, new equipment, rearrangement of school facilities or discomfort for other teachers in a system who do not wish to change.

It cannot be stressed too much that doing the activities is the most powerful learning procedure, far exceeding in effect reading or talking about the activities.

Contents

I

THE HUMANISTIC ACTIVITY CURRICULUM DEFINED

CHAPTER I

Rationale for the Activity Curriculum

THE NEED

Because the rate and nature of change itself has accelerated, the future crowds every facet of students' lives. One-fourth of the people who have ever lived are alive today. Ninety percent of all scientists who have ever lived live now. The amount of technical information available doubles every ten years. One hundred thousand magazines are published in sixty languages, and the number has doubled in the last ten years. To attain a world population of ten million took eight million years. But, from 1925 to 1965, that population grew from two to three billion. Population sociologists project that ninety percent of all Americans will live in three cities in less than ten years.

Students now in English classes will live half their lives in the twenty-first century. Half the words they read, half the words they listen to, half the words they speak, half the words they write, they will read, listen to, speak and write in the twenty-first century. Just as our own teachers could not foresee the needs of our lives, we cannot foresee our students' needs. As our needs are different from what they might have been foreseen to be, their needs will be even more different, for the pace of change keeps accelerating.

Because of the rush of change, students move through narrow and frightening paths in this uneasy age. For life in such a world, memorization of facts is an inadequate education. Accepted facts of one decade become outgrown misconceptions in the next. So, a student in an English class, no less than one in a science or social studies class, must learn to locate problems, invent questions about them, collect data, and formulate and test hypotheses as scientists and historians do. He must learn how such thinkers work and learn to do his work as they do theirs. To accept and memorize their research will not meet his needs in a life that he will live mostly in the twenty-first century, where knowledge itself will bring less security than will habits and skills of seeking knowledge. What has been useful in the past is not useful now and will be even less so in the future, but as long as parents, communities, teachers, and administrators think it is, children will be educated for a world that no longer exists. Education in the English class must cease to be delivery service for packaged learnings and assume responsibility for becoming a laboratory devoted to experimental discovery of new dimensions of experience. English education must institute a search for patterns in experience and principles of organization which have universal application.

The student gets a slow return for the investment he puts into education if the teacher insists that the greatest value the classroom can offer is to prepare him for the future. The concept of deferred satisfaction, a cherished middle class value, is being called in question even by those who have lived by it. For many in our society it has failed to produce a good life, and some who have invested in it in the form of education, especially higher education, have found it a false god, resulting in neither reliable vocational opportunity nor appropriate life style. Students must examine and select their own purposes. The teacher will find that many are abandoning the idea of goals. Deeply involved with the life of their times, they find goals irrelevant, for these refer to the future with which they are not concerned. For them education cannot be a preparation for life, since they are living now. They reason that effective education must mimic the life situations for which it prepares the student.

Learning should be a joyous part of living. The explosion of knowledge has made it impossible to continue the practice of merely passing information to students. The role of a student is to be a student all his life. This he learns to do as he enjoys enquiring, analyzing and questioning. Indoctrinating the student with an elaborate set of fixed beliefs ensures his early obsolescence. If he enjoys developing and exercising skills, habits, and attitudes and the kind of knowledge and understanding that are the instruments of continuous change and growth, he is sage in examining and selecting whatever goals he needs. He will learn what his real goals are and adopt new ways of reaching them when old ways do not work. He will safely live in the future and joyously live in the present. He is the student for whom the activity curriculum is prepared.

Hence, although English education presents difficulties related to the speed of today's change, it also presents opportunities. These will emerge as English teachers cultivate the habit of creative change, a habit of looking forward for inspiration, not back. Teachers must suspend judgments and conclusions while they discover successful procedures by trying a wide range of methods. New curricula may cause them uneasiness. Beginning teachers will find it necessary to stop looking backward to the ways they were taught, and experienced teachers will have to open their professional selves to innovation. Teachers who reject innovation and revere tradition are often more discomfited by the threat to their comfortable habits than disturbed by the effect of change on the learning of their students. But some traditions can survive only when subjected to change and evolution. The public school and schooling itself are endangered by a multitude of attacks. It is to the survival of English education within the setting of schools as we know them and to the teachers who will direct that survival that this curriculum is directed.

Specialists in the English curriculum have developed sequences and materials intended for each grade level and for students of varying abilities. A deplorable example, now abandoned by most publishers, is the traditional "grammar" book, a largely useless compendium of thinly-disguised repetitions in different colored bindings for each year of grades seven through twelve. The most important characteristic of any group of learners is how different they are from each other; hence, grade levels and materials arbitrarily assigned to them embody myths of little validity, usually invented for purposes of administrative or financial expediency. Much of what is taught as appropriate for one spot in the curriculum could be taught in some form elsewhere in the curriculum just as usefully.

Increasingly, materials are being developed for the teaching of English without assignment to particular grade or level. These exist in gratifying abundance. Most beginning or experienced teachers find a good variety of such useful materials in their schools. The problem of the teacher today is usually not in obtaining materials, but in using them successfully.

During the sixties designers of English materials supposed that success in teaching literature depended on a knowledge and use of literary criticism. Hence, many English textbooks, methods textbooks, monographs and professional magazine articles analyzed literary selections and language, designed materials for certain kinds of students such as ethnic groups or slow learners, and drew together vast bibliographical apparatuses. All these materials are useful, and the teacher of English will want to amass a large stock of them. But more such books are not the need of this hour.

Activities

Just as lecture is an inadequate way to teach, asking a teacher or a prospective teacher to learn how to use a method of teaching from reading a statement about teaching is not as effective as having that teacher go through the learning process that is required. A teacher who is going to use the activity curriculum cannot understand how to do it from reading about it. The activities that will appear throughout the text are designed to overcome this drawback to a book about teaching.

GETTING IT SETTLED: PUTTING HOOKS INTO TRUTH

3 Hours   *5 People*

If ideas you thought were true and settled forever, get unsettled when you learn new information, you may find this activity helpful in keeping up with your changing world.

Ask four other people in your class to join you in forming a group. Meet to think about and discuss these questions: Have you learned anything new in the past five years that has made you change an opinion? What? Judging from what you hear and see in newspapers and on television, have public values and attitudes changed in the past five years? In what ways? What have you noticed about values concerning sex, smoking, pollution, violence, drugs, war, minority rights, women's role in society, labor and management relations, domestic virtues, child rearing and education, money, styles of dress, and health? Are there several of these changes that people in your group feel strongly about— that you agree with, disagree with, or do not understand?

Each person should choose one change he feels strongly about. He should design a survey—a list of questions—on the topic to find out more about it and how other people feel about it. Each group member should then ask his questions of at least ten other people, the more and the greater variety of people the better. You may want to try a man-on-the-street approach, or you may decide upon a more sheltered situation, asking your questions within the school or among friends and family. You may want to avoid questions that are too personal. If you do not get the kind of responses you had expected, you may need to revise either your questions or your expectations.

Return to your group and report on what you have discovered to the other members. Discuss the problems that you encountered and the various ways you overcame them. List the ways the different people you talked to reacted to change. Collect your group's findings as a result of their surveys and bind them together in a cover. Include in the collection an introductory statement about what you were trying to accomplish and a conclusion about what you learned. In your conclusion be sure to tell about your own feelings and changes in ideas—both before and after this experience.

DICK, JANE AND TENNYSON: RATE YOUR READING

1 hour   *1 person*

To help students choose and use reading materials which satisfy their needs, whatever the designated grade level, examine the levels of difficulty in your own reading.

Make a list of all the things you read during the day, whether from the back of a cereal box or technical textbook. Arrange your items along one edge of a piece of paper in order of the difficulty of the reading. If you aren't certain about how to rank every item, here is a test you can use to find out which ones are easiest and hardest for you to read. Get a stop watch. Pick out a typical passage from each type of material you want to rank. Decide upon a fixed number of words, perhaps 50, and mark a passage from each selection containing exactly that many words. Silently read each passage and time your reading. Usually, the easier it is for you, the faster you will read it.

Think about these questions: Did you know all the words in the materials at the easy end of the list? What about the harder selections? Does the length of a typical sentence change as you move from the easy to the hard materials? In which passages are the sentences longer? What does that do to your reading? What about punctuation? Do the ideas get more complicated too? What kinds of ideas are dealt with in the easy selections? How do the ideas change as you move to the harder ones? For what purpose do you read these different materials? What does each one do for you? Make a second column on your paper, and beside each of the items you listed according to difficulty, write the purpose or purposes of each kind of reading in your life.

Try to imagine what your life would be like if you could only read materials of one level of difficulty. Imagine all your traffic signs and cereal boxes written in four and five syllable words. Imagine needing to refer to a dictionary to read the instructions on the wall of the laundromat, or the automatic car wash. On the other hand, how would you feel about reading a novel with no sentences longer than ten words?

Write a summary of your conclusions about levels of difficulty in reading and post your summary and list on the bulletin board so that others may share your thoughts.

SMART COOKIE: GIVE YOUR CLASS A GRAMMAR TEST
1 and ½ hours   *1 person and the whole class*

If you would like to find out how much of the grammar students learn in high school they will remember in college, do this.

Find a grammar book. You may want to choose one of the traditional kinds or a more modern structural or transformational one. Or you may want to combine ideas from several books. There are usually exercises and questions at the ends of the chapters in such books. Use these exercises to help you devise a test for your class. You may want to give your test orally, write exercises on the blackboard or make a worksheet for your classmates to follow. Limit your test to 10 minutes of class time because you will need to arrange with the teacher and other class members to have the attention of the whole class for that time. Try not to let your classmates know what you are going to do.

Give your grammar test. Check the papers, or have the class members do it for the numbers of right and wrong answers. Record the results in your log. How much and what kinds of knowledge do college students remember about the grammar they had year after year in grade school and high school? Why? How did your classmates feel about the test you gave them? How did they feel about themselves? How many high school students go on to college? How much will the ones who did not do as well in school remember about grammar?

Write your conclusions and personal comments in your log.

SURVIVAL KIT: GETTING ON TOP OF THE WORLD
2 to 3 hours   *6 people*

Are success and the good life things you can make happen? Here is a way to investigate this problem.

Organize a group of six people to work on this project. On a slip of paper each person should contribute his ideas about the skills it takes for a person to live successfully in today's world. These ideas might include such skills as driving a car, filling out a job application or getting along with neighbors. You can think of many. Make a composite list of your group's ideas, discussing each item and adding new ones to the list as you discover them. You may find it useful to elect one of your members to be a secretary.

As your group discusses each idea, consider these questions: What does a person need to know in order to manage the skill of living successfully? How important is this skill to his survival? To his success as a member of society? To his personal happiness? What makes this skill so important? What would happen to a person if he did not have it?

After you have completed the list, suppose your group is going to start a new kind of school, and in your school these skills are the only objectives. These are the things—the only things—you are going to expect your students to be able to do when they graduate.

Now make a second list telling what you are going to do to see that your students reach each of these objectives. How will you teach them? What will you teach them? Which skills are the special province of English teaching? Where will you teach them? How will you know when they have learned what you meant for them to learn? Will the skills you have taught them enable the students to do for themselves what they need to do to survive in their world? When they have graduated from your school, would you consider them "well-educated"? Why or why not?

Write your conclusions, along with your objectives and how you would teach them, in a report, so that the whole class can share your discoveries. You may choose to have one member read this report aloud to the class, or you may present it as a debate or panel discussion.

OLD AND NEW: CHANGE

45 minutes   *1 person*

To know about the changing world in which your students live, do this.

Use pictures cut from magazines to make a collage showing changes in our lives in the past few years. Paste the pictures onto a large piece of cardboard. You may or may not want to write words on it with a felt-tip marker. You may want to show a contrast between the ideas of some past time—fifteen, ten or even five years ago; or you may want to show only the new ideas of today. Experiment by cutting your pictures into different shapes and by arranging them in unusual ways or overlapping them. You will need to find many more pictures in the beginning than you will actually use. To find pictures which represent a wide range of change in our society look at different kinds of magazines. You will find a very different kind of picture in *Psychology Today* than you will find in *Better Homes and Gardens.*

In deciding which pictures to use and where to put them on the cardboard you may find it helpful to ask yourself some questions: Which changes are most obvious in our society? Which changes seem so natural that most of us don't think about them? Which changes have the greatest importance to young people? Are there changes you think are bad that you would like to do something about? How could you show that they are bad in your collage and show as well what you wish could be done about them? Are there changes you like and would like to see happening more? How could you express this point of view in your collage? Would your students agree with the point of view you are expressing? Why or why not?

Display your collage in your classroom.

THE MIGHTY MAGAZINE: A SURVEY
several hours some out of class   *2 to 4 people*

Prepare yourself for dealing with the interests and verbal environment of your students by surveying the magazines which surround them.

Find several people in your room to work as a group to compile a list of magazines available to young people. Here are some questions which may help you decide what you will need to know about the magazines and what it would be useful to include in your list: How many magazines and which ones are available at your school or public library? Where can other magazines be found? Would it be helpful for teachers and students to know where they can go to buy or borrow certain types of magazines? What kinds of magazines can be found? Are there some that look like newspapers and some that look almost like paperback books? What are the different sizes and shapes of magazines? Does the subject matter have anything to do with the size and shape of the magazine? If so, what? Which magazines are informative and which ones entertain their readers? Would it be useful to know what people would read these magazines? Are some for women, men, children? Do some have religious, political, or philosophical outlooks? Do some have mostly printing and others have mostly pictures? How much do the magazines cost?

How much are the subscription rates? Where can you send your money if you want them? How often are they issued?

Decide which information you want to include with the name of the magazine on your list. You may want to divide the task so that you are not surveying the same magazines as anyone else in your group. When you have finished your list put it all together. You may want to list every magazine alphabetically, or you may decide to use a different system like arranging the magazines under headings according to type, subjects or audience. Write or type your list as neatly as you can and put it in a theme cover.

Place your list on display in your classroom so that others may use and enjoy it. You may want to make copies of the list and pass it out.

THE NATURE

A new and practical look is needed at what the teacher needs to do in the English class to manage the activities of students and their relationship to materials and objectives. Beyond the old talk of what material is appropriate to a seventh or a twelfth grader or what the structure of a literary work is, both sequence and structure assume a new meaning in an activity curriculum. A mosaic of activities enables a student to give and receive a maximum number of language experiences. An activity curriculum assumes that there is no one best way to teach or learn anything but that there are numberless ways of learning, each one best for a given student at a given moment. To find this optimum, teacher and student work together, the student having a major input in choosing the time and content of his learning. If many activities are available, the student, counselled in his choices by a concerned teacher, and often in concert with his peers, will choose among them those appropriate to his own needs. As the student play-works with activities, he becomes bored with and ignores materials and activities which he has outgrown and engages in those suited to his level of growth. Properly designed learning activities appeal to his ability to make his own discrimination of what he needs. Activities must be designed around problems and materials that speak persuasively to the student.

Traditional curriculums begin with pre-selecting the objectives and the structure of what the student is to learn, an arbitrary start, often in conflict with the overwhelming power of the student's hidden curriculum—what the student learns from life by living it. The activity curriculum starts with the premise that the structure of the curriculum is the structure of the experience that causes the student to learn. The English curriculum is most effective when it tells him the same story about life his human experience tells him, when its effects on him are most like those of his hidden curriculum. What the classroom is trying to do is then reinforced by what life outside the school tells the student.

The curriculum of a school often directs attention to symbols, myths, and events which have little meaning for today's youth. The hidden curriculum of life works because students select from it what has meaning for them. The activity curriculum makes use of the hidden curriculum. It incorporates free choice and identification by the student of kinds of learning which seem to make sense because of their congruence with what he already knows or wants to know.

A counterproductive, anti-learning activity of some English classrooms is the competitive situation generated by threat. The emphasis on grades as a measure of learning worries many students, and by lowering their self-concept paralyzes their learning. Generating success and recognition through positive feedback from the activity itself, the activity curriculum mitigates the assault of the grade upon the student's ego. The student is not asked to pursue long-range objectives and compete for them but to enjoy and grow in what he is doing as he does it. Rewards are frequent and feedback immediate. Hard work is swallowed by interest, curiosity, and experimentation. The student becomes a free learner who enters diverse learning environments, engages and experiments with many kinds of roles, analyzes experience, and relies for motivation on these stimulations rather than on competition and coercion.

A talent for seeking knowledge is developed as the student learns to be self-starting and self-initiating. Emphasis on delayed gratification, order imposed by others, rigid standards, and work whose sole object is success in the eyes of others surrenders in the activity curriculum to a system that encourages immediate sensual and intellectual rewards, variety in the ordering of ideas, flexibility in selection of entering and terminating points for tasks, direct and unmediated encounter with materials and ideas, and extended self-analysis.

The activity curriculum assumes further that traditional lecture and class discussion have so many defects as classroom method that they should be used sparingly, if at all. They foster expanded teacher activity and student passivity, for only a small percentage of students participate in such classes. Teachers become misled about the kind and amount of learning being produced, and anxious students are often called on by poor questioning techniques to deliver information that they either do not have or do not know they have. The strong sometimes survive this painful and pointless treatment; the weak are crushed by it; both are scarred and crippled.

The activity curriculum shifts the stimulation of intellectual activity from the teacher to the student, where it belongs. It follows the scientific method. The student seeks problems, and, questioning the problems, he observes, collects, and organizes data. He generalizes and hypothesizes. He observes and manipulates his environment in search of solutions. He refuses to accept unquestioningly another's analysis of a question or answer to a problem. The student learns to be objective and open-minded and to accept the answers he finds. He watches himself change and learns to use these changes as subject matter for his writing and speaking. The English class becomes his laboratory.

The activity curriculum solves problems often attributed to the nature of the students but which arise directly from meaningless and mindless curriculums. An example of the flexible utility of the curriculum is its application to the problems of teaching previously-deprived groups. It creates a classroom adequate to its task of producing learning. Concern about whether anyone outside the school encourages a student's school achievement becomes unimportant. The concept of achievement is replaced by the concept of growth, and learning situations do not cause the student to look beyond his activity to the approval of others to make the activity worthwhile, but encourage him to depend on feedback from the task itself to provide satisfaction. His success feeds his self-concept, so no need arises for special activities to build it. The activity curriculum builds on what the child is, not what he is not, on what he can do, not what he cannot do. Choice and a wide spectrum of pupil interaction in activity classrooms give students access into more diverse kinds of social patterns than they experience either in traditional curriculums or in the accustomed social order. They practice new ways of participating in that order as they engage in social activity with successful results.

The activity curriculum uses traditions, rules, and structures whenever they contribute to learning and do not damage the learner and his ability to learn. But it does not use them for the convenience of the adults in the society or the school. It creates a total learning environment compatible with student interests, backgrounds and abilities not limited to but making use of any kind of books or materials already available. It is not a product of the past or organized around subject matter, but both the traditions of the past and the methods and materials of the past become its servants. Its one indispensable ingredient is the full engagement of the intellectual, emotional, and physical equipment of the learner.

If traditional ways of teaching are the best and most honest interpretation of what experience tells a teacher, then they must have some validity. And the old can mingle harmoniously with the new, giving way when the new can be managed. But real reform in the English class probably depends less on replacing old content with new than with replacing old methods with new ones. Much but not all old content is desirable and valid.

Some reform ideas have resulted in little real change. Independent study is often just a remake of contract plans, pioneered by the social studies curriculum makers of the thirties. The same materials and requirements, dull and irrelevant as ever, complete with evaluation conceived as tests and grades, ensure that some independent study programs will be as dead as other half-hearted attempts at reform in a few years when they will be seen to have made small difference. Phase elective programs often rely on materials made by teachers who conceive of change as simply a wider choice of materials and have small regard for methodologies essential to make materials meaningful. Methods, the real heart of reform, are often as unchanged as ever.

The activity classroom is more, not less, structured than the traditional classroom. A structure where every child is doing just what every other child is doing is a very simple and unsophisticated structure. But, since each human being is unique, any system of mass scheduling and instruction is inanely inefficient. Their tidiness and efficiency are an illusion maintained by pretending that individual differences are not significant. Education is sacrificed to control. A system that requires that methods as well as materials used for every child be different requires a very strong structure. But diverse options are as valuable to teachers and students in the society of the school as they are in society in general. The activity curriculum is committed to individual and small group learning, diversity, informality, spontaneity, creativity, self-motivation, play and student-created materials. From its variety of learning centers and resources, blending of subject matters, enriched environments, team teaching, individualization of tasks, and independent study, the paraphernalia of the past slips gently into limbo, and interest in learning itself replaces motivation. The activity curriculum is a philosophy, not just a procedure which rearranges the bankrupt pedagogy of the past.

Many materials are useful and pleasant to have in the activity classroom: reference books, periodicals, paperbacks, old textbooks and new ones, dictionary and stand, smaller dictionaries, thesaurus, record players and records, headphones, opaque projectors, filmstrips and filmstrip projectors, films and film projectors, slides and slide projectors, screens, maps, television sets, radios, typewriters, copying machines, developing apparatus, cameras, film, lecterns, elevated platforms, art materials, videotapes, bulletin boards, blackout drapes, writing and listening booths, lots of space . . . all these and many more, but none of these is essential. The one thing the teacher cannot do without is willingness to experiment, and a nice thing to have in addition is an educational leader—a superintendent, principal or department head—who wants teachers to experiment. Another source of strength is parents who want a change.

A teacher willing to try small things at first—one free day, perhaps, at a time, and many silent activities, until people in the school get used to noisy new ideas—can move far and fast toward the activity curriculum in one year. Activity innovation can start anywhere—with one teacher or with a whole system. Many English classrooms are self-contained and will remain so. The self-contained classroom is the classroom of countless students and teachers of English. The activity curriculum provides for change within this setting. In some schools only a few teachers want to change, and only a few parents want change for their children. A single teacher may use the activity plan to accomplish change while others maintain older ways, and no one is disturbed. In a time of transition, parents, too, have a right to choose either traditional or innovative environments for their children.

The activity curriculum, then, allows the teacher to make use of existing materials, to work independently or with other teachers on a team, to work within the self-contained classroom or in one without walls. It is wholly compatible with existing or with new building arrangements. It does not depend for success upon any particular structuring of bricks and mortar or any deployments of staffing systems. It is adaptable to either traditional or newer patterns of schooling. It meets a teacher's need to change slowly and start with ready-made materials, which may be combined with existing materials already in place. The activity curriculum does not imprison but allows change at whatever speed is appropriate for the one who is changing.

Activities

WHAT ARE YOU DOING?: I'M GROWING

1½ hours   *5 to 8 people*

To discover the different ways all kinds of people grow toward their personal goals, do this.

Find other people to work with and discuss these questions: Is there anything special you enjoy doing, like a hobby? What? Will doing it ever make you rich or successful? Why do you do it? Is this a good and acceptable reason for doing things? Do you like to wear nice clothes and have people say good things about you? Why? Would you like to be important and successful? Why? Are these good and acceptable reasons for your actions? When you are given a task to do, do you like to take your time with it and enjoy it as you go, or are you only interested in getting it finished? Are you the kind of person who enjoys the process of doing things or getting them done? Are both acceptable ways of being?

Try this experiment to see how the people in your group bring their own built-in goals to a task and how the task is worked out differently according to their needs. Arrange for each person in the group to bring a jar of rubber cement and 25 toothpicks to class. Put newspapers or notebook papers on the desk tops. Ask each person to build a construction using all of his toothpicks. You might plan to have your desks together in one corner of the room on that day.

After you have built the constructions, meet to discuss these questions: How did you get started? Did everyone build in the same way? Were you unsure of yourself? Did you know just what you wanted to do? Were you afraid your construction would be different from others'? Were you afraid your construction wouldn't stand up? Did you just want to get it done? Did you try to see how elaborate or sturdy you could make it? Who worked most quickly? Why? Did you consult the other builders? Why? Who had the best product? Why? Who had the most fun? Why? Who talked the most? Why? Was anyone bored? Why? How did each of you react to the experience differently? How did you feel during the building? What did you want to get from it? How was the experience changed for you by past experiences with building things? Was each person's way of reacting to the experience right for him? Was there one best or right way of reacting?

Ask each person in your group to write his feelings about the experience and what he learned from it on a sheet of notebook paper. Collect these sheets and staple them together for other class members to read. In this way they can share your discoveries and see the variety of your reactions to the same situation.

BEHIND YOUR FACE: YOUR HIDDEN CURRICULUM

1 to 2 hours   *5 to 8 people*

Here is a way to discover people's hidden curriculum—to know more about what it is and how it works to guide everyone's choices.

Find five to eight people to improvise some scenes with you. You need a problem, a scene to act out. Do you want a situation common to teenagers, like an argument with parents over driving the family car or a disagreement with friends over loyalties? Would you like to deal with school situations? Would you like to invent some of your own and try several?

Begin with two or three people. The group members who are not in the scene can be the audience. Make up the lines as you go. There aren't any right or wrong words to say because you make up the character and the scene to suit yourself.

But this is only half the story of what is happening to the people in your scene. What are they really thinking as they talk to each other? Do they have hidden motives of their own for what they say and do? What do they really want from each other? What is their hidden curriculum and how do they use each other to reach it? Ask two or three more people from the group to come up and stand behind the three who are speaking. This second group of speakers should try to speak the secret thoughts, feelings, and goals of the first three as they speak.

Tell each other what you have discovered about hidden curricula.

BY THE BOOK: IS IT THE ONLY WAY?

2 to 3 hours *1 person*

Here is an experiment to help you discover how people learn or don't learn.

Search the shelves of your library or newsstand until you find a magazine or book which contains instructions on how to do something that you have never done before—something you know nothing about. If you are a man, you might try a project like baking bread. If you are a woman, you might try a project like building a birdhouse or assembling a motor. Read the instructions. Can you do it now? Try it. See what you can do without asking for any help except what is provided by the instructions.

Get a spiral-bound notebook to record your progress and observations. Try to answer these questions: Do the instructions tell you everything you need to know? Does the author assume you know what you don't or know how to do what you don't? Do you ever feel frustrated when you are following the instructions? Confused? Would a child ever feel that way trying to follow a textbook or an instruction sheet on how to write a theme? Would it have been useful to you to have someone explain the instructions? Would it have helped to be able to watch someone else do it first? Would you like to have had more information on the subject before you started? How could a teacher provide this help for a child in a classroom?

Bring your project to class and tell your classmates about your experiment and what you have discovered about following the book as a way of learning.

THE EASY WAY: LEARNING DOESN'T HAVE TO BE HARD
1 week   *1 person*

If you would like to find an easy way to learn, try this.

Ask yourself these questions, thinking through the answers until you are satisfied with them: Could you learn to play tennis by reading a book about how to play tennis? How well could you do it if you had never had a chance to practice or handle the equipment? Why? How well could you learn to speak Spanish from a textbook without ever having heard the sounds of the language? Why? What would you do, then, if you wanted to learn such a skill?

Have you ever tried to study and found that you were only reading meaningless words? Try this: Choose a subject you want to study, one that would be tedious or hard for you. Now don't just read it; make a game out of it. Paint a painting of it, build a scale model of it, make a crossword puzzle out of it, dramatize it, write a funny dialogue about it, illustrate it with pictures out of magazines, make charts of it, or do whatever seems most interesting and appropriate to you.

In your spiral-bound notebook, each time after you work on this project take five minutes to write a sentence or two about what you are doing and how you feel about it. When you are finished, write a conclusion in your notebook about what you have learned and how vivid or useful this learning is to you. Give your notebook to the teacher to read, or read parts of it aloud to the class.

TEAM THING: COMPETING AND COOPERATING
1½ hours   *7 people*

This game will give you a chance to explore two kinds of learning situations found in classrooms.

You will need a group of seven people interested in knowing about learning situations. Elect one person as a leader. The other six people should be divided—either by lot or by choice—into two teams of three people each. You will also need seven dictionaries, all alike if possible. Find a spot in the room where your group can be close together, but where the two teams can sit slightly apart.

Before the game begins the leader needs to prepare a list of fifteen difficult words to be looked up in the dictionary. You will need one copy for each team. The two teams have different rules. The members of team I are, each separately, to copy the words and look them up separately in their dictionaries. The member who finishes first is to be declared the winner. The members of team II are to work cooperatively against a time limit of 20 minutes, making only one list.

After both teams have completed their tasks, the leader gives them a simple quiz on the meanings of the words by reading the words from the list and having them write as much of the meanings as they can remember.

Later, both teams meet together to discuss the results: Which team learned the most about the words? Why? Which team feels happiest about their experience? Why? How does cooperating make people feel? Is it a good way to learn? Why? Which group is more satisfied with themselves?

Plan a report to the class to tell them what your group has learned from this game.

GRADE GOODIES: JUDGING AND BEING JUDGED

1 hour   *3 to 4 people*

Here is a way you can see some problems involving grades from different viewpoints.

Try role-playing some scenes about what might happen to students and teachers who have grade problems. Find some other people who are interested in this activity. Read the situation suggestions and decide on one you would like to try or make up one of your own:

A mother comes to school demanding to know why you gave George a "C" when last year's teacher gave him an "A".

A sweet, quiet girl of average ability comes into your room after school and cries, begging you to give her an "A" on her report card so that her mother won't punish her.

You're a student who has worked very hard all semester trying to earn an "A". The boy who sits next to you never seems to do any work and often asks for more time to get his work done. You just got your English grades. He got an "A" and you got a "B".

You've worked as hard as you could for weeks, and the highest grade you could get on an English paper was a "C". There's a big grammar test in a few moments, and your mind is a blank. You wish you could get sick. You do begin to feel sick. Class is starting.

When your group has decided on a situation to try, choose which characters you would like to be. You might decide to take turns being certain characters, giving each person a chance to play a particular role. Take a few minutes to discuss the problems involved in the situations. What other circumstances could be involved that are not mentioned? What could the characters have been doing just before this? How would your character be feeling at that moment? What would he be thinking about the other character? How would he talk and move? What kind of language would he use? What would he look like? What would he wear? Would he have anything in his hands?

See if you can think of your own situations. Try being a parent, a teacher, a student who makes low grades, a student who makes high grades, a classmate, a principal, even a girlfriend or boyfriend who wants to help.

FOLLOW THE RED LINE: GRADING

5 or 6 hours   *4 or 5 people*

To deal more confidently with problems of grading, whether you are giving grades or receiving them, try this.

Organize a group of four or five people from your class. Plan a schedule for your group's meetings so that your time working together will be divided into approximately 5 or 6 one-hour segments (depending upon whether you have 4 or 5 members). During the first 4 or 5 one-hour meetings, a different person should be scheduled as the leader for each hour.

It is the leader's task to see that each group member has work to do during his hour—whatever the leader thinks appropriate—and to give each group member a grade for his or her work at the end of the hour. It is the task of the group members to obey the leader and to meet for five minutes at the end of the hour to evaluate how well the leader has fulfilled his task.

During the fifth or sixth scheduled hour, after each member has been the leader once, meet as a group to discuss these questions: In what ways was being the leader of this group like being a teacher in a classroom? Why? How was it different? When you were the leader, did you feel responsible for the group members? In what ways? Did you feel any other sense of responsibility? What were your problems? How did you solve them? How did you feel about the group members? What could they have done to make your job easier? How did you decide upon grades? Do you think your grades were fair? Did the group members think your grades were fair? Why or why not? How can you make grades fair? Should the people being graded have anything to say about how and why they are being graded? Why or why not? Are there other ways of reporting besides grades? What ways can you think of? What kinds of work or behavior is it easiest to give a letter grade for? Is this the only kind of work or behavior that is good or important? What else should be considered?

How did you feel about yourself when you were the leader? Did you enjoy it? Why or why not? How did you feel when you were the person being graded? Why? How did you feel about the leader? About the other group members? Do grades sometimes hurt the people receiving them? Why? Could hurting be prevented? How? Which leader made you feel most comfortable? Why? Which leader listened most to your ideas? How did that make you feel? How could the leader have helped you to do better? Would you have liked to know more about what he expected of you? Is a grade fair if the person being graded does not know what the basis for his grade is to be? Why or why not?

After your group is satisfied with its answers to these questions, choose one of your members to act as a secretary to write or type your conclusions. Put this paper on display in your classroom where other class members may read it and share your discoveries.

ASSUMPTIONS ABOUT STUDENTS

A teacher who chooses or makes activity cards must study students who are to use them. It is more important to find out what the curriculum of the world and the school have been doing to the student than to find out what students have been doing in school. The teacher will never escape from his assumptions about students, and these define limits to what students and teachers can accomplish together. When a teacher watches himself in the classroom, he will learn more of what he really believes about students than he will learn from verbalizing what he thinks he believes about them. A teacher's philosophy is what he does, not what he would like to do or what he thinks he ought to do.

The activity curriculum is designed to fit students as they are in schools today. Youth demand that the culture of the world as they know it appear in the experience of the classroom. Many of our youth are freed from social, family, religious and ideological restraints, from immobility, limited resources and confining responsibilities as few have ever been before.

Independent of the adult world, they spend fourteen billion dollars a year, much of which they earn themselves.

Brought up on television's ungraded reality since infancy, the student learns as much from it as from any other agency. Watching a wide variety of competence models, he learns to respect competence and relevance. He comes to the classroom brimming with information derived from filling in the dots on the screen. Entering the one-dimensional world of the classroom, emerging from his integrated electronic environment, he finds participation in a book different and less attractive than participation in television. The school, fragmented into grades, hours, and subjects, is marginally or not at all relevant to life as he sees it.

Conditioned to learn from the media, the student recognizes small difference between entertainment and learning. Whatever pleases teaches most effectively. If school learning does not please, it will lose out to pleasanter but often less ethical teachers. Having to try hard may be more of a distraction than a discipline for such a student. Learning not sensible to the student will not last, but faster, longer-lasting learning will result when it is close to his life style and experience.

Prevailing myths about the pre-adolescent try to give a precise picture of him as a potential learner. Psychology books list his characteristics. But many of the lists are weak in suggesting just how teachers can relate to learners. The seventh or eighth grader needs to be let alone a great deal more than he is in most classrooms. He needs praise, silence, and patience and love, simply expressed. He wonders if adults, including parents, really like him. Attempts to dominate his activities or possess him remind him of his recent childish helplessness. He does not want to be dependent on the teacher or other adult, but he does need security. Sometimes defiant, he likes to be accepted by mature adults.

He has a like-dislike for the opposite sex. The gang, with its secret languages and codes, is important. In a choice between parent or teacher and peer group, the gang always wins allegiance. The gang is a protest against exclusion from adult activities. He punches and fights those he likes, and his attitude is often full of verbal and physical challenge and insult. He ignores those he does not like.

Not all aspects of his being grow at the same rate, but growth cannot be safely rushed. He likes to be secretive, and this sometimes makes him seem hostile. He is often untidy, sloppy, lazy, irresponsible, and unreliable. He has a short attention span and is forgetful, especially of those things he does not want to remember. Time is unimportant to him. He is restless, active, and muscularly explosive, needing lots of physical motion, even when listening or sitting still. He is a gadgeteer and collector and fantasizes but does not abstract well. He has many anxieties about himself as a person and even thinks about dying or being killed. He wonders and daydreams and is often afraid of the dark.

In short he is very much like many of the rest of us, only in an intense and unrepressed way. The activity curriculum with its variety, emphasis on physical movement, free choice, interaction with peers and adults, immediate feedback, and short-term goals is ideal for the seventh and eighth grader.

After the eighth grade, the student becomes less open with adults. His questioning of teachers is more discreet. Sometimes he has learned to ask questions that he knows will please adults and will later be rewarded by A's and B's. But today's student is unselected and not very docile. He is more free but uncertain about how he wants to use freedom. In many ways students in high schools are socially mature and sophisticated. But they are kept from responsibility in a dependent position long after they reach maturity. Blocked from productivity, they are confined to a world of leisure, play and consumption. Their passive, subjective status limits development of their capacity for responsible action.

The adolescent develops unevenly. Physical maturity comes first, then emotional and intellectual. He must come to terms with his own body, his changes in appearance and physical function. He needs a good appearance to be attractive to the opposite sex. He needs sex information, will seek it actively, and will imitate adults. He must gain independence from parents and wants it from all adults, despite the fact that he often becomes attached to teachers. He achieves independence as he gets a job, the symbol of independent socio-economic status.

The student must relate to his own age group, and his desire for peer acceptance leads him to the achievement of social techniques. In a struggle for peer acceptance, he makes noisy demonstrations of peer loyalty, experiments in personal and social relations, and makes and rejects sudden attachments. Adolescents try to please each other, and communication among themselves is more important than communication with the adult world.

In beginning to accept themselves emotionally and physically, students of high school age are often devious, aggressive, stubborn day-dreamers. They bluster and bully and have anxieties, insecurities, guilts and fears. They shirk responsibilities. In their search for values they have trouble understanding themselves.

Today's student is the product of an age that turns out products with lightning speed. He knows the schedule of life that has produced him and that makes up his life, and he has small patience with school schedules and their emphasis on form to the neglect of reason. He already may have learned what elders have often failed to comprehend, that the world, so full of people and so small, will survive only with cooperation, not with competition. The student yearns for survival in the world of tomorrow and has no nostalgia for the competitive world of yesterday. The school pulls the student in opposite directions. It tells him the importance of good grades for getting ahead and into college. But in the world of youth there is no reward for these achievements. Sports, dates, extracurricular activities and defying the mandates of adults are the rewarded successes of his world. Even many adults reward with publicity and respect more of these values than the values they preach.

Some very bright high school students have learned that school is no place to ask answers for important questions, so they ask none. These are the psychic dropouts, those who have no interests that are socially useful, who find the routines of school bewildering or degrading and teachers overbearing, frightening, and detestable. They have learned that they get in the way if they ask questions whose answers are not found in textbooks or in the lives of teachers. Their permanent record cards are filled with words like "under-achiever," "does not fulfill potential," and "lazy." The psychic dropout dares us to judge him, but is indifferent to our judgments. His clothes are not fitted, and he walks stubbornly, deliberately, in the uptight, hustling, bell-motivated world of the school. Even when from the middle class, he imitates the poor, the oppressed, and even the unwashed. To demands for his plans, he answers with visions and songs. He sells a sense of direction for a sense of excitement. Moderation and reason he calls compromise and rationalization.

These adolescents, too, sound amazingly like other people. Their feelings, if not their values, are like our own. And they too must attain self-confidence and effective ways to structure their lives or be punished by the culture. To be effective, their classroom learnings must be related to learnings in life outside of the classroom, where the student undertakes to fulfill the developmental tasks thrust upon him by his maturing self. Then he will learn what the classroom demands, since the two demands will coincide. His eagerness to learn will be in proportion to his conviction of the importance or unimportance of the task he sees before him. If the task is forced or unrelated, it will be forgotten. And since that task must be policed to be enforced, the student will often hate the teacher-policeman as well as the learning.

The activity curriculum assumes that the way a student thinks about himself will determine how well he will learn. If he likes himself and thinks others like him, he will learn better. And the teacher cannot communicate with students until he finds out what they are like and until he finds that they are very much like the rest of us. He must help students, too, to see him as a human being with whom they have much in common. This has nothing to do with students and teachers being pals, over-identifying with each other, or pushing into each other's affairs. It does have to do with learning how to be accessible to each other when the need arises. The good teacher learns about students from the students themselves and treats their answers with care since they often do not know how to talk about themselves or will say what they think listeners want them to say or will seize any occasion to dramatize themselves. Students and teachers are partners in learning in the activity curriculum, where they experiment and learn with and from and about each other.

Good teaching builds on what the learner can do and does do, on what he is, not on what he is not. To build thus a teacher must know what the learner is and what he does. The teacher is not alienated by and from what the child is and does. The activity teacher studies the child; he does not study about the child. The learner must be seen as having the right to be what he is and as he is instead of as a divergence from some teacher-envisioned norm.

In an activity classroom a student learns that being free is not only doing as one pleases but learning how to do what one wants to do. When the exercise of authority over him is lifted, an authority which often seems to him irrational and capricious, the student tends to need less opting-out behavior—evasions or what is often called "cheating." Maturing in a free society to live in a free society means, among other things, acquiring those skills of freedom which enable the individual to perceive among a wide range of choices that one choice whose results he is willing to try to predict and whose results he desires. These skills are not learned in a classroom where teachers continually delimit the available choices or pattern their sequence and pursuit. But in classrooms where teachers are trusted and competent resources for students, learning the skills of freedom proceeds apace.

Activities

BRAIN BUDGING:
DO YOU HAVE TROUBLE GETTING STARTED EACH DAY?
10 minutes *1 person*

Try these ways to get moving—ways to get your brain or your students' working when you or they come into class every day.

Stop at the door a minute before you come in. Do you have your books and materials? If your pencil needs sharpening, sharpen it on the way to your seat. Go directly to your seat or to the activity slot area and begin your work when you come into the room.

See if you can know just what you intend to do first before the bell rings. Race it! See if you can set a goal for yourself for the first five minutes of class. Get one thing done before the first five minutes are up! You're off and running!

After you've tried these suggestions, write a line or two in your note-book about how they worked out for you. Maybe you have some ideas of your own for getting started. Try them and see if they work for you. Let your teacher know how they turned out by telling your log. Others might find them helpful too.

A PEOPLE COLLECTION: OTHER WAYS OF SEEING

3 hours   *1 to 3 people*

This will give you a chance to look into other people's life styles and to discover how their ways of seeing the world and reacting to it are different from yours.

Working alone or with a friend or two, make a collection of slides or pictures showing people whose life styles are different from yours. You may want to use a camera to take pictures or cut pictures from maga-zines and newspapers. Since pictures are for seeing, you will need to plan a display or showing of your collection when it is finished.

To guide you in choosing pictures and planning to display them, think through the answers to these questions: What can you tell about the people in a picture just by looking at it? What does clothing and hair style tell you about their life style? What can you tell from the things they are doing? From the background scene in the picture? From the facial ex-pressions? Can you divide these pictured life styles into categories of different kinds of people? What are they? How do the pictured life styles of these people make you feel about the people? Which people would you like or dislike if you met them in real life? Why? How does a person's life style affect other people's thoughts about him?

How can you make sure that the people who see your pictures will draw the conclusions from them that you want? How can you best arrange the pictures? What can you say about them? How will you say it?

Arrange a place or time for showing your collection to the class.

SLOTS AND SYSTEMS: WATCHING THEM WORK
1 hour   *1 person*

To discover how people's systems of categorizing the facts of their lives change the ways they think, do this.

Think about these questions until you are satisfied with the answers in your own mind: Are there some things you accept as true even though you do not understand how or why? Are there certain people whose words you accept as truth without question? Do you know anyone who believes something you find unreasonable and who clings to that belief in spite of any evidence to the contrary? Is it ever necessary to accept facts as truth without questioning them? Why? Could it ever be danger-ous to accept facts without questioning them? When and why? How do you know when to accept them and when not to accept them? How could people learn to make such decisions? What might keep people from learning to decide between facts to accept and facts not to accept? Are all acceptable facts acceptable forever? How do you know when to start questioning a fact that you have believed? What prevents people from questioning the things they believe? How could people learn to question old beliefs?

Do children believe everything adults tell them? Should they? Why or why not? What happens to them in the classroom when they don't?

Try this experiment with your class. Give an oral report of about five minutes straight from the encyclopedia or other reference book—but change some of the facts. (Try to choose a subject your classmates would not know much about.) Then give your classmates a short true, false, or I don't know quiz to see how many believed your false facts. Tell them afterward what the true facts were.

Tell the class about your conclusions, especially what makes people accept facts without thinking about them and how they could learn to choose between acceptable and unacceptable facts. You might want to ask for suggestions from your classmates in forming these conclusions.

YOUTH WATCHERS: KNOWING YOUNG PEOPLE
1 week   *4 to 6 people*

To find out what young people are really like—what they do and how they think about themselves and their world—do this.

Find a group of people in your class to work with. Each member will need a spiral-bound notebook, and each will need to find a teenager or group of teenagers to observe for a week. Use your notebook to write down everything that happens and all the details you notice. It will probably be most tactful not to write in your notebook when you are with the teenagers, but do it as soon afterward as possible. A small tape recorder—the kind that can be carried in a handbag—would also be a help. Spend as much time with the young people as you can.

At the end of the week read through everything you have written to see what it tells you about the teenagers you watched. What do their actions tell you about the way they feel about themselves? What things did the teenagers you watched do that the teenagers other class members watched did also? What things did the teenagers do that you might do yourself? What did they do that you wouldn't do?

How did the teenagers talk and behave when they were with adults? When they were with their friends? What kinds of pressures do adults put on teenagers? What kinds of pressures do peer groups put on them? What are the most important things in a young person's life? How can you tell? How do teenagers deal with strong emotions? What do they do to feel important? What do they do to feel safe? What do they do to get attention? How do they show affection? In all these things, how are teenagers like and not like you?

Read over your notebook to see how your ideas about teenagers changed through a week. Do you feel the same about the events you described as you did when you wrote the descriptions? Write your conclusions about teenagers and what you have learned from your week's observation in your notebook and give it to the teacher to read.

GROWING UP CAN BE EMBARRASSING: FEELING YOUNG
1 hour   *4 to 6 people*

Here is a way to put yourself inside a teenager and know what he is feeling.

Find a group of people from your class and act out some scenes that might happen in the lives of teenagers. Put yourselves in the places of these young people: You are a teenage boy whose voice is changing. What do you do in music class when the teacher tries to make you sing? You are a young girl and you have just written a note to your dearest friend telling her all about your latest secret love. How do you feel when a boy grabs the note and passes it all around the room for the other students to giggle over and you are afraid the teacher will see it? You are a fourteen-year-old boy and you are trying to convince your classmates that you are grown-up and masculine. How do you feel when your English teacher puts a sentimental poem you wrote on the front bulletin board? You are six feet tall and a football player. How do you ask pretty little Miss Smith, the math teacher, to write you a hall pass so you can go to the bathroom?

Choose one of these situations your group would like to act out. Discuss how the teenager might solve his problem. Decide what other people would be in the scene and decide which group members will play those parts first. You can do the same scene over with another cast or do a different scene until everyone has had a chance to play a part. What do these other people think and feel about the teenager? What does he or she think or feel about them? How are the characters showing their emotions in what they do and say? How are the people dressed? Do they have anything in their hands? Where does the scene take place? How can you show these things in your acting?

After you have talked about these questions, you are ready to try. It isn't necessary to practice because you make up the scenes as you go. Just say and do what feels right to you.

After you have tried role playing once or twice with these scenes, you may even want to make up some situations of your own.

Choose your favorite scene and replay it for the whole class.

WHOSE BABY ARE YOU?: A CHILD'S POINT OF VIEW
1 hour   *2 people*

Here is a way to learn how children feel.

Choose a partner. It will work best to plan this activity one day in advance so that you can gather materials you will need. For half an hour one of you will be a child and the other an adult. Then for another half-hour you will switch roles. The person who is to be the adult needs to bring an activity he might provide for a child, like a coloring book and crayons or children's story books. The adult is responsible for keeping the child occupied for the whole half hour. The child must sit still in his seat unless told to do something else, speak only when spoken to, and do whatever the adult tells him to do and nothing else. He is not allowed to do anything unless given permission. At the end of the time he must stop his work whether he is finished or not.

When you have both had a chance to be the adult and the child, discuss how you felt when you were the adult and how you felt when you were the child.

Write your answers and any other comments you have in a spiral-bound notebook, and leave them for the teacher to read.

UN-HUH: THE FEEDBACK GAME

3 hours   *3 to 6 people*

Here is a way to get other people to do what you want them to do.

Find a group of people in your class who are interested in this goal. Meet to discuss these questions: How do you get other people to do what you want them to do? How do other people get you to do what they want you to do? Do you do things more willingly for some people than others? Why? Would you rather be told or asked? Or would you rather think of it yourself? Why? How does it make you feel to be told?

Would you rather be punished for what you do wrong or rewarded for what you do right? Which would make you work harder? What kinds of punishment are used to change the behavior of children or adults? How well do these punishments keep them from doing the same things over? Do punishments get people to do things or just keep them from doing things? What could you use to reward people for behavior you like? What ways do you already use, even without thinking about it, to reward people for behavior you like?

When a friend says something to you that makes you feel good, what do you do? When you hear or see something that is interesting or exciting to you, what do you do? How does your reaction make the other person feel? Does he want to do more or walk away? How can your reactions help you get reactions you want from others? If your whole group reacted to another person's behavior in the same way, could you get him to do what you wanted him to do?

Each person in your group should have a spiral-bound notebook so that he can write down his private feelings, opinions, observations, and suggestions about this activity. Use it as a way of keeping a record of your discussions and activities.

Now test the conclusions of your discussion on some real people. As separate individuals, try getting people to do what you want by reacting in a pleasant way to the little things they do that are like the behavior you want from them. Tell your notebook about what you did and how it worked. This may also help you to see what you can do more effectively next time. Meet again to compare notes. Agree to try this system of changing behavior on some unsuspecting person you all know—perhaps a teacher. Plan a time when it will seem natural for you all to be together, and agree upon the behavior you want to encourage and how to do it.

After you have tried this last experiment and have recorded your reactions in your notebooks, choose one of your members to report to the class what your group has discovered.

TUNE IN TO OTHERS: MEETING A NEED

½ hour *1 person*

This is a way to become sensitive to the needs and problems of other people and to discover ways you can help.

Find someone with a need and help him meet it. These questions may help you: What do you have that someone else might need? What can you do that someone else might not be able to do? Could you help some one to do something for himself? What kinds of problems and needs do the people you know have? Could you help someone to feel better about himself? How? Could you help someone get along with the other people in his life? How? Could you help someone meet an obligation? How? Which kinds of needs are most important to the people involved? How can you be the most help?

If you do not already have a spiral-bound notebook just for this class, get one. Record in it the need you found and met. Tell what happened and how you feel about yourself and what you did.

FREEDOM: HOW DOES IT WORK

2 hours *3 to 4 people*

Here is a way to explore the meaning of freedom and what it means to the person who lives in a free society.

Meet with a few other members of your class to discuss these questions: Are there some things you don't do because you would get in trouble if you did? What things do you do because you would get in trouble if you didn't (like running out of gasoline if you don't fill the tank once in a while)? Make a list of things you do or don't do because it would be foolish to behave in any other way. How many of these things would have bad consequences for you if you didn't behave responsibly? How many of them would have bad consequences for other people?

In a free society where we have no rules or laws to regulate the little things of life and private dealings, why don't most people do things like going without baths or getting drunk every night? How does our understanding of the consequences of our behavior work to keep us in line?

Design a bulletin board or a display on a large piece of cardboard showing the ways people in a free society behave on one side and what consequences occur if they don't on the other. Look in magazines for pictures to illustrate the ideas.

TEACHER BEHAVIOR

This is a book for teachers and prospective teachers who are not satisfied with the way students are learning English. The teacher who accepts the activity curriculum will think less about what the department chairman, the superintendent, the community and the state want the student to know and try to find out what the student himself wants to know. He will not try to make sense of his classroom by allowing grades, I.Q.'s, reading speed, standardized tests, quizzes, final examinations, grade placement, percentiles, schedules, memos, college boards, fifty-minute periods, or assigned books to computerize, standardize, compartmentalize, or mesmerize him. He will not be concerned about where these indices place the student but will be concerned with finding out where the student's own personal time and place is and where his thinking is.

A curriculum is what students and teachers do, not what teachers would like to do, what they say or think they do, what is in the guide, or what they should do. Teachers are subject to immense pressures, and what they do is contingent upon their reaction to these pressures as well as what they know. They are the products of formal education; in-service opportunities; the numbers, abilities, and values of their students; the size, location, and administration of their schools; the instructional materials available; the quality of their colleagues, the daily preparation pressures upon them; and the expansion of knowledge in their fields.

But what teachers do is dependent on what kind of people they are as well as on what they know and what pressures they have upon them. If it is true that the world is divided into people who love people and use things and people who love things and use people—some psychologists have called this affiliation and achievement orientation—the activity curriculum teacher should be in the first group. To him students are not a challenge, a menace, or a problem to be solved. For him there is nothing in the student's life or identity that has to be surrendered before the student can be accepted. His dialect, for instance, and his dress do not challenge the teacher's prejudices. The teacher's attitude is one of interest in the student, curiosity about his work, optimism about his prospects, positive projections about his concerns and doings, and faith that the student can generate his own sense and kind of order. At the same time the teacher has confidence in himself, his own knowledge and his own ability to learn alongside the student.

Because the needs of students vary so greatly, it is impossible to specify the teacher behavior which is best under all circumstances. And an individual teaching style is indefinable. It is just the individual teacher, doing his best and being his best self to enable the student to grow and learn. Into this mix go sound scholarship, sincerity, warmth, a growing and flexible philosophy, competent methodology, adventurousness, organizing ability, and fairness. To say that something in a teacher personality always works with all students in the same degree would be absurd; however, some things do seem to work with many students.

Teacher talk needs to be managed and diminished in English classrooms. Teachers need to avoid making long speeches about anything. Extended teacher lecture assumes that teacher talk is better than what could be found in a book or put on a mimeographed sheet. A teacher who chooses lecture must examine these assumptions to see if they are true before he lectures. The mere transmission of ideas and information does not produce understanding, for understanding is not a function of ideas and information but of being in an organized relationship with these ideas. It is to the development of this relationship that the activity teacher pays constant, unremitting attention.

Not what teachers say but what students hear is important, and many students are convinced that what teachers say is boring nonsense. Communication happens when students get the teacher's message. Effective talk begins where students are. Saying true things is not communication; having true things understood is. Some teachers want to say true things and hold students responsible for hearing and understanding, but it is up to the teacher to find out what language the student understands and accepts. The teacher must identify the blocks and values of his audience. Students hear selectively, and a teacher must know their postulates for selection to get past their defenses, communicate, and be relevant. The language they hear is as varied as the students themselves: voices speaking or singing, books, visuals. Sometimes the language is wordless. Sometimes it is accompaied by a guitar. One generation's music is another's static. Sometimes the silent language of body and gesture communicates most. The style of life of the teacher communicates effectively with the young, and the teacher's rhetoric about how important his subject is will not impress the student unless the teacher embodies the worth of what he teaches.

The teacher as communicator is a teacher as listener. The teacher's willingness to listen to them helps students listen to him. The teacher should never tell a student anything the student can be led to tell the teacher. The activity curriculum teacher will be concerned with what students want to say and do say and will listen to them and respond honestly, learning from students how to be their teacher.

The activity teacher must have a sound philosophy about order and structure. When he gives directions, they must be utterly clear and simple. He is committed to explain, show, and demonstrate, being aware that how he sees a situation, problem, or idea is only one way of seeing truth. The activity teacher must believe that the orderliness in his classroom is the orderliness students feel about what they are doing. Disorder is any situation where students are bored, restless, apathetic, rebellious, or desperate.

An orderly classroom is one where the student becomes compliant, not to the authority of the teacher or the school but to the authority of his own rational choices and their results. The activity teacher never abdicates his position as leader of learning. But this leadership appears in being a model of how to learn and enthusiasm for learning as well as in knowing and using information that students do not know. The things the teacher knows that students do not know must be made accessible to students through structures which do not cause them to reject the ideas conveyed. The activity teacher finds such structures and shares responsibility for deciding which data are useful.

The teacher is a model of how students should think of each other and talk about and to each other and about their work. If the teacher appears to feel that teaching these particular students is the most exciting thing to do and that their work fills the teacher with curiosity, excitement and pride, if the teacher enjoys reading and hearing their work and responds positively to the work they do, students will look at their work with more pride and take more care with it. They will also respond more positively to the personalities and work of their classmates. Very often, cliques are a product partly of the teacher's unspoken attitude that certain students belong together or are likely to belong together. The teacher needs to encourage curiosity about differences and find them stimulating rather than threatening or annoying.

The activity teacher becomes a learning companion instead of a learning director. A strong element of teacher control is an attitude of genuine interest in the work of the student, curiosity about it, and excitement about its potential. Strong teacher control emerges from the role of the teacher as guide, advisor, listener, resource person, enthusiast, learning companion, sharer of joys, and confidant. In sharing leadership with students it is important that the activity teacher accept leaders chosen by students and not impose leaders chosen for teacherly reasons. Teachers can learn much about students and their value systems from leaders students choose. Students must feel comfortable about expressing what they think and feel, even though their thoughts and feelings oppose those of the teacher.

Teachers must devise and use a multitude of structures as they construct alternatives that involve every student. Structure must be respected for its potential to create alternatives that free creativity. A variety of fresh approaches is essential and will be forthcoming from students as well as teachers who use the activity program.

Teachers must see the alternatives they create as patterns and models which will eventually lead many students to create their own commitments. New ideas for activities will begin to come from students soon after they become accustomed to a classroom climate hospitable to ideas from everywhere and as soon as they see that tries of alternatives can be made without censure. Failed tries should be without emotional content. They should simply be experiments that did not work but that, in every case, yield information of value in constructing new alternatives. Teachers must greet with curiosity, interest, and joy times when their alternatives are rejected in favor of or used as springboards for student-created alternatives. Problems in putting student-created alternatives into effect should not be allowed to dim the joy of having and sharing new ideas.

The activity teacher must operate as a model. When teachers are learners, students tend to value learning. If the teacher values learning only for the student, his value system will not seem sincere. A student has the right to see the joy of a new idea strike a teacher occasionally if he is expected to believe that new idea times are joyous occasions. And the teacher needs to demonstrate how good learners show wonder, questioning, and doubt. The activity teacher is a professional thinker who likes to read and talk about books as well as teach them, to explore and use language as well as teach it, to free thought, not just to manage it.

The words "control" and "discipline" are important words for activity teachers. They imply a wide range of teacher behaviors, and the activity teacher must assume the stance of the action researcher in finding interpretations of these words. The teacher involved in action research decides what his goal is, examines alternative practices, and selects the one whose results will move him toward his goal most economically. Then he tests his choices, and if his projections are fulfilled, begins to construct a theory of behavior.

In helping students with problems teachers must decide whether they want to deal with causes or with effects. They have to decide what will satisfy them as results of dealing with such students. Do they want outward behavior change? What kind? What exactly is the goal? Can teachers find ways to accept student feelings even when student behavior is unacceptable? Problems shared with others have to carry the weight of added involvement. This adds complexity to solution-seeking. Hence, discipline problems should be privately dealt with by teacher and student concerned.

Students who exhibit unacceptable behavior in classrooms are simply people who have found solutions for their problems that are not acceptable to teachers and schools. Something in their social scene has reinforced these solutions in ways that have yielded satisfaction to the students. Therefore, students are convinced either that other solutions will yield lesser satisfactions or that they do not know or cannot use other solutions. If their accustomed solutions are repressed in the classroom, they manifest behaviors which teachers identify as defiance or apathy. These emerge from students' own frustration when their solutions are blocked.

The activity teacher is concerned with teaching new solutions to such students. The first step is to reinforce every element of appropriate behavior. It is dangerous to use the negative reinforcement of punishment, since this is very stimulating and rewarding to some students who have learned to find reward in this kind of recognition. The behavior which the teacher feels is nonproductive is simply encouraged by negative reinforcement.

A teacher who has not tried positive reinforcement will be astonished to see how quickly changes in student behavior occur when even tiny elements of behavior are positively reinforced. And it is a great relief to most teachers to give up the struggles attendant upon administering punishment. The teacher's reinforcement is also a model for other students who find it less rewarding to reinforce a fellow student's bad behavior with their attention if the teacher is taking no notice of it.

Although students do respond to positive reinforcement immediately, old habits of finding suffering a reward and punishment a joy take some time to wipe out. If students have learned that doing bad things makes them feel good and more like persons, they will continue to do these things which support their sense of identity and importance. However, when the teacher consistently and steadily accepts the student as a person, rewards every evidence of a turn toward productive solutions, and refuses to reward bad solutions by giving them any acknowledgement at all, students practice productive problem-solving techniques and begin to trust and gain satisfaction from them. When new ways of handling their problems offer greater and more consistent rewards, students who have had behavior difficulties do change.

The activity teacher is concerned with the teacher behavior that creates a productive climate in the classroom. This teacher has a deep respect for the students' need to feel joy and satisfaction in what they are doing and the creative power of these feelings in the human psyche. Every student is entitled to regard for his worth as a person and to sympathetic and courteous treatment along with recognition that he has assets which can be used for his benefit. This activity teacher will adopt behavior which leads to a relaxed, pleasant atmosphere, alive with freedom of inquiry, happy intuitions, and conviction of the intrinsic worth of things and people as ends in themselves.

The activity teacher will, like all teachers, be the administrator of the reward system. In valuing and prizing, the teacher is a model. This teacher will have small expectations and large enthusiasms. Learning, repeating, and recognition of facts and convergent thinking will not be prized above oral language activities, divergent thinking, and seeing complicated relationships that do not yield objective analysis. Only successes will be publicized or displayed. Evaluation will be based on whether the goals in the promise part of the activity plan are reached. Products made, problems solved, and memories stored are part of the evaluation. The conference and the log will make apparent changes in attitudes and understandings that do not result in visible products.

The teacher will help a student who feels unsuccessful to investigate why he feels this way and to make new tries based on his analysis. Willingness and ability to make new tries promptly is enhanced if the attitude and spoken or unspoken comment of the teacher is not the reason the student feels unsuccessful. If the teacher elects to question the student about his task, a non-threatening rhetoric of inquiry must be constructed. Threats are often paralyzing factors and hurdles. If the feedback from the task itself is the source of the student's negative evaluation, the move to new tasks is facilitated. Then the teacher may join the student in his new try, making suggestions for improvement and indicating fruitful lines of inquiry.

Perhaps the most challenging problem for an activity curriculum teacher is to help the student whose only measure of his own worth is knowing how many other students he excels. Such greedy uneasiness about his own worth is difficult to manage since it is often reinforced by the value system of the home and society, where the values of self depend on competitive supremacy. A student accustomed to comforting reinforcement from the reward and prizing system of grades and test results may distrust a different value system or resent being deprived of what was a satisfying reward system for him. Or he may suspect that the teacher is fooling him and really intends to start the old round of punishments and rewards for convergent thinking. The teacher in the activity curriculum must establish tangible reward products for such students while they are being weaned to dependence upon the rewards of task feedback and cooperation.

There will be days when students are apathetic and restless and do not conceal these feelings as they might in more traditional classrooms. The activity teacher will recognize and help students to see that there are times when people have these feelings, and they are no reproach to the people around them and no shame to the one feeling them. Activity cards can be constructed that help with some of these feelings. Sometimes they come from things that happen in other classes or at home, and they dissipate as students have a pleasant time in the activity classroom. At other times students have needs a classroom cannot meet, and the activity teacher simply makes them as comfortable as possible in a non-punishing atmosphere. Students in an activity classroom can begin to be easy with the fact that weaknesses, fears, anxieties, and even hatreds are feelings everybody has at some time or other. Appropriate activities can demonstrate that work, sharing, and achievement can make some of these feelings go away and others shrink to manageable size.

The activity teacher's interest and respectful attitude toward the learning of each student will be reflected in the students' respect for the teacher and for each other. This atmosphere decreases discipline problems arising from student-teacher or student-student conflict. Much of what seems to be bad student behavior results from students being success starved, having to do irrelevant tasks, not understanding tasks, or living with constant explicit or implied rebuffs. The activity classroom solves many of these problems by creating a program of varied learning tasks, meaningful and achievable. And the stress created by a teacher's attempt to keep students quiet is relaxed. This sad and banal task facilitates teaching in the traditional classroom, but is not part of creating a learning atmosphere for the activity classroom. The activity teacher will find that not all children are adjusted to the opportunities of the activity classroom all the time, but the discipline problems that arise when the class is taught as a unit and everyone is expected to pay attention to the teacher all the time do not arise.

In the activity classroom, teachers do not pretend problems do not exist. Students who say they have a problem are not told they are mistaken. Whatever students feel, they are admitted to feel. The urges they experience, they are allowed to experience. What they want, they are allowed to want. The activity teacher does not mutilate, rearrange, or exaggerate a student's feelings. Nor does he try to destroy the student's experience by means of language. Instead, he finds verbal ways to admit student feelings to examination and analysis. The creation of trust must be part of the task of the teacher in the activity curriculum. Such trust creates the climate for student learning.

An activity curriculum teacher will have his own negative feelings from time to time. The teacher must accept his right as well as his tendency to have these feelings. They are appropriate when new ideas are being accepted and are a kind of growing pain. The teacher will learn to tolerate occasional uncertainty, anxiety, or hostility in himself and in others. In the activity classroom these feelings may be more apparent than in traditional classrooms, where they are hidden and unacceptable. They may seem quite painful, but they are not more painful than in traditional settings; in the activity classroom the pain tends to be out in the open. And when it is outside, it can often be handled and dissipated. Even the act of expressing it or talking about it can dissipate it, as humor, companionship, and acceptance are expressed.

The activity teacher may wonder how safe it is for him to develop what seems to be a personal relationship with his students. Inevitably there will be those who consider his involvement with them a weakness and exploit it. But these students would have problems in traditional settings too. Difficulties will often dissolve if the teacher maintains an open attitude until students unused to the challenge of such a relationship adjust to it.

Let the activity teacher not dissipate his energies in keeping his students at a "proper" distance. Human relationships vary. Each is individual, and within one relationship changes are frequent and natural. Management and growth, rather than kinds of restriction, are key words in developing relationships between students and teachers. Respect for privacy, like openness to sharing, must be learned from experience in interaction. But in our growth we can become aware of ways to draw our circle of interest and compassion large enough to embrace all. The strong are not afraid of others, and activity teachers must be strong. They must draw their circle as widely as possible.

A teacher may find that he has feelings of rejection toward certain children. Let him test himself. Does he just admit he does not like the student? He may get rid of the student by sending him out of class. He may treat one child more harshly than he treats others. Or he may overprotect and be oversolicitous and indulgent to one. He may set special standards for one student or fail to praise him. He may make disparaging remarks or unfavorable comparisons. He may express surprise at others' praise of a student. He may adopt a martyr's stance as he does things for one student. He may speak of an older student he dislikes as a young child. He may be inconsistent in his behavior toward the student.

This rejection may result from the teacher's own disappointed hopes. Or the student himself may be unattractive in physique or attitude. The student may lack talent. For some reason the student may threaten the teacher. The teacher may not wish to teach that kind of student. The teacher may see in the child a reflection of traits he already dislikes.

These feelings must be handled by the activity teacher. The unfavored student becomes jealous, negative, and rebellious. He will be suspicious and overanxious and lack self-confidence. He will lack the inner security that enables him to recognize reasonable restraints. He may respond with timidity, oversubmissiveness, or excessive docility. He may become selfish and demanding. If the teacher observes any of these manifestations, an examination of his own feelings and behavior may reveal attitudes on the part of the teacher which can be changed more easily than can the behavior of the child. Such teacher change may work quick and helpful change in the child if the teacher disciplines his own hostility and antagonism until students sense that they are safe.

The activity classroom will function best with a minimum of rule-making. What rule-making occurs should result from teacher-student cooperation. If fewer things are made into crimes, there will be fewer criminals. The activity teacher is not tempted to consider student failure to behave acceptably as a personal affront. Only those things in the behavior of students which interfere with the learning of the class should call for intervention of class or teacher to prevent adverse student behavior. Both students and teachers have a right to input about what constitutes good working conditions. And rules should always be phrased positively in order to enlist the help of rhetoric in the cause of constructive behavior. "Do not's" should be kept to a minimum. But rule-making, like goal-setting, is a task in which the teacher needs all the help he can get from the students. Bad behavior usually comes from bad feelings, and bad feelings can often be dissolved by relaxing mechanisms suggested on activity cards. Or students can make their own. Activities can be constucted which outline socially acceptable and individually comfortable ways students can handle their aggressive feelings. These give rise to useful writing experiences when students record their feelings in their logs.

The best activity teacher moulds and disciplines that which is personal in him into an effective servant of that which is professional in him. His intellectual and affective selves are trained to respond to the call of his professional needs. That professional is most effective whose human personality has the greatest potential for making such response.

How shall we prepare such teachers? The state requires a list of competencies, and these become a list of courses that are taught to undergraduates. When they become graduate students, teachers are taught the same courses, which are then referred to as being "on the graduate level." Some English teachers become very competent in fielding the questions that arise in the field of literary criticism. A few even become competent writers. But then a haunting question arises—does ability to do imply the ability to help others learn to do?

An English teacher's problems are usually not with subject matter but with ways to get students to do things—this is called motivation, and long discourses are written on it in teacher education materials. More subject matter knowledge will probably not solve this problem. Further education in manipulating the critical apparatuses of literary scholarship, sized in various plugs of chronological segments to fit semesters, will merely prepare English teachers to approach their problems by doing more of what they already do well enough.

The English teacher as a loving and caring person is the focus of a humanistic preparation program. The teacher is prepared to be open to others, able to prize the learner as much as the learning and strong in the empathy that gets inside the feelings of others. A humanistically prepared teacher cares for those who are disagreeable and unloving as he cares for those who are easy to love, or his commitment is too shallow. He trusts and risks, in the sure knowledge that his trust will be betrayed by students whose damaging experiences in life have made them likely to choose damaging ways of dealing with others. In such cases humanistic teachers must have a caring that is strong enough to continue, though it is rejected. Their faith in themselves and others must be so secure that it becomes a charitable cloak for the cold ones who are so cold that they can only behave coldly. This kind of caring listens when it would rather talk. It is expressed in a steady faith in the humanity of others and their power to be and do good, not in their perverted will and power to do evil. It is steady in the knowledge that one cannot know how to show caring until he has been taught what it looks and feels like to care and be cared for. English, central subject of the "humanities," should be taught by teachers whose credentials as humanists are not limited to their competencies in language and literature.

Activities

A DAY WITH GEORGE: WHERE DOES THE TIME GO?
50 minutes   *1 person*

Try this to find out how an English teacher's time and attention get divided.

Make a time plan of one day in the life of an English teacher—George.

Here are some questions you might ask yourself to guide your thoughts in making your plan: If George arrives at school at 7:45 in the morning, what time does he have to get up? How long does it take him to drive to school? How many classes does George teach during a day? How long do they last? Does he have papers to grade? When does he do that? How many students and how many papers does he have? How long will it take? Does he have private conferences? How long do those take? Does he sponsor any clubs or participate in extra-curricular activities? When? How many evenings a week are there teacher's meetings at George's school? How much time does George get off for lunch? Does he get a preparation period? How long is it? Does he make out lesson plans? How much time does he spend on them? Does he type study or work sheets? Clean up his room? Work on the bulletin board? What time does George leave the building? Does he stop at the grocery store or the dry cleaner on his way home? When does he read professional literature? Does he attend a track meet in the evening or relax with his children?

George is your character. Make him do what seems reasonable to you. Now find two real teachers and ask them if George's schedule is believable to them. Ask if they have any suggestions for making it more realistic.

Post your creation, along with any additions and comments, on the bulletin board so that others in the class may share the product of your work.

EVERYBODY'S FRIEND: SHOWING PEOPLE YOU LIKE THEM

2 class periods   *4 to 5 people*

If you are interested in how people show their good feelings about each other, try this.

Find several people in your class to work as a group. Meet to discuss the question of how people act or talk to let others know they like them. Here are some questions which might help you in this discussion: What is the first thing you notice about someone who likes you? What people do you know who make you feel that they like you? What clues in their voices, faces, hands, or body movements do they give to show how they feel about you? What kinds of words do they use to let you know they like you? What kinds of questions do they ask you? How do they respond to the things you say? Are there any other ways you can tell they like you? Are there any things that would mean liking if one person—perhaps someone close to you—did them and mean something else if a stranger did them?

See if your group can make a list of the ways we can tell people like us. Now put your list to work. Ask the members of your group to use these I-like-you signals for one day with everyone they meet and talk to. During the second class period compare your results: How did you feel about the other people when you tried to show them you liked them? How did you think they felt about you? How do you feel about them now? Would you change the list? If so, in what way?

In a spiral-bound notebook record your feelings about this experiment.

WHO IS A LEARNER?: A SURVEY

1 hour mostly out of class   *1 person*

To discover how teachers are a part of the learning process, do this.

Ask some teachers about what they are learning. Make a survey. Try a variety of college, high-school, and elementary teachers. In planning what you will ask them consider these questions: What would they like to know more about? Are they studying any subject or reading about it now? Are they taking college courses? If so, what? Would they like to take any? Do they study or review what they teach before they teach it? Do they read periodicals which give them ideas for improving teaching methods? Do their students see them read and study? Do they admit their ignorance when they do not know the answer to a question? Do they involve their students in searching for answers with them to questions for which neither they nor their students have answers?

You may not want to ask all teachers all of these questions. Be sure to phrase your questions so that the teacher does not feel you are judging him. He should be made to feel by your attitude and by the impersonal and unbiased wording of your questions that any answer or even not answering is perfectly acceptable, as in fact, it is. The teachers you talk to may have other valuable information for you about teachers as learners. Find out as much as you can. Write down what you discover in a notebook.

In thinking about the information you have collected consider these questions: Do all teachers do what they expect their students to do? Should they? How do teachers feel about the importance of learning in their own lives? How might a teacher's attitudes about learning affect the attitudes of his students? How would students feel about knowing their teacher is a learner too?

Report your findings and conclusions in a short talk to the class.

TURN GREEN: RESPECTING THE RIGHT TO BE

1½ hours   *3 to 8 people*

Here is an activity for practicing attitudes of respect for life and persons which may help you to be a successful activity teacher.

Find a group of people in your class. Read this story: There is a grassy hill. The wind blows a tree seed to the hill. The rain makes the hill wet. The seed sprouts. It grows for many years. Squirrels and birds live in the tree. The tree is tall and beautiful and strong, but after a long time it becomes old. It begins to wither and die. It becomes hollow and its leaves fall off. It topples to the ground, and vines and weeds grow over it.

Discuss these questions: How would it feel to be the hill? Would a hill ever be lonely? If you were the hill would you be happy to have a seed grow on you? Why or why not? How would a hill feel when it was wet in the rain? If it could talk what would it say? Would the hill be sad when the tree died? Does a hill ever die? Imagine that you are the hill. How can you express with your body or words what a hill is? How might the tree feel about the hill which nourishes it? If it could talk what might it say to the hill? How would it feel about the squirrels and birds? What would the squirrels and birds feel about the hill and the tree which sheltered them? If you were a squirrel how would you feel and act? How would you spend your days?

Plan a skit in which your group acts out the story above. You may want to choose someone to be a narrator while the other group members act out the story, or the actors may want to speak for themselves.

Perform your skit. If you would like to share your project with an audience, invite another group to visit you and watch.

TEACHER SAY, TEACHER DO: THE TEACHER-MODEL
45 minutes   *1 person*

Do this activity to discover how you as a teacher-model can influence the attitudes and behavior of students.

To do this activity you will need to find a group of from 4 to 10 people to act as your students for 15 or 20 minutes. You may be able to find classmates, friends or neighborhood children to cooperate with you in the experiment. They should not read this activity before you do it.

Plan a situation in which you "play school" with them. Arrange seats for the students and a desk or table for the teacher so that it is as much as possible like a real schoolroom. Choose a passage, short story or paragraph to read aloud to your "class". This selection will need to be appropriate to the age and interests of your students. Plan questions to ask after you have read the selection. These can be typical teacher-questions like, "What did ____ do after he ____?", "Where did the story take place?", "What did the author want you to think about ____?", "What was the main idea?".

With your voice, gestures and expression try to give attitude clues of your feeling about the person you are talking to. Choose one person in the group—not someone who is usually considered a leader or intelligent by his peers—and show by your reactions to what he says that you think he is great. You may want to practice some of the positive and approving responses you could make in front of a mirror or with another person before the experiment. You want to sound convincing, not phony. It might be helpful to watch what other people do when they talk. How do they show respect? How do you know when someone is really interested in what you've said? Is there any way you can state your questions to that person so that you are more likely to receive a good and intelligent answer? Will the student reply with more assurance if you make him feel that you will be accepting of his answer? If the student feels that you like him, will he like himself better? If you think he is smart, will he think he is smart?

At the end of this lesson pass out sheets of paper and ask the students to rank each person in the group according to how well they think that person understood the passage. To avoid bad feelings about grades you may want to use three categories like "very well," "well," and "not so well."

How many of them ranked the person you were trying to build up "very well?" How did he rank himself? Depending upon the age of the students, you may decide to tell them about your experiment and what you found out from their reactions.

In a five-minute report tell your class about your discoveries.

TALK TIME: TEACHER OR STUDENT TALK?
several days   *3 to 8 people*

Here is a way to discover what is happening when there is talk in a classroom.

Find several people in your class who have the time and opportunity to sit in on classes being taught at the college, secondary, or elementary level. Arrange for each person in your group to visit a classroom and perform this exercise: Make sure there is an accurate clock in the room where you will be, or wear a watch with minute markings. On a piece of notebook paper number from 1 to 60 to represent each minute of the hour you will be observing. Find a place to sit in the classroom where you can be as inconspicuous as possible and can mark on your paper. Begin timing. At the end of every minute make a mark beside the number which represents that minute. Your mark will indicate who is talking at the moment you make the mark. "T" represents teacher talk,

"S" represents student talk and "N" no one or confusion. (As an alternative you may prefer to tape record a class and make such a check list from the recording.)

After each member of your group has completed this task, meet to compare your findings. Here are some questions you may want to discuss: What percent of the time was spent in teacher talk? What percent was spent in student talk? Find the average figures for your whole group. In which classroom did the teacher talk the most? In which classroom did the teacher talk the least? How were these two class-rooms different? Did the students ask the teacher questions? Did they get out of their seats and move around? How was the furniture arranged? Did the teacher praise and encourage students or criticize? How much time did the teacher spend lecturing and giving directions? When students answered questions did they give short answers like "yes" or "no" or did they add ideas of their own?

Go back to the classrooms again, the same or different ones. This time listen to what the teacher says and how he or she says it. Look at the students to see what they do and whether they are bored or interested. Listen not only to how much the students talk, but to whether or not they are saying what they think the teacher wants them to say or what they want to say. Do they talk to the teacher without being asked a question? How?

Meet with your group again. Try to reach an agreement on how much teacher talk and how much student talk there should be in a classroom. Make a list of the kinds of teacher talk and the kinds of student talk you want to have happening in your classroom when you teach.

Record your observations and your conclusions in a spiral-bound notebook and give it to the teacher to read.

THE IMPORTANT THING IS . . . : WHO SAYS?

several hours   *4 to 6 people*

If you would like to know about what different people think is important, try this.

Organize a group of several people in your class. Plan a survey to see what different kinds of people think is important and what isn't. You may want to plan a series of questions like this: "Which is more important, ____ or ____." Or, you may want to make up a short list of things you think are important to different people and ask your subjects to arrange them in order of importance. In either case you may need mimeographed copies of your list of questions. Find out if there is a mimeograph or copying machine available to you, and arrange for one of your members or an outside person to type the first copy.

Decide what you will put on your list. What things matter most to you? Getting an education? Finding a job? What things would be most important to a teenager? To a teenager's father? To a retired person? Perhaps you will want to talk to some of these people before you make your list.

Whom will you survey? How will you categorize the people you talk to? Do you need questions about age and sex at the beginning of your survey? How will you find these people? Will you go from door to door? Stand on a street corner? Can you think of any other ways?

Make as many copies as you need of your list, and have each member of your group participate in gathering information. Meet again to sort out results. What different kinds of people did you talk to? What did each group think was important and unimportant? What differences were there between one group and another? Were there any things that everyone thought were important? If you could do the survey over again, how would you change the questions? The people you talked to? Your way of talking to them?

Write a report on what your group has discovered, and elect one of your members to read it to the class.

WHAT DID YOU SAY?: A LISTENING GAME
30 to 60 minutes   *3 people*

This will help you to separate the truth of what you hear from what you think you hear or expect to hear. It will give you a chance to investigate why people hear or don't hear what others say.

Choose two other people in your class to work with. Each of you will have a different task in the game. One will be the talker, one will be the listener, and one will be the watcher during each of three five-minute rounds. The watcher will time the rounds by looking at a clock or watch. Decide which of your members will have each job during the first round. During the round the talker talks about something he knows well—a hobby, class, or even what he did yesterday. The listener listens, and after each statement the talker makes the listener repeat what the talker has given as exactly as he can. If the talker is not satisfied that the listener is repeating accurately what he said, the listener must rephrase his words until the talker is satisfied that the meaning of the statement is the same as he intended.

If there is a disagreement about what the talker originally said, the watcher may tell what he heard, but at all other times he is silent. After each round all of you may discuss what you heard or said if you like. Switch jobs for two more rounds until each person has a chance to be listener, watcher and speaker.

Now discuss what happened and the way you felt about it. Did you have any problems listening during the game? Were there any distractions from outside your group? If so, what? Did your own thoughts ever get in the way of what you were hearing? Could you prevent that? If so, how? Did your mind wander from what the person was saying? Why? What might have helped to hold your attention to what was being said? Were you confused about the meaning of what the talker said? If so, why? Did you misunderstand the meanings of the words he used? What would have helped you to understand? When you were the talker, did you get across what you wanted to say? Why or why not? Did the person rephrasing your statements take more words or fewer words to say what you said? Why? Did the meaning become clearer or less clear?

When you were a listener, how did the talker's manner of presentation affect what you heard? When you were a talker, how did the listener's reactions affect what you said? For an optional experiment in how feedback helps in listening and talking, try this same game again with the talker and listener either separated by a screen or with their backs to each other. Compare this experience to the first one in your discussion.

Write about your discoveries and how you made them in your spiral-bound notebooks and leave them for the teacher to read.

DOING YOUR OWN THING: WHAT IS IT?

20 minutes   *1 person*

Here is a way to investigate how people behave when they think they are free to do whatever they want and when they think they are not.

Use a small tape recorder, one that can be hidden if you like, to record the conversations of people in your class as they come into class. Keep recording during class. Try to arrange to take the recorder along if your class goes out of the room for a break and record through the end of the class so that you can record conversations as people leave.

Find a quiet place where you can replay the tape. Ask yourself these questions about what you have heard: How do people talk to each other and the teacher before and after class? How does this change during class? Why does it change? What things do people talk about before and after class? Are these things more or less important to them than what is going on in class? Why? What kinds of language do people use in their conversations before and after class? Does it change after the class begins? How and why? What other things have you noticed about how people behave on their own time and how they behave during class? When do they seem most interested in what is happening to them? When do they talk most? Why?

In your spiral-bound notebook write your conclusions about how people behave when they are free and how they behave when they think they are not.

FINDING WAYS: STRUCTURING A SITUATION

2 to 3 hours   *4 to 8 people*

Try this way of solving teaching-learning problems to see if it is an improvement over ways you have known in the past.

Find several people in your class to work together. If you are going to solve a teaching-learning problem, you first need a problem. Each person in the group should write on a piece of paper at least two problems he has experienced in the past in trying to learn or to teach. Take turns reading your problem situations to the group and discussing them. Here are some questions you may find useful in this discussion: Did you try to teach someone something by telling it to him? Was it something he needed to know or something he needed to be able to do? Were you able to explain it to him so that he could remember and use the information? Could he do what he needed to do with it? Why or why not? Would it have helped if he could have seen a demonstration or practiced doing the thing? If you were the learner rather than the teacher, would a demonstration or practice have helped you? Would you have remembered it better if it had been presented to you in a more interesting way? How could that have been done? Did you try to learn something by reading about it in a book? What could you or your teacher do to make reading book directions more interesting and memorable?

After your group has discussed a member's teaching or learning problem, help him think of solutions—activities to do to help him or his student learn, remember and use what they have learned. Perhaps you will have several solutions you like for each problem. Write the solutions on the paper with the problems.

Now put your system of solving learning situations to the test. After you have heard all of the problems and their solutions, choose one learning problem—something that most of you do not already know about or know how to do—and try out the activity solution on your-selves. Whatever you decided would be a good way to learn for that problem, do yourselves. Whether or not you decide to do it together or singly, at school or outside of school will depend on what it is.

Meet afterwards to talk about what you have done. Did problems arise that you had not foreseen? How did you solve them? Did you learn as much as you hoped to learn? Do you think you will remember it? How do you feel about the thing you studied? Did you enjoy what you did? Did you work hard at it? Why? What are the advantages and disadvan-tages of learning this way?

In your spiral-bound notebook write what you have done and your conclusions about the experience.

TRUSTING: HAVING A BLIND WALK

3 class periods   *2 to 30 people*

Here is a way to experience the feelings of trusting and being trusted.

Have a blind walk. Make plans ahead of time and talk to people in authority so that your blind walk will not cause problems for other people and they will not cause problems for you. You may want to have your blind walk in the school or outside, or you may want to try it while eating in the cafeteria.

Choose a partner. If a large group decides to do this, you may want to draw lots. On the first day one person will be "blind," and on the next day the other will be "blind." The "blind" person is on his honor to close his eyes and keep them closed for the agreed time. The other person is to lead him around and help him with whatever is necessary.

It may be helpful to discuss beforehand what the seeing person might do, like guiding the "blind" person through doors or telling him what is on his plate. Afterward, both partners can compare their feelings and perceptions.

On the third day meet in pairs or small groups to discuss your expe-rience: When you were the "blind" person, were you tempted to open your eyes? Why did you feel that way? Was your partner reassuring to you? Did you want your partner to stay with you all the time? Why or why not? When did you feel most safe? How did your partner help you? How did you feel about the other people in the room when you could not see them? Did you feel that you could manage for yourself, or did you feel helpless? Was that a good feeling? Why or why not?

When you were the "seeing" person, how did you try to help the "blind" person? Is there anything more or different you would do if you could do it over? Did you like being needed, or was it a bother? Did you worry about the "blind" person? Why or why not?

Did you find it easy or difficult to be trusting in this experiment? Why? Can you think of any situations in which it would be easier to be trusting? What? Can you think of any situations in which it would be harder to be trusting? What? What things could other people do to make trusting them easier? What things could you do to make it easier for yourself to trust other people? What can you do to make it easier for other people to trust you?

In your spiral-bound notebook write about the things that have happened to you in this experiment and how you have felt about them.

HOME SWEET HOME: CLIMATE MAKING

variable time   *4 to 6 people*

Here is a way to find out what makes a good classroom climate.

Find several other people in your class who are interested in classroom climate. Meet to discuss these questions: How should a good classroom climate make you feel? Comfortable? Safe? Alert? List as many of these good classroom feelings as you can. Now look at the classroom where you are. Are there bookshelves? What kinds of books are on them? How are they arranged? Do they make you feel the way you want to feel in a classroom? Are they interesting? Colorful? What about the color of the walls? Is there anything students or teachers can do about walls besides painting them? Are there curtains? Should or could curtains do anything besides keep out light? Are there blackboards? Bulletin boards? Interest centers? How could these areas be more comfortable and inviting? What about the floor? Would a shaggy old rug and some pillows be too much for it? What kind of desks or chairs do you have? What would be the best way to arrange them for the climate you want to have in your room? Visit some other classrooms and see how climate is provided for in them.

Write your observations and discoveries in your spiral-bound notebooks. Working together, write a list of suggestions for improving the climate of your classroom. Give your list to the teacher and class for discussion to see if these improvements are practical and meet the approval of the other people in the class. If any of your suggestions are approved and accepted, your group should do the work—arranging furniture, decorating walls, doors or bulletin boards, bringing in materials, or finding outside help when it is needed.

GENTLE TOUCH: WHO'S A FAILURE?

30 minutes   *1 person*

Here is an opportunity to discover how to deal with failure constructively.

Think about these questions: Have you been unsuccessful in your first tries to do something, but kept trying until you could do it well? How do you feel when you have overcome such failures? Have you ever become discouraged and given something up after several failed tries? How did you feel then? Have you ever been encouraged by someone when you felt bad about failed tries? If so, what did he say or do? What kind of comfort or encouragement could you give to someone who has tried unsuccessfully to do something? How does he feel about himself and the thing he is doing? How should he feel about himself and the thing he is doing? Should you encourage him to try again? Is there ever a time when you should encourage him to do something else—something he does well or something just relaxing? If you want to make someone feel good about himself, what kinds of things could you say to him?

Try out your theories. Find someone, a friend or someone in your class who is struggling unsuccessfully. See if there is anything you can say or do for him to make him feel better about himself and what he is doing.

Write in your spiral-bound notebook about what you have done and what, if any, results you can see. How do you feel about dealing with failure?

CHAPTER II

Getting Started

ROOM GEOGRAPHY

Although the activity classroom makes use of more rather than less structure than does the traditional classroom, the aim of the structure is different. The structure of the traditional classroom is designed to cause all
students to do the same or similar things at the same time but separately
and to make all students accessible at all times to teacher direction. The
activity structure is designed to cause each student to make individual or
small-group choices and carry out the implications of those choices with
whatever support he needs from materials, classmates, other resources, or
the teacher, whenever his need appears. The physical setting for the traditional structure requires seating students so that separation is maintained
and teacher direction mechanisms are readily displayed. The physical
setting for the activity structure is complex, as is the structure itself.

The physical attributes of the activity classroom are the activity control
board and the interest centers where the activities take place. Ideally, but
not necessarily, the activity classroom should implode upon the senses of
entering students. The way the chairs are arranged, the disposition of
visual aids, the sounds that meet the ears of the students carry a message

before the class begins. All these should be used purposefully. But the activity classroom is not a mere arrangement of furniture or a well-equipped English laboratory. It starts with a geography of the teacher's mind, with the beliefs and assumptions of Chapter I, which will assume the image of every devisable individualization possible in a classroom.

Some learning centers for the English classroom are the teacher consulting center, the activity control area, bulletin board areas, the listening area, the reading center, the reference center, the game center, the group meeting center, the log writing center, the art and media production center, and space to do skits and improvisations. Although none are essential, all would be useful.

The teacher consulting center is simply the teacher's desk with a chair or two near it and an appointment board posted nearby, where those who want to consult the teacher record appointments. The activity control area should be near the door, since students will want to gather around it as they enter but will not use it in great numbers after the first few minutes of the period. The listening area will contain any radio, television or taping equipment in the classroom and should be near an electrical outlet. The reading center will contain bookcases full of paperbacks; old, torn-up textbooks; newspapers and magazines—reading materials of all kinds. Pillows and a rug could accommodate students who like to sit on the floor. The reference center will house any reference books the teacher has— encyclopedias, dictionaries, etc. The games center is a spot where small groups may use packaged games or games invented by students. The group meeting center will be a place for planning and group discussion. The art and media production center should occupy a table near the door where students may go in and out to get water when it is needed, as it often is, without disturbing others. Space for skits may be a corner partly shut off by a screen.

The log writing center should be a table where logs are piled and students may write in them. Logs are spiral-bound notebooks, left in the class, where the teacher may look at them frequently and carry on a written dialogue with students. The log is a key feature of debriefing learning activities. Feelings are recorded, generalizations are extracted and theories arise out of activity experiences. As students record these in the logs, experience becomes learning. File folders, one for each student, may remain on this table also. These accumulate writings and reports by each student. Folders may be stored in a corrugated paper box, cut down to such a height that tops of the folders with student names on them are visible. Each class maintains a separate file box.

The activity control board starts with a large piece of corrugated paper box, perhaps a mattress box. Pockets with open tops and pleats in the sides and bottoms for cards 5" by 8" can be made of heavy paper. Columns of these pockets fastened on the cardboard are labeled "Writing," "Reading," "Language," "Speaking" and any other designations desired. Even though the control panel is labeled, the activities are not mutually exclusive. Many activities have reading, writing, speaking, and listening mixed into one realistic experience. Pockets are filled with cards which list instructions for student activities. Students may select among these activities and copy the instructions from their choice in their log, returning the card to its pocket. A student should return his card promptly so that it does not get lost and so that other students may use it if they wish. Teachers should have duplicates so that lost card information is not irretrievable.

The activity classroom may generate more noise than a teacher or school feels comfortable with. With the help of students noise can be controlled. They can invent ways to be more quiet. Can they lift instead of dragging furniture when it must be moved? Since most of them will be talking to one or just a few persons most of the time except when they are in skits or reporting to the whole group, they can practice various modulations of voice appropriate to small groups. They should understand that other classes have a right to quiet if that is their need. They should also realize that there must be places in their own classroom where individuals may go to work by themselves quietly. The movement of furniture and the movement of people should be calm and purposeful after students become used to the new system. Sometimes groups need timekeepers so that they can be reminded to move chairs and other materials at the proper time. The same person might serve as a reminder of noise level so that it remains appropriate.

This open learning situation is easier, not harder, to handle than a traditional classroom. It only seems noisy and confused because the order is in the minds of the students, not in outward silence and conformity. A conventional classroom only seems quiet and orderly. The noise and confusion there are often in the students' minds, and this disorder should not be diagnosed, as it often is, as apathy, indifference, rebellion or laziness.

Teachers may be concerned about not having enough time to prepare for teaching innovatively. Several activity curriculum features are relevant to this concern. Teachers may accumulate cards over a period of time before beginning to use them. Some activities designed for readers of this book could serve as a small starter set. As the teacher accumulates more cards made from the materials actually available from courses being taught, a varied and resourceful activity board will result. As the number of cards available for the board grows, it can be used for more and more days of lessons.

The teacher on these days can operate a counseling service for the students during the class period. An important function of the activity teacher is to orchestrate and choreograph activities of the students, grouping, separating and regrouping them into large and small groups and as individuals to achieve the best possible learning mix. Not every student needs to work with others; some are and will remain solitary workers. Others need to be shown how to enjoy group work. The teacher must become sensitive to a wide range of cues and clues that show him how to help students choose their activity. At the start of the period, teacher tasks center on getting everyone the activity most appropriate to his needs. Or, choices for a day of activities may be made the previous day. Then, while students are at work, there is time for teacher discussion with individuals of log and folder remarks previously recorded on them by teacher and students. An appointment sheet should make it possible for students who need to see the teacher to do so at a specified time. These times should be staggered to provide opportunity for the teacher to circulate among students engaged in activities to offer counsel, appreciation, and encouragement.

All of these demands upon teachers and students are quite different from requirements of classroom procedures in the past, and teachers may worry about getting students accustomed to the new system. But students accept novelty and feel comfortable with it whenever they sense the teacher is accepting and feeling comfortable with it and when it is carefully structured.

Activities

WHAT IS A LOG? WRITE AND FIND OUT

1 hour   *1 person*

If you feel uncertain about what a log is or should be and what you can write, this activity may give you some aid and comfort.

Do you have a spiral-bound notebook? If you don't, get one. It is your log. Whether you write a lot or a little in it depends on how well you like to write and how interested you are in what you are writing. It would probably be helpful to date your entries, but what system you use for ordering your log is up to you. You may want to have sections for different kinds of things, or you may prefer a chronological order. If you are concerned about whether or not the teacher can read what you have written, you might use ink and try to write neatly.

What kind of things you write in your log is also up to you. Here are some questions you might consider in thinking about what to write: Are there ideas you hear during class that you would like to write down so you could remember them later? What? Are there feelings or opinions you would like to talk about? What? Have you done things you are proud of and would like to tell about? What? Have you worked hard on a project and wanted to tell about what you have done? Is there anything you have wished you could say to your teacher? Have you some suggestions?

If you have trouble beginning, just start with whatever comes to your mind and write—anything—even if it doesn't make much sense. If you read it over, you may find something in it that does.

Now write in your log.

SIT IN: ORGANIZING YOUR ROOM, PART I

several hours   *4 to 6 people*

To find out how to arrange seats, desks, or tables in a classroom for activity teaching and learning, do this.

Organize a group of four to six people in your class and plan how to arrange the seats in your own classroom. Talk about how they are going to be used and how they can be best arranged for that use: If the teacher or some other person is going to lecture, what would be the best arrangement? How often do you think there will be lectures in your class? How much of the time will the seats need to be like that? If students are going to be working in small groups, what will the most practical way of arranging seats be? Why? How often do you think your class will be doing this kind of work? If the whole class is going to discuss something, what will the most practical arrangement be? Why? If people are doing art work, what will the most practical arrangement be? Why? How often do you think these things will happen? When the class has gone, try arranging the furniture in these ways and see if it looks as if it will work. Try arranging the seats for the next activities in your class.

What happens to your furniture arrangement if different people are doing different things at the same time? Are there certain activities for which tables would be better than desks or pillows on the floor would be better than chairs? How and when would these different seating arrangements be used? Would it be possible to plan your room so that a variety of different ways of sitting are available? What are the practical limitations? How large is your room? What kinds of seats are available in your school? What could you bring from home? Does another class use the room after you do?

Get some graph paper with one-fourth inch squares and make a scale plan of your room. Using a tape measure, measure the walls; locate and measure all the windows and doors and immovable objects. Make a basic plan of your room. Make several copies. On these plans try arranging the seats for different purposes. Be sure to keep everything to scale and plan for easy moving and rearranging. In your plans you may also try putting the movable classroom furniture in different spots to see how it affects the seating possibilities.

Post your plans on the bulletin board so that other class members may take advantage of them to arrange furniture for their work. Offer your help to people who need materials or advice for arranging seats.

SPECIAL AREAS: ORGANIZING YOUR ROOM, PART II

several hours   *4 to 6 people*

To find out how to arrange different areas of a classroom for activity teaching and learning, do this.

Find several other people in your class who would like to plan to make your classroom fit the needs of an activity program. Talking about these questions may help you with this task: What does the activity teacher do? Where should the teacher's desk be so that he or she can do those things best? What will the teacher need besides a desk? Where should these items be?

What audio-visual materials will be used in your activities? Will they stay in the room? How will you protect them from damage? If they are brought in, how will you get them from the door to the spot where they will be used? Will they be near electrical outlets? How far do they need to be from the screen?

Are you going to need books for reading or reference? Are there bookshelves in your room? Are they movable? How can you make a reading area that is comfortable and quiet? What would you need? Where could you get it?

Will there be art work done in your room? How much and what kinds of supplies will you need to store in the room? Is there a bookcase or cupboard where you can store them? Is there a table available where people may work? Where in the room should this art and media center be?

Where would the most convenient place be for keeping the file folders? Will your class use bulletin boards? How much bulletin board space will you need? Are there bulletin boards in your room? Are the locations and sizes appropriate for your needs?   Are there folding screens available to you for blocking off areas temporarily? Could you get some? Where would you use them?

How many people will be using the activity board? When will they be using it? Where should the activity board be placed so that it is accessible and convenient for everyone? How large will your activity board be? How much space do you need to leave for people to stand around it?

Will other classes be using this room at times when your class does not meet? How can you be sure that your furniture arrangement will not interfere with their activities?

After you have some definite ideas about how the areas should be arranged in the room, make several plans showing different arrangements. Use one-fourth inch scale graph paper to make your plans. You will need to measure everything.

Post your plans on the bulletin board so that they can be used by people who are using, planning to use, or constructing different areas in the room. Offer your advice and help to anyone who is working with a problem of room organization.

LIVING WITH IT: ORGANIZING YOUR ROOM, PART III

1 to 1½ hours   *6 people*

To find out how the furniture arrangement in your room affects you, do this.

Organize a group of six people in your class and explore your private reactions to the furniture organization and reorganization. Here are some questions to get your group started in your discussion: When you walk into a room, do you like to know just where everything is? Why or why not? How does it make you feel when the furniture has all been moved around? How are you used to sitting in a classroom? What are some other seating arrangements you have seen or used? What way of sitting in a classroom makes you feel most comfortable? Why? Which seating arrangement seems most practical to you? Why? How do you feel when things are going on in other parts of the room? Is there anything you can do about these feelings? What?

Try some seating experiments in your group. Arrange your chairs or desks so that you are sitting in two rows facing each other, and continue your discussion for five minutes. Try arranging your seats so that you are sitting in two rows, one behind the other as in the usual classroom, with the back row looking at the backs of the heads of the people in front. Continue your discussion for five minutes. Try a circle. Try a "U" shape. Try a "U" shape with one person sitting at the open end. What happens to the way you feel about the other people in each of these situations? How did you feel about the people who were sitting across from you in the first situation? How did you feel about the other people when you were in the usual classroom arrangement? How did you feel in the circle and the "U"? How did you feel about the person who was at the open end of the "U"? Are there any other seating arrangements that you might try? Try them and see how they work. Which way of sitting made talking the easiest? In which one did you feel most comfortable? In which one did you feel most safe? In which one did you like the other people most?

When the experiments were over and you returned to normal, what way of sitting was "normal" to you? Why?

In your spiral-bound notebook write about what you have discovered about seating arrangements.

CALLING CONTROL!: MAKE AN ACTIVITY BOARD

1 to 2 hours   *2 people*

Do this if you want to learn to make and use an activity board.

Find a partner to work with in your class. Read again the description of an activity board in "Getting Started." Collect the materials you will need. Consider these problems: What kind of paper can you get that is sturdy enough to support the weight of the cards and the handling of many people without tearing? Would colored paper be pleasing? How many columns will fit on your cardboard? How many pockets will be in each column? Will it be enough? What categories of activities will your class need? How will you make the pockets stick to the cardboard? Can you find a glue that is strong enough to hold up under the wear and tear? How will you make the pleats in the pockets? Where can you find out how to do this? Where in the room is the best spot for the activity board? Could anyone in your class help you decide?

Make the activity board and put it up in your classroom.

BE AN EXPERT: USING THE EQUIPMENT

2 to 3 hours   *1 person*

Here is a way to get to know about using audio-visual equipment and to help your classmates learn about it too.

Find out what kinds of audio-visual equipment are available at your school for your class to use. Talk to the people in charge of the equipment and find out how it is signed out and what the rules are for its use. How long can you keep it? Who can sign it out? What kind of care does it take? How long is the cord? Does it require a special electrical outlet? What kind of screen does it use? Are some pieces ever used together? How do they work? How long does it take to set them up for use? How do you focus? Rewind? Adjust sound? Speed? Prevent overheating? Where do you get slides and transparencies? How can you make them? How do you put them in and take them out? How can you use cassettes? Record players? How can you record music to go with a slide presentation? How do you splice film? Operate a movie camera? Set up a closed circuit television unit?

Get someone to demonstrate the equipment for you and use it yourself if possible. Sign it out or have your teacher sign it out and take it to the room and set it all up. See how long it takes and where in the room the equipment works best.

Plan a demonstration for the class in which you tell and show them about what you have learned.

CREATE: DESIGN AN ART AND MEDIA CENTER
several hours   *4 to 5 people*

Here is a chance to find out what goes into the making of an art and media center for an activity classroom.

Organize a group of four or five people in your class. Plan and make an art and media center to suit the needs of your class. Consider these questions: What activities might the art and media center be used for? Make a list. What are the most common tools and supplies that would be needed for these activities? Make another list. Where could you get these things? If you have to buy them, how much would they cost? Could you take up a collection among your classmates? Could you charge a fee for use of the art and media center?

After you have the supplies where are you going to store them? Is there a bookcase or cupboard in the room or the school? Have you made friends with the janitor? Could you use boxes? Is there a table available so that people can work on their projects in the room? How big is it? How many people can work at it? Where is it located? How will you clean the area? Will you have sponges? Paper towels and soap? A wastebasket?

How can you make the area an attractive part of the room? How can you keep its activities from being distracting to other people?

Plan and set up an art and media center. Have a grand opening day when you present it as a gift to the whole class. Explain to the class whatever they need to know about the supplies and furniture and how to use them.

HELP OTHERS: BE AN ART CONSULTANT

variable time   *1 person*

To become an expert at the practical considerations of handling the art media of an activity classroom, do this.

Gather information about the kinds of art projects and art materials your classmates will be using. Look through this book to see what suggestions are made for activities involving art work. Is there a media center in your room? What art materials are available? Make a list of questions you should be able to answer to help people in your class with their projects.

Here are some questions that may help you: How could you make costumes for class dramas? Could you use paper or old sheets? How? What else could you use? How could you make props? Do you know what paper mache is and how to use it? How could you make stage furniture and backdrops out of cardboard boxes? What is a collage and how can one be made? What ways can a collage be used for teaching English? What is a mural? What materials could be used in making one? What special problems would be involved in making one in class? What will rubber cement do that paste or Elmer's glue won't? What kind of scissors will not cut cloth? How can you use newspapers to protect the room and furniture during art work? What else could you use? How can you use newspapers and paper bags for drawing, collages, murals and costumes? How can people make folders or book bindings for projects? What will happen if you try to use spray paint in the classroom?

Talk to an art teacher about these questions and ask for suggestions which might help you. You may also find useful information in books about arts and crafts at your library.

Experiment. Try some of the projects you have read or heard about and bring them to show the class and tell how they were made or give a demonstration for the class. Post a notice on the bulletin board that you will help anyone who wants help with a project involving art work.

COMFY CORNER: BE A ROOM LIBRARIAN

variable time   *1 person*

Find out how to plan and arrange a reading corner by doing this.

Begin with the books. What books are in the room? Does the teacher have some to bring to the class? Do classmates have some to donate or lend? How can you get their cooperation? Are the books all in good condition? Do some need mending? How can you display the books attractively and invitingly? Are there bookcases? With flat shelves? With tilted shelves? Could you get a cheap, portable wire rack? How could you use boxes or tables? Will you put the books in some kind of order? Visit your school library and see how the books are arranged there. Can you mark the shelves?

Where in the room would be the best spot for a reading corner? Where is there the most light and the most privacy? How could you make privacy and light? Would it be a good idea to make friends with your school janitor? Could he give you cords, lamps, bookcases, boxes or other equipment you could use?

What will you do to make the reading corner a pleasant and comfortable place to read? Are there comfortable chairs? Would rugs or cushions on the floor help? How does your school or public library create a pleasant atmosphere? Are there posters or displays to interest people in the books?

Will the books be used only in the room or will they be taken home? How will you see that they are returned? Can you get library cards and pockets from your school library? Could you make your own sign-out system? How?

Plan and arrange the reading corner of your room. You may want to ask for help with furniture from other people in the room who are arranging furniture.

ON THE BOARD: BE A BULLETIN BOARD HELPER

40 minutes   *1 person*

If you or your friends have trouble getting your bulletin board displays to turn out the way you would like, make yourself a bulletin board expert.

First look at some bulletin boards in your school to see how the people who arranged them managed to put across the messages they intended.

List some of the different things people do to make you notice their displays.

How can you tell when a bulletin board is too full or too empty? What kinds of lettering look best? Which is easiest to read? Is it always best to arrange things in neat rows? How else could you do it?

What will you use to fasten your papers—pins, staples, tacks, or tape? What are the advantages and disadvantages of each? How do you feel about borders around bulletin boards? What different kinds have you seen? Which kind would you choose? Why? What about backgrounds? What are they made of? How can you change them to suit your purposes? Would you ever want to frame or mount special pictures or articles so that everyone would notice them? How would you do it? How could you find out?

What people will see the bulletin board? Does that affect what you put on it? How? Should a bulletin board have just one big important idea with lots of information about that idea? How would you know what the idea is? What ways could you find to make the idea of a bulletin board clear to the people who look at it?

After you have found the answers to these questions, tell your log about your discoveries. Then put your name in the help bank as a bulletin board helper. May all your bulletin boards be successful!

THE ACTIVITY CARD

Giving the assignment, a traditional task of the teacher, should prepare a student to work independently for a greater or lesser time. Unfortunately, many assignments do not do this. An assignment often has bad results. It is misunderstood, or students do wrong or useless things. In many cases it is insufficiently individualized. Hence, many students do not do the assignment, and, to the teacher's frustration and their own, appear in class without it. To prevent this, the teacher resorts to many devices, one of the commonest of which is the short quiz, used to find out which students have done the work and persuade the rest that they should be sure to do future assignments. Usually these are not graded until later in the day so they do not help teachers adjust lessons. Sometimes the quiz provides a grade goal for students for whom the lesson itself has little attraction.

Designing assignments of learning experiences for students involves a search for ways to package meaning. In the activity curriculum, this package is the activity card, a package which shifts from meaning as information to meaning as situation, to which the student is attracted by his inherent curiosity about meaning, into which the student inquires, and from which he develops information in the form of generalizations that occur to him as a result of his journey through the situation.

Activities and materials are rarely important in and of themselves. They are important only as they cause change in students, the change we call learning. And not all materials and activities are equally important or valuable. Quite the contrary. Some activities and materials produce more growth more economically for more students. These will be the activities used most frequently in the activity curriculum. The reader of this book will already have experienced the activity card if use has been made of the activities for Chapter I. Here is a pattern a teacher may use in making cards for students.

Sample Activity Card

Title

Time Budget   Number of Persons

Promise: The promise is a behavior or performance objective stated as a promise of student competence. The objective is a reward.
Activities: A clear, sequenced list of actions; inquiries which lead to generalizations.
Product: Log entries, folder materials, skits, discussions, reports.

The teacher must be familiar enough with the cards to guide the student who finds nothing he wants to do. He might like a "Just Read" card. Some cards may be so popular that several copies are needed. Cards used must be returned to the board. A card monitor can check that all are returned to the board before the class ends. Although the teacher does not have time and resources to make in a short time the contents of the activities for constant use of the control board, such a board is the heart of the application of the activity curriculum. Eventually, the teacher will make additions to the card file so that it can be used for more and more of the class time.

An infinity of possibilities exists for making card collections for student activities. Cards may be added from a wide variety of the teacher's own ideas and plans or from ideas gained from published materials. English textbooks, curriculums, critical reviews, and education textbooks furnish useful sources for activity cards. The *English Journal* is a gold mine of ideas. A useful collection might be constructed for each of the classics studied. The first cards a teacher makes will be good interim devices, samples, a nucleus for future building, to increase in number and variety as teachers and students increase their skills in planning their own activities. Making an activity card challenges the pedagogical imagination and competence of the teacher. It foresees the needs and thoughts of students. It reflects its inventor's sense of what is important about what is being taught. And, actually, its creation is not different from making other kinds of lesson plans.

Vast numbers of students can make little sense of the impoverished bag of learning designs in the traditional kit: lectures, assigned readings and writing, drills, and recitation. The activity card replaces these designs with a structured situation that focuses on the processes of discovering and using facts. Activity cards involve students in having experiences about which they are then questioned. Most of the facts students learn they will forget, and even those they remember are subject to increasingly speedy obsolescence. Students using activity cards learn to use the process whereby facts are collected and generated, since information in them is developed, not given.

The activity card leads the student to perceive and choose among alternatives. It is more of a guide than a leader, more of a support than a straitjacket. It cannot be truly objective but should leave the options as open as possible. From the best activity card the student gets a sense of the alternatives imposed by the task in order that the promise it offers may be fulfilled. Students learn to be free only by being free to choose appropriate ways of behaving. Understanding and using intricate patterns of freedom involving a wide range of choices requires considerable struggle. The skills of being free, like other skills, come only from practice. Activity cards provide practice in making extensive choices.

Work on activity cards leads the student to manufacture generalizations from specific examples in his own thinking and experience. He uncovers principles of combining and recombining data into useful packages of meaning adapted to his own purposes. As he generalizes, he places his meaning packages into a system which is his because he has truly learned it. He has not received it from a teacher or an authority figure.

As the student reaches the end of the task outlined on the card, he generates a product which enables him to relate his performance to the goal stated in the promise and thus evaluate his progress. His behavior during the task involves receiving language; his product involves him in producing it. He has also engaged in interactive processes with other students, persons outside of class, or the teacher. He has produced and received language, or, in traditional terms, he has "learned English." Meanwhile, shared relations with others taught him intangibles of human relationships, provided interest in his task, encouraged creativity and individuality, stimulated sustained attention to long-term problems, and provided human approval motivations and social experience. A teacher alone could not provide so many human values to so many students for so long a time as they can provide for each other.

A teacher gets good things to happen to students in activity experiences by asking the right questions. The teacher, as activity card maker, is primarily a deviser of questioning strategies. Silence, boredom, and confusion indicate that wrong questions have been asked. Good questions are a bridge between what the student does and thinks and the generalizations he should make about what he does and thinks.

Good questions are often those for which the teacher has no answer, not those whose answers come neat and prepackaged. Many useful questions admit of many or even no answers. Questions that may be answered by yes or no should appear on an activity card only where a commitment is needed to develop further ideas or logical patterns. The teacher should work to expand his skill in formulating good questions all his professional life. It may take some time to accustom students to playing with open-ended questions when they have been accustomed to give answers verifiable "in the book" or by the approval of the teacher. A teacher's respect for a student's in-depth answers and his response to them can show the student that this kind of answer is respectable. Questions must not threaten, and divergent answers must be without penalty if students are to be willing to make the maximum number of tries.

The questioning process in the activity curriculum takes advantage of principles of programmed learning: individual pacing and confidence-building success appear in each step, and steps are so small that movement from one to another does not end in paralysis or frustration. Some redundancy is needed in a series of questions students are to confront alone. Then, if they have wandered, they can backtrack.

Questions should link literature students read and the speaking, listening, and writing they do to ideas they can discover from their own experience. Such discovery provides a satisfying feedback, encouraging the student by making him see the importance to him of issues that arise in his classroom experience. In the case of literary and philosophical problems, he becomes aware that clear, unambiguous answers are not always the best, most truthful, or most useful and that important questions often have no final answers. They lead to further questions. They are hospitable to exploratory, tentative response. A student may find that it is sometimes better to find out how to ask questions than how to answer them. He sees that an answer for one person is not always useful to another, and an answer useful at one time or under certain conditions may not be a good answer for another person or under another set of conditions. The student realizes that men of good will and good scholarship will differ on important issues. Students and teachers can learn together that the vigor with which they pursue investigations they hope will lead to truth, not the vigor with which they support their prejudgments is the measure of their will to learn.

Students need maturation of judgment to understand the essential ambiguity of all important issues and the frequent necessity of choosing between alternatives, none of which completely resolve difficulties and many of which entail new problems as they solve old ones. Traditional curriculums often aim at teaching values, prepackaged and prechosen. The activity curriculum directs the student to engage in the process of valuing. It assumes no omniscient position that values a student will need may now be defined, formulated, and fed to him. It assumes that if he has practice in defining, formulating, and digesting his own approach to valuing, he will be ready to meet his needs for valuing in the future.

No student has to finish everything on a card. Most cards are designed so that the student who does everything will have the most growth, but there are exceptions. There may be discrepancies in times listed for the activities. Not all students work at the same rate, and some do a more complete job than others. The teacher may want to indicate a wide range of times. He may consult students about this problem. Some cards may be designed for one person but may furnish good discussion materials for a group. The teacher needs to be flexible and experimental, and encourage students to be so. The aim is to do and grow, not to finish, complete, or cover. The focus is on the student, not on the material. Ideally every student should read, write, speak, and listen every class period. Cards should combine these skills.

Students who have learned in patterns where they were judged in terms of how many activities they completed may want to judge themselves on how many cards they finish. It may take some time to reinforce the behavior which values exploiting all the possibilities for growth inherent in one card before turning to another. The behavior of the teacher must direct students' attention over and over to how much they are learning, how much they are growing, and how many new ideas they are gaining and using, whether these come from one card or many. Also there is value in letting a student who wants to do some of the activities on a card and not others to exercise this option. He may want to return later and finish some of the activities after he has gained insight into their value from doing other activities. Openness of options, maintained in an atmosphere which encourages constant self-examination and accounting for his decision, helps a student to see that his goal is learning to make useful decisions, not just creating products.

After the first use of the activity cards, adaptations will occur to the teacher, and he will change his application of the system with every class he teaches. But to plan the study of a unit or a piece of writing, the teacher might follow this procedure the first time the activity cards are used. First, he will make literature cards applicable to the writing being studied, providing for a range of interests and abilities. He can add cards relating to listening, writing, and speaking. Study aids from textbooks are a useful source of ideas. A few blank cards may be left for students who want to make their own.

Teachers must see card packs as materials to be manipulated and changed to fit the focus of their own need, scholarship, and experience. Cards should be constantly reviewed, selected out, or added to as teachers and students find some useful and others less so. Cards can be used for small experiments in independent study, as enrichment devices for independent study packets already in use, as alternatives to the "questions at the end of the story" sections of anthologies and in a hundred other ways to complement curricular arrangements already in place. This system allows independence to grow as teachers and students are ready for it. No sudden calls need to be made on teacher time or skills, but both teachers and students can grow into the ability to design their own plans as fast as they become ready to do so. Activity cards are tentative, subject to manipulation, change, and reconstruction by teachers and students who should use them, when they are ready to do so, as ever-adaptable springboards for their developing creativity in designing options. Teachers and students should work together to choose and make new options, always enlarging the areas of choice and alternatives and choosing together from among them more wisely.

Not many days will pass in using the activity curriculum before students and teachers will begin to invent new cards and revise old ones. Students who use cards should be encouraged to make suggestions about productive or unproductive parts of the activities, how they can be made more useful or more fun. Alternative methods of doing activities can be suggested on additional cards. There should always be a supply of clean cards available for anyone who wants to rewrite a card. When teachers and students begin to add new ideas to the cards and bring new ideas for new cards from their lives outside of class, the activity curriculum begins to show that it is successful. It becomes organic and growing. When the teacher finds that everything he sees or listens to or reads reminds him of a card he would like to add to the control board, he has embarked on a curriculum project that will last the whole of his professional life and lead him to accumulate files and files of activities related to all the materials he teaches. Such files could be accumulated in English departments in schools as ways of sharing ideas and helping new teachers. They might even be collected in large school systems and take the place of the bound list of books and pages that constitute many system-wide curriculums.

As teachers and students work together on new reading or language materials, cards which the teacher decides to put in the rack will change. Certain cards will be chosen because they contain more or less structure, call for more or less abstraction, or provide appropriate activities for a certain kind of student. Individual students may be referred to certain cards by the teacher or by students who have used them. A classified advertisement column in a class newsletter could be run to advertise testimonials from students who liked certain cards.

Cards available in the rack and the sequence in which cards are put out by the teacher will determine the sequence of class learning activities. Student needs can be assessed by the teacher as logs are read, new letters and materials in folders are evaluated, and class performances of skits and reports are made. Individual conferences between teacher and student, very short if this is made necessary by numbers, are essential. Each new activity will grow out of needs discovered in previous activities.

The teacher should keep a record of cards that go well with certain units or pieces of literature. Inadequacies need to be recorded so that cards may be supplemented or changed when there is time. The teacher should ask students who want to do so to write log evaluations of the cards. Some students like to evaluate, and others do not. A card can be designed for those who would like to evaluate. The activity teacher must create in his classroom a learning climate of flexibility, inventiveness, and ingenuity which will extend to both teacher and students and help all enjoy their school day.

Activity cards should lead the student himself to sense his own needs as he becomes aware of the processes through which he passes as he learns, seeing his ideas and feelings as they develop. He should learn to cherish and be proud of his own growth and find ways to talk about it in his speaking and writing.

Homework in the activity curriculum is the bridge between life as the school prescribes it and life as it is tested under the duress of life circumstances. For instance, there is no drill or exercise in language, but there are opportunities to see how language operates, to test what has been learned about language in the classroom. Life experience is the laboratory of language learning. Traditional homework produces little advancement in learning and generates much discomfort among students and parents. Homework is present in the activity curriculum, and many cards require activities which have to be carried on outside of class, but these will be found to ask for collection of outside data to be used in the classroom, or they will request verification in the outside world of data which have been collected in the classroom.

Activities

CARD BUILDING, PART I: BEGIN WITH A NEED
35 minutes   *1 person*

Here is a way to get started making lesson plans or activity cards.
Before you can make a lesson or activity card you need someone to

make it for, and the person or persons you are designing it for must have a need which a lesson or activity can help them meet.

Begin with the people in your class. What are their learning needs? How can you find out? Try a survey. Ask each person in your class what he would like to be able to do by the end of the semester. Write some on these needs in your log. Can you divide the needs into categories? Which needs would be easiest to satisfy by the usual kind of school lesson? Why? Which needs would be the easiest to satisfy by an activity involving the person or other people? What kinds of processes or activities could help the people in your class meet their needs? Would any of the needs be impossible to design a lesson or activity card for? Why?

From the needs you have listed choose one for which you could design an activity card. What kind of activity could you find that would fit that need? How will it get the person from where he is now to what he needs to be able to do? Perhaps you can think of several different activities for this need. Jot down these ideas in your log, even if they seem silly at first. If you have trouble thinking of activity ideas, look through the activities in this book to see what sorts of things you might use.

When you have exhausted your ideas, forget about them for awhile and do something else. When you return to this work, read over everything you have written. If you think of any new activities or changes in the ones you have, add them. As you read the activity ideas, ask yourself these questions: By doing this, will the person learn to do what he needs to do? How will it help him? Is the activity suitable for his age and interests? Does he have the knowledge and skill to be able to do it? Does he have enough time to do it? Where will he do it? Where will he get the materials? Will the activity lead him step by step to learn what he needs to know or to be able to do? Will he be able to use what he has learned again in other situations? As you think about these questions, you may decide to cross out some of the ideas or improve them.

If you are satisfied with any of the activity ideas you have discovered, use them for the foundation of one or more activity cards to be used in your class. If you do not feel certain about where to go from here, try "Card Building, Part II." If you are not satisfied with your ideas, you may find it helpful to find some other members of your class who are making activity cards and compare your efforts.

CARD BUILDING, PART II: BEGIN WITH A GOAL

20 minutes   *1 person*

To give direction and purpose to your activity card writing and to your student in his activity card reading and doing, do this.

If you have an activity you would like to use for a lesson or an activity card, you must already know something about the person or persons you are designing it for, and you probably have some ideas about what they will be able to do when they have finished it that they could not do before. So that you will have these ideas clearly before you as you work on your card, supply the missing words for this sentence and write it in your log: "When ____ is finished with this activity, (he, she, or they) should be able to ____." If the person using the card will be able to do more than one thing, use this sentence over as many times as necessary. If it seems appropriate, you may also want to add how well the person should be able to do it.

Check your activity idea to be certain you have told the truth about what it will do for the person. If you haven't, change the activity or the goal—or both—until they are consistent. Ask yourself if your goal or goals are valuable to the person who will be doing the activity. If it passes this test, turn your goal into the promise which you will write at the top of the card. Tell your reader what the activity will do for him.

Here are some questions to think about which may help you find the best words for your promise: How do you want the person who reads this to feel about what is on the card? Are there any words you do not want to use because they might have unpleasant associations for your reader? Are there any words you could use to make him feel comfortable? How can you convince him he will like the activity and yet be truthful? What is the most simple and exact way to tell him what he will get from the activity?

Write your promise in your log beneath your teaching goal. Now finish your card.

HAPPY WORDS: CARD TITLES

30 minutes   *2 people*

If you have an activity idea, here is a way to find a title for it.

Find a partner to work with and get paper and pencils. Each of you has an idea. Now you need to sell your idea to the other person. Imagine your partner is going to be looking through the cards on an activity board tomorrow. If your card is there with the others, how will it catch his eye? How can you make him pick out that one and read it? How can he know at first glance that this card will help him with something he needs to do? How will your title convince him he should take the trouble to read the rest of the card?

Practice writing some titles for your activity to see if you can solve these problems. You may want to write your titles in two parts, one just for fun to get your partner's interest and the other to tell him what the activity is about. You don't need to wait until tomorrow to see if your titles do what you want them to do. Test them on your partner. As you try out your titles on each other, you may find it helpful to ask yourselves these questions: Would the title make you want to read the card? Why or why not? Do you mind if it's silly or funny? Does your title tell the truth about the activity? How could you make it say more exactly what you mean? What words could you use to make it appeal to young people? Could you use literary devices, slang or words from popular slogans as attention-getters?

Trade activity ideas with your partner and see if he can suggest a good title for your card and if you can suggest one for his. Did you find any titles that you liked but that didn't fit this idea? Start a title file. On an empty page somewhere in your log write down all the good-sounding titles you thought of. Someday you may have just the right activity to fit that title.

Write some of your favorite titles in large letters and post them around the room to see if your classmates notice them and what their reactions are. You may even get some helpful suggestions. If other people in your class also post their title efforts, you may all enjoy and learn from seeing what others have done.

QUESTIONS AND ANSWERS: THINKING ABOUT ACTIVITIES
40 minutes *3 people*

Here is a game that will give you a chance to practice the questioning strategies of good card-making.

You will need three people. In the beginning two of you will play the game while the other keeps score. Then, you will trade places, until you have played the game three times and each of you has been the score-keeper once. Each of the two players chooses a topic that he feels informed enough to answer questions on—perhaps a hobby. Flip a coin to decide who has the first turn as questioner. The person who is to begin asks his partner questions on the partner's topic for a period of three minutes. The scorekeeper watches the time.

The problem is to ask only questions which do *not* have "yes" or "no" answers. The person answering the questions should try to be honest and unevasive in his answers. The scorekeeper keeps record of the number of answers other than "yes" or "no" that are given during each turn. At the end of three minutes the questioning and answering partners switch roles. Here's a hint for questioning: It is hard to answer "yes" or "no" to a question that begins with "how," "what," or "why."

When you have played the game three times so that everyone has had a chance to be the questioner once, count the good answers to see who was the most skillful questioner. Then, discuss these questions: Which questions were the most thought-provoking? Why were those questions better? How can good questions make good answers? Does a good questioner ask something he knows the other person cannot answer? Why or why not? If a question can be answered by one word—even though it is not a "yes" or "no"—is it a thought-provoking question? Why or why not? How can you tell when you have asked a question that has made the other person think? How can you tell when you have asked a question which excites his interest? What do the other person's reactions tell you about the success of your question?

Try what you have learned about questioning by writing an activity card.

CARD SHARPIES: SHARING YOUR WORK

30 to 50 minutes   *4 to 8 people*

Here is a way you can improve your activity card writing, find new ideas for more cards, and get practice in card writing.

Find some other people who have also been writing activity cards. Each person decides upon some part of the card he has written that he is not satisfied with. He copies his card onto a piece of paper, leaving out the part he does not like.

Trade papers with someone else in the group. Fill out the missing part of his card while he fills out the missing part of yours. Try it again. Trade with a different person. Do this as many times as seems reasonable for the size of your group and the interest you have in it. You have practiced card writing, and you have collected several different versions of the problem part of your card.

With your group, discuss some of the difficulties of card writing and their possible solutions: Which parts of the cards did most people have trouble with? Why? How did other people solve these problems? How did other people interpret what you had written? What discoveries did you make that will help you write this card or others in the future?

If there is space on the bulletin board in your room, post some of these cards with their different solutions to writing problems for other people to compare.

HELP!: START A HELP BANK

1 hour *1 person*

Here is a way to help yourself with your learning needs and to help your classmates too.

You need some 5 by 8 inch cards and a shoe box that will serve as a file for them. Write "Help Bank" on it, and put it in a spot in the room where it is accessible to everyone. The purpose of the help bank is to make it easier for people in your class to help each other with their work.

If a person wants to be in the help bank, he gets a blank card from the bank and writes at the top of it something that he could help other people do. He might be able to help as a proofreader, sign maker, builder, artist, or audio-visual expert, or use any skill his classmates might need in their work. He can list as many things as he can contribute, but each should be on a different card, so cards can be arranged according to the kind of help. Whenever these people need help on something they are not so good at, they come to the help bank to find a card by someone who is good enough to help them.

Your task is to be the help bank librarian. Arrange the file so that people can easily find the kind of help they want, and help them find it if they have trouble.

Present your help bank to the class. Explain to your classmates what it is for and how to use it.

GLAD
I DID IT AND I'M MAD: CARD EVALUATION
SAD

10 minutes *1 person*

If you have done a card activity, tell your log answers to these questions:
1. What was there about the title of the card that attracted you?
2. Did you understand the goal? Did the questions and activities relate to it? Did it tell the truth about what happened to you

when you did the activities? Did attaining the goal seem important to you?

3.   Were the questions good? Did they lead you in the direction of
     the goals without any gaps that you could not jump? How much
     help did you have to have from others? Should the card have
     some helps on it that are not there? What are they?
4.   Did the card deal with something that mattered to you? What
     was it? Did you really want to answer the questions and do the
     activities? Which ones were best, and which ones were least
     effective?
5.   Write a few sentences of advice to others who would use the
     card. Should they choose it? What will they get out of it? Will
     they like it? Write an advertisement of the card for the bulletin
     board.

GET WET, THE WATER'S FINE: HOW TO USE AN ACTIVITY CARD
10 minutes   *1 person or a group*

To help your students use activity cards, here are some suggestions you
can try the next time you come to class.

So that you won't get caught in a rush at the card center, come to
class with some ideas about what you want to work on. Do you have any
questions that you haven't been able to find the answers to—questions
about how people talk or think, about books, poems, plays, or even what
it has all got to do with you? Do you have some kind of problem with
language that you wish you could solve? Write down three things you
would like to know about or improve in. Take these with you to class.
Look for them under the subject heading that they seem to fit into best.
Pick out two or three cards. Take them back to your seat to read them
and decide if you want to do any of them. When you have decided, take
the extra ones back right away so that others can use them.

Look at the suggested time and numbers of people involved. It may
take you less time or more, depending upon how difficult this task is
for you and how much care you put into doing it. As for the number of
participants, that can often be changed to meet your needs if you
change the activity a little.

The title may help you to know if you are really interested in this card,
but just underneath the title is a promise which tells you what you can
expect to get from the activity.

Your card may start out with questions. Those are for you to think
about, ask other people, discuss with a group, and look up in books.
In other words, try to find the answers in any way that satisfies you.

Some cards have lots of questions and some only have a few. Your card may start right away with an activity for you to do and have the questions later. Some cards are mostly activity and some are mostly questions. That depends on what the promise is.

Each card is like a recipe. If you can't get one ingredient, it is sometimes possible to substitute another. But the most important thing that goes into this recipe is you. You can't possibly get more out of it than you put in. The card doesn't do anything; you do.

At the end of each card is a section which tells you what objective you should reach. This might be something you do, something you make, or something you write in your log.

Before you start to do anything on the card be sure that you read through the whole card once. Then you will know exactly where you are going and whether or not it is practical for you. When you need special help, don't forget to consult the help bank. And if you feel uncertain, why not join a group?

Now try it.

THE TEACHER BEGINS

Deluges of books justify change and advocate various kinds of freedom in schools. But teachers who feel locked into curriculums, book adoptions, self-contained classrooms, and communities who value tradition need practical help. A teacher who wants to change at the start of the semester or start of the year has chosen an optimum time to begin the activity curriculum.

It is best not to tell students or fellow teachers that you are going to do something different or that students are going to be free in your classroom. Freedom is not a thing which may be bestowed by a teacher on a class. It is a long and complicated process and requires far more structure to operate than a repressive atmosphere.

To operate in an activity classroom effectively, students must be retrained, but this will take less time than many teachers think. For what we ask them to do in an activity classroom is what they are likely to want to do and what they would do if left alone to choose. We are using natural inclinations, for when students are free to choose, they choose to be free. Freedom is choice, and the process of teaching students to be free is the process of constantly widening the range and effectiveness of student choices, starting modestly and growing new ways to choose as students develop competence in using freedom.

A good way to begin with a new class is to set goals. This process starts with a discussion in the class about what English is. Each day, decisions a class has made about what English is are fed back to students on the board or on mimeographed sheets, and discussions are renewed until agreement is reached. This may take several days. When students begin to look at English with teachers, they often decide that English is, as other scholars have decided, language, literature, and composition, or as modern thinkers are beginning to say, speaking, reading, writing and listening, ways of receiving and expressing language.

Having reached this conclusion, students have decided what it is they are going to study during the semester. This is the time to divide any cards a teacher has made into the classifications that students have chosen and post them under these classifications on the activity control board. Students should then be invited to consult the board and choose activities that they would like to do. They will see that, if they are to do these, they need work space, and their help can be enlisted to divide the room into interest centers. They can be asked to contribute any materials they have to the centers—old books, etc.

The next step in setting goals should come after students have done some work on the cards and begun to ask about grades for their work. Another full class session is then indicated to deal with the problem. Students can begin to check the promises on the cards to see if they have done what they intended to do when they started. Since they have decided that English is reading, they must decide how well they would like to be able to read and how far they can go toward that goal this semester. The same process will outline hoped-for progress in writing. They will examine such questions as what it means to read or write well. All these questions are of vital import to students, and they must have input in deciding them.

Each student may want to set his own goals in his log. These, as well as class goals, can and should be revised frequently. They can be added to if progress proceeds well, subtracted from if they were unrealistically high, or jettisoned altogether if they were inappropriate. Constant reference to goals set by the class and by individual students should be part of every student-teacher conference and every student choice of daily activity.

Most students accept competition with their classmates as their primary measure of achievement. The activity teacher may want to use the help bank system to suggest an alternative value system. The problem called "cheating" needs to be reexamined. It may be that any assignment that permits cheating is a bad one. If a student can circumvent his own growth or feels he needs to do so, he cannot be encouraged to learn. He needs to feel good about seeking help, when he needs it, from other people as well as from books or from his memory. And students need to learn how to help others in the only way that is really useful, helping them to help themselves. All need to learn to value group achievement which seeks, includes and values the achievements of each member of a group. These are values in themselves, not just by-products. Students need to explore how they feel when they help and receive help and when they show that they recognize and value achievements of others. These are the satisfactions that build a community, whether that community be in a town, a country, a world, or a classroom, and teach the skills of finding strengths not weaknesses in others. An atmosphere of safety pervades the classroom where assignments are packages of success for all, not just success for some and despair for others. Reluctant students are encouraged when they see that their peers can do and enjoy doing tasks. The will to do becomes contagious. Although there is a premium on competency, there is also a premium on caring about the opportunities and contribution of all. Reductions of tensions and jealousy are reflected in a reduction of disruption.

If the teacher wants to start using the activity curriculum in the middle of the semester with students who have already been accustomed in the class to traditional methods, another approach recommends itself. Let the teacher begin with a carefully structured activity day. In the planning students should have much input, planning the activities, making the control board, designing the interest centers. Activities used should be sure success-getters, ones that will work well with the students so that they will have immediate feedback of success. Activities should be chosen for their potential in solving whatever problems administrators and fellow teachers see as the greatest problems of the school. When teachers start with what they are sure they and their students can manage well, they will be able to build on their successes and what they have done that they feel comfortable with when they consider more radical departures from habits of the past. It is important that teachers do not use any rhetoric of radical change to students, fellow teachers or administrators. Such language rouses fears and opposition, threatening those who are unready to change. If students and their teacher are successful with one activity day, more may be scheduled until the class is absorbed into the activity curriculum.

Activities

IN THE MOOD: GETTING YOUR CLASS STARTED

5 minutes per day for 1 week   *1 person*

Discover ways of getting a class relaxed and in a mood for creative thought.

Plan warm-up activities for your class or group. If you are planning to do this with the whole class, arrange with your teacher or planning committee to use the first five minutes of each class period for a week. If you are working with a group, you will also need to provide extra time in your schedule of events.

Begin your warm-up plan with music. Listen to tapes or records until you find one that fits your purpose. How do you want the class to feel when they hear the music? What kind of music would be too distracting or too exciting? How would you know if it is too slow or relaxing? How do you feel when you listen to the music you have chosen?

Try shaking to the music. Shake a hand; then an arm too. Shake both arms. Shake your head, your shoulders, your feet. Move to the music, not in any particular way. Just sway if you feel like it. Was it good music to shake to? If it was, you are ready to try this kind of warm-up with your class or group.

When you first do this some people may be shy about it. Tell them they may move and shake as much or as little as seems comfortable for them. It may help your classmates to get over their first-try shyness if you arrange before you begin to have two or three confederates who will be the first to start the exercise. If they seem to be enjoying the experience, it will be easier for others to join the activity.

At the end of the week ask everyone who participated to tell his log how he felt about the acitivity.

ROAD MAP: GOAL SETTING

45 minutes   *4 to 6 people*

Here is a way to practice goal setting.

Find several other people to work with. Talk about your individual goals for this class: What is this class supposed to teach you to do? Is that what you want to learn from it? Is there anything else you hope to gain from it? If so, what?

On a separate page of your log see how many things you can list that you would like to be able to do as a result of what you learn in this class. Appoint or elect one person in your group to be a secretary. Ask each person to read his list or give it to the secretary. Have the secretary make a composite list, writing down the goals suggested and putting check marks by the ones used by more than one member to show how many times this goal was suggested.

Have one member read these goals to the group. Discuss these questions: Did you hear any new goals you wish you had listed? Have the secretary check them. Would some goals be impossible to reach? Which ones? Why? Would some goals be silly, selfish, or not worth reaching? How could you improve them? Which goals do most of the people in your group agree with? Why? Are these goals things that you would be able to do or demonstrate when you finish the class? How will you know when you have reached them?

As a group, choose not less than five or more than ten of these goals as your official group goals. Agree on how they should be worded and write them in your logs. Consider what you can do as individuals or as a group to reach these goals. If you have some ideas about how to reach your goals, you may decide to turn them into activity cards.

The next time you are trying to choose an activity, open your log to your goals page and ask yourself if the activities will help you reach your goals. If you can't find any that will, you may want to write your own.

BENEATH THE SCENE: INVESTIGATING STRUCTURE
40 minutes   *1 person*

Do this to find out what you need to do to structure an activity class.

Find out how your class runs. Watch what happens in your class. Talk to the class members. Talk to the teacher. Ask what he does every day before the students come into the room. How and what does he prepare for class? Why does he do what he does? Who makes sure all the equipment and furniture is what it needs to be and where it needs to be? How is this done? When and where does the teacher read logs? When and where do the students write in their logs? Do groups of students meet and work outside of the classroom? If so, when and where? How do students make arrangements to work on large, messy, time-consuming, or noisy projects? When and where does the teacher have conferences? How much time during each period does the teacher spend giving advice and helping with individual problems? What do the teacher and the students do after class? How is the time during class divided? When do students or groups start working and when do they quit? What else do they do? How do the teacher and students know when it is time to do all these things? When do people give reports, look at the bulletin board, visit the activity board? Does anyone check to see when supplies are getting low? If so, who, and what do they do about it? What keeps everything running smoothly—or does it? If it does, why does it? If it doesn't, why not?

Write what you have discovered in your log, and make your discoveries work. Put your name in the help bank as a planning helper.

A PEOPLE PLAN: ACTIVITY DAY

several hours   *4 to 6 people*

Do this to find out how to plan an activity day in a traditional classroom.

Find several other people to work with. Plan to have an activity day in a traditional classroom. If you know of any teachers who would be willing to try your plan, prepare it for that class and ask the teacher to use it. You might invent an imaginary class for your activity.

Consider these questions as you talk about your plans: How can you prepare the students for the atmosphere, the decisions, and the physical freedom of an activity classroom? If you will have discussions ahead of time, when will that be? How long will it take? What questions will you ask students? What questions do you expect them to ask you? What will the answers be? How will you involve the students in the preparations for the activity day? What could you show them or demonstrate to them? What decisions could they make about how the room and activities will be organized? How far in advance does this need to be done? Who will make the cards and the activity board? Who will decide what activities are on the cards? How will all this fit into the structure of the classroom and the school? What furniture and equipment will be used, and how will it be used? How and when will it be moved? When will students use the activity board? How much time will be left for the activities? Would it be practical to get cards and form groups one day and do activities the next?

Have you thought of any other considerations yourselves? What kinds of problems might occur? Go over and over your list until you have covered every possibility. After the activity day, will there be an opportunity for the students to discuss their reactions? Will they have logs where they can write their reactions?

Would it help you to sell your plan to the teacher and the principal who needs to give his approval if your plan is typed and makes a good impression? Would your teacher be impressed by a list of objectives also? How will you know if the students have profited from this experience?

Obviously, this plan will cover more than one day. The time element is part of the plan. Write your plan and make at least two copies, one for the teacher and one to leave in the room so others in the class can see what you have done. The members of your group might also find it useful to make private copies of the plan. You might want to use it yourselves someday.

After the activity day visit the teacher and talk to him about how he feels about the experiment. Ask him if he would like to try it again. How did the students react? Would they like to try it again? What advice can he give you about next time? Does the teacher feel that the objectives were achieved?

If your plan was not used in a real classroom, write in your logs how you think it would have worked and what the answers to these questions would have been.

DECISIONS, DECISIONS: GRADE MAKING

variable time   *4 to 6 people*

Here is a way to find out what grades mean, how to use them, how to set the criteria for them, and in general, how to live with them.

Form a group with several of your classmates to work on this activity. In your group discuss these questions: Who would decide on the grade? If the teacher decides, should the student have anything to say about it? If so, what? And how much? What should a student be graded on? Willingness to work? The quality or quantity of work produced? His ability to produce work? What things can your group think of that you have been graded or not graded for in the past?

With your own class in mind make a list of criteria that you think the members of your class should be graded on. Write your list at the top of a long piece of paper—you may want to tape another piece on to the bottom of yours—and post your list on the bulletin board with an invitation for class members to add new ones of their own.

The next day discuss your list and any additions to it. Agree on ten of these criteria that your group thinks are most important. How would you arrive at a grade from these criteria? Would each item have the same value? Would some count more than others? How would you judge whether or not a person in your class measured up to these criteria? How well should he do these things or know these things to get an A, B, C, D, or F? How would you know how well he does them or knows them?

Since each one of you knows himself best, use these criteria to arrive at a grade for yourself. Write your grade and how you determined it in your log. Later you may want to use this entry as the beginning of your own system of grading.

A TOGETHER TALK: CONFERENCE

1 hour   *2 people*

Whether you are going to be the teacher or the student, this may help you to face student-teacher conferences with confidence.

Find a partner and talk about these questions: Why does a student want to have a conference with a teacher? Why does a teacher want to have a conference with a student? What things does each one want to learn about the other? What does each one expect of the other? If you are a student, what do you think the teacher is thinking about you? What are you thinking about him? What questions do you ask him? What do you expect him to ask you? How do you speak when you talk to the teacher? How do you expect him to speak to you? If you are the teacher, what do you think the student is thinking about you? What are you thinking about him? What do you want to ask him? What do you really ask him? What do you expect him to ask you? How do you speak to him? How do you expect him to speak to you?

List the different reasons a teacher and student could have for wanting a conference. Ask yourselves the above questions for each of these reasons. Do any of the answers turn out differently when there are different reasons for the talk? Pick out several of the reasons you like best. Try to imagine what the teacher in these situations would be like and what the student would be like. Pretend that one of you is the teacher and one is the student. Act out what you think would happen when the two of you talk. Try acting out several different conference situations.

After you have acted out a scene, discuss these questions: How did the teacher and the student feel before the conference? How did each of them feel afterward? Did the conference do for them what they wanted it to do? In which situation do you think the teacher dealt best with the problem? Why? In which situation did the student deal best with the problem? Why? How did the student and the teacher feel about each other at the end of each scene? Was it good that they felt that way? Why or why not? How can teachers talk and act so that students have good feelings as a result of conferences? How can students talk and act so that teachers have good feelings about them?

In your logs write your conclusions about conferences. Choose the most successful of your teacher-student conferences and present it to the class.

CARD PLAY: BE A CARD HELPER

variable time   *1 person*

This will help you become skillful at using cards, categorizing them, and finding the right ones for the needs of individuals.

Become an expert on the activity cards in this book. Notice which cards are placed in which categories. Look at each card. Read the time it takes, the number of people needed and the title. Read the promise and the whole card.

If you find any cards which seem to be in the wrong category, read them carefully and find a place to relocate them if it seems necessary.

Put your name in the help bank as a card helper. Be sure to write on the help card what you can help people do. Write in your log how you feel about being a card helper: How do you feel about the people you help? How did you feel about yourself when you helped them? Were there things you wished you knew? Were you glad you knew what you did? Do you think those people you helped would like to help you on something they know and you don't? Will they be able to do their cards without you next time?

II

RECEIVING LANGUAGE

CHAPTER III

The Student Reads

Teachers who help students receive language pay attention to three aspects of student reading: a student's desire or lack of desire to read, the special opportunities to receive language provided by each genre, and the relation of what the student is given to read to life as the student can observe it.

In the junior and senior high schools the problem of teaching reading is more and more the problem of reaching learners who have been through all the standard procedures which have not worked, a problem of reaching kids who can read but will not read. All that teaching decoding can do has been done. Why can't they read, and if they can, why don't they? The answer has often been for the school to do more and harder what has failed before, use more developmental reading, more clinics. These have a place, but they have been around for a decade, and they have not made a real difference in numbers of students who do not read. Many teachers and more students are desperate. In their mutual frustration they visit constant indignities upon each other.

Sound and touch learning were as important as sight learning in preliterate culture, but the coming of print downgraded them and made sight learning all-important. While teachers in English classes urge students toward verbal facility, they must respect as well nonverbal sensitivity and imagination, which interact with reading skills. The range and delicacy of those perceptions are revered by the young, but because the printed book is still the chief means of preserving and advancing knowledge, students must gain reading skills as well.

Some students in secondary school, perhaps as many as fifteen or twenty percent in some classes, cannot read. Many causes, among them emotional blocks, poor instruction, limited backgrounds, slowness of intellectual response, physical illness, or inadequate language maturation of the brain underlie lack of reading ability. Certain students will always read more than others. Some students do not want to read and never will want to read. They want to see films or television, look at pictures, or see comics. Some have seasons of reading, when their life style either abolishes reading or encourages it. Growth in reading ability increases in many people throughout their lives, and one theory says that at certain ages happy children do not read at all.

Forcing past natural attitudes toward reading will probably have small permanent positive effect. Hence, the activity teacher will not worry students about their reading. But that teacher will do many things to make students comfortable about their reading and with the idea of reading and will give practical helps to boost reading competence.

SELECTING READING MATERIALS

Access to books should be easy, and selection should be assisted by a concerned teacher, who is himself a reader, a wide reader, and a reader of literature that youth likes. The English teacher is a model in this as in other language behavior. In order to develop taste the student must believe he can choose good books. A good book for a student is a book he feels good about choosing and one that is treated with respect by his teacher. Taste starts not with what students should read but with what they will read, and teaching a student to like the best does not mean starting with the best.

In 1909 when the American copyright law began to operate, English teachers taught selected and docile students a body of standard classics, which were largely in the public domain. There was no thought of clarifying the student's contemporary experience or sensitizing him to the developing world through literature. But critics of various historical periods are far from agreeing about what a classic is, and the estimate of what is best often changes with the century or even with the short term fashion. Hence, the "standard classics" approach to the teaching of reading and literature is fading.

The "adapted" classic has a place. Many of these books have great stories and characters, who exist importantly quite apart from the language and full exposition of the author. Students can enjoy and should know many of these books they have neither the time nor the ability to read. The adapted classic allows the slow reader to know the great old stories and characters he would never meet if he did not have the abbreviated version. Certainly he will not know the book as the close reader of the original would know it, just as even the close reader of a good edition does not know the book as the scholar who studies facsimiles or originals of the author's manuscripts knows it. These are all matters of degree. But the reader of the adaptation will know something about the book, and he has a right to whatever access to great literature his ability permits and his life style makes desirable.

Censorship of what students read is often a problem in schools. To understand and cherish the heritage of values out of which the modern world has grown, the leading edge of culture and communication in the current scene must be explored and relevancies established. Probably students should read whatever books they want to read, and no censorship should be exercised beyond that arising from recognition of individual differences and standards of appropriateness mutually decided upon by teacher and student. We cannot screen ideas that are thrust upon youth by advertising and the media. We cannot supervise and restrict their movement. We cannot protect them from ideas but must prepare them to handle ideas of all kinds. Educational processes must develop standards and values which students internalize. They have to fix their own guidelines and develop inhibitions rather than obey prohibitions.

In settings which will develop those guidelines it is important to remember that one who cares more for what is good than he does for what is true loses both goodness and truth. Works which should be censored are those which swerve from the truths of the human heart. A good piece of writing may not do this, even though it may present those truths in idiosyncratic ways and under circumstances of the writer's own choosing. We lose the trust of youth if we guard them from ugly truths and expose them to pretty lies. The dirtiest book is one that falsifies life.

The dangers of reading words that relate to sexuality, defecation, and the deity are vastly overestimated. Most students hear lots of this kind of talk. Many of them read a lot of it but remain unconvinced that they want to use it. At one time writers used euphemisms—like the television bleep, whose only effect on the listener is to distract him while he translates and returns from the sense of unreality imposed by the unreal language.

The aims of the censor cannot be attained in a day when advertising and the media function as they do. Editing and euphemism breed cynicism and contempt among young readers and suggest to them that they are not expected to take school-chosen materials seriously or believe schools are supposed to have anything to do with life as it is. If parents or the community are offended by books that seem dirty to them, students are offended by bland, moral, and meaningless texts. They use a censorship too on such materials. They just turn them off.

When the student reads materials that adults hope he will not like and will not read, adults must not make scenes, destroy the materials, or shame him, or he will think he is evil. But, he will not quit reading the materials; he will just be more careful to hide what he is doing from adults. Teachers should get student reading out in the open and help students determine what effect the reading has on them and why they want to read it. Some students are so curious about sex they read fiction books about it because they cannot get other kinds of information. Fiction may mislead them. They may need nonfiction books to which they may be guided and which will meet their need far better.

A writer who writes of a certain kind of people must tell the things they do and say and the way they do and say them. Writers have to use the words that the people they write about would use, or the conversation they put in their characters' mouths is false. If they did not use these words, they could not write about many important and interesting characters. There are many visions of the world, and even though adults have chosen the world view they wish to contemplate and intend to contemplate no other, students must have a choice. To make a choice, a student must see the many faces of man.

A teacher is sometimes more disturbed than he needs to be over a school's censorship of a single book. Let this teacher turn from thinking about how much that book would mean to his course and become concerned, not with whether the school is going to let him be free, but whether he knows enough to be free. No one book is the source of what a student needs to know about life, so rich and various is literature. Let the teacher cultivate the freedom he is permitted to pursue and that no one may deny him, the freedom to read even more widely in this literature, to search for and find new books that his students will enjoy and the community will accept.

Let the teacher read new ideas pouring out of current scholarship about how to teach literature. If he does not do so, he creates his own censorship, for if he does not know these ideas, he is not free to choose them. The least free teachers are those in bondage to the most relentless of tyrants, their own ignorance or apathy. Unless this bondage has been dissolved by diligent preparation and mastery of critical materials on whatever he is teaching, protests that the teacher be allowed to teach some special piece of literature or his academic freedom will be impaired ring false. Sound scholarship demands a proper humility before the fact that the field of literature is incredibly varied, and within its broadly ample confines is material acceptable to all, which can teach any lesson about literature, material flexible enough to meet the need of any student yet acceptable enough to soothe the agitation of the most rigid moralist. Those from whom we demand freedom have a right to demand what use we intend to make of it.

Response to literature starts with what a student enjoys and understands. Literature is created to give pleasure and understanding and his activities in the classroom should make this apparent to a student. Enjoyment is the key to understanding because it provides genuine interest. A good book gives the student a truly pleasing and profitable experience. Enjoyment must precede appreciation, or appreciation will be second-hand, received information that will not affect what the student does about books. Making a student read something he does not like convinces him that reading is an unpleasant chore which he will do only when he has to.

A teacher must be sure students will like the books he teaches if students are to think reading is a good thing to do when they are allowed to make a choice of how they will spend their time. Students must not be allowed to think that good books are dull books and that people that have literary taste like only dull books. Forced labor and discipline must not be part of the reading experience. An eager reader is not created by guilt feelings but by the feeling that if he doesn't read, he is missing something valuable.

Many students do not meet books in their lives outside of school. For them books are just part of the school world. If books are to move into students' lives outside of school, they must interact with values students believe are important. The high school student who does not want to read is often one who has been discouraged from making reading choices based on his own interests and personal experiences. Book selection should make the first order of business the learner's present taste and past experience. The student today will not take seriously the world of the classroom and the things that go on in it if his sense of what is real is countered there by forced reading of genteel classics. Many of these deny his interpretation of experience outside of school which is full of activities important to him that are never mentioned in approved texts.

All kinds of reading are respected in the activity curriculum. Many varieties of books are good books for students to read. No one book and no one kind of book is necessary for a particular student to read or necessary to his understanding of any particular literary concept. No one book prepares a student for life or even for college. Some books can be read by all or almost all students and some by only a few students. The activity curriculum tailors the reading list to the individual student. All books are legitimate fare: picture books, picture-story books, stories of other lands and people, historical fiction, realistic stories, biography, plays, poetry, essays and a host of others.

For many students only the present holds interest. The student does not see the same vision of his country, his people and the world as his teachers do. For him long-term goals and the institutions founded on them may have little relevance. He may be outside the religious value system and see himself as a speck in the uncaring cosmos. It is there he must find the skill to live, not by denying it or filling it with the fancies of another time but by acknowledging and surviving its immensity and indifference. He distrusts words which try to color dullness and hide lies. For him the exquisitely ordered worlds of Milton and Spenser no longer exist. Hence, the activity curriculum constructs a reading plan which recognizes the absurdity of presenting the British-American literary tradition as the only heritage of all students. World and ethnic literature and the literature of the young about the young are at least as important.

Students like stories that meet their human need for security, acceptance, and competence. These do not have the same outward appearance in one place as another or for the children of one culture that they do for another. But they are universal needs of man and are desired in some form in the vicarious experience of reading as well as in the real experience of life. For a child of a minority culture, reading books about his own ethnic background is satisfying. He needs to have the skills he has learned for survival in that culture recognized. These may be very different from those approved by the majority culture of the school and reflected in its literature.

There are many ways of teaching reading. None has been found superior to all others for all children. Every method should be used to help students who have reading problems. To become a cherished activity, reading must be done under pleasant circumstances and result in students having good feelings about themselves. Hence, the reading corner in the interest center pattern is important. The reading situation should be comfortable and relaxed. Many students need music to read by, and they can bring transistors or tapes which can be played on earphones. This has the added value of shutting the reader away from other sounds in the classroom.

A reader should always be encouraged to find out what new words mean. Some students who have an unreasoning dislike of the dictionary can ask the teacher or other students about words, and such enquirers should be as politely treated as any other persons who ask questions. In a rich, comfortable, secure reading environment, students will fulfill whatever potential they have at that time for learning and liking to read widely and well. They will explore their way to maturity in reading and become independent readers if it is within their potential to do so.

There are a multitude of ways of thinking and talking about reading students have done. There is nothing inherently wrong with the book report if it is only one of the multitude of ways. Students must be encouraged to find all these ways of thinking. Teachers in the activity program do not try to see if the student has read every word and knows everything about the book. Students who start a book they do not like may stop reading it, explain why they do not care to finish it, and shop around for a book they like better. Some books should be read in parts, with parts skipped over. What he reads and enjoys is the basis for a student's understanding of a book, and what he reads without enjoyment will yield little in the way of permanent understanding of literature or love of reading. Students will read more books if they like and focus on the process of reading than if they pay attention to the results of reading—what they are going to do with the book after they have read it.

Frequently in the junior high school and on occasions in later years, reading aloud is a useful activity for teachers and students. In every case it should be carefully prepared. The teacher of English should be a good oral reader. If he is not, he should avail himself of the training that will make him so. Practice and listening to one's practice on a tape is helpful if the teacher is guided by the thought that reading aloud which sounds most like conversation and has the rhythms of ordinary speech is most effective. Training and practice with materials should precede performance. Dismal around-the-class reading exercises are at best dull and at worst embarrassing and destructive. Material to be read aloud should suit the talent of the performer. Much reading aloud can be choral, where children who make mistakes will not be embarrassed by being heard by others. Hard words can be practiced in advance and color and style in performance planned. Reading of conversation is more interesting when students discuss in advance how they would feel and how their faces and bodies would look when they say what the characters will be saying.

Activity cards are appropriate to many plans for teaching literature: thematic unit, chronology, genre, masterpiece, or just textbook following because it is a method not a materials oriented approach. The goals of the teaching will probably be all or some of these in varying degree, depending on the desires of teacher and students: to enable the student to have faith in reading as a means of solving some of his problems with life and leisure, to know and enjoy a wide variety of literary types, to understand how the time and the place of the writer affected his world view, to understand a large reading vocabulary, to read with speed appropriate to comprehension of the material, and to distinguish the interaction of some of the elements of plot, setting, character, and style and how these are revealed. A student should probably have by his last year in high school some ideas about literary forms, literary terms, and the ideas and art of whatever number and kind of the great works of literature he is capable of accepting.

Instead of using language which distracts the student with terms about literary merit, the activity teacher will talk about activities which will show the student how to judge whether a book communicates truly about human experience, whether its assumptions about man are valid, whether the human experience being communicated is important, and whether the language of the book is interesting and appropriate. That one book has more literary value than another can be discovered by the student if that book is appropriate to his experience and if its literary merit is founded on fact not fashion. The themes of great literature are in children, in all of us. Activity cards must be designed to cultivate these potential themes in students and make them articulate. This cultivation encourages the student to search constantly for new ways to enjoy and read different kinds of books.

Activity cards should make it possible to study reading and literature in many different ways. For instance, strictures among some literature teachers against the use of biographical information have been so severe as to verge on the ridiculous. But biographical or historical information about the writer and his time, so long as it interests the student and he sees it as relevant to the writing he has read by an author, is a useful addition to his literary study. Of course, it is important that he learn not to overinterpret such data. He can be led to understand that, just as all writing grows out of experience, no one can be sure how much any one facet of the writer's life influenced his writing, that all such attributed influence is speculative, even when the writer has himself said that he was so influenced. Many writers do not understand what makes them write as they do, although the writer's own analysis of himself must be taken along with other evidence when determining the genesis of his work. All this kind of information helps to account for the way a writer's work is done, what he says and how he says it, and how it affects his readers. These are good things for readers to think about.

Activities

USING TIME: WHAT DO YOU DO WHEN YOU HAVE TO WAIT?
variable time out of class   *1 person*

Find out for yourself how students can use reading to fill in the empty spaces in life when there seems to be nothing to do but wait for something or someone.

Lots of us have to wait for other people, in line, on public transportation, in doctors' offices. How do you use that time? It doesn't have to be dull. Try reading. Get a paperback and carry it with you in your purse or pocket. In a pinch, especially if the situation does not encourage concentration, newspapers and magazines can also help to fill the waiting time with interesting thoughts.

Read in your extra moments for one week. At the end of the week write about the experience in your log. How did you feel about reading under such circumstances? What were the reactions of other people to your reading? What did you read? Did you find that you preferred to read a certain kind of literature? If so, what? Did you encounter any problems? If so, how did you solve them?

SHOPPER'S GUIDE: CHOOSING A BOOK

60 minutes   *1 person*

This will help you guide students in finding the right books for them.

Think about these questions: What kinds of books do you like to read? How do you choose a book for yourself? Do you know where to find the kinds of books students might be interested in? Be sure you know where various kinds of books are located in the public library. Are all libraries alike? How would you find a book in an unfamiliar library? Are you making your own collection of paperbacks that you have read and would like to lend to students? Do you share and trade such books with classmates?

What kinds of books will your students like? How do you know? How can you help someone who does not have the same interests as you? How can you find his interests? How can you tell by just looking at a book what kind of person might be interested in it?

Does your librarian keep a set of covers from new books so that those who are hunting a book can read the "blurbs" on them? Have you investigated some of the book review sources in the library so that you could hunt there for books that might interest a reader? What are these places where books are reviewed? Make a list of them for your ready reference in the future.

How will you help students find books that suit their needs? How can you encourage students to try books that are a little different from the ones they usually choose—a little longer or harder or about a different kind of person? How can you encourage students to be persistent in reading books that are challenging to them and yet feel free to return books that are dull or too difficult for them? How can you encourage students to examine their own book choices? How could you arrange for students to share their book choices so that anyone in the class who wants a certain kind of book may be referred to the person who has read that kind?

Write one or more activity cards to be used by junior or senior high school students in selecting books.

A PERSONAL THING: YOUR FAVORITE QUOTATION

50 minutes   *1 person*

Here is a way you can demonstrate for your students the importance of personal involvement with language.

If you sometimes find things when you are reading—words, sentences, lines—that have special meaning for you, dwell on them, cherish them, think about them, even save them. Have you found any quotations lately in any of your reading that appeal to you? How could you explain to another person why you like them? Do you agree with the ideas they express? Do you like the sound of the words? Why? Write two or three of these quotations in your log and explain in your own words why you like them.

To enjoy your quotations even more and to share them with others, try these suggestions: Frame one and put it on your wall or desk. Make a collection or a scrapbook of quotations. Try writing favorite quotations in cards you send or at the tops of letters you write. Paste a favorite quotation on the front inside page of your notebook where you can read it every day. Illustrate your favorite quotation—use just one picture or make a whole collage about it. Write your favorite quotation for a friend and ask him to share his favorite one with you.

Try one or more of these suggestions. Tell your log how you feel about using quotations.

LIBRARY EXPERT: MAKING A CHART

60 minutes   *1 person*

You will be better able to help your students find materials they need if you do this.

Take a 40 minute segment of your class time to have a good "snoop" around your school or public library and see where everything is located. Ask the librarian for help if you have questions. Start at one end of the room. Take a sheet of paper and make a chart, naming each part of the room as you come to it. You will find these things and more.

Where are the reference books? What would your students use them for? What different kinds of reference books are there? What is the use of each? Is the same information found in several different books? Are there tapes, microfilm, or records in this library? Where are they? How are they used? What are they used for?

Where is the checkout desk located? Are there other places where the librarian keeps supplies? Are there free materials like magazines for cutting? Where is the job information? Are there special displays? Where is the school or college information?

Where are the card catalogs? How do you use these? Is there a picture file? A pamphlet file? Where could students find subject matter books for courses they take? What other courses are represented? Is there any special order in which the books are arranged? Where are the fiction books? Where are the biographies?

Are there some listening areas in the library? Are there special study places? Where is the pencil sharpener? The wastebasket? The drinking fountain? There may be other areas you want to chart—doors, windows, directions, for instance.

How can you be sure that your students will get the most from their library? How can you structure a situation in which they can learn about it?

Post your chart on the bulletin board in your classroom for the use of others. Design one or more activity cards which your students could use to learn about the library.

GREAT GUESSING: WORD GAMES

20 minutes some out of class   *2 to 20 people*

This activity will add to your store of reliable games to interest students in vocabulary building.

Try these games with your classmates—as many or few as you can find to participate. Choose a word. Say "I'm thinking of a word"—and then describe it. Tell how it starts or ends or how many letters it has and add clues until someone guesses it. Then let that person think of a word. Sometimes it is fun to think of words in categories or words that rhyme. Try some of these, then think of your own:

"I'm thinking of a word that rhymes with _____."

"I'm thinking of a word that means the same thing as ____."
"I'm thinking of a word that is as hot as ____."
"I'm thinking of a word that describes ____."
"I'm thinking of a word that begins with ____and ends with
____."
"I'm thinking of a word that is something to eat." (This can be to
wear, to ride in, to look at, and so forth.)

Now try your games outside of class. Try them with relatives, neighbors,
young people, old people. Find which groups of people like which games
best and why. Record your discoveries in your log so you can refer to
the information later.

A DECK OF GODS: FUN WITH MYTHOLOGY

1 hour or more   *4 to 6 people*

To find a way of making mythology interesting to students, do this.

Find a group of people to work with. Working as a group, design a deck
of mythology playing cards. Before you begin, you may want to decide
what kind of mythology your students would like to know about. What
cultures besides the Greek and Roman have mythologies?

Make your playing cards out of ordinary file cards or buy blank cards
in a novelty store. A deck of playing cards is divided by numbers and
suits. How would you divide your cards into categories? Would you
pattern your game after animal rummy or old maid? Would you play it
like poker? Could you design your deck so that gods and goddesses
represent each number and face card? How would you decide which
ones to use and which to leave out? What information about the god or
goddess would you include on each card? Would you mix different
systems of mythology in one deck? If so, how would the students keep
them straight? Would you use events in mythology and heroes as well?
How will you find pictures to represent these characters and events?
What different games could you invent for your deck of cards?

Make your cards and invent at least two different games to play with
them. Write the rules to go with the cards and play the games in your
group.

Write about the experience in your log. Did you learn anything about
mythology from making the cards and games? What? What could students learn from playing the games? What could they learn from making
the cards?

A NEW ROAD: WRITERS AS EXPLORERS

50 minutes *1 person*

If you do this, you may be able to help students find their own answers to questions about the personal aims of writers of literature and what private truths writers are searching for.

Think about the process of writing as an exploration: What is an explorer? What is he trying to do? Is he always sure of the place where he is going? Or how he is going to get there? Or what he will do when he does? Find some examples to support your answers. What makes an explorer start out on his journey? What moves him? How do you know?

Did you ever explore? Why? Was it frightening to not know exactly what was going to happen next? Did you know what you hoped to find when you got there? How willing were you to risk taking wrong roads?

What are the risks a writer takes when he explores new ideas? What kinds of ideas might these be? What works have you read where a writer explored new ideas? If you were that writer, how would it be frightening to write in a way that no one else ever had before? How would it be rewarding? How would you feel about your writing? Would you want other people to see it? Why or why not?

Read some poetry by e. e. cummings. How do you feel about it as a reader?

Write "Private, Stay Out" on one page of your log and fold the page over to the center so that no one can read it. On that page explore some private feeling. Just begin and don't worry about where you are going until you get there.

MESSAGES TO UNKNOWN READERS: GRAFFITI ON THE WALL

several days *1 person*

Here is an approach to literature you may find useful because it comes not from textbooks but from the every-day world of students.

Think about these questions: Did you ever see writing on walls? Where? Why do people write on walls? Who are they sending messages to? Why? What kind of messages do they send? Do they sign them? Why or why not? Are the feelings expressed on the walls different from those in student themes? What are the differences?

Be a graffiti collector. Where, besides walls, do people scratch or scribble messages? Can you find any of these messages in your classroom? Get a notebook or tablet to write graffiti discoveries on, and look for graffiti. Look at floors, desks, window sills, blackboards, sidewalks, sides of buildings, windows, fences, sides of cars and trucks, backs of shirts. Paste a large sheet of newsprint near the pencil sharpener in your classroom and invite your classmates to contribute graffiti for a week.

Classify all the graffiti you have collected as to subject and make a small booklet for circulation in your class. Is some of the graffiti funny, sad, silly, stupid? Are some things repetitious and trite? Are there some items people would consider offensive? What will you include and what will you leave out of your booklet? Should you censor it? How much and why?

Circulate your graffiti collection. What reactions did it get? How could you arrange a situation in which junior or senior high school students could discover and use graffiti? What could they learn about language and the way literature works as communication? How? In your log write your answers to these questions.

TRUE FOR YOU: TELLING OURSELVES THE TRUTH

45 minutes   *1 person*

To help students be honest with themselves when they read, do this activity.

Think about these questions: Is it sometimes more comfortable to believe something that is really not the truth? Can you think of any times when this might be so? Are there things you should have done today that you did not do? Did you tell yourself that these things could wait for another day or be avoided altogether if you just waited? Was this true? What kinds of things do we tell each other to make ourselves able to avoid truths we do not want to face?

Are there characters in fiction who do this? Who are some, and what happens to them? Did you ever read a story which had a clear moral which was pointed out in some obvious way? Did the facts in the story prove what the moral stated or could they have pointed to some other outcome that was disregarded? Do you like happy endings? Why?

Why do people want to believe in things that turn out well? What dangers are there in believing things that are not true? Is there ever a difference between what people say they do and what they do? Between what they say they believe is right and what they do? What stories have you read with people like this?

Try this experiment: Read a short news article (one with an emotional content) aloud to the class. Pass out paper and ask everyone to write his answers to some simple fact questions that you ask about what was in the article. See how different the answers are. How many people were hearing what they wanted to hear in what you read? If some violent act was committed, how many people of the same sex as the criminal switched the person's sex around?

Discuss the results in your log and with the class.

BOOK BAG: MAKE A CHRISTMAS BOOKLIST
40 minutes   *1 person*

If you would like students to collect books of their own, but if books are too expensive, here is a way you can get some books for yourself and experiment with a scheme that may help your students as well.

You may want to tell your gift givers what books you would like to get for Christmas. What kind of books do you enjoy? Do you have a favorite author? A series? A subject? You might want some reference books of your own like the ones you use most at school. Then you might want some paperbacks for just reading.

In making your list, try to find the exact name of the book, the author, the publisher, and the date it was published.

You may want to post your list on the bulletin board. Or you may get another to join you in this activity and submit your lists to the newsletter, asking that your names be kept secret so that everyone can guess who would be most likely to want the books you have listed.

UNLOCKING WORDS: WHAT THE ENDINGS TELL ABOUT WORDS
40 to 60 minutes   *1 person*

Do this activity to help students recognize the meanings of words when they are reading and find the best way to say what they mean when they are writing.

Look up the word "use" in the dictionary. How many forms of this word are there? Make a list. Which is the action word? Which is the one naming the agent or instrument? Which is the act or result? Which is the descriptive word? Are there several? Which shows manner, comparison, quality, contrast? Here's the list. Put them in the categories above: use, user, using, usage, usable, usability, useful, usefully, unusable, disused.

Do the special endings work with other words? Which ones? What about beginnings? Do they have their own special ways of changing word meanings? Can you find some? Which one is in the list above?

Draw some conclusions about which endings indicate certain ways words are used—to show action, describe, name, and so forth. Write what you have discovered about beginnings as well. Either do this in your log or as an article for the newsletter so that the class can share your word discoveries.

KNOW YOURSELF: WHY DID YOU LIKE THE BOOK?

30 minutes   *1 person*

This activity will help you to organize your own thoughts about the book you have read and to have ideas of what you are looking for in reading when you choose your next book.

There are many reasons for liking a book. Is it hard for you to tell just why you like a book? Was there anything in this book that made you change your thinking or feeling about anything in particular? Give as many examples as you can.

Were you able to say about anyone in the book, "Yes, that's just like me—or just like someone I know"? Give examples. Was there anything in the book that made you see how someone else might feel or think or behave that you had never thought of or understood before? Did you meet any people unlike anyone you ever knew? Did you read about places that were new to you? Give examples—as many as you can.

Did the book make you want to know more about anything? Always give more than one example if you can. Did you get any valuable information from this book?

Try to summarize the yes answers you have given to these questions in a statement for the card file of book recommendations and write a recommendation for the bulletin board.

TEACHING FICTION

The first task of the English teacher is to teach the student to read, but teaching the student to read soon becomes the subtle and demanding task of teaching literature, launching a reader into a lifetime development of taste and imagination. As soon as the reader begins to realize that reading is more than identifying printed words with things, he has begun to appreciate literature.

A prospective teacher is usually adequately equipped with information from his college classes about the standard works in English and American literature written before 1950. Many teachers feel that they are not so well-equipped with an understanding of literature written since that time. Literature of the usual anthologies and standard paperbacks admitted to the classroom rarely speaks the voice of today. And classic literature which speaks the voice of all time is frequently edited or reinterpreted to avoid the cries of despair, negativism, or ugliness that inhabit darker visions and are the authentic sounds of our time.

Student anthologies are censored by the need to sell a commercial product to power groups whose inclination is to use schools to reinforce the received majority vision of our culture. This vision of how the human experience is to be conveyed excludes the experience of many students. It results in their alienation from what they are given to read in school. Moreover, exclusion of part of the literary heritage which does not accord with the accepted version of what man is all about ensures that the anthology will present a value system and vision of order not only at variance with the experience of most students but with the vision of our culture seen by many Western writers.

Certainly anthologies present well the conventional version of Western and American majority culture. And good teaching can be done with them. But the number of students for whom this vision of the world is the acceptable vision, who share this code of values, and whose life experience confirms and does not contradict it is shrinking. What of them? What of their life style? Is their value system to be denied by all that they are allowed to call literature? If so, they will identify literature as lies someone wants them to accept as a price tag to accepting students themselves, and they will treat it with contempt.

It requires courage to include the smartly flipped values of much modern literature in classroom study, to expose its excessive search for all that is weakest in man. To reveal the banalities and self-righteous pretension of much modern literature requires a sure knowledge of what one is doing. And we do not fulfill this responsibility when we ignore films and books that attract the attention of everyone but people in the classroom. The well-published forbidden fruit of the film, the adult book store, and the peepshows which seem available in every small town are an environmental happening, literature of a kind that engages the attention of the young only a little less than it does their elders.

Modern literature seems to emphasize a special style rather than the substance of plot, setting, and character, sounds as well as words, a revolution against optimism and an obsession with doom, a dramatization of evil in terms of violence, a dark vision, never outlined with even the faint promise of light or marginal possibility of redemption, a moral chaos where as Sophocles says, "Whirl is King." These present little a traditional teacher can deal with in a traditional setting. But failure to do so measures the lack of relevance that many students see in English. Students are exposed to a popular culture and a popular literature which says that human beings are animals and the more animalistic they seem, the more it proves that nobody is being fooled, that man's natural state is hating and treating others with violence and enjoying their pain, and that hate itself is a more believable emotion than love.

Literature differs, however, from philosophy, in that it does not use language as a range of signs but as a source of meaning in itself. But when we look to current literature to justify our insistence on order and form in writing, we find few current works which fit the formula we commend to students. Few pieces have the closed design, motivation, sequence and results that express logical structure. Writers are inventing new ways to express what they want to say because traditional structures cannot contain their vision. New ideas about what is grammatically useful are emerging. Contemporary writers say they have to decompose by incoherencies, shatter forms, violate conventions, and explode language to express their vision of language today and its function in the world. Paperbacks have brought these variations from safe, conventional schoolbook literature into some classrooms. These accommodate the anti-novel, the plotless novel, and the film whose ambiguous intent does not fit into standard categories.

For the modern writer the world does not make sense, and this vision of mindless chaos he communicates. He sees man's destiny to end in pain, fear, and death, as it does, despite personal piety and virtue, religious hope, public charity, and the ameliorating graces by which man glosses experience. Perhaps this dark and bitter vision is not yours. Yet there is no point in denying that it is the dominant artistic vision of our time. And it is hard to refute the evidence adduced by its proponents. Certainly we cannot refute it with the arguments that we travel around the moon, and that the world covets the riches we greedily and unsatisfyingly consume, while we cannot give all our children free education, adequate medical care, or, in some cases, food. These facts reinforce the writer's sense of our inability to order priorities, a sense which pervades the chaos and despair of his vision. The modern writer says that if man is not the creator and preserver of chaos, he must stop acting as if he is.

The literature of the American Dream is another problem of the English classroom. It is filled with an ethic of work, religion, clearing wilderness, and killing Indians and animals. Anyone can be President or rich, and natural resources and women are to be "tamed." Greatness is in building cities, forming industrial giants, and having wars. The American of literature is a man of simple action in accepted spheres, trusted or hated for his power and willingness to wield it. His folklore abounds in the violence, conquest, seduction, and manipulation he uses to assert his freedom.

Ideological romances tell of Americans who invent their own law in finance, business, politics, and war. Such writing creates an easy moral feedback, whose aim is to sentimentalize and beautify in a world without real cause and effect. Doubts are repressed and complexities simplified, while the reader fails to assume the responsibilities of an adult, one of which is to lie to oneself as little as possible. All this literature is fed to a generation which knows that everything that is faced is not thereby changed but that nothing can be corrected and changed until it is faced.

One answer to the problem of teaching literature today lies perhaps in teaching some neglected values in the classics of the past. These have been obscured by pedagogical filters, whose urge to flatter the prejudices of the majority culture has caused editors and teachers to edit out much in classic literature which is no stranger to what is happening in the world today and its literature. Perhaps by studying these classics we can pierce the vicious hollowness of the lie that violence is without suffering and show that profound feelings can be aroused without recourse to literary tactics that arouse nausea and disgust. With each vista of the human heart revealed leading to another view ahead, the infinite subtleties of human-hood as the great writers have seen them lie open before a student.

A bridge between the literature of today and the literature of the past is acceptance of the implications of many of the classics, implications often played down in the text editions to match the vision of the American dream of goodness and success. Teachers today must teach the story of man in conflict with chaos and with order as it has been written in great literature. Let us teach the *Iliad* as well as the *Odyssey,* for the *Iliad* has no dirty, yellow Trojans or one hundred percent Greeks, just men who, with varying degrees of skill and sorrow, like men in other wars, kill each other.

Works of literature impel compassion, fear, tenderness, delight, horror, and laughter. But the same book which does one of these in one age may accomplish another in another age. For the sixteenth century, *Don Quixote* was a farce. For the eighteenth century, it was the history of man. The nineteenth century found it a parable of the two planes on which man lives his life: the quest for the ideal and the material necessities. Readers still endow with new meanings the Homeric epic and the *Divine Comedy.* Sometimes the meaning for which the artist consciously strives is not the achieved meaning. The artist's will to believe is defeated by his artistic insight into reality. The ebb and flow of his imagination reveals meanings hidden even from the artist himself. The mind and the imagination of the writer are informed with intuitions about the nature of reality which are not the products of his conscious thought and which survive the conditions of the age of his work's creation into the age of new concepts with undiminished power to tell the way man and life are. D. H. Lawrence warned critics to trust the tale, not the teller.

While a curriculum based on the significance of the past selects and edits writers to prove that significance, a curriculum of literature for today's youth evolves as conditions change and relies on students and teachers to join in studying that change and its significance. If today's problems are war, alienation, racial strife, religious renewal, technological advance, work ethics, and law and justice, these must appear in the curriculum. If we do not let them appear, our curriculum will join irrelevant official cultural styles of the past which exited to oblivion in other periods of change. From 1840 to 1940, for instance, middle class society held an official cultural outlook, stagnantly refusing creative innovation. Vital and significant cultural life in the Western world went on outside the official canon. In literature there were Flaubert, Baudelaire, Dostoevsky, and Joyce; in music, Rimsky-Korsakov, Debussy, and Stravinsky; in the visual arts, Degas, Rodin, and Picasso. Others joined them to create a new cultural style for the age without regard to the taste and ideas of officialdom.

There is thus much in today's dark literary vision which echoes what great writers in every time have told us. The ridicule of naive optimism, the fascination with corruption, is as characteristic of Hawthorne, Melville, Poe, and Faulkner as it is their literary heirs. There are no better guides to the underground of the human psyche than Baudelaire and Dostoevsky. Melville speaks of a baptism not of the Father and Son but of the devil. His portrait of the writer, "Bartleby, the Scrivener," has but one answer to the modern world—"I would prefer not to." Melville says that Hawthorne's work says, "No" in thunder, that the devil himself could not make him say yes and that all men who say yes lie.

There are other no-sayers in the literature of the classroom. Huck Finn says no to womankind, to the family, and to organized society. And teachers have taught it as a children's story! Great writers have not failed to say of the causes dearest to them what is always and everywhere true of all causes, that they have been imperfectly conceived and inadequately represented and will be betrayed consciously and unconsciously by even their leading spokesmen. So Dante turned on Florence, Moliere on the moderate man, De Sade on reason, Shaw on the socialists, Tolstoy on the reformers, Joyce on Ireland, Faulkner on the South, Graham Greene on the Catholics, and Pasternak on the Russians. The Greek poet said no to the belief that life was explicable in terms of the Homeric gods. The

Christian poet has often had to deny that society is or can be really Christian.

But English teachers need to be careful about the traditional concept that there are such things as timelessness and universality. That these are obsolete concepts sociologists have been saying for some time, but those in literary fields have not been listening. The English teacher who sees his role as the transmitter of ancient culture is equally obsolete. Those who refuse to see that truth is not eternal place themselves in the position of having to prove the truth of a truth that is no longer true. Humanity does not depend on the past, but on willingness to be human in the present. That is what students expect. Teachers need to be sure that they are not teaching that to be true which they know is not true but wish was true.

Literature explores, seeks, and creates meaning in human experience with all its diversity, complexity, and strangeness. By choice and arrangement of materials, the writer tests ways of seeing and responding to life. By arrangement of the flux of experience and the temper of his treatment, he says, "This is the way man responds to experience, succumbs to it, alters it, or explores it." Literature always assumes the importance of man's experience, even when, as in tragedy, it finds much of that experience evil.

The study of literature is dedicated to the proposition that every man is an object of concern because he is a man; the operations of conquest, killing and destruction may not be talked about in literature apart from the sufferings they occasion specific people. But a mere catalogue of vice and catastrophe in a book or a play is not closer to the quality of tragedy than an insurance report of an accident. In literature these are not abstractions but concrete in the experience of individuals. Great literature deals with their particular suffering in the general catastrophe. It never departs from its focus on their fate. It traffics not with the view of people as personnel. It opens windows on the stranger and the enemy and shows their shared humanity. It deals with the infinite complexities of life, not with oversimplifications of those complexities. A writer's visions, not his observation alone, are the source of literary truth, and it is not the writer who sees only the facts who writes good literature but the writer who sees through the facts who comes nearest to interpreting the landscape of the human heart.

The inferior writer creates characters who live outside the reader and become objects of curiosity. The good writer creates characters that live inside the reader and become extensions of his own experience, enabling him to enter emotionally into their lives. Because literature exists both in and outside of time, going outside the time and place it portrays to suggest all time and persons, it fulfills the desire of man to live beyond his own brief moment. The reader's contact with life is enlarged as he chooses a literature which adds another kind of life to his, enables him to be at one with others and makes their memories his own, cultivating the grace of his moral imagination and thrusting him outside the paranoia of self.

In literature he sees for awhile how someone can have, and what it feels like to have another view and what the world looks like from another angle. He tests that outlook against what his own experience has told him and often finds another's view of the world may have more power than he thought. Literary experience acts as moral and ethical prompting on the temper with which students face experience. The student deepens his knowledge of others and of himself. He finds life is more of this and more of that than he had thought. The flow of his sympathetic consciousness leads him into new places of the spirit. He learns not by logic but by metaphor and imagination. His moral will is invigorated as literature illuminates, deprecates, or reinforces certain acts and conduct. Literature develops the moral imagination so that a student can feel his way into the hearts of others and can become someone other than himself. He finds that good causes and bad ones have always been abroad in the world, that there are many ways good men may mistake one for the other, and that some ways of combating evil nourish the very menace they seek to uproot.

But English teachers cannot claim that literature, read and understood, will always make man moral and good. Events of our own age press against conventional claims for moral values in the study of literature. Matthew Arnold contended that the best that has been thought and said would refine the resources of the human spirit. But the ultimate barbarism grew from the core of Western culture. Nazi masters of iniquity listened to Beethoven and Bach as they crafted lampshades of human skin, newly flayed from the bodies of murdered Jews. Men of Auschwitz read and loved Shakespeare after a hard day at the ovens. Two centuries after Voltaire proclaimed its end, political torture remains a normal process of political activity. Culturally developed moral intelligence does not eventuate in political and social morality. Trained and persistent commitment to logical values, written words, and the capacity to identify with imaginary sentiments may even dim immediate sensitivity to the hard edge of circumstance. Assumptions regarding the relevance of literate culture to moral values is in question.

From the shadows of our own frightening century, the modern writer speaks—a shadow of twenty million Russians murdered by their own government and fifty million by the Chinese, six million Jews killed in the German ovens, thousands incinerated in an instant in Hiroshima and Nagasaki, hundreds burned in a night at Dresden, after the strife which had occasioned the bombs had already been decided, millions who follow the blood sports in which the infliction of pain and death upon a fellow creature whom it is as easy to love as to kill is sought by man for his pleasure, fun, and excitement; in this shadow we cannot say moral sense is the product of literature.

For English teachers these realities demand a modest approach to claims about the subject they teach and the will to embark upon a lifelong commitment to search for ways to teach so that habits of moral self-examination and self-discipline become a force in their students. The activity curriculum constantly demands that students choose activities which give a concrete promise and examine how they feel and respond to each part of the activity. It is a practical method of pursuing this commitment.

A teacher who is going to teach literature cannot understand how to do so from reading about it. That teacher must have experiences he wants students to have in order to understand how they work. For beginning teachers this is of great importance, since they must build a bridge between many of the things they have been taught about literature in their college classrooms and what can be taught, for instance, in the seventh grade. Many aspects of college experience with literature are not appropriate to public school teaching of literature. Students who have been carefully told what to think about literature may be tempted to use this method on their students. The best way prospective teachers can gain perspective on teaching literature is to use activities themselves until the necessary approaches become natural to them. The literature activities listed here should be springboards for students and teachers who want to manufacture their own activities.

Activities

SHARE AND SMILE: READING TOGETHER

2 weeks   *2 people*

Try this activity to discover ways you can help students enjoy sharing reading ideas.

Find someone in your life outside of school—a parent, brother, sister, or close friend—who will agree to try this activity with you. What does this partner like to read? What do you like to read? What kind of book does your partner think you ought to read? What would you like to see him read? Make a bargain with your partner. You choose a book for him to read and ask him to choose one for you.

Arrange to meet for at least half an hour every day for the time you are reading the books. During this half hour read to your partner any passages you particularly liked or disliked or did not understand, and ask him for his opinion of them. If you have your own copy of a paperback book, you may find it helpful to read with a pencil at hand to write down comments in the margins so that you will remember them later, or you might want to use a separate piece of paper.

If you live in the same house with your partner, try reading some whole chapters aloud to each other. You read aloud to your partner from your book, and then he reads aloud from his. Be sure the listener feels free to interrupt with comments. You may find this reading aloud useful as a diversion while one of you is doing tedious household chores. There are many opportunities when hands are busy, but minds are not.

After you have finished the books, consider these questions in your log: When you began reading it, did you think you would like the book your partner had chosen? Did you like it? Did your feelings change in any way about the book you had chosen for your partner to read? If so, how? Did you feel any differently about the person you read with after the experience? Did you know anything more about him? Did you know anything about yourself that you did not know before?

What might a high school or junior high school student learn about a parent or a friend as a result of such a reading experience? Could such an experience change his feelings about reading in any way? If so, how and why?

BOOK STRETCHING: *RUN, BABY, RUN*

2 weeks   *2 to 20 people*

If you have only one copy of a popular book like *Run, Baby, Run* and many people in your class want to read it, here is an activity that may help you stretch your book to fit everyone's needs.

What is the book everyone at your school is talking about now? Take a survey in your class to find out how many people have read it and how many people want to but haven't a copy. How many people in the class have copies? Have you tried the library? Where else could you find one?

Are there some people in your class who like to read aloud and who do it well? Could they read your copy or copies of the book to people who want to hear the story? If you have only one book for the whole class, could these people take turns reading it aloud? If you have more books, would it be possible to have several people reading aloud at the same time to different groups? What would the people who had read the book be doing? Could they help in any way? If so, how?

If only a small group is reading the book, where and when would they do it? If the whole class or most of the class is doing it, would they spend the whole class period or only part of the period reading? How much and when?

Organize a group or groups in your class to read the book in this way. If you are a listener, how can you get the most out of what you hear? Should you ever interrupt the reader to ask questions and make remarks? Why or why not? What happens when you do? What happens to your ideas about the story? What can you do to make the reader's job easier?

What ideas and events in the story are important to you? What is not important to you? What do you want to remember? How will you remember those things? Set aside a time each day after the reading to write in your log about the things that were important to you.

After you have finished reading or listening to the book, reread what you have written in your log and discuss your reactions to the book with the other members of your group. What events in the main character's life caused him to change his ways of thinking or feeling? Which events in his life led him to important decisions? What were the decisions he made? What were the results of his decisions?

With the members of your group make a list of the most important events in the story. If there are other groups in your class also reading that book, compare your list with theirs. Narrow your list of events so that there are about the same number of important events in the story as you have members in your group. Ask each member to choose one or two of the events which are especially vivid in his mind.

Get a large roll of paper and make pictures on it. You might decide upon chalk, paint, crayon, or markers—whichever is most practical in your circumstances. Find a place where you will have space to unroll it on the floor and work. This might be outside or in the hall. Line yourselves along your paper so that your events will be in the sequence as they occur in the story. Draw scenes to illustrate your events. Does your mural tell the story? You may also decide to title or quote from the book under each scene to give your viewers help in understanding your illustrations. Find a place in your room or in the the school where you can put your mural on display.

GOOD GUYS AND BAD: THE HERO'S CHOICES

2 hours   *4 to 8 people*

If you do this, you may be able to create situations in which students can critically examine behavior choices in literature.

Find books to read which have heroes or dominant main characters. As you read, discuss these questions: What are man's most important emotions? What are the strong emotions and desires of the main character of your book? Is he or could he be led to make wrong decisions because of these emotions? How does he manage his emotions? What decisions do they lead him to? Does he ever act first and think later? Is that a kind of decision? Can you tell when he has made a decision that is going to cause trouble later in the story? How?

Does your hero sometimes do violent things? Why? Did you ever do anything violent? Or want to? What kind of experience led you to feel that way? What happens as a result of the violent acts that someone does? Do many people suffer? In your story does violence cause suffering? Is the suffering shown so that you feel it? How does it make you feel about the character whose decisions led to the suffering?

Are the people who make wrong choices always bad or evil or weak people? What people in literature do you remember who were very strong or otherwise good but made one or more bad decisions that spoiled everything? Did you ever choose to do something you thought would bring good results, but it brought bad ones? How can we tell which choices are really right?

Is your hero sincere? Who is more dangerous, the man who is a vulgar brute, hypocrite, or cynic or the man who commits evil, believing it to be good? Which is your hero? Is the strong idealist who is willing to sacrifice all for his belief a dangerous man? What heroes have you studied who were like that? If one has a good aim in view, how far is he justified in going to pursue it? How far do we have to go before we become like the thing we are trying to destroy?

As you read and discuss, choose one character whose decisions cause strong feelings in the members of your group. Plan to conduct a jury trial to see if his decisions were evil. Who will be the jury and the witnesses? Will they be characters from the book? What will the charges be? And the punishment? Who will be the prosecutor? The defense attorney? The judge? Plan to act out your trial. Where will your courtroom be? Will you have an audience? Set aside a time—five or ten minutes—for the participants to decide upon their testimony or parts.

Act out the trial. You may be surprised by the conclusion! If a recorder is available, you may like to record your trial on video tape. It will seem different when you see it as a spectator.

LOOK BEHIND YOU: THE AMERICAN DREAM IN LITERATURE
several hours   *4 to 8 people*

Here is an activity that will give you some ideas for planning activities and discussions about American literature.

Form a group and choose books about early America to read. As you read meet during class to discuss these questions: Why did the early settlers come to America? How were their ambitions like or unlike the ambitions of the members of your group? Can you find any evidence that the American pioneers had the same kinds of dreams as the members of your group? What did their desires and dreams cause them to do? What bad things did they do? How did they treat the people who already owned the land?

What kind of stories did they tell about what they had done to convince themselves it was all right to treat the original owners of the land as they did? What are some of these stories? How did their desire to justify what they had done affect the rise of the "Western" novel and film and television story? How were the original owners of the land shown in these stories?

Look up the "Letter from Chief Joseph" in your library. Plan a skit in which you show the Indian viewpoint in a land dispute. The setting might be a council of chiefs who are going to sign a treaty. Here are some questions you might want to consider in making your plan: Why weren't the needs of the Indians considered in the American Dream of a new world? What sort of feelings did the pioneers have about the future? What might they have thought would make their sacrifices worthwhile, even if they would be gone by the time things were better? Have their dreams been realized? Have some bad things resulted from the way they treated the natural resources and land? What would they think if they could see the product of their dream? Is there any way you can show the outcomes of the pioneers' dreams in your skit?

KNOWING BY SEEING: FILMING YOUR BOOK

several weeks   *1 or more persons*

Try this activity to be able to help your students in using film in the interpretation of literature.

Make a short film about a book you have read. List a number of scenes in which you can show the ideas, places or characters from your reading in picture form. Arrange them in a sequence that will carry your meaning. Your list of scenes is known in the film industry as a scenario. Plan your scenario with two things in mind—what you would like to show and what you can find for your picture making. For your film you may want to stage some scenes with your classmates.

You may decide to make either a slide presentation or a movie film, depending upon the equipment available. If you make a film instead of a slide presentation, you will need a film camera such as a super 8x and a film editing and splicing outfit. It is difficult to make a film for a movie in the sequences you want to show the scenes.

Whether you decide to use slides or movie film, you will also need to plan for a tape with narration or music or both as a background for your presentation. This will need to be carefully timed so that the appropriate sounds occur during the right scenes.

There are many books on film-making available from the library, and you may be able to get some materials from your local camera shop. Investigate your community for camera clubs at schools, churches, or the YMCA. These may provide aid and information of use to you or your students.

Show your film or slides for your class. Tell your log about the problems you encountered and how you solved them. What problems would you expect to meet if you planned a filming project with an English class in high school? What ways might you solve these problems?

INSIDE THE CHARACTER:
A DIARY FROM YOUR BOOK

50 minutes   *1 person*

To discover how you can involve an individual student in a book he is reading and encourage him to become a creative and active reader, do this.

Read a book which has a main character. What are the most important points in the story? At these times in the story was there a lot at stake for the main character? Suppose that his character kept a diary. Write his diary showing what he thought at these critical periods in the book.

Was he afraid? Was he foolish? Self-sacrificing? Heroic? Did he have a selfish motive? Was he trying to defend or protect someone else? What were his ambitions? How did he see himself? Was he confident and sure of what he was doing? Were his thoughts cold and calculating? Was he sentimental? How many of his true thoughts and emotions would he admit to himself, even in a diary? How would his feelings show in the words he used in his diary? Would he pray or swear or laugh at himself? Would he write about his girl friend or his mother? Would he philosophize about the state of the world? Would he think only about the problems of tomorrow?

Make your character's diary as much like the real thing would have been as possible. Put it on display in your classroom so that other people may see how a book diary can be made.

ADVERTISE YOUR BOOK:
MAKE A POSTER

40 minutes   *1 person*

Here is a way to become familiar with one of the things students can do to respond to their literary experiences.

Have you seen any psychedelic posters? Sometimes the outside of a music album is a good place to find one. How are they different from other posters? Are the colors different? How? Do you like the colors and the way they are put together? Why or why not? How do they make you feel? Do they do what the person who designed them meant for them to do? How do you feel about the shapes? Is most of the space filled or are there empty spaces? Make a statement for your log about the colors and shapes of psychedelic posters.

Choose a book that you have read that you would like to advertise. Collect a number of the ideas in your book you would like to share. Can you think of a visual image to represent each idea? What are the important emotions of your book? What colors express those emotions best? What kinds of shapes express those emotions best? Should your poster have hard sharp black lines or soft gentle lines? Should your poster show a lot of mixed-together things or only one simple thing? What would best show the feelings and ideas of the book? Use cut-outs, drawings, or paintings for your images. Be sure you clearly write or print the name of your book on the poster.

Hang your poster on the bulletin board. Does it do what you wanted it to do? Does it get attention? Does it say what you wanted it to say about the book? Why or why not?

WHAT MIGHT BE:
READING A SCIENCE FICTION WORK

30 minutes   *1 person*

If you would like to be able to guide your students in reading science fiction critically, do this.

Think about these questions: What desire of man does science fiction express? Why does man keep wanting to go beyond his limitations? What are some of the science fiction ideas that are stale and too much used? What qualities of man are especially shown by science fiction? Does some science fiction criticize things in our present lives that seem bad to the writer? How is this done? List some things that science fiction writers criticize. Do they also manufacture dreams of the way they think things ought to be or ought not to be in the future? What are some of the things that they predict? What do they show that is frightening? What that is good?

In what way were the Greek myths a kind of science fiction? Is invented science a kind of magic? See if the hero of a science fiction book is in any way like the hero of a myth. What ways are they alike or different? What do both kinds of literature have to do with people's dreams and how the way they are compares with the way they'd like to be?

What kind of science fiction would you like to write? Is there something we would like to have that we could imagine into a story that would make life better in the universe? Tell your log how you would make it better if you could.

ACROSS TIME AND SPACE: UNIVERSAL SYMBOLS

1 to 1½ hours   *3 to 6 people*

To help students realize that there are some ideas that do not change very much, do this.

Form a group and discuss these questions: Have you read any myths? You will find that the gods and goddesses stand for certain ideas and characteristics that relate to everyone in all time. What are these ideas? It might help to get some myths and look at them in your group.

These universal ideas are found in the things that matter to all men. Have the members of your group read any pieces of literature in which these universal concerns are important? Share with each other the books and stories you have read in which you found these ideas. You may want to read from a book to the group. Did you find many of these examples in books that were written long ago? Why is this so?

Make a list of the universal ideas and classify some of the books you have read or some of the ideas and people in the books under those universal ideas which fit them best. You might make a display or bulletin board arrangement of your findings for the rest of the class, or report on your information in the newsletter.

ANOTHER WAY TO TRUTH: PARABLES, ALLEGORIES, FABLES

1 hour some out of class   *1 person*

If you want parables, allegories, and fables to be useful and interesting for your students, this activity may help you.

Look at some of the stories that Jesus told to show his followers how he felt about what they should do about common problems in families and daily life. Find the one about the prodigal son. Do you suppose there was actually a man of Jesus's acquaintance who had this experience? Why did he tell the story? Find the one about the ten talents. What is meant to be understood by this story? Are some things not so accepta-ble being compared to familiar things to make a point? What is the point?

Look up the little play, *Everyman*. It is a very old play. What things in it represent ideas? How do you know? What point is being made by the old writer?

Do you know any fables? What kinds of characters are in them? The Greek writer Aesop wrote many of these. Look up some of them and see if you can see what is meant by the stories that are told about animals. Why did the writer use animals instead of people? How does he make sure you get the point? Do you like this way of making sure you don't miss what he means? Why? Are there any modern stories which have characters in them that are more than just the characters in the stories, who represent ideas the writer wants to convey?

Have you ever heard of a book called *Animal Farm* by George Orwell? It is an example of how a modern author has used the fable or allegory to put across a message about modern problems. You can find other examples. The cartoon section of the newspaper offers a few.

Make a collection of literature which shows modern ways of using parable, allegory, and fable forms. Bring your collection to school and put it in the reading corner for a few weeks so that your classmates can share in your discoveries.

SPECIAL MEANING PACKAGES:
SYMBOLISM IN LITERATURE

40 minutes   *1 person*

Some kinds of stories may just seem silly or not make much sense to your students unless you can help students find ways to see that stories sometimes mean more than they seem to mean. This activity may make it easier for you to help students read and enjoy these stories.

Sometimes the writer, for the sake of getting ahead with his work, wraps up several meanings in a special event or place or person. For instance, a character may be both the character he portrays in the story, and he may be symbolic or a meaning package bigger than his part in the story. He may be a symbol of all people who get caught in the problems he has. In the same way, a place or event may be bigger than itself.

Find some meaning packages in your reading that may mean more than they seem to in their place in the story. What kind of stories that you have read use all the characters and events in this way? Did you ever read any animal fables? What did some of these characters represent? You may want to look up some of these.

Tell your log about the stories you have found and what kinds of meaning packages you have discovered in them. Write your conclusions about why it is sometimes useful for writers to write this way.

A BOOK LOOK: WHAT DOES
OUR LITERATURE SAY ABOUT US?

1 hour   *1 person*

This activity may provide you with some ideas for guiding students in discovering cultural significance in literature.

Think about these questions: How would you express your feelings toward some of the unpleasant things you read about? When people say "It's disgusting!" are they talking about the bad thing itself that is being described? Are they indignant about the fact that evil exists—or that someone has written about it? Which is more disgusting, that such things happen in our world or that someone writes about them?

Does the dramatist or writer feel as bad about the evil as other people, or does his writing about it mean he approves of it? Why would he want to write about it? What would he hope to accomplish?

Is it always true that a writer condemns the evil he writes about? What other reasons might he have for showing violence or evil? How can we tell the difference between a writer who writes of evil in order to exploit people's fascination with it and sell his work and the desire of a writer to expose and denounce evil by showing it vividly?

Are more people writing about such things today than in other times in history? When in human history are there more likely to be such writings? Where will future generations go to find out the real tone and temper of our age? What things will they think about us from the writing we have left behind?

What tells us most of what we know about the Greeks? The Egyptians? What do we call the sixteenth century: the Age of ____? The early Greek times we call the Age of ____? Why? Where will future generations find a true picture of us? What picture of us would they find in old television stories?

Imagine that you are a historian of the future—two hundred years from now. From that future point-of-view write a report or a film scenario of what our age was like.

LOOKING AHEAD:
MAKING PREDICTIONS

several hours   *3 to 5 people*

If you do this activity you will discover ways to help students extend their abilities to make predictions about their reading.

Organize a group to work on prediction-making. How do you find clues in what a situation is to tell you what it will become? Does your school have windows overlooking a street where people might cross? Can you practice making predictions about which people will cross the street and which will not? What are the clues in that situation that can help you predict? If you are watching people walking down the hall, can you predict which doors they will enter? See how many things you can find in your room to make predictions about? Tell your logs about your predictions and how successful they were.

Try your predicting skills on a book. Find several copies of a book that you would all like to read. Read the first chapter or section of the book either as a group or individually. Meet as a group to talk about the first chapter. Look for clues which will help you make a prediction about how the book will be completed. Write your predictions in your logs.

Finish reading the book. You may want to do this as a group activity or you may prefer to read separately. Set a time limit for finishing the book. Agree upon a day when you will all meet to discuss the ending of the book and predictions about it.

How was the prediction you made in the beginning like or not like the author's ending? Why was it like or not like his? Did the clues in the first chapter which led you to make your prediction mean what you thought they meant? Why or why not? Were there other clues which told you more about what to expect later in the story? If so, what were they? Why do you think the author ended the story the way he did? Which version seems most consistent with the feelings and actions of the characters? Why? In your discussion remember to support your answers with examples from the book.

Write your conclusions to these questions in your log.

OUT OF SIGHT: WHAT DID
THE WRITER LEAVE OUT?

2 hours   *1 person or a group*

To be better able to help your students make inferences about what they
read, do this.

Select a book to read, and think about or discuss these questions:
Does the writer tell you every event that happens during the time period
of the book? Why? How does the writer decide which ones he will include
in order to tell his story and which ones to leave out? How would you
decide?

Does the author always tell you what a character was doing before he
appeared in the story? Does he put clues in what the other characters
say and do? Do you ever picture in your mind what the characters were
doing even though the author didn't tell you?

Pick out one section or chapter from your book and see what the
writer has left out. Are there characters who are not in this chapter or
are not in all of it? Are you not taken with them in detail to see where
they go and what they do? Who are they? Are you informed about what
has happened elsewhere that you as the reader do not see? How does
the writer make you know what has happened to the characters' thinking as well as what has happened to them outwardly? How does what
they say about others reveal the kinds of people they are themselves?
Give examples from the book in your log showing how the writer uses
clues to show what he does not tell.

Choose a scene which you know must happen in the lives of the
characters but which the writer expects you to know or ignores or tells
about only briefly. Knowing how these characters feel about what happens to them in other scenes in the book, how do you expect them to
feel in this scene? Knowing how they behave in other scenes, how do
you expect them to behave in this one even though the author has not
told you exactly what happens? Trying to imagine with your eyes and
ears what the characters would see and hear, write the scene in your
log as you think they would happen in the story. Can you find clues in
the words or actions of the characters just before this missing part
which might help you uncover their feelings during the scene you are
writing? Can you find clues in later scenes which reveal what happened
during your scene?

Improvise or act out your scene for another group that has not read
this book. Doing this may help you see why the writer left it out or even

make you wonder why he did not include it. You may use this technique in studying a play as well as a story or book.

TEACHING DRAMA

Traditionally, the study of great tragedy helped man see what he and what society might be if he did not control himself. *Macbeth* tells of the cold-blooded murder of a kind and generous superior, father and patron to the man who murders him. Society itself is a conspiracy to prevent man from committing criminal acts. Tragedy is a process of persuading ourselves and others not to have tragedies. In the fall of a great but imperfect man we see the extreme possibilities of life. Tragedy exposes important and extreme impulses and emotions and shows us how to manage them. Released from the equilibrium of ordinary life, we get a socially acceptable substitute for real tragedy.

One way to contain the human need for violence is to institutionalize in drama the expression of violence. Good art shows the relationship of suffering and violence. Vulgar art shows suffering and violence side by side but does not relate them. Drama provides the ritual, the sacred place apart, where man may exorcise the devils of violence, guilt, and revenge, without real evil consequences. The theater is a collective psychoanalytic experience, where the fearfulness within man is acted out on stage. It relates the social self to the anarchic self within.

Tragedy uses language in a special way to show how ineffective language is to control events. When characters make an attempt to control experience through words, they fail. Words cannot keep down experience. Tragedy centers on the predicaments of the hero, an enlarged self that had an enlarged place in society. The driving dreams of the hero overrun the conditions of society which make the dreams of the hero possible and try to contain them. The tragic hero is the product of society, who, pursuing his possibilities, disrupts society and is destroyed by it. He tries to appropriate more of life than is his share. His words are undercut by reality, and the irony of fate emerges.

The study of current drama and the way it is presented poses a special problem, for much that we are trying to do in the classroom now is involved with the drama and the use of oral language. We can learn from the modern stage the use of improvisation, sound, multi-media, and audience involvement.

Traditional conventions and literary style were designed to order experience and leave the audience with a sense of the orderliness of life, whether it be comic or tragic. Plays today leave the viewer in doubt about the nature of order and even about his own perceptions. Structure and order become irrelevant. Major plays in the Western tradition, from Aeschuylus to Ibsen, take their concern from certain beliefs about God, ethics, and society and aim to reconcile the reader emotionally and intellectually to the system of belief they explore. Change is reform advocated within a recognizable context, even if it be revolution.

Theater today is often a choreograph of picturesque gyrations, sacred ceremonies, magic, unwritten scripts, improvisations, sexual obsessiveness, massacre of language, noisy, attention-getting mechanisms, indifference to artistry and skill: not adversary demands upon human thought but the very qualities that keep man degraded and philistine. Spectacle without beauty and gesture without intelligence replace individual dissent with stereotyped assertions and obliterate with simple-minded nihilism complex moral, political, and social issues. But theater, which abounds in hippie and Jesus-rock musicals, nude tableaus, oriental dances, Yoga exercises, high decibel music, and actors who pull out of character to address the playgoers, shocks an audience into awareness, moving it into the stream of the drama's consciousness.

Perhaps we would be more comfortable if these things did not happen and the conventions of another day were maintained on the stage, but they do happen, and students often feel very much at home with them, as witness the phenomenal success of "Jesus Christ, Superstar." These gain and absorb the attention of students, while the classroom goes calmly on as if they did not exist, and teachers, if they think about them at all, hope that, if they are sufficiently mechanical and repetitious, they will go away. But will they? What is the student to make of the fact that the classroom excludes them from consideration, but the best critics do not?

If we do not prepare students to see plays in which film blends with stage acting, in which actors hum, buzz, drone, or do Balinese dances during the narrator's speeches, how will they know that a pop literature in which people do these things is often mistaking departures from convention for liberation? Students must learn to investigate how they feel when these things happen and what the purpose and effect of such instant literature is. They must examine the vision of the new literature which does not produce thought because it does not deal in ideas. But it does deal in feelings—what they value most. They can examine the feelings to see whether they add the richness to life that we all seek in artistic forms.

Without some sensitivity to the life style of the young, we will be unaware of the power of the visually arresting, momentary immediacy of the modern approach to dramatic art, and we will be unequipped to help them question what it does with the attention it compels, whether it really has anything to say, whether the shocked response it evokes moves them other than into another vacuum. They can learn that surprise and shock are not deep emotions, that technology, kookiness, and dalliance, a cast that screams, snarls, spits, fumes, mocks, and grovels cannot forever substitute for calculation, liberating thought and self-examination. And they need to practice judging whether such drama has anything to say or has added anything to their lives if their only response to an inquiry about it is, "Well, you know, I mean, like, it's heavy, man."

Elements in modern drama that disturb are meant to do so. In its own way it is saying what Faulkner echoed of Shakespeare, "Life is a tale, told by an idiot, full of sound and fury, signifying nothing." Yet surely the sufferings of the characters of Faulkner are of a different dimension from those of an *Easy Rider*. Or are they? And are the sufferings of a *Macbeth* as relevant to the student as those of a *Midnight Cowboy*? Unless we accept the drama of one age as moral protest, we are in a shaky position to insist that the drama of another is so. Our credibility is at stake if we accept the drama of the past as legitimate moral protest but say that the drama of our own time is not.

We need to look honestly at what is being said by the drama of the day—when something *is* being said. Protest drama assumes a legitimate moral position when it says that a view of ourselves as we are is a first step to a vision of ourselves as we might be, when it cries out, "Say if you dare that the world is not like this, or prove by what you do that it is not or need not be like this. But if you cannot deny this dark vision, say so; quit lying to yourself and others. Stop reinforcing with actions that which you deny with words, which order experience only when they describe what is actually happening."

When drama study in the classroom goes on as though no drama has been written since 1960, can students sense how artistically, intellectually, and humanly fraudulent are some of its manifestations? The classroom too often ignores what is open on the street, the newspaper, the television, the film. Surely there must be urgent talk in the classroom of whether the reader or viewer feels cleansed, renewed, full of the strong desire to overturn evil after seeing in repeated detail, lingeringly, the machines of human torture. There must be talk in class about whether the presentation of man as incoherent, inarticulate automaton of chaos helps him live more effectively.

The serious dramatist sees the practice of his art as a moral activity.

Diction, structure, and point of view serve a viewpoint, or they have no value. To lie in the theater is the unforgivable act, yet sometimes an audience forgives lies if they do not recognize lying or if they need the lies. To fulfill its obligations, serious drama must often be negative. But much drama we have chosen for classroom presentation is cheerful, positive, and affirmative and sustains belief in the redemptive nature of endurance, piety, and hard work. A serious dramatist tells the truth and accepts the implication of that eternal gap between the imagined order of the work of art and the actual chaos of the life it pictures or imitates. There is an eternal discrepancy between dream and fact, the best man can imagine and the best he can achieve. Weak drama of the classroom often composes a pseudomyth, not to express, as does real myth, wonder and terror, but to enshrine sentimental reassurance. What life refuses, it grants. These prefabricated dreams are the drugs of the literary world and attain in the reader the indifferent stupor characteristic of every drug. They assure him that everything is progressive, optimistic, rational, kindly, and humanistic. Students know this is not true.

The strength of the modern writer's dark vision and its compelling evidence is not combated by the literary gap in English classrooms between the evidence of life as students live it and drama in textbooks. The student very logically concludes that school drama is talking about a world that does not exist—at least not for him—and that teachers who feed it to him do not know what they are talking about, although he will humor them in their delusions in order to please them and get a diploma. He comes to believe that the price of access into adult life is the acceptance of lies. That price many youth, in a runaway trek across the country, refuse to pay.

Naturalist drama, starting with Ibsen, exploring society by exploring character, advocated change, reform, but reform within a recognized order, within a drama taking place behind a "fourth wall on the stage." Modern drama, whose actors join the audience or are joined by them, dissolves the stage illusion in search of a new sense of self. Reality is not imitated but created. Traditional perception of art is from outside its frame. Now drama moves inside the frame which has eliminated audience, actors, and artistic categories.

In much the same way, the activity curriculum obliterates the frames of category which divide subjects and studies, teachers and students who are free in the activities to create their own forms and shape their own values. The student, like a modern audience, works amid conflict and challenge, finding ways to form his values and a self-perpetuating and self-enlarging habit of permanently challenging what seems to be and what has been said with what might be. If we are successful in the drama we create and call an activity classroom, freedom will create a new order which constantly renews ability to feel and connect.

Activities

IS WRITING APPROVING?:
CENSORSHIP IN LITERATURE

1½ to 2 hours   *1 to 4 people*

Doing this activity will help you deal with your students' needs and questions involving censorship in literature.

Work alone or form a small group for this activity. What is the purpose of censoring a play or book? Conduct a survey among your classmates, friends, and the "man on the street" about censorship. Ask these people if there are any kinds of books they think should not be allowed in the school library. You may want to ask about both high school and college libraries. Ask a school librarian if there are any kinds of books the library does not stock because they are considered unsuitable. Ask why they are unsuitable.

Discuss or think about these questions: What do people who censor books think will happen to people who read them? Do you censor your own reading? Are there books you do not want to read because you consider the ideas in them dangerous? Do people usually think such books would harm them if they read them, or are they thinking that others would be harmed if other people read them?

Which is more important, fighting bad conditions or fighting books which talk about bad conditions? Do books which show the evil make it attractive or unattractive? Do they help or hinder the fight against bad conditions? What about the obligation of a work of art to show life as it is? How far should a work of art be free to do this if some think it furthers evil for a picture of evil to be presented in a lifelike way? What if a book presents a picture of attractive and pleasant people who do things that are disapproved of by most people without showing such people as frightening, distasteful or contemptible or even coming to a bad end? Does this make people who read the book think it is all right to do bad things?

Plan and write a news article in which you tell about the results of your survey and your conclusions about censorship. Either print your article in the class newsletter or circulate it in the class.

NEW AND OLD: TELEVISION OR STAGE?
2 hours or more   *1 person*

If you do this, you may be able to help students who see more of television than stage plays to enjoy both kinds of plays and find out how they are alike and different.

Choose a play that you have studied and feel comfortable with. Compare it with a television show. You may want to read these questions, go home and watch the show, and answer the questions the next day in class. Is the opening of the television show more or less likely to have an exciting beginning? What are some of the devices used to create excitement in television shows? You might have to look at several television shows to find these devices unless you can remember some of them.

Why does the television writer have to create one of these exciting starters even more than a stage writer does? In some television shows the placement of the commercial at the start is especially planned not to interfere with the beginning. How is this done? Why? What do you do if you do not like the start of a show on television? What, then, can a writer do to keep you from responding in this way?

What kind of action or words keep your attention? Do you have any examples of older playwrights who have done something like this to attract and keep audience attention? You might read over the opening scene in *Julius Caesar* for an example. If you want to know why Shakespeare thought it was important to have a scene like this, read something about the kinds of audiences he had and how they behaved.

After a television play gets the attention of the viewer, what is the next problem of the writer? When will the first break occur? What will happen to the audience during that break? What will the writer want to get done before that break to make sure he gets his audience back afterwards? Will he use large or small numbers of characters? Why? What kinds of conflicts will he use most often? What kinds of conflicts occur on the shows that are shown week after week as serials? Why?

Would the exposition be most likely to occur at the start of a television drama or would it be better to arrange this necessary information so that it could be given in some other way or at some other time? Why? How and at what other times could it be given?

Could you change your play into a television script? Try it. See if you can make it into a half-hour television program. Remember that making it fit into the time is all-important. Plan for commercials. When you have finished, see if you can find a group in your class to perform it.

JUST RIDICULOUS: COMIC CHARACTERS

1 hour   *1 person*

If you do this, you will be better able to help students discover why and how writers use funny characters in drama and literature in general.

Ask yourself some questions: When you are watching a film, television program or play, are there some characters you know are ridiculous as soon as you see them? How do you know? When you are reading, what clues does the writer give you that someone is supposed to be ridiculous?

Are there certain kinds of people in stories and plays and on television that we always recognize as ridiculous? By what characteristics do we recognize these comic characters?

Find three examples of such characters in literature you have read lately. Is this use of what is called the stock character an inventive and creative literary device or a tiresome and uncreative one? Give reasons for your answers for each example. Could the use of stock characters be more justified at one time than at another? Why?

Make up several stock characters of your own. Give them names and write a description of each one. Draw pictures of your characters or get an artistic person—perhaps from the help bank—to draw the pictures according to your directions. How would each of your characters behave in a play? Would they serve a good purpose in the play? Would you enjoy being in the audience during their performances?

Post the pictures of your characters along with their names and descriptions on the bulletin board in your classroom.

DRAMA MAKING: ACTING OUT PICTURES

30 minutes   *2 or more people*

Here is an experience that will prepare you to help students get started in acting and role-playing activities.

Find two or more people to work with. Look through some magazines for pictures which show two people doing something together. What are they doing? How did they get there? Are there other people in the picture? What are they saying? What could they be feeling? What kinds of lives do they live? Discuss these questions and see if you can create a story to go with the picture.

Work with a partner or as many people as you need and have in your group to act out your picture-story. Decide what problems the people in the story have and try to show by your words and actions how they react to their problems. Do they solve them? Why or why not?

If your group is large enough, other members may want to act out the same scene to see if they can improve on it, or they may want to find a different picture and act out that one.

After you are satisfied with your skit or skits, present them for an audience—another group or the whole class.

IT HAPPENS HERE: IMPROVISING SHAKESPEARE

1 hour   *2 to 10 people*

Try this to find one way your students can enjoy Shakespeare.

Choose a Shakespearean play that you might use with your students. Decide upon a scene that happens in the play or might happen in it. Plan to improvise this scene. List all the things that the writer had to get done in advancing the plot, setting, characters, and theme in this particular scene. Choose the characters you will play and let each person know what part of the jobs he is responsible for during the improvisation.

If he is responsible for plot activities, he must convey certain information and perform certain actions. If he is responsible for characters, he must let the audience know what kind of person he is or someone else is by the things he says or does. If he is responsible for setting, he must refer to it in some way or react to it. If he is responsible for theme (and everyone should be responsible for it in any scene), he can express it in words or act it out or show it by his attitude to what others do.

Since you do not have to memorize in an improvisation, you can spend your time thinking up words and ways to make these things happen.

Either play your scene before the class or tape it for later playing.

IDEA BAG: FINDING AN IMPROVISATION SITUATION

25 minutes throughout the day   *1 person*

This activity will give you ideas for helping students find improvisation situations.

Think about these questions: Before anything dramatic is interesting, what does it have to have? What does any dramatic situation have to have to be interesting? Are there any such situations around your school? Do you have any conflicts or know of any between students? Are there any disagreements with teachers? Are there any conflicts over school rules? Are there any boy-girl problems? Are there any cliques in school? What trouble do they cause? Are there any school affairs that seem to be worrying any groups—students, teachers, parents? All these are good subjects.

At home are there any conflicts between parents and children? Between various children in the family or the neighborhood? Are there disagreements about allowances, dating, curfews, grounding, clothes, hair length, manners, jobs, cars, responsibilities in the home, fears? In the community there may be good material for improvisations. Are there racial tensions, religious conflicts, social class barriers, or other items where differences appear?

Where could you get material on these things? Where are you that you could overhear conversations about them? At home? At lunch? Shopping? On the bus?

Collect ideas in a small notebook for a day and see if you don't have lots of material to use. Be sure to write down enough about each situation so that you will know what it is when you read it at the end of the day.

YOU CAN DO IT: MEMORIZING

variable time   *1 person*

Try these ideas yourself and see if you can use them to help students memorize parts in choral reading, skits, scenes from plays, or poetry.

Here are some tips professional actors use who have to memorize several pages of script each day. First be sure you know the meaning of every word and every part of the passage. Then you have only to read it aloud under certain conditions over and over. The number of times you will have to read it before you will find you know it will depend on how closely you follow these special rules.

Stand and walk around as you read. Read aloud as loudly as you can. As you hold the book with one hand, gesture and talk. Work in front of a full length mirror and look at yourself in the mirror every time you feel sure enough of the lines to look away from the book. Don't push yourself, but do look away as much as you can from the book. When you know the materials, you will find you are talking to yourself in the mirror. And you won't have any trouble forgetting half way through as you do when you try to memorize line by line.

Be sure to follow as many of the directions as you can. It will shorten the time you have to put in at the drudgery of memorization. If you are learning lines in a skit or play, you will need to learn the cues or who speaks just before you and what the last few words are that he says. Try to get someone to help you by reading the other lines when you practice, or just memorize the cues as you learn your own lines.

Now join a group of people who are going to put on a play or skit, or prepare a reading to give before the class. Use what you have read on this card, and record in your log how these directions worked for you.

FOLLOW-UP: TALKING ABOUT AN IMPROVISATION

10 minutes   *a group or class*

To find useful things to talk about in the discussion following an improvisation or other class presentation, complete the activity on this card.

When you are watching a dramatic incident in a film or in a skit, do you ever think, "That's not the way to do that. I would do it differently"? When you talk about the improvisation, you might suggest or ask others to suggest different ways of doing whatever was done. If the problem in the play was solved in one way, ask if there are other ways to solve it.

Were there other actions the characters could have taken? You might even replay the scene with other or the same actors doing it another way. What were the actors feeling and thinking as they played the roles? Is there usually more than one way to solve a problem? Does everything we do have consequences? What would be the consequence of what was done in the skit? For each person in it? Would another solution have other consequences? If we can control what we do to solve problems we confront, what control does that give us over the consequences? Was there anything any of the actors wanted to say that they did not say? Why? What would have happened if they had said these things? Would the consequences have been different?

After the discussion tell your log how you felt about the improvisation before, during, and after the discussion.

FEELING HAPPY, FEELING SAD: WHAT IS COMEDY?

2 hours   *3 to 7 people*

To find some ideas to help students discover why people feel happy or sad when they watch a play or read a story, try this activity.

Talk about these questions: If you are sitting in a safe comfortable chair watching, or maybe reading about, disasters happening to someone else, why do you laugh, or cry? You know that the character the disasters are happening to is imaginary. Do you ever forget? When do you remember? Do you feel relieved when you remember? Do you laugh?

One writer has said that man is the only animal who laughs and weeps because he is the only animal who is aware of the difference between the way things are and the way they might be. What do you think of this statement?

Do you ever laugh or cry at a play or television drama or film because you see that the characters could behave differently and so suffer less? Or do you laugh because you are relieved that what might have happened did not? Give examples for your log.

Some television shows are not performed before real audiences, so the producers use "fake" or "canned" laughter to make it sound as if there is an audience when you see the show at home.

Pretend that you are the producer of such a show. Find the script of a one act comic play, and decide where the laughter should interrupt. To test your skill, act the play for your class, and see if a real audience laughs where you thought they would.

FINDING THE SKELETON OF A PLAY:
WHAT MAKES DRAMA SPECIAL?

2 hours or more   *1 person or a group*

If you or your group are reading or viewing a play, or planning to, you may need some help in knowing what things to look for. This activity will help you.

Read these questions and try to answer them in your mind. Then make a little list of your own, using this one to guide you. List the questions you think the play ought to answer.

At the start of the play what kind of information does the writer give the audience? What do the characters talk about first? Are the events they mention events that have happened before or events that are going to happen? Which are mentioned most and first? Why does the writer do this? Do characters call each other by name or give facts about each other that you would need to know? Do they refer to people who are not there? Do they tell about any events to come? As you read the play, or review it, find examples to support your answers—whether you are answering these questions or your own.

What conclusions would you draw about what kind of information the writer must give at the beginning of the play? What other kinds of information appear at the start? Do you begin to get a feeling of fun, sadness, fear, or some other mood? Do characters talk about the place or the time? Are there other clues given to place and time in the play? This information and the lines needed to set it up are called exposition.

After the playwright gets this job done, what will be his next task? It's a job he has to do or everyone will go home and stop listening to his boring play! Will there be more or less talking in this part of the play, compared to the amount of action there was in the first part? Why? Do the characters seem to accumulate problems or solve them in this part? This part is called the rising action. Do the problems get worse and worse until you think they can't get any worse? At what point are the problems most complicated, or at what point is there the most tension and excitement? In what act and what part of the act does this moment occur? This is called the climax.

Then what final job does the writer have? What does he have to do to finish the play? Does the character always solve the problems? What other kinds of endings besides those satisfactory to the character are possible?

Using these questions or your own, see how they apply to your play. What, if anything, do the answers to these questions have to do with the way the play is divided into acts and scenes? What things are true of plays that are not true of any other kind of writing? Write your conclusions in your log.

CALL IT FUNNY: COMIC SCENES AND PLAYS

45 minutes   *3 to 5 people*

If you would like to know more about comedy—what makes it interesting, why people laugh at it, how authors make it work—try this activity.

Have each member of your group read or watch a comic scene, television play, or stage play. Then, have each member tell the group about his comic scene or play. After hearing about these experiences with comedy, discuss these questions in your group: In a comic scene do we at any time feel that the characters are in danger of any kind? Do we experience suspense? Have each member give examples to prove his point. Draw conclusions about the use of suspense in comedy. Does the threatened disaster occur? How do we feel when it does not?

What *kind* of disaster is threatened, one that will make the character appear ridiculous or one that will destroy his life? Draw conclusions about the kinds of disasters that comic writers use.

How do you feel when you see that the character is going to be rescued? How do you respond? Does your relief make you laugh?

Use examples as you tell your logs your conclusions.

YE GODS, GHOSTS, AND GHOULS: HIDDEN FORCES IN SHAKESPEAREAN PLAYS

45 minutes   *1 person*

If some of the supernatural devices Shakespeare uses to show the hidden forces in his characters' lives seem strange to you, maybe this activity will make them more understandable.

What characters appeared in Shakespearean plays which a modern writer would not use? What was their purpose? Give some examples, perhaps from *Macbeth* or *Hamlet* or *A Midsummer Night's Dream*. What were the many purposes these characters served in the plays? Give examples. You may want to do some research.

Would audiences of modern plays accept these creatures? Did you see *Jesus Christ, Superstar*? Is there any similarity between the ways the ancient plays presented gods and this play?

Make a report to the class on the difference between the modern and old ways of handling hidden forces in drama. Use any method you prefer of getting your information across. Write it, say it, record it, make a bulletin board or display out of it, or act it out.

CUTTING UP: COMEDY

45 minutes some at home   *1 person*

If you don't see why some things are funny or if you would like to know more about what makes people laugh at the things they do, try this activity.

Do you like to watch comic shows or plays? What does a comic play do for you? Could it have any other purpose? Why does the writer want you to laugh? What things does he make you laugh at? Does laughing at someone or something make you feel any differently about it or him? In what way?

Look at one of the comic plays you have read and see if the author makes you laugh at certain things in order to make you have certain attitudes toward them. Did he want you to change in any way because you had laughed at these things? Did your attitudes change?

Are television commericals sometimes funny in ways that meant to get you to change an attitude? What about cartoons? Find some cartoons that have a serious purpose of this sort underneath their humor. See if you can tell what the purpose is. Political cartoons are particularly serious ones. Where can you find some political cartoons?

Paste some political cartoons in your log and tell about their purpose.

TURNING EVENTS OVER:
THE GREEK WRITER AND HIDDEN FORCES

several hours   *5 to 10 people*

This activity will show you a way to use Greek drama with English students and to involve students in analyzing and acting activities.

Find a group of people in your class and consider these questions: How does any writer find ways to show the forces inside of his characters or in his characters' experiences? What kinds of forces would not escape the reader's or viewer's notice in a real scene with real characters?

Do some research to see how methods of showing these forces might vary according to different historical times in which writers write. Have members of your group report to the group on ways that have been used during different times.

In ancient plays and stories how were forces that governed man's life made visible? In the plays of Aeschuylus, the ancient Greek writer, they appeared right on stage. The members of your group should find examples to share.

What effect did this physical presence of supernatural force have upon the audience? What purpose did it serve for the writer? What influence did it have upon the lives of the characters? What would the audience go away believing? How would it affect their lives? When events occurred in their lives which they could not explain or which turned the course of their fate, what conclusions were they likely to draw?

Do you think that a modern audience would believe in this kind of supernatural interference in man's fate? With your group design a modern situation in which forces of destiny behave as they did for the ancient Greeks.

Create a modern situation with a modern problem in the form of a skit or one-act play. Handle your situation as one of the ancient Greek writers would have done. Act out your skit for the class.

TEACHING POETRY

The literary genre that is often most difficult for teachers and students to enjoy is poetry. That the teaching of poetry in the English class has been neither successful nor adequate is attested to by the dislike many students have for poetry and their complete failure to connect their own poetry in their music with anything they have known in school. A favorable response to poetry cannot be engendered by some of the standard approaches: reading silently from anthologies, analyzing technical matters, or paraphrasing. And no one should be assigned to read a poem. The will to read it must be the reader's, or the poem is lost.

The teacher must develop in himself the feelings about poetry that he wants students to have. The focus is not on material to be mastered but on response to experience. If, however, poetry plays little part in the life of the teacher outside the classroom, he is not likely to be able to make it play an important part in the classroom, because he does not really believe it is important, and he cannot make someone else believe it. Perhaps he should not even try to do so.

Those who read poetry expecting it to be like prose have problems. Prose offers explicit abstractions and generalizations, but poetry offers a set of facts or a situation from which the reader must draw inferences. Poetry is like life; it is not linear; many of the words and experiences are not immediately intelligible and are never paraphrasable. Poetry offers a set of facts without many hints of why they are significant or worthy of the reader's notice. Poetry demands involvement as well as intellect and experience; it is not subject matter; it requires not just reading but awakened sensitivity.

Poetry is not a subdivision of literature printed in columns instead of across the page and intended mainly for girls and teachers. It is not fantasy and make believe but a special way of knowing, as it has been since the Hebrews and Greeks. We cannot know an apple by reading a definition of it. We must see it, taste it, and digest it. So it must be with a poem, which translates experience into insight. A prime purpose of poetry is to discover and impart knowledge. When Wordsworth described a daffodil, he told us, this is what a daffodil looks like and this is what it feels to look at a daffodil. The poet sees that all things have relationships, that people have feelings about them, and a thing is not described unless feelings are taken into consideration. Knowing about feelings is as important and as valuable as any other kind of knowledge. A poet's knowledge of a daffodil is as valuable as that of a botanist.

Some students can be led to discover the poetry in themselves if teachers believe it is there, search for it, and recognize it when they find it. Versification is not this kind of poetry; it is more akin to mathematics or games. A poem is not about ideas but about having ideas and feelings. The poet believes that life can assume pattern and order, given the proper words. He explores with language his experiences and his own states of mind. Poetry is an attitude, a spirit, a collection of responses which lead to words coming from the emotional content of experience. A poet sets down experience so that he can share it with others. He creates an object with words, explores reality, and makes sense of his experience. He packs the largest meaning into the smallest space and uses the perfectly chosen concrete image to do so. And it must be expressed in sounds as natural as birdsong. Poetry is the form in which preliterate culture was expressed, and it has been speculated that the first language was not related to ideas but to the lovely sounds primitive man discovered he could make when he wanted to express his feelings. If the teacher can make these things happen to the student, the student himself will write poetry, for youth is returning to poetry and often feels deeply about it and music that expresses it.

Poems used must be those whose experiential content is familiar to students. Students whose experience is only of the industrial and urban world are unfamiliar with images of the past which so often came from nature. But poems are shorter than other genre, so it is easier to duplicate varied collections for the classroom than it would be in the case of novels or long plays.

Activities

WHAT'S THE DIFFERENCE?: PROSE AND POETRY

35 minutes   *2 people*

This activity may give you ideas for structuring situations in which your students can make discoveries about the nature of poetry.

Get a partner. You will each need to prepare for this activity outside of class by looking through some old newspapers, magazines, and books. Find between five and ten short selections of poetry and prose. Try for variety. See if you can find at least one poem that doesn't rhyme and one that does. Can you find a funny or silly one? A sad or ugly one? A far-out one? A traditional one? Try the lyrics from a song. For prose also look for variety. Try sentences or paragraphs from books. Can you find instructions on how to do something? A recipe? A news item? A conversation? A description?

Take your collections of prose and poetry to class. Have one person close his eyes and listen as the other reads each of his selections. After each selection has been read, the person with his eyes closed guesses whether what has been read is poetry or prose.

Did you guess them all right? Why or why not? Can the person reading make prose sound like poetry or poetry sound like prose? If so, how? What does the person writing a poem do to make it sound like poetry? What are the sounds that make you know you are hearing a poem? Just rhyme? Did you guess the poem that had no rhyme? Why? Are there any special words used in poems that do not seem so much used in prose? Are the words put together differently? If so, how? How did the poetry make you feel? How did the prose make you feel? Why? Make a list of all the things you can think of that help you know when you are hearing a poem.

Have you discovered anything new about poetry and prose and what happens when someone hears a poem that doesn't happen when he hears prose? Record your feelings and conclusions in your log. What could students do to make these discoveries for themselves?

SHOW AND TELL: PICTURES IN POETRY

50 minutes   *2 to 5 people*

Here is something you can do to learn to help your students discover the imagery of poetry.

Do you remember show and tell in primary school? Did you ever try to tell without the show? What happened? Were your listeners interested? Why or why not? Does a poem tell or show? How can you tell? What are the parts of a poem that tell? What parts show? Discuss poems you have read lately and show the group parts that tell and parts that show in your poem.

Does poetry tell or show more than prose? Which does a poem do more, give a philosophy or show you a specific event? Is there ever a philosophy in a poem? Find examples to support your answers. Why doesn't the writer just tell you what he wants you to believe instead of showing you a picture which makes you have to draw your own conclusions?

Why isn't the poet afraid you will miss the point? Is a poem more of an idea or a happening? Why? Isn't this more trouble than just saying what he wants to say straight out? Then why does a poet choose to make his point this way?

When you were discussing the show and tell parts of the poems, did you all agree on what the poems were showing or telling? Why? Choose one poem about which you all have strong feelings. Talk about the pictures that poem brings to your minds. How are your pictures of the poem the same and how are they different? Are there limitations on the ways a poem can be interpreted? If so, what? What decides what a poem cannot mean? Can a poem ever mean more than a poet thought it meant? How do you think the pictures the poem brings to your mind might be different from the ones in the poet's mind?

Make plans for everyone in your group to bring cardboard or construction paper and several magazines with lots of pictures in them from home. Share your magazines, looking through them to make a collection of pictures which best represent the pictures the poem makes in your mind. Each person in the group should make his own collection according to his interpretation of the poem. Paste your pictures on the cardboard or construction paper in a way that makes sense to you. Ask each person to explain to the group why he chose the pictures he did.

POETRY OR BASEBALL: PLAYING THE GAME
50 minutes   *1 person*

Do this and you may be able to help your students discover how and why poems are made.

Make a list of terms used in baseball. Are these ever used at other times besides when people are talking about baseball? When? What other meanings do "pitch," "strike," "first base," and "left field" have when people are not talking about baseball? Ask at least ten other people what these words mean to them. How many of them talk about other things besides baseball? Make a list of these other meanings in your log.

Begin with another sport—boxing. What do "throw in the towel," "knockout," and "hit below the belt" mean that isn't about boxing? Write a phrase that says each of these things in other words. How is this paraphrase you have written different from the way it was said originally? In what ways is it less effective? Did it take more words to get the meaning across? Was it as vivid? Did it raise as much feeling in you and as many pictures in your mind? Which way of saying it made the clearest picture in your mind? Why?

Choose a poem you have read or would like to read. Try saying what is said in the poem in your own words. What happens to the poem? Does your paraphrase work to get the idea across as well as the poem did? Why? Does it say everything and make the reader have the same feelings as the poem did, even though it may be longer? Why? Can a poem be said some other way? Why? What things are lost?

What does it mean to take something literally? Can you take a poem literally? How else can you take it? When Shakespeare says, "All the world's a stage," is he talking about the theater? How do you know?

Newspaper reporters tell about actual happenings. Look in your daily newspapers to see if they also use expressions which literally mean one thing to mean something else. See how many examples you can find.

Choose one of these newspaper articles or a paragraph from one and arrange the words into a poem. Paste the original article in your log, and put your poetic version beside it.

MOON, SPOON, JUNE: HOW DO POETS USE RHYME?
several hours   *1 person*

If you do this, you may find ways for students to analyze and enjoy the use of rhyme in poetry.

Did you ever try to make up rhymes? Think of all the rhymes you can. Is a rhyme all it takes to make a poem? Why or why not? The English language causes some problems for rhyme makers. Are there some words you would like to use in your rhymes, but you can't find any other words to rhyme with them? Some words are easy to rhyme. What are some of these words that appear in many poems? Make a list and see how many rhymes there are for them. Your list may include "moon," "star," "life," "love," and so forth.

Capable poets have been working with these words for several centuries. What has happened to the possibilities for doing something new with them? There are other things that rhymsters can do to find original ways of using rhyme. Where could a poet put a rhyme instead of at the end of a word? Give an example.

Try a short poem making the vowels rhyme and letting the consonants go as they will. Try another one keeping the consonants the same and using different vowels . . . run, rain, Rhine, ran, ruin . . . are examples. Then there are almost rhymes . . . summer, somewhere . . . Make your own list.

Look at some modern poems and at some written in the previous century. Do modern poems use more rhyme than older poems? Why? If a rhyme is used, it should sound natural and inevitable.

If there are so many problems with rhyme, why do poets use it? A long time ago, before most people could write and poets were not able to write their poems down, they had to depend on memory. What help would rhymes be to a poet then? Why do teachers use rhymes and songs to help small children learn the ABC's and the months of the year? Could rhymes be an attention getter to an old-time storyteller-poet? Would they seem to demonstrate magic powers? Was that important? Why?

Pretend that you are one of the storyteller-poets of long ago carrying gossip and entertainment to small communities. Make up a story and put it to rhyme. Then memorize it. Either record your poem on tape or recite it for an audience from your class.

GET THE BEAT: RHYTHM IN POETRY

1½ hours   *1 person*

If you do this, you may find ways to help your students enjoy reading poetry.

How do you experience rhythm as you live through a day of your life? Make a list in your log of all the ways you experience rhythm. Do you like to dance? To listen to music? What does listening to rhythm do for you? Do you tap your foot? Jingle your keys? Rattle your change? Tap your pencil? Why?

What body functions have rhythm? Ask someone who is an authority on the way the body works. Does this give you any clues about why a poet uses rhythm? Why do small children clap their hands, chant in sing-song voices, stomp their feet in unison when they play games? What can a poet accomplish with rhythm that he cannot accomplish without it?

Find a poem with a strong rhythm and try reading it aloud to a drum beat. Find someone with musical experience to accompany you with a drum beat while you read the poem aloud. You might be able to find such a person in the help bank. You will need to practice your performance just as you would if you were going to sing a song.

Read your poem to the drum beat for the class. Be sure to share your discoveries with your classmates by telling them about what you have learned about rhythm and by giving them a chance to ask you questions after your performance. Offer to help anyone who wants to try the same activity.

PART OF THE CROWD: CHORAL VERSE

several hours   *10 to 30 people*

Try this to find out how you can involve shy, uninterested, and uncertain students in reading poetry aloud.

Assemble a group of people to participate in the choral reading of a poem. Choose a poem that has a good story in it and has lots of repeated parts so that your listeners will enjoy hearing it and you will have parts that you can all say together. Many songs, poems, and even selections from the Bible can be used for choral reading. Your group may want to test several different ones until you find just the right one for your reading. Two poems often used are "Overheard in a Saltmarsh" and "The Negro Speaks of Rivers."

Talk over your chosen poem until all of you understand every part of it. It's hard to say anything very well if you aren't sure of what it is you are saying. You may want to check the pronunciation and meanings of new words. Try writing them down in your log as a reminder.

Decide which of you feels sure enough of himself to take the solo parts. You will need both boys and girls for this. Then pick out the parts for heavy and light voices. Sometimes you can use the whole group or just two or three together. How can you have variety and still keep the meaning? You may want to make a plan which shows who will speak during each part of the poem. Try writing the words of the poem out in the way it will be read, with symbols or letters beside each line of the poem to show who reads that part. Make a copy for everyone to see. Will you need a director to keep you together?

Record your reading on tape and listen to yourselves. Are there parts you want to read fast or slow or louder or softer? How will that change the effect of your performance? Can you understand every word? You may want to ask someone who does not know the poem to listen and tell you which words he cannot understand. You can mark these words on a copy and practice until you are sure each word can be heard.

You may want to add some body language to individual or group lines. Are there words that seem to suggest movement? Should everyone make movements or should only certain people do it? How can you tell what the effect on the audience would be? Should some speakers make entrances as they speak or should all stand with the group as they speak?

Would your performance look and sound better if you memorized the performance? Will the audience be able to hear and see you? Would standing on some steps help? Will you want any background or props? Will you wear any special clothing?

When you are ready, invite an audience and give your performance.

Write about your experience in your log. What problems did you have? How did you solve them? What problems would you expect if a high school English class did this? How could they be solved? How do you feel about what you did? How do you think a student would feel? Why?

WHY FIGHT?: COMPARING VALUES

2½ hours   *4 to 6 people*

Use this activity to discover a way of dealing with topical issues through poetry.

Form a group of people from your class. Find a copy of "Charge of the Light Brigade" by Tennyson. Choose one person to read it aloud to the group or take turns reading it. Also read "Next to God, America" by cummings.

Discuss these questions: What attitude does each of these poets take toward patriotism? Which is most like yours? Does the other point of view have any validity? Why? What is patriotism? What things does a patriot admire? Do most people who consider themselves patriotic have other attitudes that they usually hold? If so, what are they? How do they feel about religion? How do they feel about the country's leadership? How do they feel about heroes of the country's past? Are there certain words or expressions they tend to use to describe their feelings, themselves, and their country? How do they feel about those who do not share their ideas about these things? In searching for the answers to these questions you may find it helpful to talk to some people who have strong feelings of patriotism and to some who do not.

Is a person a patriot who sees many faults in his country's past or present actions? Why or why not? Are we citizens of the world as well as of a country? What kinds of attitudes would lead to the best kind of world?

After you have each found satisfactory answers to these questions, discuss your personal answers and the answers of the people you talked to. If there are differing points of view in your group over any of these issues, plan a panel discussion in which you will present your different points of view for the other class members.

Present your panel discussion for the class.

A ROCK HISTORY: ROCK LYRICS, PAST AND PRESENT

several hours   *1 person*

Here is a way to use a student's interest in music to get him involved in poetry. Try it yourself.

Do you have a record collection? Do you know someone who has a big record collection? How far back does the collection go? Rock started nearly twenty years ago. During that time many different kinds of lyrics have been written.

Start a collection of the lyrics on records and work on it whenever you can find a collection larger than your own. Sometimes you can use the listening booths in shops.

How can you classify your lyrics? By the people who recorded them? By subject? By date? What will be the most unusual subjects? Can you find differences in the lyrics from different years? What are they? How do the lyrics change as they become more modern? How and when do the changes happen?

When you have collected several dozen lyrics, make a small book for circulation in your class. Write a preface for your book, discussing the classifications you have made and any conclusions you have reached about differences between older and newer lyrics.

Could you write a card for a teenager on making a collection of lyrics? How will you appeal to his interests? What problems might he have? How can you guide him through them? How can you be sure you will tell him everything he needs to know but let him make his own discoveries? How can you be sure he will be able to do the things you expect him to do? What will he learn by doing them? Write your card for a teenager in your log or on a 5" x 9" card. Save it to use when you teach English.

SPREAD A LITTLE JOY:
FUNNY POETRY

10 minutes   *1 person*

Here is a little something you can do to see how poetry can be fun.

Do you have a favorite funny little poem? Why do you like it? What makes it funny to you? Share your enjoyment by telling someone else about it.

Read your funny poem to someone else or let him read it. Does he think it is funny too? Why? Does the poem have any serious idea behind the fun? If so, what is it? What does the poem make you think of? What did it make your friend think of?

Is your poem silly? Why? Is there anything funny about how the words are put together? How does a poet find a funny way to put his words?

Post your poem somewhere for others to enjoy, and tell your log how it felt to share a happy thought.

MEANING MADNESS: WHAT DOES A POEM MEAN?

2½ hours   *4 to 8 people*

To help students feel comfortable with their own ideas about poetry, do this.

Form a group of people in your class who would like to be more comfortable with what they think about the poems they read. Discuss these questions: Does a poem mean the same to every reader? Why? Can it ever mean to any reader what it meant to the writer? Why? What determines what a poem means to anyone?

If the words on the page are the same to everyone, what is different? Do the words on the page say the same thing to everyone? What makes the difference? Try this experiment: Find some examples of modern art in the library or from magazines. Pass a picture around the group, and have everyone write down what the picture means to him. Compare answers. Try it several times. In what ways are the answers the same and in what ways different? How is modern art like poetry? Why doesn't everyone see the same thing?

There were some things in the pictures that everyone saw, and there were some physical limitations upon the kinds of things you might see. Are there limitations on the ways a poem can be interpreted? What? What decides what a poem cannot mean? Can a poem ever mean more than a poet thought it meant? How could this happen?

Try the same exercise with poems that you did with the pictures. Let every member of the group choose one poem to be talked about by the group. Compare and discuss different meanings.

Pick the one poem about which you had the liveliest discussion, and plan a panel discussion on its meaning before the whole class.

POETRY PLEASE!: READING A POEM ALOUD

2 hours   *1 person*

If you would like to help students read poetry aloud and feel more confident about it, do this.

What subject could you talk most interestingly about? Is it one you know better than you know most things? How does this help you to speak well?

If you are going to read a poem well, you need to know it well. How can you know a poem well? What would you need to know about it? Make a list of what you need to know about it.

Do you need to practice before you read? After you have chosen your poem and are sure that you understand the meaning and know how to pronounce all the words, try practicing into the tape.

If you feel strongly about something, do you sound more convincing when you talk about it? What are you thinking about when you speak about something that is important to you? When you read, try thinking about the ideas behind the words you are using. Does this make you speak more slowly or faster? What does this give your listener time to do?

Listen to your tape and make notes of things you can improve next time. You might want to be sure to stress important words and phrases. How could you pick these? How could you remind yourself to stress them? How do you stress words with your voice? With your body? What things do you do with your voice to show punctuation?

In a poem is there anything that tempts you to punctuate when there is no mark? How can you keep from doing this? You might try to write out the poem in paragraph form if you find you are doing too much pausing at the ends of lines.

Do you want to present your poetry reading before an audience when you have used the tape to prepare yourself? The tape cannot see you. An audience can. Will you use gestures? How will you stand? Will the expression on your face change from one part of the poem to another? Will you look at the audience? What will you wear?

These are some things you can do with your voice to express certain feelings. What can you do to express excitement? Tension? How do you express calm and relaxation? What do you do with your voice when you are expressing just telling a story? When you let your voice go up, what is being expressed? If you want to express determination, or conviction, how will you use your voice? Practice in front of a mirror for gestures and with a tape recorder for voice until you feel ready to read before an audience.

Read your poem. Choose an audience with whom you feel comfortable, perhaps a group in the class that is also interested in poetry.

POEM PLAY: A DRAMATIC POEM

2 hours   *3 to 8 people*

To help students deal with a poem that consists mostly of conversation, try this activity.

Find a dramatic poem and produce it as a play. Cast the parts. In your rehearsal try to read the lines as though they were not poetical but real conversation. If there are some non-conversational parts, you may need a narrator.

What would help you to get the feel of it as a conversation rather than a poem? Perhaps it would help if you saw the lines written as conversation. Have each person write himself the "sides" he needs. Sides were the lines of an actor in the old days of the theater. On these sides there were just the name of the character who spoke before the actor, the last three or four words he spoke (called the cue), and the lines of the actor whose sides they were. This system kept producers from having to make full copies of the play for everyone. It may work for you. Try it. Be sure to write the sides in conversation form, not in poetic lines.

You may select an audience and invite them. Read the poem into the tape for later presentation or just present it for yourselves. Tell your log what you chose to do and why.

GETTING DOWN TO ESSENTIALS: IS POETRY TRUE?

50 minutes   *3 or 4 people*

If you are interested in what makes poetry different from other kinds of literature and how students can enjoy it more do this activity.

Did you ever wonder whether literature was true—true like physics and chemistry for instance? What was true for chemistry twenty years ago is not true now. Chemistry textbooks need to be updated.

Which is more useful and valuable, a poem just as it was originally written or one which has been brought up to date and changed for readers today? Would it be a good idea to do that to Shakespeare? Why? Do you think people could just discard the way it was written and modernize it?

What is it that gets outdated in science, but doesn't in poetry? Find a poem about an object that could be described in a botany book—a flower perhaps. Then look up the description in a science book. Discuss the differences between the two descriptions. Does the poet talk about something that goes beyond the flower or the object that the poem is about? Does he say things about his own feelings? About life? Why don't these ideas get outdated?

What conclusions does your group reach about the value of a statement of poetry and a statement of science in its likelihood of going out of date and being found to be no longer true in future generations? Report your conclusions to the class.

READING NON-FICTION

To live, work, and play effectively, students must read to gather information. And they can learn that information production can reflect the same clarity, precision and grace they find in other forms of literature. A well-conceived and clearly-labeled chart in a business report is as suggestive in its way as that chart to the purpose, content, and theme of Macbeth given in the initial scene of the gleeful and plotting witches. Material for teaching non-fiction, immensely diverse, forms an endlessly gratifying source for individualizing reading.

The English teacher should make a list of the sources of reading materials available to students, starting with a survey of reading students have done in recent weeks. Items found in the survey be can categorized, and categories should be supplemented whenever students read new materials. These vary from stop signs and billboard advertisements to encyclopedias and scientific manuals. All are respectable student reading, and students should use them as stepping stones to more reading and to analysis of intent, content, and value.

As students study biography and autobiography, they investigate the relations of man to events and people in his life. As they read travel and accounts of exploration, they investigate the relation of man to the physical environment. As they read editorial essays, they examine the purposes and devices of those who would persuade or convince them. As they do information-concept reading in their texts in the content areas, they learn the relationship between having ideas and thoughts and getting information from others' ideas and thoughts. As they use maps, graphs, charts, and cartoons, they learn the use of non-verbal printed symbols and how to draw from them implications and perceive implied relationships.

The teacher of English may want to help his students solve their reading problems in other content areas. In fact, teachers in other content areas may expect English teachers to have taught their students how to read materials in other content areas. But content areas deal with expository writing, and much of what is taught in English class is narrative. The expository mode specifies and directs. The literary mode suggests, implies and deals consciously with ambiguities of all sorts. The main-supporting ideas pattern of the expository mode in content area paragraphing is not the paragraph pattern of the story. Literature is read for pleasure and vicarious experience. Content area reading is usually for information. Content area reading is designed for a convergent response, for a logical approach. Hence, reading literature is not a very efficient skill-building experience for teaching students to read in content areas.

Although a reading laboratory serves somewhat the student's content area needs, content area teachers need to reinforce and reapply what happens there, for reading has no content of its own; it is a process of acquiring information designed to solve problems and as a source of recreation and enjoyment. Skills taught in the reading laboratory are often taught in contexts different from those used in the content areas, and these skills must be made to transfer; they will not do so automatically. The English teacher can further this process by teaching directed reading of content area material.

Many content area teachers use inquiry methods. Hence, in reading for a class, students have a purpose, a problem to be solved. The student should survey what he already knows about the subject before he begins to read. He will then be looking for clues to information relevant to his needs: headings and titles will indicate hierarchies of importance; the index and table of contents will guide him to information he is seeking. He will skim to find answers, holding questions in mind as he hunts specific answers, stopping from time to time to ask himself questions and to answer those which the text raises, reflecting on what he reads and reading selectively.

A student needs to read critically in content areas, to identify clues that tell him what a writer wants him to believe and to make conscious decisions about whether he wants to believe it, to decide how much power the viewpoint has and should have, to decide how much credence it should be given and whether he wants to withhold judgment until he has further data. He needs to see the blurring inevitable between opinion and fact and find his way as near to what he can accept as truth as possible by testing what he reads. He must distinguish central ideas from ideas used to support them. He must use devices for stimulating memory, organizing and relating what he reads as he goes along, summarizing and note-taking.

When he looks for corroborative materials, the student needs to locate ideas related to what he wants to know and reject what does not meet his purposes. He must check and cross check information from library bibliographies and reference materials. He must determine when he has sufficient materials, whether he should look further, how reliable and recent are materials he has consulted and what questions remain to be answered. When consulting a variety of reference materials, he must compare them, finding discrepancies and checking qualifications of writers. He investigates both sides of controversial questions. He interprets non-word materials. Perhaps he reads fictional literary materials for enjoyment, adding new dimensions and enlarging information. These kinds of reading are a source of endless numbers of activity cards which teach students how to find information, extract data, judge its validity and appropriateness, apply it to their needs and enjoy the manner of presentation if it is aesthetically pleasing.

Activities

FACT FUN: READING A NON-FICTION BOOK OR ARTICLE
40 minutes   *1 person*

Do this to find ways to help students read non-fiction books or articles critically and with enjoyment.

Choose a non-fiction book or article that you have read lately, or find one and read it. Consider these questions: Why did you choose to read this particular book or article? What problems is the writer trying to solve? What solutions does he offer? Do you agree with them? Why or why not?

In the writing is there a sentence or a group of sentences which state his position? What do they say? Did the writer fail to solve some of the problems? How did he account for those he failed to solve? What facts are brought out in this book that are effective in pointing to solutions? Does the writer show how he became convinced of the validity of the solutions he advocates?

Is there any point at which the writer seems uninformed? Or misinformed? Is he illogical? Is his discussion incomplete in any way? Does he leave you with unanswered questions? How about the writer himself? Does he have sufficient background to be an expert?

List the things that have made the writer an expert. Does he keep up with new developments in his field? Is there evidence to indicate that he does? If so, what? Does he write in words that the ordinary reader can understand? Does he stick to topics he is an authority on and not give opinions on others? What kind of proofs does he offer? Does he use some verifiable facts? Documentation? What are these?

Does he give all the alternatives and show why he rejects the solutions other than the one he chooses? How can you check what he says against what others think or say on the subject?

Imagine that the author of your book or article is coming to speak to your class on the subject he wrote about in the selection you just read. You are chosen to introduce him and what he has to say to your classmates. What would you say? How would you convince your classmates they should listen attentively? Would you mention other articles or books your author has written? If so, which ones would it be appropriate to mention? Introduce your author to the class and see how many people say they would like to hear him talk or read his article or book.

TRUE AS LIFE: GETTING THE MOST FROM YOUR BIOGRAPHY
variable time   *1 person*

If you do this, you will be better prepared to help your students read biographies.

Review a biography you have read recently or find one and read it. Is your biography about a special kind of person who did special things? Was the person all good or all bad? In what ways did the author show you this? What special things do you think the author wants you to see about the person?

Do you think there were any things he knew about the person that he left out of the book? Why would he do that? If you were the author, how would you decide what was important enough to talk about in the book and what wasn't? If you knew something bad about the person, would you tell that too? Why or why not? What would it do for your book? For the people reading it? Would you try to show what made your character look better or smarter or braver than he was in real life? Why or why not?

Do you like to read a biography that shows a great person in a true to life way? Why? How does it make you feel about yourself?

Try doing what a biographer does. Choose someone you know well and write a short biography of him. You may want to ask this person and some other people who know him well questions about his life, or you might want to spend some time with him just to see how he fills his days. See if you can write about this person as you know him without showing him to be better or worse than he really is.

NEWS VIEWS: COMPARING NEWSPAPERS
2 hours or more   *3 to 6 people*

You may find this activity useful as a beginning for your own plans to help students read newspapers more critically.

Form a group of people in your class. Discuss your ideas about news and newspapers: How do you get news about what is happening in the world? How can you be sure you are finding out the truth about what is happening? Ask several different people from your group and outside of your group to tell what has happened in the news today. Compare their accounts.

Get several different newspapers for the same day. Ask your school librarian if you can have a copy of one of the national newspapers your school library takes for the same day. You may have to buy one at a downtown newsstand. Three from which you might choose are *The New York Times, The Christian Science Monitor,* or *The Wall Street Journal.* If you have trouble getting one, try a local stockbroker's office for a *Wall Street Journal.*

Compare the papers. What international stories are handled and where are the stories about them? How about the national news? What feature articles and feature pages are in each paper? What comparison can you make about the number of columns devoted to local news? How do the ads differ?

Find a story in each paper about the same event. Compare the number of inches of column space devoted to it. Are some facts about the event in one paper that are not given in the other? If so, why? Are there any facts given in one paper which seem to contradict the facts in another?

Does the headline always give the true interpretation of what is said in the body of the story? How do you account for differences if there are any? What kind of information you read in the newspapers is likely to have the greatest differences—news stories or stories for entertainment? Why?

Compare the editorial pages of the newspapers. Are there any differences of viewpoint there? What is the difference between the editorials and the news stories? Which ones seem to tell the viewpoint of the newspaper most openly? How might the viewpoint of the paper appear in the selection, writing, headlining, or displaying of news stories? Do newspapers ever editorialize in the way they present the news? How? What does it mean to present news "objectively"? Is it possible? Why or why not?

Try it yourselves. Make your own one-issue newspaper in which you try to tell objectively all the news of your school, community, and class. Type your finished newspaper, and post it on the bulletin board for all the members of your class to read.

AD GLAD: WHAT YOU READ IS NOT ALWAYS WHAT YOU GET
45 minutes   *2 people*

Do this to help students understand the real messages advertisers use to sell their products.

Bring a stack of newspapers and magazines from home. Take 20 minutes or more at the beginning of class to look through the magazines and newspapers for advertisements. Find an ad which you agree appeals to the "everybody's doing it" spirit. Discuss how much it affects you. Can you think of a time when you might use such an appeal? Find an ad which "name drops"—which says one should use a product because someone famous does so. How effective is this argument? Whom might it influence? Find an ad which associates some unrelated idea with some accepted value like patriotism or motherhood. Who is likely to be affected by this argument? Find a condemnation of something by associating it with a distasteful idea like communism or some human weakness.

Pick out an advertisement which you both think would sound good as a television commercial. Practice reading it that way. Plan to stage your commercial for the class. Decide if you need any props or added actions. Perform your commercial for the class.

After your performance pass out pieces of paper to the class members and ask them to answer these questions: How did the commercial make you feel? Why? Would you be more or less likely to buy the product than before? What did the commercial really say about the product that would help you make a wise buying decision?

Record the results in your logs.

TAKE YOUR NEWS LIVE: YOUR OWN KIND OF NEWSPAPER
1 hour or more   *4 to 7 people*

Here is a way to become an expert on newspapers and how they are made so that you can help your students read them with greater understanding.

Form a group to make a one-issue newspaper for your class. You may be able to make copies for all your classmates if you have access to a copying machine, or you may decide to post your newspaper on the bulletin board where people can read it as they come into the room.

Plan what kinds of news you will include in your newspaper and how you will arrange the items. You might find it useful to look at some newspapers to see how they are arranged and what news they tell about. What news would be most interesting to the people in your class? What news would be easiest to find out about? How could you use events that happen in your class or school? Could you have editorials? Human interest stories? A literary section? Is anyone in your group interested in writing about social events, homemaking hints, politics? Is there someone who likes to draw? Could he be a cartoonist? Will someone proofread? Who will make the decisions about what should be included and what should not? How do you write a good title for an article? You may want to choose an editor and an proofreader. How will your newspaper look when it is finished? How can you be sure it will be pleasant and easy to read? Do you have a member who knows how to type or has good handwriting?

Post your finished newspaper on the bulletin board or pass out copies to your classmates. In your log talk about what high school students might learn about newspapers if they made their own newspaper. What problems would you expect high school students to encounter if they did this activity? How could they solve these problems?

READING AND LEARNING: YOUR DRIVER'S TEST BOOKLET
1 hour   *2 people*

Do this and you will be able to help your students prepare for their driver's tests.

Find a partner. Pretend that you are both high school students who will be taking driver's tests soon. Each of you should get the little booklet that gives you the information you need to pass the test. Be sure you use an up-to-date one, since some new shapes have been added to signs.

Talk about these questions: Why are the safety experts so eager to have drivers know the signs by shape as well as know what words are on the signs? What are the four kinds of licenses you could get? Which one are you trying for?

The booklet has many sections, each one dealing with one aspect of driving. What is the label on each section? Make a list of these labels. Is there a table of contents? Is there an index? Use the index as a test. Have your partner read it to you or read it yourself to see if you know about each item in the book. From each section of the booklet make a list of important facts and record them in your log. Get a colored marking pencil and underline the facts you think you do not know well enough to pass a test. As you become sure of each new fact you have marked, put a check mark in front of the sentence that tells you the fact.

Make a test for your partner while he makes one for you. Plan a certain time or day when you will take the tests. If possible, add a test drive as a part of your testing, each being the examiner for the other.

Just before you take the test, carefully review the sentences you have marked. If you are going to have a test drive, make a list of the things

the tester will want to see you demonstrate—the book tells you these—
and try them in the car.

Give each other your tests, and good luck! Tell your logs how you did.

PLANNING AHEAD: MAP READING FOR A TRIP

1 hour or more   *1 person*

Here is an activity to prepare you for helping students read maps.

Think about a trip you are planning or would like to take. Get as many
maps as you can for the places you would like to go. Filling station
attendants will often be helpful in giving you maps when your family car
is filled with gas. If your family has a credit card with a major oil
company, you can write to them, telling them where you want to go, and
they will send you maps with the routes marked. They often mark the
shortest route and the most scenic one in addition so that you may take
your choice.

Some maps tell many things besides the road mileage. Make a list of
the information you can find on the maps you have chosen. Which of
them will help you on your trip? Do you have a map with small areas
enlarged in inserts which can help you get around large cities?

Plan where you would like to stop for overnight stays during your trip.
If you often stay at certain hotel chains, you can reserve in advance or
get a list of the hotels from the local member of the chain so that you
know where you will find a place to stay.

Check your library to find out about parks and other places of interest
in the cities you plan to visit. See if there are official sources of information about the places you plan to visit—like state tourist offices attached to state capitol offices which send free information to anyone
who writes an enquiry. In Canada each of the provinces sends material
to anyone who enquires. The addresses can be obtained in your library.
Some cities have materials that are available through chambers of
commerce.

Gather all the information you can from every source. You may find
some new sources not mentioned here. Tell your log all the sources you
find so that when you need information on another place you will have
a ready list of sources where you can enquire.

Organize your materials into an envelope in the order in which you
will need them on your trip. That way they will always be available
whenever you need to read them. Have a good journey!

SPECIAL STUDYING: READING IN SOCIAL STUDIES AND SCIENCE
1 hour   *1 person*

If you want to become more able to help your students with their studies in subjects other than English, do this.

If you are taking a science or social studies course or would like to read about these subjects, find a science or social studies book and answer these questions: Is the print sometimes different in different parts of the chapters? Why did the editors put certain things in different print? Look at some books with different kinds of print in different places until you are satisfied that you understand how and why your book is printed that way. In each of these books how do titles and phrases in blacker type relate to the rest of the chapter?

Are the chapters in your book divided into sections? See if you can find a key sentence that introduces each section by telling what its main idea will be. This is not always the first sentence. Are there key words in each paragraph that point to the important ideas of the section? What are they? Choose one chapter of your book and see if you can find these key words in one section or in several paragraphs. If you find any words you do not understand, be sure to find out what they mean.

Are there study helps and questions at the end of the chapter? Answer these as fully as possible to use them as study helps. Ask the teacher about any you don't understand.

How was reading this chapter different from reading a chapter in an English book? Were there differences in the ways the sentences were written? Were there special words used that are used only by people who are talking about this subject? If so, what are they?

Make a small dictionary of the special words used only for this subject so that you may use it in the future and so that your students may use it as a model. With each definition, be sure to give examples of how each word is used in a sentence.

ANSWERS AWAY: USING A REFERENCE BOOK
1 to 2 hours   *1 person*

Doing this may help you to guide your students in their research.

Begin with a question—perhaps about a course you are taking— whose answer you cannot find in your textbook. Look up the answer in the encyclopedia or other reference book. If you do not know which reference book to use, ask the librarian or teacher for advice. Find the answer you need.

Will you be using this answer to write a report or paper? To give a talk? What will you say if someone asks you where you got your information? What will you do if you need to come back to this spot in this book again to check on what it says? If you are looking up several items, how will you know which came from which book? To help solve these problems write in your log the name of the book, its publisher, the date of publication and the page on which you found the answer.

Read what the book says several times, long enough that you will be able to tell some of the ideas there without looking at the page. Then close the book or turn the page and see how many ideas you can remember and write in your log.

Now that you have put it in your own words, plan to give a short talk or write a report using what you have discovered. You may want to look up some other information on the same subject to go with it. If you plan to use several different ideas from different sources, try writing your information as you did in your log, but on cards or half sheets of paper. These will be easy to rearrange and put in the order you want to write or say them.

Write a short report or give a three-minute talk to your class.

TEXTBOOKS ON TRIAL: WHAT'S IN A TEXTBOOK?

2 to 3 hours   *4 to 7 people*

To be able to guide your students in adapting their reading methods to suit their reading materials, become familiar with the kinds of non-fiction reading materials students read most—textbooks.

Form a group to survey textbooks in a variety of content areas. Each member of your group should choose a subject. Find two or three high school textbooks on the subject you have chosen. You may be able to borrow them from the library or from high school students or teachers. To discover how these in your chosen subject area are like or unlike books about other subjects, make a descriptive list of all the facts you can find about each one. Here are some questions which may help you.

How large is your book? Does it have a hard or soft cover? Why? Does it have a book jacket? If there are words or pictures on the book or book jacket, what do they tell about the book? Is there a preface? Why is it there? Would it be of any value to a student? Why or why not? Is there an introduction? What does it say that a preface wouldn't say? What other information can you find on the first pages of the book that would or would not be useful to a student? Does your book have a table of contents? What does the table of contents tell you about the structure of the book? Is the book divided into parts or units that are larger than chapters? How are the chapters or topics grouped? Are there sections or topics or subtopics within chapters? How could these groupings be useful to students who are reading or studying the book? How is the arrangement of material in your book related to the subject? Are easier concepts placed first? Is there a chronological order? Does the book move from general to specific or from specific to general?

Choose a chapter or section to examine closely. Are there devices used in the text to point out facts or ideas? Are new or important words italicized? If different kinds of type are used, when and why are they used? Would a science book have more italicized words than a literature book? Why? In which subjects would you expect to find the most diagrams, the most pictures, graphs, charts, and tables? Are there informative headings, summaries or marginal notes? Why and how could these be used to tell students what to look for or linger over? Are footnotes used to give information or explain ideas? Will students read the footnotes? What will they miss if they don't?

What do you find at the end of the chapter or section? Is there a list of references? Would the books or articles listed be useful or interesting to high school students? Is there a summary? Are there questions or activities? Will these help students understand what they have read? How? Is there a glossary of terms? Would it be best to have a glossary at the end of each chapter or at the end of the book? Why?

Is there an appendix at the end of the book? What kind of information can students find in an appendix? What kind of information would you expect to find in an epilogue or postscript? In which kinds of textbooks would you expect to find an appendix, an epilogue, a postscript, or a bibliography? Why? Is there an index in your book? How are the items listed? What can you look up in it? What kind of textbooks might have two indexes, one for names and another for subjects?

Present your discoveries to the class as a panel, each of you reporting on the traits of textbooks in the subject he has chosen. You may want to meet first to discuss your discoveries and plan how much time each of you can spend talking so that the others will also have enough time to speak. Try to show how books in your subjects are like and unlike books in other subject areas. Be sure to plan for time for questions from other group members or from classmates.

A NOTE TO REMEMBER: NOTES FROM READING

2 hours   *1 person*

To help students learn to take useful notes from their reading, do this.

Your students may use books from the library or rental books in which they cannot write. They may need to pick out important parts to use later or memorize. There are times in teachers' lives too when such note-taking is necessary.

Find a book on a subject that you would like to know more about. Get this book from a library or borrow it from a friend. Buy some cards and use them to write your notes on. They may be 5" by 8" or smaller. At the top or end of the card note the subject of your reading, the "Louisiana Purchase" in American history, for instance. Write the name of the book and the pages so you will know where you got the material if you need to find it again. Then note the main ideas from your reading: names, dates, events, new ideas, viewpoints, facts that you might need for tests or reports. If you are reading a book which is concerned with ideas reather than statistics or facts, you may find it useful to pick out the main idea of each paragraph and put it in your own words. Now take notes on a chapter from a math book and on a chapter from a book in still another subject area.

Which book was the easiest to use for note-taking? Why? In which were the ideas most clearly organized? Is it easier to find the meaning in long sentences or in short ones? Why? Is it easier to take notes on facts or on ideas? Why?

In your log write your conclusions about taking notes to remember important facts and ideas.

ACRONYMS: INITIALS FOR NAMES

several days   *1 person*

To help your students understand the use of initials for names in their reading, do this.

Find examples of names that have been formed by combining the initials of words. These are often used by government agencies. How many can you find in today's newspaper? One famous acronym used during World War II was CINCPAC—Commander-in-Chief, Pacific. Collect your own list from newspapers and news magazines.

Do you suppose some groups invent names that can be made into pronounceable initial-names? What combination of vowels and conso-nants do the initial-names have to have to make sure they can be pronounced? Do some of the initial words have real meanings that are related to the organization?

Put your acronym collection in a scrapbook or in your log. Write some of your own. Make up your own acronym names for the people, groups and activities in your classroom.

WORTHY WORDS: HOW ARE DICTIONARIES MADE?
several hours   *2 to 5 people*

If you would like to help students use and enjoy dictionaries, do this.

Form a group and talk about these questions: If you were going to make a dictionary, how would you do it? Where would you look to collect your materials? What kind of materials would you need? Is a dictionary more of a historical or a legal document? Does it give laws or describe how something is or has been done? How can you find out what a word means and how it is used? What people will you listen to? Is a person who has and uses an object or an idea a better judge of how to pronounce it than someone who only knows about the word? Why? Then where will you look for your authorities? Check the *Webster III* dictionary to see what kind of people the lexicographers quote as using the words they define.

Special fields of interest sometimes have their own special dictionaries. What ones do you know of? Here is a way to learn about dictionaries and do something for the people in your class at the same time: Form your group into a dictionary committee. Ask class members to post in a special spot on the bulletin board words they have found in their reading which are interesting, unusual, or troublesome to them.

Collect these words for a month and make your own dictionary from them. Include information you think your classmates would like or need to know about the words—perhaps the class member who found the word and the title of the book where he found it.

ESSAY LAND: EXPLORE IT!
3 hours   *4 to 6 people*

To help your students discover the pleasure and value of the essay, do this.

Form a group and discuss these questions: What is an essay? How is it different from a poem, novel, drama or any other form of literature?

Why do people choose to say what they have to say as an essay? What do they want to make you think or feel? Do they ever try to convince you of something? Do the writers of essays ever write just to let out feelings and ideas that are inside them?

If you want to find an essay, where do you look? Where in a newspaper might you find an essay? Do you ever write essays in your log? How are those essays different from the ones you find in magazines? For what purpose did you write them? Find some examples of essays from magazines, books or your own writing. Bring several examples with you the next time your group meets.

Share the essays you have found. You may want to take turns reading them aloud, you may want to explain them or you may want to pass them around to be read silently. After you have shared your examples, talk about these questions: Why did you pick the examples that you brought? How do you feel about the subject? How do you feel about the person who wrote the essay? Would you like to meet him? What would you say to him? Do your feelings about the writer change your feelings about the subject? If so, how? What does the writer say in the essay that lets you know what he is thinking and feeling and what kind of person he is?

What problem did the writer choose for himself in your favorite essay? How did he let you know about his point of view? Did he just tell you or did he plan his essay so that you would agree with him before you knew his point of view? Does he give facts to support his ideas? Does he use details, description or examples? If so, find some. Underline them, or make a note to remind yourself of the devices this writer uses. These notes may be useful in helping you compare the methods of this writer with the methods of others. Did he give arguments for his own point of view or against someone else's? Does your writer hold up ideas for you to compare or contrast? Does he explain everything he brings into the essay, or does he sometimes leave you in doubt? Does he make his ideas more interesting by telling a story or incident? Do you understand all the terms and words he uses? Does he use literary or historical allusions? If he does, how do you feel about them? Does he quote from an authority? Why? What are the writer's reasons for feeling the way he does? How does he show his reasons? How does he show his opinions? Does he draw conclusions or summarize what he has said? Do you agree with his conclusions? Do you think he has shown what he wanted to show? Did you change any opinions or ideas as a result of the essay? Why or why not? How did the essay make you feel as you read it? Why?

In your log write an essay telling what you think the perfect essay should be like and justifying your opinion.

CHAPTER IV

The Student Listens
and Views

A student whose training in listening comes from hearing a teacher dispense instructions and information designed to help him know how and even what to think is not likely to develop substantial skills in creative or analytical listening. Because the student will spend far more of his time listening to language than he will spend in reading, writing or speaking it, his skills of listening deserve at least as precise and thorough attention in an English classroom as do the skills of reading, writing, and speaking. And good listening requires as much imagination and creativity as writing, reading or speaking well.

A student's cultivation of listening skills results in better relationships with others, efficient information gathering, improvement in speaking, writing and reading, and greater enjoyment of the media. Ways to hear and ways to see are allied skills, and both should be taught in the English classroom. Purposes for seeing are much the same as those for listening, and teaching visual perception is not, in practice, very different from teaching auditory perception. Many activities serve both purposes.

LISTENING TO IMPROVE HUMAN RELATIONS

Listening activities lead to better relationships with others, and improve the students' ability to carry on two-person or small-group conversations.

The student should learn to listen supportively, analytically or creatively to what others are saying and to vary the components of his listening in the same way he selects an appropriate rhetoric or vocabulary for his speaking behavior. He must choose an attitude appropriate to each listening occasion as he would choose to skim or reread in his reading activities. Thus he will listen as actively as he communicates in other language areas, as actively as he reads, speaks or writes.

To improve his communication with others, the listener must turn his thoughts from himself to the speaker. Looking past his own preoccupations, he clears his thoughts to listen to another successfully. Testing his fulfillment of this requirement, the listener will consider whether his listening is a mere wait until he can begin to speak or whether he is genuinely attentive to the speaker. To discipline the argumentative self or the self which wishes to change the subject to another closer to his own interests matures the student and adds to his ability to control his behavior. And to listen creatively to that with which it is his first response to disagree expands and matures the student's sense of the worth of others.

The listener should be able to identify the mood of the speaker and the mood the speaker wants to encourage in his listener. Activities which engage the student in talking and listening with his classmates should lead the student to hear what is meant by what is said, to judge critically the information he is given by others, to seek areas of concern where agreement with others may be reached and to define ways of resolving differences. Many of the activities proposed in the chapter about reading and speaking and some of those suggested for writing are appropriate to teach listening. But the activities presented in this chapter will be directed to developing specifically the sensitivity to others that is necessary to successful listening.

Activities

LISTENING AUTHORITY: BECOME AN EXPERT

several hours   *1 person*

To help students discover the importance of listening in their lives, find out what research says about listening.

Your teacher or librarian may be able to give you some suggestions about where to look. The *Reader's Guide to Periodical Literature* or the *Education Index* are good places to begin. Perhaps your library has microfilm as well as books and magazines. Be sure to look under all the related topics you can find. Try "communication," "group dynamics," "media," and "perception."

In reading all the materials you have gathered, what will you look for? Would it be useful to you in motivating students to be able to tell them what percent of their lives most adults spend in talking, reading, writing and listening? What else would be interesting to your students? What facts should you tell them? What could they discover for themselves? What should you not bother them with?

How could this information be used by students? How could it help them to listen better or want to listen better? How could this information help you as a teacher? Would it give you more confidence to know these facts? Could you plan activities more wisely on the basis of this knowledge?

From what you have read, choose information you think would be useful to your own class of prospective teachers.

Present this information to your class either in the form of a newsletter or as an oral report. Be sure to include suggestions for using the information in the classroom.

WHAT'S LISTENING?: HOW LISTENING WORKS
1½ hours   *2 people*

To help students discover different ways of listening and learn how to adapt their listening habits to suit their listening needs, do this.

Explore the different ways people use listening. Find a partner. Each of you should make a list of everything he does for one day. You may want to keep a notebook or log with you for this day so that you can write down your activities before you forget about them. How many activities on your list involve listening or talking? Pick out all activities that involve listening and list them along the left edge of one or more sheets of paper, and make four columns after each item. Label these columns "passive," "appreciative," "responsive," and "critical."

Examine your lists. Were there some times when you just listened without really thinking of what was being said? If so, mark these times "passive." Were there some activities during which you enjoyed listening? If so, mark these "appreciative." Were there some activities during which you "talked back" either orally or quietly to yourself? If so, mark these "responsive." Were there some times when you interrupted or wished you could interrupt to disagree? If so, mark these "critical." Were there times when you combined two or more of these ways of listening?

Compare your list with your partner's list. How did he listen in similar circumstances? How is your listening like his, and how is it different?

Talk about these questions: How did you each feel in the different listening situations? Did you ever wish when you were listening that you could have some feelings you did not have? Why? How does the way you feel about something or someone change the way you listen? How do you feel when listening to a television program? How do you feel when you listen to the commercial? What things do you hear and what things do you "tune out?" Why? What do you hear when you listen to a popular song? To a lecture? To your best friend? Why? What do you tune out in each case and what do you hear?

What is the best way to feel about listening when you want to learn from what is being said? Why? What is the best way to feel about listening when you want the person you are listening to to like you? Can the way you listen change the way a speaker or your fellow listeners feel? How?

Write your conclusions about these questions in your logs.

WHO LISTENS? WHAT DOES IT TAKE TO LISTEN

10 minutes   *1 person*

Doing this may help you interest students in listening and in trying to improve listening habits.

Is there someone in your life that you ask for advice when you need a listener to your troubles? What kind of person is this, or what kind of person ought he to be? How does he make you feel? Describe him in your log. After you have talked to someone else about your problem, how do you feel about it? Has talking about a problem ever led you to the solution? What does a good listener do to help you solve a problem?

Is there any person in your life you would not ask for advice, even though he might know how to give you a good answer? Why? Do you know anyone who talks a lot but makes you feel unimportant when you try to say something? Do you like to talk to that person? Why? How do you want to feel when you say something?

If other people want to feel the same as you want to feel, what can you do when they are talking to make them feel that way? Try putting yourself in other people's shoes when they talk. Find a group or another person to work with on some other activity. Listen to everything your group or person has to say in the same way your ideal listener would listen to you.

At the end of the class period tell your log what it was like to be a good listener. Was it difficult? Why or why not? Did you succeed in being the kind of listener you wanted to be? Do you think you helped other people in the group feel good about themselves? Why?

A GOLDEN RULE: LIKING WHAT YOU HEAR

15 minutes   *1 person*

Here is a way to listen that makes the world an easier, happier place to live.

Try to listen for the good in the conversation and actions of others. Hear them as you would like them to hear you. Begin where you are—in class. It's easy to find someone to listen to. You may want to join a group working on another project. Whatever you are doing, when it is your turn to listen, try to find something important, intelligent, and good in what the other person is saying. If you find yourself thinking critical or disagreeable thoughts, remind yourself to be as generous in your mind with the faults of the other person as would like him to be with yours. If you find yourself bored, remember that you might also be boring. As you go through the class period, work at holding to good thoughts and feelings about other people and what they are saying.

At the end of the period or after it is over, take 10 minutes to write in your log. Did you find it easy or difficult to listen to others as you would like them to listen to you? Why? Did this way of listening change the things you said and did? If so, how? How do you feel about the other people now? Did you discover anything new about yourself or other people? If so, what?

SENDING SIGNALS: LISTENING WITH YOUR WHOLE SELF

30 minutes   *2 or more people*

Here is a game you can use to help students become skillful listeners and speakers.

Find a partner. If you can, choose a quiet secluded spot to work. Think of a message, a simple idea like "I'm thirsty" or "I like your dress." If you could not talk or write, how could you get your message across? Try to communicate your message to your partner without talking. When you are both satisfied that the message has been correctly received, switch roles so that each of you has been on the receiving end of a message.

After the game, you may find it useful to talk about these questions: Did each of you understand the messages? How? Do some people use other ways of delivering messages than by words? What are some ways people speak with their hands, heads, faces? With other parts of their bodies? What kinds of messages are easiest to convey with gestures? Why?

Did you make any sounds that were not words? What are some sounds people make that are part of all languages? If you could use sounds but not words in this game, how could you show meaning with your voices? If you are talking to someone, what clues do you have to his thoughts and feelings if he speaks very slowly and draws out the words? What do you think is going on inside of someone who cuts words short? Why does a person speak through his nose? What does it make you feel about him if you are listening? What happens to you as a listener when someone speaks with a raspy voice? What effect does abnormal loudness or softness have on a listener? What about high and low pitch?

Repeat the message game, but this time use sounds that are not words or sentences. You might like to imagine that you are primitive people who do not yet have a language. You need to communicate by the way you talk.

When you have tried the game this way, you may find it useful to talk about this second experience. In what ways was it easier to communicate with sounds than gestures? In what ways was it harder? Did you have any problems understanding the messages? If so, why? If you are the person sending the message in an ordinary conversation, what can you do to see that you make the impression you want on your listener? If you are the listener, how can you get the message the sender intends?

Give a demonstration for your class, showing emotions with gestures, expression and physical attitude. Try a conversation using nonsense sounds in front of the class, and see how many people can discover what you are saying to each other.

THE SILENT SPEECH: TRANSLATING GESTURES INTO LANGUAGE
15 minutes   *1 person*

To make your students more alert to what people really mean when they talk—the things they do and don't say with words—do the activity on this card. You will also find out some ways in which you do or don't get across the message in your mind when you are talking.

Make a list of all the body language with which people convey their feelings and thoughts. Start with these two if you like: a shrug, a clenched fist. List as many as you can think of. Look in a picture magazine or look at a television program to find the many kinds of body language people use. Try turning the sound down on the television set in order to watch more carefully.

When the list is as long as you can make it, write at least one statement a person might say to replace the body language. Which would best convey the impression the person wants to give, body language or verbal language? What are some occasions when using one or the other would be better? Are there some occasions when using body language would be dangerous or even have an effect opposite to the one you want to produce? Are there some occasions when words can produce a better effect than body language? What are they?

Tell your log what philosophy you have for using words to replace body language.

I CAN SEE WHAT YOU ARE SAYING: FEELINGS TALK
10 minutes   *2 people*

Here is a way to find out how people let others know about themselves and what they are feeling.

Have you ever noticed that a friend was happy, sad, angry, or disappointed before he said anything? What are some of the physical signs that tell you what other people are feeling? How do you know, even without her saying a word, when your mother is angry? When you see your best friend walking down the hall, can you tell whether he is happy or sad? How? Can you tell what kind of mood your teacher is in when you see him? Would it be useful to be able to detect people's feelings even more than you do?

Picture in your mind how each of these people would stand or move and what his facial expression would be:

1. a shy student entering a new class
2. a student receiving a passing grade on a project he feared he had flunked
3. a man looking at the dented fender of his new car
4. a student confused by directions on an assignment

To help you imagine them, ask yourself about them. What is each of these people feeling? About themselves? About other people? Why do they feel that way? Would everyone feel the same in those situations? Think of several different people you know and how they might react differently in the same situation.

Now demonstrate each of these mental pictures to a friend and see if he can tell you about the characters on the list. Did he guess the feelings you were trying to show? Tell your log your conclusions.

ALL EARS: HEARING YOUR GROUP

1 to 1½ hours   *4 to 5 people*

Try this to find ways you can help students use listening to improve their group work.

You will need a tape recorder. Form a group and choose a topic for your group to discuss. You might want to use this as an opportunity to talk about an activity from another part of this book. Record your conversation on tape for 15 minutes. It will help you to know who is speaking later when you listen to the tape if each person identifies himself before he talks.

Before you replay the tape, ask yourselves some questions about your discussion: Did some people seem to enjoy talking and others not? Are some people quiet because they are afraid they will not say the right thing? Do some people seem to like to hear themselves talk, no matter what they say? Are some subjects easier to talk about than others? If so, what are they? When are you most likely to talk even if you don't usually want to? Do you feel you have to answer questions even if you aren't much of a talker? If you are an active talker, is it hard to talk after you have asked a question until you have had an answer?

Were there times when no one talked? Why didn't they? Who talked first? Why? How does it make you feel when no one talks? Is there any way you can get other people to talk? Does everything you say have to be important or even make sense? Did people in your group ever say things that did not make sense? Did some people laugh or make other sounds that were not words? What meanings did these sounds have? Did anyone say something foolish or embarrassing? If so, did you think any less of that person because of it? Why or why not?

During the conversation did everyone in the group seem to understand what everyone else was saying? Why or why not? What are some ways that people can become confused about what someone else is trying to say? Did you try to plan what you were going to say? If you did, how much of the conversation did you miss? Did you feel that other people in the group were interested in your ideas? How could you tell? Were you interested in theirs? How did you show them? Did you ever want to interrupt? Did you follow the impulse? How did you feel about interrupting?

After you have satisfied yourselves about the answers to these questions, play the tape and see if any of your answers need to be changed or if you discover some new questions and answers. Each one of you may want to keep a tally of how many times during the discussion he talked so that each can see his own group personality.

What can you do as a group member to improve your listening and to make it easier for others in the group to listen effectively? Can you be a good talker without being a good listener? Why?

Write a newsletter report sharing your discoveries and conclusions with the rest of the class.

TALK FOR TWO: CONVERSATION LISTENING

15 minutes   *2 people*

When you have finished this activity, you will be able to guide your students in using listening as a means to better and more enjoyable conversations with others.

Choose someone in your class that you would like to know better. Ask the person to talk with you for fifteen minutes.

Start the conversation by asking about something you know will interest the other person. Some good questions start like this: "How did you feel when you . . . ?" "I have been wondering how you . . . ?"

Then listen. Look at the other person as he speaks. Remember the most important aspects of the conversation for you are listening . . . not listening to your own plans to answer what he is saying, but listening with your whole mind to what he is saying. Listen to what his body is saying as he speaks and to what he might be thinking and does not, for one reason or another, actually say.

Never interrupt as long as he will talk; but if he seems stuck for an answer, or further talk, nod or murmur encouragingly. Find things in his answer that will help you lead him to talk as you remark, "Did you really . . . (repeating some statement he has made) or "How did you feel when . . . ?"

If you want to disagree, find a point of agreement first and then add "but sometimes I wonder . . . " Never contradict or use a flat no.

These conversational actions cause the other person to become uncomfortable and unable to converse well. Politeness is a concern for the other person's comfort and is a basic element in good conversation.

Afterward, record in your log some of your own feelings about this conversation: How did you feel before you began it? About him? About yourself? About the conversation? How did you feel during it? Did you have to hang onto yourself to keep from interrupting? Were you distracted from what he was saying by your mind arguing against it? Did you become interested in what the other person was saying? Did you become more or less comfortable with the situation as it went on? How did you feel after the conversation? About him? About yourself? Was this different in any way from the way you felt in the beginning?

SUGAR TALK AND VINEGAR TALK: WHAT IS THE DIFFERENCE?
40 minutes at different times   *1 person*

This activity will help you guide your students in listening for the ways their word choices affect their relationships with others.

Think about these questions: When you sit around the house in your old clothes, are you being comfortable or sloppy? What's the difference between the two? What person might call you sloppy? What people might call you comfortable?

When you disagree with other people, which ones might call you stubborn? Bullheaded? Determined? Does the use of any of these words tell you more about the speaker or the one spoken about? Why? What can you tell about others by the words they use?

When you urge someone to do something, are you a nag or a helper? If you save money, who would call you stingy and who would call you thrifty? If you talked a lot at a party, who would call you a show-off, and who would call you a person with a good sense of humor? If someone punished his children, who would call him a brute and who would call him a good disciplinarian? If you wear expensive clothes, who would say you were trying to impress people and who would say you were well dressed? If you are quiet, who would think you were being moody and who would think you were being thoughtful?

Why are there two or more sets of words for the same thing in these cases? Which kind of person do you like best, the one who uses sweet words or the one who uses sour words? Why? Is there a right time to use both kinds of words? If so, when? Here are some other word twins: fat or plump, plain or ugly. Are there some you use often? What ones do you hear other people use? Can you find any in the newspaper?

Listen to the ways you and people you talk to use sugar and vinegar words. If you do not eat what is on your plate, which will you say you are doing—watching your diet or not liking the food? Why? When might you use each one?

For one day listen carefully to everything you hear at home, at school, on television, even what you read. In each case are sweet words or sour ones being used? Why? Did the speaker's choice of words have the effect he wanted on his audience? Would you have chosen the same words he used in these cases? Why or why not?

Record the results of your listening in your log.

MAN-ON-THE-STREET: WHAT DO PEOPLE THINK?

2 hours   *2 people*

Here is an activity to help you explore listening as a means of knowing and understanding the thoughts of others.

Find a partner and a tape recorder. Plan a fifteen minute tape of interviews with people you stop on the sidewalk or in the hallway of your school. Here are some questions to help you with your planning: Where will you do your interviewing? What kind of people will you be talking to? How will you get them to stop and talk to you? What will you tell them about yourselves? What will you ask them? How can you stay away from topics that might be too personal or controversial? What topics do people usually like to give their opinions about? How can you keep one person from talking too long? What kind of language should you use so that no one will be offended by the way you ask your questions? Write some questions out first and try them on friends. Then choose the ones that had the best results. Which one of you will ask the questions? Who will hold the tape recorder and microphone? Could the way you dress affect the answers you get or the willingness of people to stop and talk to you?

You will probably need to spend much more time standing and waiting for people and talking than you will actually use for your fifteen minute tape. You may even decide to try interviewing on two days to see if you can improve on your techniques of questioning.

After you have finished your tape, you may want to edit it to take out harsh sounds, empty spaces and other technical problems, or just cut down the time. For this you need two tape recorders.

Play your finished tape for the class or for another group.

LISTENING TO GATHER INFORMATION

A teacher of listening provides experiences that give students insight into effective, economical ways to gather accurate information. This kind of listening occurs in a variety of fairly formal situations demanding sustained attention. Listening to media advertising requires many of the same skills.

Activities designed to help students listen effectively to formal speakers teach students to direct their attention and mental action to a speaker's words and behavior. The listener should be ready to listen when the speaker begins. A good listener avoids being distracted by attention getters other than the speaker-side conversations of other listeners, the listener's own doodling, outside noises.

The introduction a speaker gives to his talk focuses initial listening attention. It often indicates the speaker's purpose. He may recount an anecdote or make a startling statement in some way related to his topic. The listener needs to assess this relationship. Perhaps the speaker intends only to create a receptive mood in his listeners. But the need to create such a mood may also be a key to the purpose of the speaker, to what he wants from his listener.

Although the listener's objective may be to assimilate information, remembering individual facts will only minimally help him know and understand what is being said. The listener must identify the main points the speaker is making or the central issues he is raising. These must be distinguished from supportive points or the facts that support main points. A good listener does not so concentrate on one point that he misses others but tries to move with the flow of the speaker's thoughts. If the listener takes notes, he must not get so involved with details that he misses main points. In taking notes, he may want to divide his paper lengthwise and use one column for main points or principles and the other for facts given to illustrate them.

A good listener suspends judgment about what is being said until he has heard all that the speaker has to say. He constantly analyzes the speaker's ideas, relating them to his own ideas, evaluating them in terms of what he already knows, and looking ahead to project what the speaker's next points will be. The listener must not block out ideas he does not like or give undue emphasis to ideas he finds particularly appealing. Nor may a good listener reverse the meaning of words the speaker uses which may have special emotional content for the listener.

Although a listener should pay close attention to the speaker's facial expression, gestures and vocal inflection, the listener must not become distracted by aspects of the speaker's delivery that he finds unappealing. An effective listener controls his reactions to the mannerisms of the speaker as carefully as he controls his differences with what is said by the speaker.

If there is a discussion period after the speech, the listener should plan questions whose answers will clarify confusions and stimulate the speaker to expand his remarks. These questions should inquire honestly for further information. They should not challenge, and they should not make it appear that the questioner wants to display his own knowledge or seem to know more about the subject than the speaker. When there are several listeners, one should not dominate the question period.

Those who listen to a report from a classmate have special responsibilities. They must learn an attitude and a rhetoric for commenting on the work of fellow students. They will follow the teacher's example in their comments. Most comments should be positive and avoid judgmental language. The days when listeners, whether they be teachers or students, speak disparagingly of the "posture" or "delivery" of report-givers are or should be over. The use of rating sheets whose columns classify from "excellent" to "poor" on such items as "gestures" and "organization" are likewise quaint hangovers from the past, pedagogical artifacts of a time when it was supposed that telling a speaker what was wrong with him would forthwith make him better.

The student who has unfortunate or distracting mannerisms will usually give these up when he has more confidence, a confidence which comes when he thinks his audience is truly interested in his ideas. This interest is displayed when listeners use positive comments in referring to the speaker's work, comments, for instance, that show curiosity about the speaker's ideas or research and refer to their own eager response to what has been said. When students or teachers comment negatively about a speaker's work, it is often because they do not know how to listen for the real substance of what that speaker is saying or because they are not in control of a rhetoric for making positive comment. Positive comment, the result of creative listening, uses such patterns as, "When you said . . . , you made me wonder . . . " or, "I felt as you talked . . . " or, "Did you find out anything about . . . ?"

To teach listening provides an economical and pleasant method of improving the performance of speakers. Students who have skills of listening and response can reinforce the effective speaking of their peers so that speakers can know what is effective in their performances. Classmates should listen carefully to a fellow student making a report, identifying those aspects of idea and delivery which they find appealing and should accumulate questions which display interest in what has been said. These positive responses provide a sound basis for a discussion which follows the speaker's presentation. Skills gained in these listening activities become useful in small-group discussion as well.

Listening to and viewing the media demands the development of defensive listening habits, necessary because of the aggressive and sometimes misleading information presented. These habits of response in the listener may be in contrast to the positive responses recommended for live, peer-group listening situations. An attitude of guarded, critical, questioning examination must be cultivated by the listener to calls the media makes upon him for action. Examples of these demands are abundant in commercial or political speaking. So sophisticated have these appeals become that special analysis is needed to uncover their subtle and often charmingly misleading attempts to influence his behavior. Effective listening activities suggest ways the student may develop insight to protect him from undue intrusions of the media into his will to choose wise behavior for himself. He must develop processes for sifting appropriate and useful information from false or useless claims.

The list of skills for listening is almost endless, comprehending most of those appropriate to other language arts. But insight into listening, like insight into other language arts, is best gained by practice, so the English teacher who is to teach listening should practice as many of these activities as possible. Those he does not have time to perform he should read and visualize with care in order to see the kinds of student activities he can derive from them.

Activities

ARE YOU READY?: PREPARING FOR LISTENING
30 minutes   *1 person*

Here are some ways you and your students can prepare yourselves for listening experiences.

If people in your class are giving reports, be a listening helper. Find a person who is planning to give a report to the class or to a group. If he has not already done it, help him find a time to schedule his report. Find what events will occur before his report and after it to make sure nothing will interfere with his presentation.

Consider how you can help him involve his audience in active listening and responding. Would he like to use a game or skit in which the class will be involved? Could you help him make a mimeographed form so that the whole class can know what he is going to do and say next or can know what they can do or say next? How will the audience be informed of the title, topic, sources, and main points? If you do make a form, will there be a place on it where listeners can jot down comments and questions they want to ask later? Will there be technical terms or words which might be difficult for listeners? How will you see that their unfamiliarity with those words does not interfere with their understanding of what they hear?

Where will your speaker stand or sit? How can you be sure that everyone can see and hear him? Does he know how to pronounce all the words correctly? Could you listen to his report first to be sure the words sound right and the ideas make sense? Will the reporter answer questions afterward? What kinds of questions might be asked? How could you help the reporter to prepare for them? How could you help the audience ask questions which clarify, elaborate and support the speaker's ideas?

Do you feel that the report was a success? Describe in your log its successes, and mention items that could be improved.

FINDING YOUR WAY: A SPEAKER'S SIGNPOSTS
25 minutes   *1 person*

To enable your students to sort, choose and remember information which is most important to them in a speech or report, you may want to use an activity similar to this.

Plan to listen to a speaker on television, radio or in your class. Be sure to hear a speaker who will talk several minutes. Does someone introduce the speaker? What does the introduction lead you to expect? How is the information given useful to you?

What information is usually given in the first part of a talk that is essential to understanding what is to be said? How does the speaker let you know how he wants you to react to what he is saying? How does he tell you his purpose? Is he trying to convince you, inform you, persuade you? Does he want you to do something? Is he trying to impress or entertain you?

How does the speaker let you know when he is going to start to talk about a new idea? What words does he use? Does his voice get louder or softer when he is making an important point? Does he pause to emphasize a word or idea? What kinds of gestures or facial expressions tell you that he is saying something he wants you to remember? What are the important points of his speech? Does the speaker repeat, review or summarize his points?

Record your answers to these questions in your log. You might find it useful to make a list, chart or outline of the signposts you discovered so that you can refer to this page in your log when you need to listen to a speaker again or to guide students in their listening.

HAPPY LISTENING: WAYS TO ENJOY A SPEAKER

10 minutes   *1 person*

To discover some ways of thinking and listening to speeches so that you can help students enjoy speakers more and understand better what they have to say, try this activity.

Listen to a speech or a report, and ask yourself these questions: Does the speaker have a topic you are interested in? What interesting facts does he reveal? Do you always hear him well? Are his explanations clear? Do you feel comfortable and relaxed as he speaks? Do you feel stimulated and excited? Do you feel curious and want more information? Is his voice pleasant? Does the speaker use a familiar dialect or one that is new in some ways or strange to you? It is easy to listen to speakers of our own dialect, but it is interesting to listen to speakers of other dialects just as it is nice to eat a new flavor of ice cream once in awhile.

Is it apparent that the speaker is interested in what he is saying? Does he seem to have enough words for whatever he wants to say? Does he have a pleasant appearance and manner? Does he summarize well so that you can understand and remember what he said?

Have these questions in your mind while you are listening. Think about them and choose some comments from your thoughts—some things that you think the speaker would most like to hear—and tell them to him after he speaks. Later, comment in your log about what makes a good speaker.

YOUR HEAD HEARS: LISTENING WHEN IT'S IMPORTANT

10 minutes   *1 person*

If your students sometimes miss important things they need to hear, this may help you help them keep their minds where they need to be.

List the times today when you would be in difficulty if you did not hear and understand what was being said by someone else. How can you be sure you will hear what will help you? Are there some people you listen to more carefully than others? Why? Do you have to try to listen when important things are being said, or does it just come naturally? Is it easier to listen to some speakers than to others?

Try this the next time you want to keep your mind on important things being said: Get as close to the speaker as you can. Look at the speaker. Try to think about the meaning of the words as he says them. Try to imagine that you are inside of him and the words are your thoughts. Whenever your own thoughts start to get in the way, push them out.

Try this exercise whenever you can during the day and see if it helps you to listen in classes. Tell your log how it worked for you.

HEAVY WORDS: SORTING OUT PREJUDICE

15 minutes   *1 person*

This activity will help you find ways to alert students to words which foster race prejudice in their own speech and the speech of others.

Using a thesaurus, make a list of different words for black and of words for white. Which has the most words that refer to evil, black or white? How do you explain this difference? Make a list of the words for yellow. Yellow is the color for what people? Why do you suppose we have all these bad understandings of the word yellow?

How can we avoid the prejudice trap that seems built into our language? Can you make a list of special terms using these words that you want to avoid in your own speaking?

Record your list and your comments about prejudice words in your log.

BEING A SPONGE: LISTENING FOR INFORMATION

1 to 1½ hours   *a small group*

This activity will provide you with insights you can use in helping students listen for information effectively.

How do you hear information? Imagine yourselves doing everything you would usually do in a day—but without being able to hear. What information would you miss if you could not hear your alarm clock ring? If you could not hear the weather report? If you could not hear a child cry? What kinds of instructions and directions do you follow every day? How do you know what other people are thinking? Make a list of all the situations you can think of which might occur during a normal day that require your listening for information.

Compare your lists. What are the most common ways you listen for information? When is listening for information most important? When is it least important? Choose from five to ten situations which you agree are the most important. For example, you might choose listening to the news, listening to your mother or other members of your family, listening to your boss when he's telling you what to do, listening to your spouse or sweetheart telling you about all the latest news, listening to a friend who is helping you with lessons or listening to readings and reports. In your situations is there a talker and a listener? Are there sometimes several talkers and several listeners?

Invent a little scene to go with each of your listening situations. What does the talker want to communicate? What does he think about the listener? What does he say? How does he say it? Why does he choose to say it as he does? What does the listener want to hear? What does he think about the speaker? How much and what does he hear? What thoughts of his own get in the way of his listening? Do his feelings change what he hears into what he wants to hear? Does he accept everything the speaker says as truth, or does he question and analyze it? Do the words of the speaker simply pass through his head like rows of corn, or does he try to fit them into what he already knows? How does the listener react to what he is hearing? Does he smile, frown, yawn, nod, interrupt, question, agree, disagree, wiggle, scratch or tap his fingers? How does his physical reaction indicate what is happening inside of him? Does his physical reaction tell you if the information he is hearing is useful to him? Why or why not?

Using your group members as listeners and speakers, act out several of your listening situations. Be sure every person has a chance to try several different roles. Afterward, talk about how it felt to be the listener or the talker. Did you react the way you thought you would? Why or why not? Did other people in the scene react the way you thought they would? Why or why not? What did the members who were watching think you were thinking? How well did you listen? How well were you listened to? What was difficult? Why?

SPIN IN: TRY TAPE

2 hours   *1 person*

If you would like to discover ways to use a tape recorder in helping students learn to listen effectively, do this.

Locate a tape recorder; a small uncomplicated one is best. Tape something you would like to learn about—a lecture, a speech, a reading, a play. You may be able to get already prepared tapes or cassettes at your library. To give yourself a more challenging experience in learning only from tape, try not to be present at the orginial event from which the tape is made. You might ask a friend to make the recording for you. The tape should play for at least 30 minutes.

Listen to the tape. Try to concentrate on each idea so that nothing escapes you. If your mind begins to stray from the words of the recording, stop the tape and rewind it to the spot where you began to think of something else. Start again. If some words are not pronounced clearly or do not seem to make sense to you, you may also want to rewind and replay.

When you have listened to the tape for the first time, ask yourself some questions: How many times did your mind wander from the tape? Why? What did you do to help you concentrate on what was being said? Would it have been easier or harder to concentrate on what was being said if you had been present at the event rather than listening to a tape? Why? Would it have been easier or harder to concentrate on what was being said if you had been reading the words from a printed page? Why? What are the advantages of listening to a tape over being at the real event? What are the advantages over reading? What are the disadvantages of tape?

Listen to the tape again. Was it easier or harder to concentrate on the ideas the second time? Why? Did you learn anything the second time that you missed the first time? What sort of information did you notice the second time that you did not notice the first time? Did you do anything other than just sit while you listened? What could you do that would not interfere with your listening?

Listen to the tape again. What did you discover about the tape the third time you listened to it? Were you tired of listening to it? If so, what did you do about it? Was it harder or easier to concentrate on the words and ideas when you were hearing them for the third time? Have you learned everything from your study of the tape that you wanted to learn? Why or why not? What do you think you would learn if you listened to the tape a fourth and fifth time? What is the best time and situation for listening to a tape? How could tape help a student with his studies? Could tape be useful to everyone? Why or why not?

Organize your conclusions about listening to tapes for information into a talk. Record your talk on tape, and play the tape for the class.

ROAD MAP: LISTENING TO DIRECTIONS

30 minutes   *2 people or more*

This activity will help you plan for students to talk and listen with more careful attention to detail.

Have you ever asked someone for directions on how to go somewhere and become even more confused than before? To practice giving and listening to directions, do this: Choose a partner. Get a road map. Locate on the map a starting point and a destination. Plot a course between the two spots. Be sure that you take several different roads and go through some cities and towns. Do not let your partner see the map while you are plotting the course. Your partner will need a blank sheet of paper, a pencil and something to write on, perhaps a notebook or cardboard.

Sit back-to-back or so that you cannot see your partner's paper and he cannot see yours. Now give your partner directions on how to get from the starting point to the destination. He should try to make his own map to follow on the trip. He may ask questions. When he has finished, compare the two maps and decide whether or not your partner would reach his destination following the map he has made. Ask your partner to plot a new course to another destination, and trade places so that you each have a chance to give and receive directions. Since everyone gives directions differently, try this activity with several different partners for a wider experience.

Tell your log what you have discovered. In what ways did being the speaker differ from being the listener? What can the speaker do to make his directions easier to follow? When you were the listener, did you ask questions? What were they about? What questions got the most useful answers? Did you ever get confused about a direction your partner had given? Why? How could the confusion have been avoided?

GOOD VIEWING:
DOCUMENTARIES AND NEWSCASTS

3 hours   *1 person*

Here is one way you can analyze newscasts or documentaries on television which will enable you to guide students to look for positive values in their television watching.

Plan to watch the news at the same time for several days in succession. Each day watch the news on a different channel. Try to view also at least one documentary during these days. In your log record your reactions to what you have seen, using these questions as a guide.

Does the newscaster have a pleasant personality? In what ways? Did this increase your enjoyment of the news? How? What ways were the news events made to seem more real and dramatic when you saw them on television? Did this increase your information about what had happened? Did it increase your pleasure as a viewer? How does it make you feel about what is happening in the news?

On which events did the newscaster spend the most time? On which ones did he spend the least time? Why? What did he talk about first? Why? How many of the news stories dealt with violence? With dishonesty? With disaster? With scandal? How many of the stories dealt with the theater, the arts, literature or education? How many news stories told about the bad things that people do? How many told about the good? Why? How much of the good and how much of the bad should be in a newscast? Why? Would it be possible to tell the truth about the news if you said only good things? If you said only bad things? Why?

On which channel was the news most true and close to the real picture of life as it is in our world? Why did you choose this channel?

Make a collage on a large piece of cardboard for display in your classroom in which you show the good side of the news. You may want to use clippings, pictures and articles from magazines and words or pictures you have made yourself which illustrate good happenings in the news.

HEARING AID:
CRITICAL LISTENING

45 minutes   *1 person*

You will be better able to help students judge whether they should believe what they hear if you do this activity.

Listen to a speech or television address by someone who is asking for action from his listeners. Perhaps you can find a political speech. Ask yourself some questions about what you hear: Why does the speaker want this action? What qualifications does the speaker have? Are they qualifications in the field he speaks about or does he just have some general reputation? How much of the speaker's persuasion is based on valid ideas and how much on his personality? How much of his persuasiveness is based on his attractive delivery and how much on his ideas? Are you distracted from what he says by an unattractive delivery?

Embody your answers in your log comments. Be sure to refer to your speaker specifically.

OH SAY CAN YOU SEE: POLITICAL LISTENING I

1 week   *4 to 6 people*

Find ways to help your students listen to political speeches as you try this.

Do you ever listen to political speeches? Where do you find them? Does anyone run for office in your school? How do these candidates let you know their views and what they will do if they are elected? Do they use any devices besides speeches? If so, what? Do you have a favorite political candidate or political philosophy? Have you ever tried to convert someone to your political point of view? How did you come to have that point of view?

Have an election in your class. First take a poll to find out the political parties or views of the people in your class. Find candidates who will agree to represent the political factions your poll has revealed. The members of your group will need to become campaign managers. You may want to schedule speeches and/ or debates, pass out handbills or put up posters, write a political platform, or plan a rally. You may want to give help to other class members in listening wisely.

Here are some questions you can discuss in your group or with the other class members as a guide to listening for making up your political mind: Will your expectation that you will agree or disagree with the speaker affect the way you begin to listen to him? How? Does your speaker start by saying anything that shows his listeners may not all agree with him? Does he appeal to listeners he thinks will agree with him? If so, how? How does he try to win over those who do not agree with him? What kind of feelings in his listeners does he make appeals to? Are these good qualities in the listeners? Are they qualities like unselfishness and desire to serve and help or are they qualities like greed and fear and pride? Which would you rather have in a leader— ability to appeal to your good qualities or your weaknesses? Which is the best kind of leader? Why? What qualities is a leader likely to bring out in his followers? Why?

At the end of the week hold an election. Judging from the results of the election, do you think the people in your class were wise listeners? Why or why not? Tell your log.

MAKING UP YOUR MIND: POLITICAL LISTENING II

25 minutes   *1 person*

To be able to help students listen intelligently to political speeches, try this activity.

Think about these questions: What do we mean by having an open mind? How can you be open-minded when you listen to a speaker? How can you keep your feelings about how a speaker is dressed or how he talks from interfering with your hearing of what he has to say? If you don't like something a speaker says, do you stop listening? Do you forget about what he is saying while you argue with him mentally? Would it help if you took a pad and pencil so that you could write down questions to ask him later? How can you be certain you are not misinterpreting what he is saying? Have you ever changed your ideas about a speaker as you listened to him? What did he do or what could he do to make that happen? Is he more likely to change what you think by what he says or by how he says it? Why?

Arrange to listen to a political speech in your class or out of it. What devices does the speaker use in what he says and how he says it? How does he try to convince you that his point of view is right? If your mind begins to wander, is it because you are thinking faster than he is talking? How could you use that extra thought-time to make sure you are getting the most information from what he is saying? Could you review, analyze, evaluate, question?

What call for action does the speaker make upon you? Will you do what he says? If you will, why? Will it be because you already intended to do so or because he changed your mind? Were you able to wait until you had heard everything he had to say before you made up your mind?

Write a short letter to the speaker telling him why you did or did not agree with what he said. Remember to be positive and constructive in your remarks.

ONE WAY OR ANOTHER:
LISTENING AND READING

45 minutes   *1 person*

Give your students a good start in enjoying and understanding literature by finding out what reading and listening can do for you. Try this activity.

Read a scene from a Shakespeare play and then listen to a recording of a cast performing it. What different feelings do you get from each experience? What are the disadvantages of reading? What kinds of problems did you have? What are the advantages of reading? Is it sometimes helpful to go back and read something over? To check the spelling or the punctuation for clues to the meaning? What else? What are some disadvantages of listening? Advantages? Is the language easier or harder to understand when you hear it?

In your log make a checklist for listening and reading. Show the advantages and disadvantages of each as you discovered them in your experiment. Also write your conclusions. Would you choose to read or to listen if you could only do one and wanted to know as much about the play as possible? Which was the way the play was meant to be presented?

ASK THE EXPERT: HAVING AN INTERVIEW

1 hour   *6 to 30 people*

Try this with your classmates to discover how your students can practice listening for information with each other.

Think of one topic that you are an expert on—perhaps it is something you can do well, a place you have lived, a hobby or a subject you have always been interested in. Pass a paper around your group and ask everyone to write his topic on the paper. Pass the list around a second time and ask each person to write his name beside a topic he would like to know more about. Each person who has written a topic will be interviewed by the person who has written his name beside the topic. Since everyone has written a topic and has put his name beside someone else's topic, each person will be interviewed once and will be the interviewer once. Start to pass the list around one more time, asking the person who wrote the first topic to stand beside the person whose name is written beside his topic. The second person will do the same and so forth until everyone is paired off. (This will be half-way through the list.) Spend fifteen minutes interviewing each other in these combinations. Then pair off according to the combinations on the second half of the list. You may want to give the interviewers a few moments to think about the questions they want to ask before they begin the interview.

In your logs discuss what you learned about the other person and his topic. How can a person who is interviewing make the interviewee feel comfortable? What can the expert do to make the interviewer feel comfortable? What kinds of questions get vague answers? What kinds of questions get informative answers? Did you understand everything the other person said? Why or why not? When you were the one talking, did you have to stop and explain what you meant? How was your style of interviewing different from the style of the person who interviewed you?

When did you feel most comfortable—when you were an expert or when you were the interviewer? Why?

Tell your log how to be a good interviewer.

A WORD FROM THE SPONSOR: WATCHING TV COMMERCIALS
2 to 3 hours   *3 to 5 people*

This activity will enable you to help students watch commercials critically and to evaluate more realistically the information they receive in commercials.

Meet with a group and make a list of commercials you can remember seeing lately on television. Agree that you will each watch as many of the listed commercials as you can when you are at home. During the next class session meet again as a group. Talk about the commercials one at a time. The following questions may help you in your discussion:

What does the commercial try to sell? How does it try to get you to buy the product? How many times is the product mentioned in the commercial? Why? How is the product shown in the commercial? What is happening to it? What are people doing with the product? How does that make you feel about the product?

How is the commercial matched in tone and atmosphere with what is on the program? What is the setting of the commercial? What kind of language does it use? Who is it addressed to? What kind of music is used in it? What kind of people are in it? How do you feel about the people? Is that how the sponsor wants you to feel about them? Why or why not? What do the actions of the people have to do with the product or why you should buy it? According to the people in the commercial, what does the product do for them? Besides the people in the dramatization, is there a voice that narrates? How does this voice help convince you to buy the product? Are famous people used to get attention for the product? In what way should we imitate these people?

Is there any appeal to your desire for social acceptance, good health, independence, economic security, comfort, time saving, sex appeal or other human desires? Does the commercial threaten any loss if the product is not used? Will one lose friends, fail to marry, spend money, time or energy needlessly? To what extent do these needs direct your own behavior?

What facts does the commercial give you about the product? (You may want to watch the commercials with a notebook in your hand to jot down these facts.) How much of the commercial is fact and how much is feeling? Compare several commercials that advertise the same kind of products—like different brands of detergent. What facts do the commercials give you by which you can judge which brand is best for your needs? Could you improve any of the commercials you have discussed? How? Could you make them more honest? More informative? How? Would they sell the product as well? Why or why not?

As a result of your discussion, define a "good commercial" and a "bad commercial." Show the class what the difference is by making two skits, one an example of a "good commercial" and one an example of a "bad commercial."

LISTENING TO IMPROVE READING, SPEAKING AND WRITING

Cultivating listening skills improves a student's speaking, reading and writing abilities. A student who applies listening skills as he hears speeches and participates in small-group conversations appropriates skills needed to improve his own speech as he evaluates the speaking of others. Good listeners become better talkers because they are aware of how their own listeners feel. As a student increases his sensitivity to the differences between ideas and attitudes held by different speakers, he becomes more aware of his need to meet the needs of his listeners. He is more curious not only about ideas but about the effect of ways of expressing ideas, in dialects and their implications, in slang and its uses and disadvantages, in the uses of cliche, aphorism and pun. This awareness adds to his control of verbal response to others and theirs to him.

When the student improvises and even when he uses a script for dramatization, he will be most successful when he really listens to the one who is speaking, and he will have less success when he merely waits until his own cue for speaking is given. The good listener listens to the whole body message of the speaker: eyes, feet, hands and posture send important messages. The listener must speculate, using all possible clues, on why a speaker says what he says. And he must listen to what is left unsaid and to why it is left unsaid, to what is implied as well as what is explicitly spoken.

We receive vastly more language than we produce, but this reception of language through listening increases our ability to produce a variety of kinds of language. Long before a child learns to know words through their shape by reading, he learns to know words through their sounds by listening. The teacher of listening must use this natural, early-established habit of the learner.

To increase his vocabulary the learner needs to hear words used in a variety of contexts and to receive new words as part of new experiences in which those words have meaning. Activities should include television listening and listening to cassette tapes which students can make for themselves. Cassettes can be played while a student is driving or doing other things. He should know that some actors use this system to learn lines. If a student is studying materials whose language is too difficult for him to read—as is the language of a classic play by Shakespeare, for instance, for a slower reader—he should listen to it as well as read it or while reading it. Or he should view it, if a film can be obtained.

Finding the central and supporting ideas of a speaker or making these clear in his own writing makes use of the same skills as listening for the ideas in a speaker's presentation. Main and supporting ideas are located similarly. Student writing often improves when the student records his ideas on tape and plays them back before he writes them. Some students can organize their ideas, arrange them in time, place or importance sequences, and edit them effectively by making short films or tape and slide shows. The skills involved are the same as those used in writing the traditional theme, and practice of them in a setting of visuals is much more attractive to some students than in writing. The collage is a similar device with similar advantages.

Reading skills, too, are closely related to listening skills. But the differences as well as similarities between the two methods of language reception should be explored in activities. A listener may find he is more affected emotionally by a speaker than he is by a writer. Speaker attitudes indicated by facial expressions, voice tone, bodily gestures and even the attitudes of the rest of the listeners in an audience affect the reception of the message of the speaker. The reader is helped, as the listener is not, by being able to review what he has read and by editorial guides, headings, print devices, italics and paragraphs. These must be inferred by a listener.

The ways the student receives language and analyzes it will profoundly affect his ability to produce it happily and effectively. Activities should lead him to identify the multitude of ways meaning emerges from the language and the ways these meanings affect him. He then becomes increasingly able to use these same methods of revealing meaning in the language he produces in his writing and speaking. Reception of language forms the support system for producing it, and the teacher of English must plan listening activities that will serve as a support system for student production of language.

Activities

BABY TALK: VISIT TO A NURSERY SCHOOL

2 hours   *1 person*

If you do this, you will be more prepared to help students investigate their language.

Call a nursery school to see if you can spend an hour visiting. If you cannot visit a nursery school, you may be able to visit a family with small children. Take a notebook and/or a tape recorder with you. Find a child who is three or four years old and playing alone. Using your notebook and/or tape recorder, record all that he does and says for an hour.

Replay the tape. Reread the notes. Did the child play quietly or talk to himself? If he talked, what did he say? Did he use good sentences? Did he ever say the same sounds several ways over and over? Why did he do this? Why would he do this? Do you ever practice something over and over until you get it right? Did he make any noises just to be making noises? Why? Did he talk to any other people or did they talk to him? Did adults talk to him in the same way they would talk to another adult? Did he talk to adults in the same way he talked to himself? Why? What kind of response did he get when he talked? Did the child use language to get something he wanted? How successful was he? What could he say to get attention? To please an adult?

How does the child know when he says something right? Why does he speak out loud? Does he learn language from the sound and the music the sentence sings? Is there a certain music to a language? Can you tell when someone is speaking a certain foreign language even when you do not know what he is saying? How? Why does a child talk to himself about what he is doing?

What conclusions do you draw about how a child learns language? Share your discoveries with the class by reporting your results in a newsletter article.

DO YOU BELIEVE OLD SAYINGS?: CLICHES

45 minutes   *2 to 4 people*

Here is an activity which may help your students recognize the cliches in what they hear and say. Try it.

Form a group of from two to four people. Have you heard these expressions lately: "A stitch in time saves nine" and "Whatever is worth doing is worth doing well"? What does each of these sayings mean?

Does everyone in your group agree? Ask several people in the class who are not in your group. What disagreements did you find? Do you believe both the sayings are true? What exceptions might there be? Do any of you play games you like but are not good at? How does that fit the "worth doing well" statement? Can you think of other exceptions?

What other expressions do you hear people say every day? Make a list of as many as your group can find. Why do people use such sayings as these instead of thinking about the situation and making a statement that fits just the one thing they are talking about? What advantages are there to using a TV dinner over using one that you cooked yourself, item by item? Do you use packaged cake mixes or start from "scratch"? Why use mixes and TV dinners? What savings do they make? What are the disadvantages? How do they limit you? How about prepackaged thoughts such as those mentioned above? What purpose do they serve? When are they not so useful? Will you want to use them in writing as much as you might use them in talking? Why?

Write a skit for your group using nothing but cliches for the dialogue. Perform your skit for the class.

SLANG USAGE: WHAT DID YOU SAY?

1 to 2 hours   *3 to 5 people*

If you would like to get your students to listen to and use slang with discrimination, here is an activity to help you.

Form a group, and discuss these questions: Do you ever use slang? Are there any special words you use with people who are close to you—words that have meanings beyond what they mean to other people? If so, why do you use those special words? How does it make you feel to use them? How does it make you feel when someone else uses special slang words you do not fully understand?

Is slang a dialect? Where does slang come from? Who uses it? Why? What makes some groups develop a complicated slang that is almost a separate language? What groups have done this? Make a list of your favorite slang and the places where it is most useful. Where does each word come from? Where did you get it? Have you ever used any other slang? What then is one of the drawbacks of slang, in writing for instance? Have you heard any slang words that come from combining two words or parts of words? Does some slang come from making a word that sounds like the meaning? Does some slang help you make your emphasis clear by exaggerating?

Working together, make a list of all the slang words you know, and write a slang dictionary for your class. Be sure to alphabetize your dictionary. You may also want to include more than one meaning for some words.

TEAMING FOR MEANING: WORDS THAT ARE ALIKE

20 minutes   *2 people*

If you would like your students to listen more carefully to words, what they mean and don't mean, how they are alike and not alike, how they change when you put them together with other words, try this game.

Find a partner and talk over these questions together: Are there words that mean the same? Name some. Do they have any differences? Can you think of situations in which those words would not mean the same? Are there really any two words that have exactly the same meaning? Does any one word mean quite the same in any two different places where it is used? Try using one of your words in different sentences. What does it mean in each? What do we do when we translate from one language to another? Do we translate just the words? Why?

Try this little game: Find a sentence—an ordinary sort of sentence that you might speak—for your partner to translate. Your partner's problem is to say exactly the same thing (in English) without using any of the same words. How many more words than were in the original sentence does your partner have to use? Does the meaning come out quite the same? Now let your partner find a sentence for you.

Tell your logs about what you have discovered, and how you feel about it.

FINDING A SPEECH COMMUNITY: VARIETIES IN LANGUAGE

1½ hours   *4 to 6 people*

If you do this activity, you may be able to help students discover how language works in the social context of their lives.

In your own class organize a group and discuss these questions: Do you know any persons who speak differently from other people? Are they people who belong to some special group? Do they make a living in a certain way or come from a particular country or region in your country? How many different ways of talking can you find on television? What is the difference between a dialect and an accent? How would your way of speaking sound to the people who sound strange to you? Do you have an accent or speak a dialect? Does everybody? Why or why not?

Choose a person you know from television or life whose way of speaking is different from yours, and as accurately as you can, try to describe how his speech is different. Are the sounds he uses in speaking different? If so, how? Does he use unfamiliar words for certain things? Does he speak faster or slower? Are there other differences? Find as many as you can.

What makes some people who speak the same language speak it differently from others? Find all the reasons you can for the differences. Consider the countries in which their ancestors lived, whether they have lived in isolated groups, educational backgrounds and any other matters that may have affected the speech of that group of people. How many speech groups are there in your school? In your town? What are they?

What effect does their different speech have now on the lives of these people? Are they more or less able to have access to the things they want in our society as a result of their speech? Does their way of talking help them to have a sense of identity? Do some people want to maintain their group differences? Under what circumstances might they be an advantage? You may want to talk this matter over with someone you know who speaks differently. Be sure you do not offend anyone by the questions you ask.

Using one or more small tape recorders, record as many of the different kinds of speech you have talked about as you can. If you have several recorders, you may want to make individual field trips to places where your recorder can "hear" people talking. Bring your tapes back to class. Listen to them as a group and edit them to make a collection of the most distinctive kinds of talk.

Play your tape for the whole class. You may also want to share your conclusions about the problems and advantages of speaking a distinctive dialect.

ENJOYING A DIALECT: BLACK SPEECH

20 minutes *1 person*

To help your students listen with interest, pleasure and understanding to speakers of black dialects, investigate black dialects for yourself.

Black speech has added many interesting ways of speaking to the general dialect. Are there any special ways of speaking or words you use that started in black speech? Get one of your black classmates to make a list of words in black speech for words you use in your dialect. Make a double column list of these for the bulletin board.

Think about these questions: Why is the black speech so complete in the number of words it has for standard words? When someone lives separately from others, will his speech differ more or less from the speech of the main group? How does this explain the differences? Can the black classmate speak your dialect so that you can understand him? How do you explain his greater versatility? Is the difference between the school language and his dialect greater than the difference between the school language and your dialect? Which of you has to be the more expert language user to make the transition from home to school?

Ask your friend to speak several sentences and then you speak several sentences into a tape recorder. See if you can get someone who has another dialect to speak into the tape also.

Listen—not to the words but to the sounds that are made. Is there a difference in the rhythm and music of the sounds as well as the words of different dialects? How would you describe those differences?

SOUND SENSE: YOUR VOICE AND PUNCTUATION
50 minutes   *2 people*

Here is a way to use listening to help students find the sense of what they read and write.

Find a passage from your reading that has lots of punctuation marks. Try to discover what the writer wanted you to do when he put in the message of each mark for you to read. To find out how these punctuation messages work, it helps to read the passages aloud.

Each of you should read a passage aloud to the other, paying special attention to the writer's punctuation messages. Afterward, talk over these questions: How did your voice tell you the difference between a question message and a period message? Between a comma and a period? Were there some times when your voice couldn't tell you the difference between kinds of punctuation messages? What were they?

When you are reading aloud, which is the best way to deliver the writer's message with your voice—thinking about lowering your voice because there is a pause indicated by a period or thinking about the overall idea that is being communicated and letting the punctuation appear automatically? Will it appear automatically? Can you train yourself to respond to the idea so that your voice does what it needs to do? How can you help each other do this? Listen to your voices when you read to be sure the idea gets through.

After you have practiced finding the punctuation sense with your voice, try reading a strange passage slowly to your partner to see if he can write it down putting the punctuation in it that the writer intended. Let your partner do the same for you. Do this as many times as you think is useful to you.

Talk to your log about your experience with the sounds of meaning. Were some passages easier to read or punctuate than others? If so, why? Were there some passages whose meaning you could not clearly decide? If so, why? What discoveries did you make about the messages of punctuation? How could students make these discoveries?

IN GOOD SHAPE:
PUT-TOGETHER WORDS

35 minutes   *1 person*

To help students improve their spelling and speaking habits, become an expert on the ways words are combined by listening to their sounds as well as by looking for their different forms.

Think about these questions: Are some words obviously combinations of other words? Look around the room and find such a word. Did you find blackboard? What others can you find? Make a list of all the combination words you find or hear in one day.

Were these words always together? How did they get together? Were they written together at once when they began to be associated or was there an in-between step? Of what use is a hyphen? Can you tell if a word is hyphenated just by hearing it? Why? In the history of words when two words are put together, at what stage does the hyphen show? Is there one written in this activity? When will the two words get together without hyphens? Listen to people talking. What tells you if words are written together, with hyphens or separately? If you were writing language the way it sounds, how would you write it? Try a few sentences.

In everyday talk do words sometimes get used together as one word when they are still used in writing as separate words? What about "gotta" and "haveta"? Can you think of others? Do the sounds of words change when they are put together and become compound words? Do the spellings ever change?

When people want to invent new words for new ideas do they sometimes put together old words to have new meanings? What about "sit-in"? Can you think of some others?

Write an article about put-together words for your class newsletter or bulletin board.

BETTER LETTERS: LISTENING TO LETTERS

30 minutes   *1 person*

To help students improve reading and writing, try this activity.

Are letters like "t" or "l" always the same even though they appear in different words? Say "little" to yourself. Now get someone else to say it by writing it on a piece of paper and asking him to pronounce it. Try this same thing with "wet." Is the "t" sound the same? How are they different? Could you make a rule for the difference based on what kind of sounds are around the letter?

Try this with the other consonants—all the letters that are not vowels. Find how they sound when they are the beginnings of words, when they are in the middle of words and when they are at the end of words. Are there differences based on what other sounds are beside them? Try to formulate as many rules as you can for various sounds. One good one is "p," which sounds very different when it is associated with different other sounds. Is the sound different from the letter? Say "p" as a letter. Then say it as a sound. Is it different? In this experiment are you working with sounds or letters?

Write your conclusions in your log.

THINK SOUND: WHAT DOES IT DO TO MEANING?

30 to 45 minutes   *1 person*

To discover ways of helping students acquire the habit of using their inner voices to clarify meaning in what they read and say, do this.

Think about these questions: What are the two meanings of this sentence? "Uncle Sam made me a soldier." How would you say it if your uncle made you a toy? How would you say it if you were in the army? Say the sentence both ways to yourself. Can you hear the difference in the ways you say it? Do the pauses change? You may find it helpful to read the sentence into a tape recorder and listen to it. You need to think the different ideas when you say the word in order to hear them.

Try these two sentences: "Mr. Jones watched a baseball arch through the air." "Mr. Jones watched a Roman arch through the window." Does a pause or emphasis make the differences? How? Why? What differences are there between Green Bay Packers and green bay tree? Where is the pause? How can you read the sentence, "He gave her dog biscuits"? Can you know what happened until you hear the sound? What conclusions would you make about the importance of sound to meaning?

To illustrate what you have discovered make a tape to play for the class or plan a short talk in which you demonstrate the ways sound can give meaning to sentences. See if you can make up some double-meaning sentences of your own.

SOUND SAMENESS:
SPELLING AND SOUND I

40 minutes   *1 person*

Prepare yourself to help students with spelling problems by investigating the relationship of sound to spelling.

Are there words that are spelled alike and sound alike but have different meanings? Here are some spell-alikes which have different meanings and sounds. Can you untangle them? tear-tear, lead-lead, read-read, contract-contract. Find some others and add them to the list for your log.

Are there words that sound alike but are spelled differently and have different meanings? You can make a list that you can play games with. What is wrong with an advertisement for a department store that asks for a "stationary buyer"? Would your travel folder talk about "hallowed spots of Grease" or "Greece"? Would it make a difference? Might someone think you would not be able to find your way through a country if you couldn't find your way through a word?

Because these words sound alike, people very often confuse them in their writing, with strange results. Often newspapers and magazines like to reprint these funny or strange mistakes in their humor sections.

Make a collection of such word mistakes in your log, or put them in a scrapbook.

SOUNDS CAN BE CONFUSING:
SPELLING AND SOUND II

25 minutes   *1 person*

Prepare yourself to help your students with spelling and writing problems by doing this activity.

Think about these questions: Do you know what a ghoti is? The "gh" is pronounced like the "gh" in cough. The "o" is pronounced like the "o" in women. The "ti" is like the "ti" in nation. What then is a ghoti? Then why don't we spell in whatever way we want to? What would happen to literature or writing which is handed down from one age to another? Would we be able to know what was really meant after a writer died? What if we all spelled as we speak? Do we all speak English alike? How do you pronounce "what?" Does everyone? Does yours sound like "waht" or "wot"? Do you say the "h" at all? Does anyone? Have you ever read a book by Dickens? He uses the word "very" a lot of times. People in that time said "werry." Wouldn't that have been confusing to read in our times when no one says the word that way?

Sometimes the sounds of letters get confused, not because everyone says them that way, but because the sounds are very similar. In these phrases can you put the right letters where they belong?

his mine was not working   wearing a banaba on her head
cedars, birches and populars   a wicked basket
mole on the bread   a hash fell over the hall
weave on your loon   a parking meteor
a scrawl on her face

If you were working on these spellings from the sounds of the words, what percentage of the words would you be able to correct? Count the words in a sentence or in several sentences in your own reading. What percentage of them can you sound out successfully? Even when you cannot sound out all of a word, can you sound out most of it? What conclusions would you make about the usefulness of being able to sound out words? What does this mean for spelling?

Write your conclusions in your log.

NET ONE: FISH OUT
THE MAIN IDEA

2 hours   *4 to 6 people*

If you would like to help students find the main ideas in their listening and reading materials, try this activity.

Form a group, and ask each member to bring a paragraph from a book, magazine or newspaper to class with him the next time it meets. Take turns reading your paragraphs aloud to the group. After each person has read his paragraph, you should all write a title or headline for it in your logs or on pieces of paper. Before you go on to the next paragraph, take a few minutes to discuss your choices. Here are some questions which may help you:

What was the main idea? How do you know? Was there a sentence or phrase in the paragraph which contained the main idea? If there is such a phrase, when would you expect to hear it—at the beginning, the middle, or the end? Is the main idea repeated in the paragraph? Does the writer choose any special words or use words in a different way to let you know that this is the important message of his paragraph? How can you make your headline or title say the most about the paragraph in the fewest words? What kinds of words carry the most meaning? What happens to adjectives, adverbs, articles, prepositions and passive verbs in titles and headlines? Why?

Could you play this same game with pictures rather than headlines and titles? Each one of you should make a collage illustrating the main idea of a paragraph you have heard. You may want to do this at home or you may agree to bring glue, scissors, paper and magazines to class so that you can work on your project together.

Display your collages along with the paragraphs they illustrate in your classroom.

MIND MAKING: LISTENING TO REMEMBER
30 minutes   *a large group or class*

If you would like to help your students remember what they hear, here is a game you can play to experiment with your own listening memory.

Ask everyone in your group or class to make up a fictitious name and vocation for himself. Set aside a 15 minute time period during which you converse with each other, learning the names and occupations of as many of your classmates as possible. At the end of the 15 minutes, return to your seats and write as many of the names and occupations as you can remember. Allow 10 minutes for writing. At the end of this time ask each person to tell his fictitious name and occupation. Check yourself. How many did you remember?

Tell your log about the problems and/or successes you had in listening to remember. Which is easier, remembering what you hear or remembering what you see? Does it help to repeat what you want to remember? Did you use any mental tricks like rhymes or sound-alike words? Were these distractions that interfered with your memory? How do you feel about trying to remember so many names and occupations at once?

LISTENING FOR ENJOYMENT

In our culture, seeing and hearing for enjoyment form central components of man's leisure time activities. To expand this enjoyment should be a function of the listening curriculum. The child's earliest and most natural pattern of language growth is in his ability and opportunity to talk and listen to others. It is amazing that teachers have resisted, downgraded, ignored and discouraged this natural activity of the student and failed to use it as a vehicle for language learning. Long ago the urgent desire of the student for conversation with his peers, so long forbidden in most English classrooms, should have tipped curriculum makers that the student who insists on talking, often to the constant resistance of his teachers, is obeying an inner command, related to his developmental tasks which it is useless, foolish and counterproductive to resist. Exploitation of the potential for language growth in pleasant two-person and larger groups has a built in motivation and should be regarded as a basic tool for language learning.

Language as sound should pour constantly in an abundant stream over the student in the English class. Conversation, choral verse, taped verse, music, films and plays should be exploited fully. That music is used at all times and on all occasions by young people to accompany their activities should incite their teachers less to wonder than to imitation. Music to write by and music to read by should be a standard fixture in all English classes. Earphones enable the student to individualize his listening and can be of great value in reading and writing centers of the activity classroom. Listening done outside of class should be integrated into class activities. The television set has been the companion of most children as long as they can remember. Reference to this source of listening experience should be integrated into many other kinds of English experiences.

Thinking or musing that takes up many hours of time of every person is a kind of continual listening to our own thoughts. Many teachers lament the seeming apathy of student daydreamers. But these students are often obeying strong inner compulsions to solve developmental tasks appropriate to the stage of life through which they are passing, tasks which must be accomplished before they can go on to tasks the world outside their thoughts, including the world of the classroom, assigns them.

But listening to their own thoughts affects the things students say and do, how they react to others and how others see them. The English teacher who is teaching listening should make use of this inner listening in activities that will help the learner to use his musing and "daydreaming" to improve his thinking, speaking and writing. Almost all small children talk to themselves, some almost constantly. Adults do this also, especially when reacting to worry or stress. Social pressure pushes this habit underground in the adult, but the inner voice and the inner ear are far from stilled. To help the student bring to the level of conscious control this submerged conversation with himself is a worthy objective of the listening curriculum. A number of activities are suggested that will help the prospective teacher to know why, when and how he speaks and listens to himself so that he may teach his students to listen and speak comfortably with themselves.

Activities

ON THE AIR: BE A DISC JOCKEY

2 to 3 hours   *1 to 5 people*

To help students listen to their favorite disc jockey programs with a greater understanding of the verbal and organizational skills involved in producing their entertainment, do this.

Find a group or work alone. Plan a fifteen minute disc jockey program. You will need a radio to listen to so that you will have models to guide you in planning. You will need a tape recorder to record your program, and you will need a record player and records. If you have a group, you may want to listen to the radio together or you may decide to listen separately at home. Choose one member of your group who has good handwriting to be your secretary. Discuss these questions: the answers will help you in your planning:

How many minutes of a fifteen minute segment of a disc jockey show are spent on commercials? How many different commercials would you expect? What products are advertised? How many minutes of the fifteen does the disc jockey usually spend talking? How many records can you play and still leave enough time for the disc jockey and the commercials? How can you plan for the exact amount of time your records will take? Will you also want to include a news summary? Would it be helpful to decide what station your disc jockey will inhabit? Would it be useful to choose a particular time of day?

Before you plan your program in detail, you need to decide upon the records you will play. Your selections may depend upon the records you have at home as well as the musical tastes of your group members. Perhaps you will want to vote on the selections. Choose someone to be your disc jockey. You will want other voices for the commercials. Whom will you choose? Will you need background music or sound effects for the commercials? Who will write the script? How will you move smoothly from one part of your program to another without moments of silence? Can one person be responsible for the record player? Do you need a director to give cues? Does each person need a copy of the whole script or just the parts which involve him?

When you have taped your program and are satisfied with the results, play the tape for the class.

WHAT MAKES IT FUN?: LOOKING AT TELEVISION

40 minutes   *1 person*

To make students more aware of their viewing tastes and habits, plan activities in which they can investigate the likes and dislikes of people they know.

Take a survey among your classmates to find out what the most popular television program is for your class. What makes it popular? What kind of program is most popular with you? Why? What kinds of feelings do you have when you see it? What makes you feel satisfied about it? What things do you feel better about when you see it? Make a list of things that make people feel good when they watch television. Do people have some needs for good feelings that television programs can't meet? Which of the needs for having good feelings are being met? Does meeting these needs make the difference between a popular and an unpopular program? Why?

Write a recipe for the most popular television program in the world. What kinds of things would it have in it? Why?

TV PATHFINDER: MAKING TV RECOMMENDATIONS

40 minutes   *1 person*

To prepare yourself to help students make wise viewing choices, do this activity.

Make recommendations to your own class of programs you think they would like to watch. How long in advance will you need to plan for this activity? Will you give recommendations at the beginning of the week, or would you like to make recommendations each day? Is there a time set aside for announcements at the beginning of classes or once a week? Are such announcements usually placed on the bulletin board in your class? Could you write your recommendations on the blackboard?

How will you make decisions about what your classmates should watch? How could you find out about their interests and needs? Would it be helpful to preview some programs to see what they are like? Does the Sunday supplement section of your newspaper contain reviews of coming television programs? Sometimes it reviews programs a month in advance. What information can you find in the *TV Guide?* National newspapers and news magazines may also contain reviews of coming television programs. If you find conflicting reviews of some programs, you may want to pass on that information to your classmates.

Give your recommendations to your class. Be sure to watch your choices yourself, and tell your log if they fulfilled your expectations.

WHY WATCH?: GETTING TO KNOW COMEDY

1 hour   *1 person*

This activity will help you find some ways to show students that comedy can be important to them, and you may help them understand why people like to watch situations and people that are funny.

Do you have certain favorite television shows—ones that you wait for all week? Do you grow fond of certain characters? Even though you are fond of them, do you always agree with them or even approve of them? Give examples in your log.

Are some of these comic characters? Can we see the ridiculousness of someone without liking him less? Did you ever do something ridiculous? How did you feel about it? When you have done something ridiculous, are you willing to let other people know about it? What are you afraid others will think about you? Is it possible that they can continue to like you or even like you a little more because they know they can do silly things too?

When you see comic characters acting silly and making themselves seem foolish, do you feel more comfortable about yourself? Would other people feel that way too? Does this good feeling also make you feel better about the ideas the play is about?

Make a survey of people in your class to find their favorite comic characters from television. Take an opinion poll in your class to see which one makes people feel best about themselves. Is this also the most popular? Write your conclusions about the survey.

NEW AND OLD:
HOW IS A TELEVISION PLAY DIFFERENT FROM A STAGE PLAY?

2 hours or more   *1 person*

If your students don't see as many stage plays as television plays, they may enjoy both kinds of plays more as a result of knowing some ways that they are alike and different. To help them, do this activity.

Find a stage play and compare it with a television show. Is the opening of the television show more or less likely to have an exciting beginning? What are some of the devices used to create excitement in television shows? You might have to look at several to find these devices unless you can remember some of them.

Why does the television writer have to create one of these exciting starters even more than a stage writer does? In some television shows the placement of the commercial at the start is especially planned not to interfere with the beginning. How is this done? Why? What do you do if you do not like the start of a show on television? What then can a writer do to keep you from responding in this way?

What kind of action or speaking keeps your attention? Do you have any examples of older playwrights who have done something like this to attract and keep audience attention? You might read over the opening scene in *Julius Caesar* for an example. If you want to know why Shakespeare thought it was important to have a scene like this, read something about the kinds of audiences he had and how they behaved.

After a television play gets the attention of the viewer, what is the next problem of the writer? When will the first break occur? What will happen during that break? What will the writer want to get done before that break to make sure he gets his audience back afterwards? Will he use large or small numbers of characters? Why? What kinds of conflicts will he use most often? What kinds of conflicts occur on shows that are shown week after week as serials? Why?

Would exposition be most likely to occur at the start of a television drama or would it be better to arrange this necessary information so that it could be given in some other way or at some other time? Why? How and at what other times could it be given?

Take a story or one-act play that you have read lately and change it into a half-hour television program. Remember that making it fit into the time is all-important. Plan commercials. When you have finished, try to find an acting group to present your play.

WIDE VIEW: SEEING A FILM FROM A BOOK

2 hours out of class   *1 person*
½ to 1 hour in class

Do this and you will be more able to help students get the most from their film viewing, whether they are seeing a film from a book they have read or any film.

View a film of a book you have read. Think about these questions: Have the leading characters been changed? How? Have minor characters been eliminated, added, or altered? Have relationships been changed? Have any identifying characteristics been changed? Have religious, ethnic, or political factors been changed? Has the place of the events been changed? Have settings become more luxurious or more poverty-stricken? Have simpler or more explicit explanations been used? Has dialogue been transferred from one character to another? Has a descriptive passage been transferred into dialogue? Have the goals of the characters been changed? Have they and their motivations been made more simple or more complex? Has the original theme been altered or eliminated? Have incidents been added or eliminated? Have action scenes been added or taken away? Has evil been punished and good purposes rewarded? Has the value system of society been upheld? Account for as many of these changes as have occurred by seeing if they are caused by the commercial needs of the programmers or the need to vindicate some special moral stance.

If you have difficulty remembering just what the film did or did not show, you may want to talk over these questions with other people in your class who also have seen the film.

Did you agree with all of the changes that were made in the film version of the story? Why or why not? Tell your log how you would have done it: or better still, choose a scene from the film that you thought was handled wrong and do it the way you think it should have been done. Write your own script, and get an acting group in your class to act it out.

MOVIE SHOPPING: FINDING A GOOD MOVIE

½ hour in class   *1 person*
some time out of class

If you would like students to become discriminating in their choices of films for reviewing, become a film critic yourself first.

How do you choose a film you want to see? Did you ever choose one because of a newspaper review? Collect some reviews from the local and other newspapers and magazines. Select a film from some of the recommended ones. View the film. Decide what it was that made the critic like the film, and see if you agree.

Record your criticism in your log, and make a comment for the bulletin board in your classroom. Pin your comments beneath the original review, telling your agreement or disagreement with it. You may want to repeat this activity with another film. If you do this, also repeat your agreement or disagreement with the critic's opinion. If you're going to convince your readers that your opinion is as good or better than his, your examples and arguments must be as convincing as his.

FILM FACTS: LEADING A FILM DISCUSSION

several hours   *1 person*

You will be prepared to help students enjoy and learn from films if you lead a discussion among those in your class who see one.

Find out if there is a film scheduled to be shown to your class. If there is not one scheduled, talk to your teacher about arranging for one. Preview the film, or films if there is a series. If the film is part of a series, you may wish to work with one or more other students, each of you taking a film or part.

Consider these questions: Is there any more information you can find about the film? Are there reviews of it? Does your teacher have a Teacher's Guide to the film that you could use? Is it based on a book which you could read? Does it show places or famous people that you could read about in the library? Collect as much information as might be interesting and helpful to the class to add to their enjoyment and understanding of the film.

Does the film deal with materials your class is studying? How is it related to your class work? Will you need to point out this relationship to make it more clear? When would be the best day and the best time in the period to show the film? Would the film be a good introduction to the materials it deals with? Would it be best as a concluding note in a unit of studies? Would it be relevant to the studies of one group in your class and not to others? Is there a special room in your school where some of the people in your class could go to see the film without disturbing others?

Practice threading the projector and being careful with the equipment. Be responsible for getting the equipment and returning it. Synchronize the sound and the start of the film after the leader so that you have a professional presentation.

In a short handout or on the board suggest to the rest of the class what they should look for in the film. Have them watch for any differences between what they have read and what appears on the film. Is a film a different way of showing an idea than print? How? What advantages are found in each? Are there differences in what you can do with film or print? What? Is there a difference between what a reader and what a viewer feels as he reads or listens and views? What is it?

Write in your log a summary of the ways in which film is able to help students understand a story or an idea that print does not. In the case of the Encyclopedia Britannica films good scholars suggest interpretations of the Shakespeare plays. Perhaps you think there are other interpretations equally good. Discuss them with other students and tell your log about them.

MUSIC TO SEE BY: FINDING MUSIC FOR YOUR FILM OR SLIDE SHOW

60 minutes   *1 to 6 people*

If you want to get your message across better and discover how your students can make film or slide shows more interesting, try this activity.

What music makes you feel happy? Sad? Are there songs that make you feel angry? Patriotic? What songs make you feel in other ways? How do songs without words make you feel that is different from songs with words?

What is the mood of your pictures? Are you trying to get a message across? What is it? How could music help you say the things you are trying to say with the pictures? How could lyrics help? Should the music be fast or slow? Or both?

What if the music is finished before the pictures are, or the other way around? How can you be sure that won't happen? How much time does it take to present your film or slides? How long are the musical selections you want to use? Can you use only parts of some? Can you put some together? Which ones seem to sound best next to each other? Which picture will be on the screen during the most exciting parts of the music?

Decide what songs or parts of songs you want to use, and record them in the order you want to use them on tape. Time the tape to fit the pictures. Then play the film and tape together. If you don't like the way they fit, make adjustments. Now present your show.

WISE WATCHING: VIEWING SKITS

15 minutes   *1 person*

To help students be better skit watchers—for their enjoyment and for the enjoyment of the whole class—try this activity.

Were you ever afraid of being in a skit? Why? What things did you think the audience might do that you would not like? What would being a good audience member mean? What things would an audience member do if he wanted to help the cast of a skit? What things would he not do? How can you keep from laughing when someone is playing a part that is not at all like him as you know him in real life? Could you concentrate very hard on thinking he is the person he is playing instead of the person you know he is? Is he having to concentrate this way on his character? Try doing this and see how successful you are.

Tell your log how you feel about this. Is it as good a feeling as giggling? Why?

ACTIVE AUDIENCE: WATCHING ROLE-PLAYING

25 minutes   *1 person*

Your students will enjoy watching role-playing more if they are actively involved in what is happening. Do this to discover some ways of involving them.

Find out when a group in your class will be role-playing and plan to become an active watcher on that day. Read these suggestions over several times before the role-playing event so that you will remember them as you are watching:

Think about what you would change in the scene if a role were played differently. If one character were acted differently, how would the characters react to him? Can you think of more than one possibility? Would the outcome be different? How? What do you think the character is thinking as opposed to what he is saying? What makes you think so?

With permission, you might stand behind one of the speakers, speaking his thoughts as he speaks his words. Or, you might find another cast or ask the first cast to reenact the skit, allowing you to act a role which you would play differently from the way it was originally played. Does the outcome change? How?

Comment in your log on your feelings as you listened and as you replayed.

SOME SOUND: ENJOYING POETRY

2 hours or more   *2 people*

If you would like your students to enjoy poetry, here is an activity that can help you.

If studying poetry sometimes seems dull or difficult, listening to it may be more fun and easier than reading it. Find a partner. Share some of your favorite records with him, and work together to write the words from the songs you both like in their poetic form. (Whether you work in class or out of class may depend upon the availability of a record player and a spot to listen to it.)

Make a scrapbook collection of your poem-songs. Consider these questions: How much of a poem is sound? How different are the poems when they are on paper? How will you know how to arrange the words on the pages? (It might be helpful to look through some books of poetry to see the different kinds of arrangements of lines and words that are possible.) How will you place the poems in the scrapbook? According to their subjects? Their styles? The date of the song? Will you make any comments of your own in the scrapbook to explain your collection?

Put your scrapbook in the display corner of the room so that your classmates may enjoy it also. You may want to share your discoveries with the class by playing recordings of some of your selections for them and then reading the words as poetry for comparison.

ONCE UPON A TIME . . . :
LISTENING TO STORIES

variable time   *3 to 8 people*

If you want to introduce your students to the joys of listening for fun, this activity may help you.

Form a group to tell and listen to stories. If you have a favorite story or anecdote, tell it or read it to the group. While others are telling their stories, listen. See if you can listen with your imagination. Let go of your own story you are planning to tell and everything around you. Put yourself inside the world the storyteller is trying to show you. Don't worry about whether there is a plot or the characters make sense. Just enjoy the story for what it is as it comes to you.

Think about what you can do as a listener to make the telling of the story more enjoyable for everyone. What can you do to show the teller you are interested and approving of what he is saying? How can you encourage him? Could your appropriate or inappropriate reactions affect the enjoyment of the other listeners? How? What can you do to keep outside noises or movements from distracting your attention?

Keep a record in your log of your feelings about your story telling and listening.

LOOK ALIKES—WORD ALIKES: FINDING SIMILARITIES

several hours *1 person or a group*

If you would like students to see the world around them with greater discrimination, here is a way to do it with pictures and words.

Find a group or work alone. Think or talk about these questions: Why doesn't everything in the world look alike to you? How do you tell yourself that one thing is different from another? How do you know? How can you tell that gray is different from blue? How could you describe the difference without the words "gray" and "blue"? How is an apple like and not like a rubber ball? Do babies know all these differences and likenesses when they are born? How do they find out?

Find two pictures which have two images that look alike—for example, a ruff of smoke and a cauliflower. How could you express this likeness in words? If you have a group, each member may want to try it. Now find some pictures of your own and say what the alikeness is in words. You might take a camera and make some slides or movies, making pictures of similarities. Then express them in words.

Make a slide talk with a tape or a film with a tape or a picture book showing your alikenesses in pictures and words.

WHAT DO YOU SEE?:
TALKING ABOUT PICTURES

15 minutes *2 people*

If you complete this activity, you will find it easier to help students talk about, write about and describe what they see.

How do you decide what a picture is about? Do you read the caption or do you already have a good idea before you see the words?

Choose a partner and each of you find a picture that you like from a magazine. Find a picture as full of people, things, and activities as you can. Do not let your partner see your picture. Describe to your partner all the objects, people, and actions in the picture and let him write a caption or title for the picture. You do the same for his.

Compare what you have written with what the caption and written materials with the picture say. Were you close or far from what the paper or magazine thought the picture said? Maybe you like your caption better!

REVEALING WORDS:
TRIP TO AN ART GALLERY OR MUSEUM

several hours   *1 to 10 people*

To be able to help students listen for prejudices, tastes, values, and attitudes which are revealed in comments about what they see, try this activity.

Form a group of people from your class who would like to visit an art gallery, a museum or a zoo. Plan a field trip. You may want to write letters or make telephone inquiries to gather information about the best time for your visit, the rates and about guides, guidebooks or other information which may give you additional interesting facts about the sights you will see.

Plan to take two small hand cassette tape recorders. (Taking two is insurance against dead batteries, fouled tapes or microphones that don't get turned on.) Keep your visit short—not longer than one and a half hours—because you will spend at least that much time listening to the tape afterward. Before your trip try to plan the sequence of your viewing, and appoint one member of your group to keep a log of the objects you have seen in the order you have seen them so that you will know what is happening on the tape when you listen to it. Try to record comments and reactions of other visitors as well as of persons in your own group.

Arrange to meet, in or out of class, to listen to the tape together. One of the advantages of listening to a tape is that you can stop and replay interesting or questionable parts or discuss what was said and then continue on. Using the log of your visit, retrace your field trip according to its sounds. After each sight or event during which comments were made, stop the tape and discuss what happened. Here are some questions which may be useful to your discussion:

What can you tell about the object being viewed by the comments made about it? What words or sounds tell you how the speakers feel about what they are seeing? When you hear your own reactions, are you surprised at what you said? Why? Do you feel differently about the sights you saw now than you did when you made the comments? Do some speakers on the tape influence the reactions of others? If so, how? What can you tell about a person by the words he uses to express his feelings? Find a critical comment. What does it tell you about the speaker's values? Find an approving comment. What does it tell you about the speaker's values? Are some people usually critical and others usually approving? Why? In what ways do people's first impressions and first reactions tell the truth about their feelings? In what ways might first reactions be misleading? On what basis do most people judge a work of art? Did you compare one object to another? What details do people notice first? What do they remember afterward? Did you react differently to the exhibits or animals at the end of your visit after you had seen many than you did to the first ones you saw? If so, why?

Choose several portions of the tape which your group agrees reveal values and attitudes of the speakers. Replay these selections for the whole class and explain their significance.

LISTENING TO WHAT YOU DON'T SAY: YOUR INNER VOICE

45 minutes   *1 person*

To be able to guide your students in acquiring a respect for and enjoyment of their unspoken thoughts, do this.

Practice listening to your own thoughts. Read a short story or an article from a magazine. Do you accept or believe everything the author says? How do you respond to what seems unreal or untrue? Do you interject arguments of your own or carry on an inner dialogue with the author? What do you, or would you, say to him? If you are reading from your own copy of the magazine, try writing notes to the author in the margins. Some famous people have used this system of expressing their inner responses. How do you feel about it? Tell your log.

If you are reading a story rather than an argumentative article, do you put your own words in the mouths of the characters if the author has not supplied them? Do you imagine what you would say if you were in the characters' places? Listen to your own thoughts as you read. What do they say? Tell your log.

When you are talking to other people, do you always say aloud what you say silently? Try this experiment. Find a group to work with in your class. As you are working, listening and talking with the other people, listen to your own thoughts. Why don't you speak all of your thoughts aloud? Are you afraid others will disapprove or think your ideas silly? What makes you feel that way? Are you ever afraid your thoughts might hurt someone else's feelings? What do you or would you do then? Do thoughts ever pass through your mind too quickly to be spoken? How do you feel then? Are other thoughts too fragmented or incoherent to speak aloud? What would happen to you if your words came out in fragments or incoherently? Have you ever been with someone whose words did not always make sense when he talked? How did you feel about him when that happened? Are there times when you would like to speak, but don't because someone else is speaking? How do you feel about people who interrupt when others are talking? Is there ever a good time to do it? Are there some thoughts that are too private to be spoken? How do you feel when someone else reveals his private thoughts to you? How would you feel if your own private thoughts slipped out? Why? Are there some situations in which private thoughts may be talked about and some situations in which they may not? What makes the difference? Are there some private thoughts you would not talk about in any situation? What can you think and do in the privacy of your own mind that you could never do or say in any other way? Are there times when you like to think your own good, happy, pleasant thoughts just because it makes you feel good? What does it do for you to be able to retreat into your own pleasant thoughts and shut out the rest of the world?

In your log write your conclusions about what your inner voice does for you.

AIR CASTLES:
LISTENING TO IMAGINARY SOUNDS

30 minutes   *1 person*

If you do this activity you will be more able to help students listen and think imaginatively.

Imagine you are in a place where there are many sounds—choose your place carefully so that your mind will know what kind of sounds to tell your imagination to hear. You may find a picture in a book or magazine which suggests many sounds to you and try to imagine the sounds while you look at it. Whichever method you use to help you imagine sounds, just sit for at least 10 minutes concentrating on the sounds your imagination hears until they are clear in your mind and your imagination has nothing more to add. Perhaps you would like to start with the quiet sounds first and work your way up to the loud ones.

Does the clock tick or the water drip? Does the motor on the refrigerator run or the cat purr? Does the wind rustle the leaves or distant traffic roar? Do insects buzz? Can you hear your own footsteps or your breathing? Are there other people? Do they talk and move? Is there machinery working? Follow each sound step-by-step in your mind.

In your log write a description of the sounds you have heard and what they meant to you. Did you imagine the sights which went with the sounds? Did your sounds turn into a scene or story?

III

PRODUCING LANGUAGE

CHAPTER V

The Student Speaks

Through interaction with his culture, an interaction largely accomplished by speaking and listening to others, a child creates his sense of self. The small child learns language easily and quickly through self-initiation, involvement and immersion in oral language. But when he goes to school reading and writing, although less important than the other receiving and producing activities of language, dominate his activities in learning English, at the expense of speaking and listening.

Teachers like to talk, and they think what they have to say is important. Students think what they have to say is important too, and many of them like to talk in ways of their own choice, with persons of their own choice, at times of their own choice. This desire should be used, not suppressed, in the English classroom. From attempted suppression arise problems of apathy and rebellion. Avoidance of this suppression and the prevalence of oral language activity, along with the arrangement of learning centers and abundance of valid learning materials and activities is the characteristic most differentiating humanistic activity classrooms from traditional classrooms. The activity classroom is centered on student talk, not teacher talk. Important questions in the humanistic activity curriculum have multiple answers, different answers for each person examining them, or answers which have many parts, the search for which is shared. Finding and checking these answers requires student talk.

Humanistic teachers teach as if the point of education is that the one educated begins to be different and do things differently, to make full use of what he is and can be. At one time teachers thought that the student would do things differently if he could, however temporarily, recall or recognize certain information. Now many think that this is not so, that a change of behavior involves feeling differently as well as knowing differently. To accomplish this change the teacher must have access to the student's realm of feeling as well as his realm of knowing. In this former realm are tucked away the wellsprings of need and desire to change. Oral language interaction between students taps this wellspring.

Students in a humanistic curriculum study the language they themselves speak, observing what it does and how it works. They find that they have no means for persuading, informing and understanding their fellows as effective as language. By their handling of words they will be revealed to others. When they are not speaking to others, they speak to themselves, thinking in words. And as their proficiency in using language grows, they will enjoy using it as they speak, read and write.

Many objectives for growth in oral language proficiency emerge from a humanistic curriculum. The student establishes for himself a variety of dialects and manipulations of language conventions appropriate to his needs, along with techniques for expanding those varieties whenever it may become necessary to do so. Some students enjoy becoming acquainted with historical, anthropological, sociological and psychological features of language. The student may also profit from learning appropriate vocabulary to describe and analyze varieties of written and spoken English. Most important of all, he should develop the desire and ability to control the beauty, power, grace, flexibility, clarity, and precision of language available to him as a speaker of English.

EXPERIENCING AND SPEAKING

Students in humanistic English classes investigate what language really is and how it works in their experience to relate what they say to what they think. Language is the vehicle of thought, and most of what man knows about thought is what language tells him. Man does not have to have words to think, but he tends to think in the words he has and to confine his thoughts to the channels created by the language he knows. His thought finds concrete existence and form in words.

The structure of language is a factor in the way the child understands reality, and the language he uses to describe reality conditions how he perceives that reality. He sees the world in the ways he thinks about it and believes what he believes about it because of concepts he can express in his language. Man sees what he believes because that is all he has a name for. He recognizes only faintly and inexactly the pattern constituting an event for which he has no name. Unless their linguistic backgrounds are similar, observers are unlikely even to see the same picture of the world.

The child's language, then, enables him to categorize his experiences. By the words and linguistic structures he uses to define experience, he attaches meaning to it. As he manipulates sound, syntactical, and vocabulary systems, he extends his awareness of relationships and creates his world. He makes a constant verbal analysis of ordinary life, and the name of a situation and the linguistic formula by which it is analyzed cue his behavior toward a phenomenon. He organizes his experience and regulates his actions by language. By his language he traces the consequences of his behavior, enlarges his knowledge of himself and identifies with the experience of others. Mediating his activities through words that move between experience and concept, translating the concrete into the abstract, he changes the realities he senses into verbal symbols. A kind of elemental machine, at birth, he becomes a self through these experiences, which he interprets and conceptualizes through language. He is entrapped, enmeshed, entangled by the symbols and syntax of his language, through which he classifies experience and the features he perceives in the objective world.

Much of the way the child speaks is learned verbal behavior, determined by a cultural process. The bonds between his thought and his language originate and grow in the evolution of his speech. The small child talks to himself while he develops a concept, and he speaks as he manipulates objects. Thus, he forms and fixes concepts, and around his language his concepts grow. Language is his response to what the world offers and tells him. Developing thought and speech meet when the child is around two, and his babbling speech begins to turn into the inner speech of the adult. But as he contends with his problems, he may again speak aloud to himself. Macbeth, Brutus and Hamlet spoke soliloquies, and the businessman addresses his shaving mirror with the speech he will give at his board meeting.

Because he categorizes experiences in the designs available to him in his language, and his sound systems are the surrogates of experience, the child matures in language proficiency as he manipulates a chain of terms that define control of his environment. His organization of language reflects the organization of what he sees, feels and hears. Sights and sounds of his everyday life, through analysis and synthesis effected by his language, become classified and organized as events.

Language is the child's method of discriminating response. His words and concepts change each other; the instrument makes possible the product, and the product refines the instrument. By language he relates new ideas to those he has learned and creates a context. By language he files and structures experiences. Experience and language interact as language symbolizes experience, but always the experience must be there before the symbol is created. The word-blocked child is really the concept-blocked and experience-impoverished child. Not more words but more experiences which he can clothe in words are needed before he can expand his use of language, for language growth depends upon constant feedback from experience.

Thus, as the language user controls experience by naming and describing it, he imposes a pattern through language on the amorphous mass of his human experience. Speaking and understanding in a variety of experiential situations, the child develops a sense of logic in events and words and learns to use language to speak of the world he inhabits. Children's language moves from the specific in experience to the generalization in thought, through the language they have available to respond to experience. From experience they consider possibilities, formulate hypotheses, reach conclusions and make judgments. The ability to handle abstractions grows from previous concrete experience. A child learns by doing and talking about what he has done. The activity classroom exactly fits this natural process by providing experience and open-ended discussion, as well as ample opportunity for debriefing verbal experience. Students talk about their experience to their logs in mono-log and dia-log, to their fellows in small and large group discussions and to others outside of class. This talk, both tentative and explicit, leads to meaningful statement in formal writing and speech. And present talk becomes grist for future thought.

Activities

TALK AND TELL: WHY DO YOU SPEAK?

1 to 1½ hours   *1 person*

To plan more effective and realistic speaking activities for your classes, consider the reasons why people—you or your students—use oral language.

When you communicate do you have a purpose? What are the messages you send to other people? Do you ever say the real message with your gestures or tone of voice? If so, why? Do you ever talk to make yourself feel good? Do you ever say what you think will make someone else feel good? Why? Do you ever talk to impress other people? To convince them or persuade them? How would you talk to your best friend if you wanted him to loan you money? How would you talk to a child who had broken his toy? How would you talk to a fellow worker on the job? How do different situations and people change your reasons for speaking? How do different reasons for speaking change what you say and how you say it?

Think of the different reasons you have used speaking during the past week. Try to remember at least four situations involving different people and reasons for talking. What words did you use in those situations? What was your tone of voice? What were your feelings about the other people? Did your talking accomplish what you intended?

Describe these scenes in your log as if they were scenes from a play. Include stage directions and dialogue. Later, when you want to do some acting with a group, you can turn to this page in your log for some scenes which are already prepared and true-to-life.

THOUGHT POWER:
CAN YOU THINK WITHOUT WORDS?

15 minutes *1 person*

To be more able to help students increase their thinking power by increasing their word power, do this.

Think about these questions: How much do words help you think? Could you think about a wave if you did not know the word? What about a syzygy? Can you think of one of those? Of course you can't, not until you find out what it is. After that you will be able to think of one right away. Look it up and see.

Musicians have many terms to describe the features of music, but to the untrained listener these may be only pleasant sounds. Grammarians have many terms for the features of language so that they may think and talk about these features. Is it easier to think and talk about language, music, mathematics or any other subject when you have many words to describe the way it operates? What advantages might a person have in thinking if he knows many words? How important is the ability to combine words into good sentences that work? Could sentences help you think? How? Does the musician hear more in music because he has more words to tell him what to hear? In what way do we see what we have names for? Can we see things we do not have names for? What do we see? What might someone see who does not have a name for it? If you visit a museum and see strange objects made by primitive people, do you read the sign or label so you will know what the object is? Do you see it differently when you know its function?

What conclusions do you draw about your ability to think without words? What happens to your ability to think when you increase your vocabulary? Of course, that means that you use the words you learn—just learning them and forgetting them would not increase your thinking power. Some people say that if you use a word three times in the first twenty-four hours after you learn it, you will own it forever. Try it!

Make a list of words you hear or read today that you would like to add to your thinking vocabulary. Write the words and their definitions on slips of paper and carry them with you, as book marks or in your pocket, for the next twenty-four hours. Use them whenever you can. The next day tell your log if you feel comfortable using your new words.

WHO? ME?:
MAN TALKS TO HIMSELF

45 minutes some time out of class   *1 person*

If you would like to help students discover how writers make their characters seem like real-life people whose thoughts you can understand, do this activity.

Think about the answers to these questions: Do you ever talk to yourself? Are you sure you don't? Do you talk to yourself in your thinking—maybe replaying a scene in which you think of things you might have said and done but did not do? Maybe you imagine scenes in which you behave in certain ways with certain people—scenes in which you are the kind of person you would like to be. Does everyone do this? Why? How does it help us? What help does it give us in either changing or accepting what we do and have to do in real life?

Watch yourself for a whole day to see if you ever talk to yourself—in your mind, or in whispers or mumbles. When were you most likely to do it? What kinds of things were you thinking about when you did it? Were these more or less important things to you and in your life? Were they concerned with people you were at peace with or with people you were worried about? Is it healthy to talk to one's self? Why? What does it do for us?

Did any of the characters in plays you have read talk to themselves? Consider Shakespeare's plays. What characters talked to themselves? What do we call such talk? What were the subjects of the conversations? What were the circumstances when they occurred?

Tell your log some of your conclusions about when and under what circumstances people talk to themselves.

WANTED!: YOUR SPEAKING NEEDS

20 minutes *1 person*

If you examine your own speaking needs and goals, you will be better able to help students find and examine theirs.

Think about these questions: Are you completely satisfied with yourself as you are? Why do people want to be different? Can you recall events in your life which made you decide to change? Is there someone you would like to be like? Are you ever embarrassed when you talk to others? Would you like to be able to express your feelings more easily? Do you ever speak in haste and later regret what you've said? Do you ever wish other people would pay more attention to your ideas? Would you like to be popular at parties and tell jokes well? How do you feel when you meet strangers? How would you like to feel when you have to give a speech or report before a large group? Would you like to improve your salesmanship or convince others to vote for your candidate? Would it help if you could be more flexible in your word choices? Are you always satisfied with your dialect? Make a list of all the ways you would like to change your use of language.

Examine your list of speaking needs to see what you can do about them. Be both student and teacher to yourself. Give yourself advice about how to solve your language problems. Do you need to acquire self-confidence in speaking? If so, find an activity to meet that need. The activity suggestions in this book may help you.

Write your advice to yourself in your log and use it as a basis for choosing your oral language activities.

LANGUAGE STEW: YOUR MANY LANGUAGES

1 hour *1 person or a group*

To help students become more flexible in their use of language, investigate the importance of setting to language choices.

Think or talk about these questions: Do you speak with members of your own sex in a different way than you speak with members of the opposite sex? Why? Do you share a hobby with others? Are there special words you use with them to talk about what you are doing? Do you have any other special word or language groups?

How do you talk to your employer? To your students or teachers? To friends or your sweetheart? How close to the English of school teachers is the English you ordinarily speak? How do you account for the differences? Are there times when you speak school English because it fits other places besides school? How do you talk at church? How would you talk if you were applying for a job? How would you talk if you were a high school student? How could a high school student use different ways of speaking in different situations?

What differences are there between the way you speak when you speak to several people or a group and the way you speak to one person? Are you aware of what you are doing when you shift from one way of speaking to another?

Make up a character—an ordinary person whose life is a lot like yours or one of your students'—and pretend that you can watch everything he does and see everywhere he goes for one day. What kinds of people does he meet? How does he talk to them? Write down samples of the different conversations he has during the day. If you have a group, you may want to act out these different conversations to show how your character's speech changes according to his situation.

KEEPING UP: DOES LANGUAGE EVER CHANGE?

2 hours   *1 person*

Here is an activity that may help you prepare for students whose interests lead them to wonder about the historical features of language.

Find a copy of *The Canterbury Tales* by Chaucer. In most editions there is a copy of the first eighteen lines of the *Tales* just as Chaucer wrote them and as the people spoke English in 1300. Compare it with the way we speak and write English. What conclusions would you draw about how English has changed? Does it still change? What evidence do you have? What causes language to change? If it is easier to say a word in a certain way, will people who use and hear it often say it the easier way? What happens if many people adopt the new way? Do you say Dee′troit or Detroit′? Which is easier? Which is the wave of the future?

But there is another influence on language to keep it from changing. Society wants all speech to be understandable and clear, so it insists on the preservation of older ways that seem clearer. Compromise moves oral language faster than written language to new forms. New words constantly come into language. Some new words last and others vanish. Which ones are most likely to last?

Look in a large dictionary to see if our words have changed in the ways you think they should. Where else could you find information about why and how language changes? You may want to ask your librarian or teacher.

For those in your class who have not done this activity, make a chart showing five words which were commonly used in Chaucer's time but are not used now, and explain why they are no longer used. Then show five words which were used then and are still used today. Show how and why the meanings of these words have or have not changed and why they have lasted. Also show five words which have been added to our language in the past 25 years, and show why they were added.

PEACE WORDS:
DO YOU USE WORDS TO SUBSTITUTE FOR ACTS?

1 hour   *3 to 7 people*

Help students solve problems with words rather than with less reward-ing or aggressive behavior. Do this activity.

Form a group to plan a skit showing how words might be used instead of violent acts in some conflicts. Begin by discussing these questions: What are some of the problems in our society that could be helped by replacing violence with talk? What does the violence accomplish? How could talk help? Choose one situation you would like to use for your skit. What are the needs of the people involved in this situation? Are their values different? How? How do these groups feel about each other? What would convince them that compromise would serve their interests? What problems might they have in understanding each other? What prejudices might interfere with common sense? How could compro-mises be reached in spite of these difficulties? Could the two or more groups be represented on neutral ground? Would an arbitrator or disin-terested third person to act as a referee be useful? Would it be neces-sary to assure each party that he was being treated fairly? Are there any special words the participants should avoid in the interest of diplomacy?

Perform your skit. You may even want to try several to see how different sorts of problems work out. Tell your logs how you feel about the results.

IT'S GOOD TO BE YOU: SPREADING GOOD FEELING

15 minutes   *a group*

Try this activity with your group to discover how students working in groups in a classroom may build each other's sense of self-assurance and well-being.

Take 15 minutes before your group begins some other work project to discuss these questions: Do you want the other people in your group to think well of you? How will you know if they do? Are they more likely to think well of you if you are approving of them? Why? How do they know what you are thinking about them? How can you show another person that you like him and approve of him, even though you might not agree with his ideas? If one member of your group forgets to be courteous and respectful of others' rights, how can you help him without making the same mistakes? What can you do when you are listening to another's ideas to let him know that you think he is an important person? Can you find ways to let other people know that you are a good person and that your ideas are good without saying that someone else is bad or his ideas are bad? How do you feel about someone who says bad things about others? How do you feel about someone who says good things about others? Why?

Try phrasing your comments in your group today in positive ways, for example: "I like that idea because . . . ." "In your opinion, would this be true also . . . ?" "How do you feel about . . . ?" Try to lead the conversation away from disagreements and suggest alternatives to ideas you don't like.

When your group has finished its project, tell your log how you feel about yourself and the other group members.

TALK IT OUT: TALKING TO A CHAIR

15 to 25 minutes   *2 people*

This activity will give you an experience in using language in the classroom to solve personal problems.

Do some situations seem so full of strangeness and bewilderment that you are confused about what to do? You will not be surprised to know that many other people feel that way too, especially young people, who may lack the experience to give them confidence in new situations. Modern life has many such situations, and we have to find ways to handle them. Try this to develop some techniques: With your partner, sit on either side of a vacant chair, and each of you talk only to the empty chair. Don't talk at all to each other!

Here are some questions you may want to talk about afterward with your partner or write about in your log: What kind of feelings did you get about the chair? Did there seem after awhile to be someone in it? How did you feel about the person on the other side of the chair? Were you more uncomfortable or less so as time went on? Did you keep to the rules and talk only to the chair? You should not expect good results unless you did. What did you talk about? Did what you talked about change as time went on? Why? If you like, try this again or with a different person on the other side of the chair to see how the change affects your feelings.

COFFEE TIME: HAVING A CLASS COFFEE HOUR
several hours   *4 to 6 people*

Doing this activity will give you an experience in planning social events in the classroom for students to practice language skill in a realistic social situation.

Form a group to plan a coffee hour in your classroom. Talk to the teacher and other students to get their approval and cooperation. Will you want to invite others to your coffee hour—relatives or another class? Will you need the other class members to bring food, coffee, money or help clean up afterward; or will your members do those tasks? Will you need the permission of someone higher than your teachers? Who will ask? How will you do it? Will you need to send invitations? Should you talk to the school janitor first? Who will welcome guests? Who will introduce them to class members? What will you say? How can you prepare yourself to remember names? Will your guests have seats or will they stand and mill about? Will you plan an activity for them? How will you see that no one is left out of the conversations? Will you have background music? What will the guests do with their coats? Would it be helpful to each member of your group to have a different task? Would it be helpful to have some people whose tasks are to keep conversations going and see that no one feels left out?

After you have had your coffee hour, make an activity card that you think high school students could use to plan a social event for their class—perhaps a coffee hour for parents or an exhibit of their work. Consider the problems you had and how you overcame them. Try to consider also verbal skills, like making introductions, which high school students might want to practice.

SPREADING THE WORD: MAKING THE CLASS ANNOUNCEMENTS
15 minutes per day for 1 week   *1 person*

To find out how it feels to give the class announcements so that you can better aid students in doing it, do this activity.

Arrange to give the announcements in your class for one week. At intervals during each class period check with the teacher, group leaders, and individuals for items that need to be announced at the end of the class. Post your name and perhaps your telephone number so that anyone who needs an announcement made can tell you. Plan to make announcements of important events ahead of time.

Is it best to make announcements at the end of the period or at the beginning? What are the advantages of each system? Can announcements be made best orally or should they be listed on the blackboard? What are the advantages and disadvantages of each? Could you record announcements on a tape to be played, and play it at the end or beginning of the period? What advantages would there be to this method?

Make your announcements. If a tape is to be played, notify everyone when it will be done and make certain that there is enough time to hear it. Call attention to any announcements you write on the blackboard also.

BRAINSTORMING: WHAT IF . . . ?

1½ to 2 hours   *3 to 5 people*

To help students use talk to extend their abilities to think creatively, do this activity.

Form a group, find writing materials for each person and arrange your seats in a small circle if possible. Ask each person to write on his paper three questions that begin with "What if . . . ?" Your questions may be silly or they may be very serious: What if Thomas Edison had died before he invented the telephone and the light bulb? What if grass were purple? What if all people had only one eye in the middle of their foreheads? What if pollution goes on happening? What if all the people in the world had enough to eat and there were no more poverty? What if we could take a knowledge pill and suddenly know all we needed to know? What if there were no trees?

Ask for a volunteer to read one of his questions first. Ask each person in the group to give his answer. Ask the next person to read one of his questions for the group members to answer, and continue around the circle until everyone has had a chance to ask one of his "what if" questions. At this point you may have new ideas for questions you would like to ask. Write your new questions and continue around the circle with them again.

Which questions received the most interesting answers? In your logs write your favorite "what if" questions and the answers you found interesting. Could you make a story out of them? Could high school students use ideas like these as sources for their writing?

PUTTING IDEAS TOGETHER: THEORIES

variable time *1 person*

To be more able to help students formulate theories and organize their arguments logically, do this activity.

Do you ever make theories? Think about your own theory-making processes. Could you ever have thought something like this: "People are walking down the hall. They are people I have seen in my class; it is 8 o'clock; it must be time to go to class"? What would prove this supposition to be true? How many times during an ordinary day do you put facts together and arrive at a supposition? On the basis of what you see people doing in your class, can you formulate theories about what they are going to do next? When you choose a book in the library, how do you make a judgment about what will be in it? If you must drive through the city, do you make a theory about the quickest route to take? Are your theories always proven right? How important are past experiences in your theory-making? Are there any times when past experiences can't be trusted? When do habit and emotion interfere with your theory-making?

Become an observer of your own thoughts for one day. Can you trace your actions to the thought theories behind them? What are the facts in your experience that led you to make the hypothesis become a theory?

In your log describe as many of your theory-making thoughts as you can for one day.

MINI-SPEECHES: GETTING USED TO SPEECH MAKING

15 minutes per person *3 to 10 people*

After you have finished this activity, you may be able to make both planning and delivering a speech less frightening for students.

Make up a dozen slips of paper and write a topic that interests you on each. It should be something you have heard discussed around school lately. Put the slips in a box; mix them up and let the first speaker draw. Give him ten minutes to make up a short speech on the subject. Five minutes after the first person draws, another should draw. Then everyone gets to draw ten minutes before he speaks. He goes off into a corner to make up his speech. If you plan all this carefully, each person will come back into the group to talk every five minutes, after the first person speaks; and everyone will have ten minutes to prepare.

You may need someone from the help bank to help manage the

business of the drawing, while the others concentrate on their speeches and being good listeners to the speakers.

Tell your log how you felt before, during, and after giving your speech. What did you think of the topic you drew? If you could have changed it, how would you? If you could go back in time and relive your speech, what would you do differently? What advice would you give to the other speakers?

SEEING IS BELIEVING: USING VISUAL DEVICES

10 to 30 minutes   *1 person*

This activity will help you teach students to make their reports or presentations more interesting and easier for their audiences to understand.

What are some of the symbols that are not words that make ideas clear? Make as long a list as you can. What kinds are used in math classes? In social studies classes? Did you ever make a graph? What kinds of things can you show on a graph? Would a design help your presentation? What kind of speech would be helped by a cartoon? Could you use a map? Can you use pictures or other visuals to help "sell" the ideas in your presentation as a billboard promoting a product does? How?

If you do not feel you could make these things but would like to use them, see if someone in the help bank has some skills in making some visual devices for you.

When you prepare your report or presentation, plan to use some of these devices. Afterward, tell your log about it. Were you pleased with the results? Did you put the message across as you wanted? What would you do differently if you could do it over?

AUDIENCE SENSE: MAKING IT EASY FOR YOUR AUDIENCE

10 minutes   *1 person*

To help students improve speech making and report giving, complete this activity.

Are you going to have an audience? Who? What kinds of things would they like to hear? How can you make it easy for them to enjoy what you have to say? How should your voice and movements be to make the audience feel comfortable? Can they all hear you and see you? What are some of the things you will be sure to do? What about your information? How will you be sure they understand your main points? Will they want to? How will you excite their curiosity? How will you keep their interest? Will you emphasize important points? How? Would it be a good idea to summarize? Why? Will you want to ask if there are any questions? At the end only or along the way?

As you plan your speech or report, ask yourself these questions and try to fit the answers into your plan. Keep thinking about the people on the other end of what you are planning to say and how you can make it clear and enjoyable for them. Now give a speech!

SEEING IS BELIEVING: PLANNING A VISUAL DEBATE
1 hour   *1 person*

You will increase your ability to use visual aids and help students use them if you do this.

Select a controversial issue on which students may reasonably disagree. Describe the magazines and kinds of cut-out pictures that students could use to present both the negative and positive sides of the issue. Be specific about listing 10 to 20 kinds of pictures for both sides. Talk to a visual resource person in your school to find out about the various ways pictures may be prepared and presented as visual aids: laminations, slides, collages, posters and so forth.

Show how the debate could be arranged. Who speaks first in a debate? When in the argument would the visual aids be useful? Should they be used to gain attention? When would they be distracting to the audience? How could they be kept out of sight before and after they were needed? How many minutes of the debate time should be spent handling the visual aids—getting them out, explaining them, and putting them away? Should some visuals be saved for the rebuttal? How can you be sure that students will talk to their audience and not to their visual aids? Will other equipment be necessary—an easel, projector, or screen? Make a list of materials students need for this exercise. Will they need cards to read? A pointer? A desk or podium?

Show how this exercise could fit into a larger unit of study. Would it be useful as an introduction, an exercise, a culminating experience? How?

Make a written plan which a group of students could use for a debate.

THE PERSUADER: BEING CONVINCING WHEN YOU SPEAK
40 minutes   *1 person*

If you would like to be able to show students how to sell their points of view to others, do this activity.

Plan a five minute speech to convince your class about something that is important to you. The people you are trying to convince are not very different from you. Use the answers to these questions to guide you in choosing ways to present your arguments: What convinces you when you hear an argument? Do you ever say, "Prove it to me!"? What kinds of evidence do you accept as proof? Because someone says so? Who says so? Whom do you accept as an authority? Do you like a speaker to give examples or illustrations? Are you convinced when he tells you about something that happened to him or a friend of his? What about statistics? What do statistics mean? What kinds of statistics could you use? Where do they come from? Should you always believe them? Do you always understand them? Do you believe every word that is written in *U.S. News and World Report?* What reasons can you give your listeners for believing what you say? Would it help if you have support from several different sources for what you are saying?

Give your speech. In your log write suggestions which might be helpful to a high school student who wants to make a persuasive speech.

GETTING THE PICTURE: WHAT DO YOU SEE FIRST?
1 hour   *2 people*

Investigate how you see so that you may better help students with their struggles to bring their global impressions into the concrete realm of language.

Find a partner and plan to do this activity. Each of you needs to look through magazines at home and choose several large color pictures to bring to class at the next meeting. Choose pictures which have a strong emotional mood and also detail. Do not let your partner see the pictures before the activity.

Ask your partner to turn his back while you place one of the pictures face down on a desk. With your partner watching, turn it over just long enough for him to see it. Replace the picture, face down. Ask your partner to tell you what he remembers about the picture. When he can think of nothing else, show him the picture again. Ask him what he noticed this time. Trade places, and this time you look at your partner's picture. You may want to do this several times with different pictures.

Afterward discuss these questions: How often do you study life for details? When you write or talk about an event, how often must you do it from memory? What were the first words you said about the pictures? Which is easier to notice first, the over-all mood or the details? Why? What were the hardest parts of the picture to remember? Did differences in the pictures affect what you noticed first? How? Did talking about the pictures change the way you felt about them? How? Did talking about them impress them on your memory? Did you ever describe something that you later discovered was not in the picture? Why might that happen?

ALL ALONE: GIVING A SOLILOQUY

1 to 2 hours   *1 person*

If you do this activity, you will be better prepared to help students with their dramatic speaking activities.

Find a soliloquoy that you would like to recite for your group or class. Read the lines, trying to put yourself in the character's place. What has happened to him in the past to make this point in the drama necessary? How is the character feeling about the other people in the story? How is he feeling about himself? Do his feelings change as he speaks? Does he arrive at a resolution? Picture him in your mind as you read the words he speaks. How does his expression change with each thought? How do his gestures show his emotions? Does he pace up and down? Is he steady on his feet? Does he waver? Does he sit? Do his shoulders slump? Does he raise his eyes to heaven or look downward? Does he look into space at something his audience cannot see? Does he see visions in his own mind or is his gaze fixed upon happenings or people on the stage? Is his voice loud or soft? Is he overwrought or listless? You may want to practice your soliloquoy in front of a mirror.

Give your soliloquoy. Tell your log how you felt. Would a high school student feel as you did? How could you help him deal with those feelings?

LIVING POETRY: NARRATING A DRAMATIC POEM

1 to 2 hours   *1 person or a group*

If you do this activity, you will be better able to help students who want to dramatize poetry.

Form a group or work alone to present a dramatic poem. "Death of the Hired Man" by Robert Frost or "Get Up and Bar the Door," an old English Ballad, are examples of choices you might make. Whether you are planning to work as a group or alone, you will need to plan how you will show the action of the poem to your audience. If you have a group, you may want to have one person read the poem while the other members act out the scene in pantomime. Or, you might want to have different members speak lines. If you are working alone, you can still mimic different characters by adopting a different stance and expression for each one. You may want to change your voice or have props which you switch for different characters. Some entertainers have used hats to help the audience identify different characters. Or, you may find background music that will help your audience visualize your poem's drama.

However, whether you are working as a group or alone, do not let the supporting scene, actions, props or music overshadow the reading. To be sure of your effect on the audience, practice and have a friend or two view your performance before you give it to the class.

Present your narrative. Be sure to record your problems and how you solved them in your logs so that when you are helping students, you can find ways to avoid problems you had this time.

SELL YOURSELF: MAKING YOUR FOLDER PRESENTATION
20 minutes   *1 person*

Prepare yourself to help students think about and talk about their language learning by presenting a talk for your teacher about your class work.

Consider these questions: What do you want your teacher to think and feel about you as a result of your talk? Have you prepared summaries, materials, a log, samples of your work, in a folder so that your teacher can see proof of what you have done? How can you make your folder a good advertisement for you? What arguments can you use to persuade your teacher that you have learned what you should as a result of this class? Can you set forth your objectives, what you did to attain them, and your proof of your efforts? Can you use this talk to demonstrate what you have learned? How can you be sure you will be able to remember everything you want to say? How can you be sure you will be able to find just the right items in your folder to show? How will you choose your words? Will you want to dress in any special way? Will you be expected to shake hands? What questions can you expect your teacher to ask? Are there any questions you want to ask?

Prepare your talk and your folder. Make an appointment to talk to the teacher.

TELL THE TEACHER: TEACHER CONFERENCE FIRST AID

15 minutes   *1 person*

Here is one way to solve the problem of not being able to schedule a teacher-student conference. To discover its advantages and disadvantages for you as a teacher or student, try it.

Have you ever had problems finding a good time to talk to a teacher? As a teacher, you may find your schedule filled. Arrange to have a tape recorder conference with the teacher of this class. It's much easier to find a time to listen to a tape than to a live person. Leave the tape on the teacher's desk with your name attached or spoken into the tape to identify yourself. Then, tomorrow, collect your tape and see what answer the teacher has left you.

To know how your students might feel about taped conferences, analyze your own feelings about them. How did you feel about not being able to give or receive any immediate feedback? Were you satisfied with what you said and the answers you received? Why or why not? Were there any technical problems? Would students feel comfortable with this system? Why or why not? Tell your log.

LANGUAGE HELPER: JOIN THE HELP BANK

10 minutes   *1 person*

Here is an activity which may give you practice in helping others with language problems.

What special language skills do you have that might be helpful to others? Schedule an interview with the teacher to see how your skills might be most helpful. Then write an advertisement for the help bank card file stating your name, your special skills, and the conditions under which you will give help—such things as previous appointments a day in advance or an appointment out of class time.

Don't forget to tell your log about what you discover as a result of helping others.

SPEAKING IN GROUPS

From the beginning, language is the child's prime social instrument. Growth in it parallels emergence from the self-centered to the social world, and language growth is greatest when there is interaction of minds and personalities. Language skills develop as the child feels a need to communicate. Children pattern and repattern, but adult reinforcement and pressure returns them again and again to culturally accepted patterns of language. If a child is to learn language well, he must be listened to attentively by adults and peers who respond to him, appreciate his efforts, and encourage him. They will not criticize him or make him feel that his efforts to use language are accompanied by pain, failure, or embarrassment. The child will speak most and grow in ability to speak well if he feels secure in his speaking and believes he can use language to achieve his purposes. Verbal play, puns, and word fun help him grow. The internalization of his external dialogue brings the tools of language to bear on the stream of his thought. His perceptions, conceptions, and intuitions about the objective world arise from the socialized speech he engages in, his most important experience.

The humanistic activity teacher respects the ability of all students to communicate. Schools often underestimate students' verbal competence. But if students communicate less with school officials and within classes than they do with their peers and outside of classes, their failure is a function of the school, not of their own inadequacy, and the school setting must be reconstructed so that they do there what they do elsewhere within their dialect groups and with their peers. Students' classroom lapses into apathy, silence or confused, incoherent noise demand a change in the school before students will change.

Students need constant classroom talk if language growth is to occur, and if the school insists on silence in the classroom, or if the teacher believes that students grow best when he is talking and students are quiet, growth in the language proficiency of his students will be retarded. To unleash his linguistic skills, a student needs endless conversation about his experiences with his peers and with adults in a nonthreatening atmosphere. Student-student talk is needed by those unready to talk to teachers. A demand for classroom silence destroys the best instrument for student growth in language proficiency that the classroom affords. It constrains the natural instinct the child has to pursue what he needs most, verbal interaction, that source of his earliest and most natural avenue of language growth. The activities of the class should channel this urge to communicate and use it for the growth of the child, not stifle it into silence.

For the humanistic curriculum in English the primary resource of experience for students is interaction between students. From this oral language activity, percepts develop. Interactive speaking experience gives each the feedback that stimulates him to constant action and appraisal of his actions. It is virtually impossible for one teacher to furnish a roomful of students the stimulation and constant feedback that a class of students can furnish each other. Yet this resource is constantly sacrificed to the brave but futile struggle of one teacher to accomplish interaction with all students. Teachers fight a losing battle to see how many students they can get to participate in a class discussion, when it is obvious that only a few can participate. If several participate, they can do so only infrequently in the form of class "recitation."

The student learns to speak if he is motivated to speak of his own world. From his own experience comes the need to discuss it, and meeting this need, the student grows in language maturity. The student must be thrust into situations where relationships between the ideas he is experiencing cause him to seek ever more sophisticated sentence structures to express them. Social sharing is fundamental to this teaching and learning of language, and opportunity for such sharing is vital to the development of language proficiency. The class must be organized to use, not thwart, the natural desire of students to interact with other students. The very irrepressibility of this urge is a clue to its importance and to the student's knowledge of his own best avenue of growth.

Interaction with peers enables students to gather information, select pertinent ideas and relationships, reorganize these into solutions for problems, attain openmindedness, and grow in willingness to explore solutions with a critical attitude. When a student has had an experience with language, he should have opportunity to explain to others how he has achieved it, both for his own reinforcement and for their edification. In such a situation he debriefs language experience, seeing where he has come and how he got there.

With the philosophy that peer interaction is most likely to produce language growth, the activity teacher will make constant use of small group activity as a device superior to individual work or teacher-directed, large-group activity. It produces learning needed in life because it is like life. It increases the number of students who respond verbally and makes them respond more often. It makes students more active in producing oral language, the basis for all language learning. It frees the timid from fears engendered by adults or large groups. It controls the dominant through group pressure and decreases the teacher domination characteristic of traditional classrooms. It replaces unnatural, forced pressures with natural pressures arising from interaction with peers.

Discussion must have a clear goal, purpose, progress and conclusion. But the teacher should limit sharply his participation in small-group activities. Such participation is more likely to be destructive than not. He may, on occasion, ask questions and suggest materials, especially where there is deadlock. He can prod, goad, and encourage search. He can urge comparison of ideas. He can suggest structures for forwarding consensus. He can help students foresee results of their decisions and their choices, not by telling them what those results will be but by insisting that they make forecasts which are reasonable and logical and do not ignore the implications of the data they have gathered. He helps students evaluate their actions. But the activity teacher does not give truths, correct answers or interrupt.

Students who talk out problems can be led to examine the use of evasive language or gobbledegook. Listening to or using these linguistic evasions deadens awareness of reality. Students may begin to think that words mean nothing and not expect them to mean anything. It is difficult to help students to see what language really means when an atom bomb test is called "Operation Sunshine" or Viet Nam generals say they must destroy a village to save it. Examining what is said to them and by them, students assess realities which lie behind words. Language must be seen as a way to help people do good things instead of bad things.

As the primary skill of English, speaking should pour in an endless stream over every language arts activity. However, traditional activities of courses in public speaking—the elitism of competitive teams and contests, the spoken rote with various devices inserted to simulate spontaneity—are outdated to the point of quaintness. Cooperative, not competitive, speaking sharpens skills in greatest need today. Reaching consensus, not putting another and his ideas down, is the aim of today's speech. Thus, cooperative and informal speech skills are the objective of the humanistic English class. Students learn to speak to others in ways which reflect their own sincerity and thought, listening courteously and sympathetically and attempting to find points of agreement and ground for consensus, not sharpening disagreements. They form habits of speaking in ways that will help their listener's self-concept and build his good feelings about himself and others, not ways that intensify or create unease. Furthermore, the student is not taught vocal variation or gesture as decoration for his speech, as ways to lend it credence, but as ways to be more fully honest about what he believes and to enhance unity between what he feels and how he expresses what he feels. An ethical dimension should be apparent to students.

Nor will oral language ability produce dramas which are used for school fund-raising campaigns, as school dramas have so often been. Nor is it part of the dying sensitivity fad, although the fringe excesses of that phenomenon should not close our thought to useful things that might be learned from it. Theories about acting out and creation of roles help students to build new roles for demands of the lives they will live, new ways of playing old roles and new understandings of the roles others play. Students must learn to make endangered institutions of society work, by playing creative, effective, and satisfying roles in them. To such aims classroom drama is directed, developing insight and generalization as part of the language growth of the student.

Shakespeare's Jacques was right. All the world is a stage, and all the men and women are players. And students who are to become effective men and women on the world's stage need more and more varied abilities to enact the increasingly varied roles they are called upon to play, as they extend the arena of their activities. Students need to learn how they are capable of reacting and how to react more creatively and variously. Throughout life they accumulate new roles. The humanistic classroom must provide occasions when they can try out a large repertoire of possible roles and judge which ones fit them best. Confronting a rapidly changing experience, a student must change, shift, and adapt roles, learning new ones and adding to his store of ways to answer the world. His process of maturing is a kind of role expansion, through using roles consciously and unconsciously. Bringing this process to the level of conscious thought enables students to increase their control over it.

British schools have used drama importantly in the teaching of English. Suggestions of British educators about oral language have been echoed by many educators in this country, but they have not been widely followed. However, humanistic curriculum makes oral language experiences a central element in classroom activities.

Ancient man knew the importance of acting out to help man know the meaning of his world and to control it. High on the walls in the ice age caves of Spanish Altimira is a picture of a beast whose image was pierced by an arrow by the primitive painter. His painting acted out the results he hoped to obtain in hunting. The Greeks acted out in religious ritual their problems and their solutions. Medieval drama embodied rituals celebrating the miracles of faith. Although drama in our own time has lost much power to move and change behavior, the classroom can resurrect this power where improvisations and acting out are important in teaching English.

A useful structure for oral language learning is the game or simulation. These games are different in their aim from English games of the past that were ways to teach spelling and other aspects of the language arts. They do not have as their aim the production of a winner. Everyone wins, in the sense that everyone gains insight into himself as a result of the game.

In simulation a central problem is identified and stated. Those concerned in the problem are identified by role. A point of crisis in which an action concerning the problem must be taken is selected, and those concerned in the problem constitute the roles participants play in the simulation. They act out viewpoints implied in each of their roles, engaging in conflict and conflict resolution mechanics devised as they play. After the group makes its decision about the crisis situation, the group debriefs by analyzing the process through which they have passed, gaining insight into each of the roles and viewpoints represented and the feelings of each participant as he pushed his role to victory, defeat or compromise.

Because traditional games produce a winner whose triumph is considered appropriate, they encourage and reward competition. Learning simulations encourage cooperation by showing that winners are not always justified and triumphs over others are not as effective in human relations as careful treatment of minorities and compromises that take into consideration the rights of all. Winners do not necessarily feel good about winning nor do losers always feel bad about losing. In many cases there do not need to be either winners or losers. Simulations often create communities or groups who deal with real problems. There is involvement with many roles. Role switching allows each to explore how others feel. The simulation should eventuate in dispelling conflict, self acceptance, and regard for others.

The humanistic teacher who uses the endless resources of oral language activity has a strong opportunity to build reservoirs of trust in students. Students' lives are saturated by ecopopulation pressures, the acts of violence and injury men perpetrate on each other, and there is little in their lives to reinforce attitudes of caring for others. Too often students have lost patience with systems, laws, and orderly processes. They escalate negative behavior and open defiance because they feel frustrated in making complaints. If human frustration is to be handled short of chaos, we must create a climate and systems that dissolve distrust and forge new values from the fragmented rootlessness of a physically mobile society, with its frozen social, economic, and class structures. Students who have had a part in inventing and operating systems that work are more likely to believe in systems, in whatever works for compromise, accommodation and consensus, and in resort to law for stability and structure. They learn to invent communication avenues, avenues of change, decreasing tension and distrust. The teacher can work by example to show that they can avoid even wanting to stifle points of view unlike their own. Participating in oral language activities in the classroom, the student should cultivate hospitality, not hostility to ideas of others.

Activities

ROSE COLORED GLASSES: WHAT CAN YOU CONTROL WITH WORDS?

2½ hours 2 or 3 class meetings   *3 to 6 people*

To help students use language as an effective tool and to help them see how they as well as others use it to modify experience, investigate the ways people use words to control what happens to them.

Form a group and discuss these questions: In church what do people try to control with words? How would you describe church ritual as attempts to control what happens to us with words? How do political speeches try to control events with words? Why do people talk about the weather so much? Are there any words people say that are designed to ward off supernatural happenings? What kind of people most frequently make such attempts? What kind of people are most likely to believe that words are magic? Why? Can you give some examples of the belief that if you talk about an event in a certain way often enough, it will become true? Can saying something painful make it happen? Why or why not? How does saying something painful in a nicer way affect how we feel about it?

If you want to believe something, does writing it down make it seem more real? If you want to believe something, does finding someone to agree with you make your idea right or your belief true? If you read contradictory statements by two authors, which will you choose to believe——the one whose idea agrees most with your own beliefs or the other? Why? If you hear on the five o'clock news that your house has burned down and rush home only to discover that the story was a mistake, how was your world changed during the time that you believed the story? If words make you believe a falsity is a fact, do you behave as if the fact were true? How would it be true for you if you believed it and how would it not be true? Would you be wiser if you checked first to see if the story were true, before you acted on the information? In real life would you?

Together, make a list of ways people try to control what is happening to them as you observe this for one day. You may want to observe yourselves—how much you try to overcome difficulties by talking in a certain way. Meet again as a group to discuss what you have observed and how successful the efforts of people to control their worlds are.

Choose several situations in which people attempted to control their experiences with words and act these out in your group. According to how you feel about your acting success, you may or may not want to act out one or more scenes for the class as a whole.

KICK THE HABIT: WHY QUARREL?

30 minutes   *3 people*

To be more able to help your students in their communication problems with each other, do this activity.

Have you ever been involved in a quiet talk that gradually turned into a quarrel? What were your feelings when things were quiet? Did you become frustrated? Why or why not? What do you think the other person was feeling? What happens when a quiet talk turns into a loud quarrel? Can you remember how it happened? What do the two people have to be feeling? What do they say to each other to make those feelings happen?

What could you say to someone if you wanted to hurt him or make him angry? Have you ever said things like that on purpose? If you were trying *not* to quarrel, could you think of any things to say that would make the other person feel good or that might show him that you respect him, his point of view, and his right to express it? What could you say to him?

When you get involved in quarrels, does it happen most with younger people, older people or with people your own age? Would you say the same things to an older person to make him feel angry or good that you would say to someone your own age? Why or why not?

Now try out your answers to these questions by acting out some quarrel situations. Find two friends and go to the "talk corner." Think of some person you quarrel with often and ask one of your friends to pretend to be that person. Describe to your friend the person he is supposed to be, and describe for him the circumstances in which you most often quarrel. Start a dialog with him pretending to be in that situation.

Your other friend is the listener. His job is to listen and even to take notes if he needs to so that he can tell both of you afterward about the things you said and how you acted that caused the greatest good and bad emotions in each other. After you have acted out the scene, ask your two friends to switch places and try it again. Then ask one of your friends to be you and you be the listener.

Did you discover things you did not know about your own behavior? How did you feel when you were watching your friend play you? Why? How did your friends feel? Did you discover anything about making people feel good or bad when you are talking to them? What? How do you want them to feel? How do you feel when you quarrel? Why? What can you do to prevent misunderstandings when you are talking?

Discuss these questions with your friends. Then tell your log about what you discovered and how you feel about it.

QUICK!: WHO GIVES THE ORDERS?

variable time   *3 to 8 people*

Do this to help students sort out their feelings about situations in which they must either give or take orders.

Meet as a group and read this story aloud or pass it around so that everyone can read it.

"Orderly, get me a tank of oxygen. Quick!" This was the command that the young intern barked out as he ran up to orderly Sam Smith who was, at the time, carrying out his normal duties in the operating room suite. Being a member of the operating staff, Sam was used to emergencies. He immediately dashed down the corridor to get the tank of oxygen.

Sam returned in a matter of minutes and asked the intern what he should do with it. The intern told him to take it to the amphitheater, where it was needed for a class demonstration. Sam, upon learning that there was no emergency in one of the operating rooms, flatly refused to take the oxygen tank to the amphitheater, telling the intern that this was not a part of his job. The intern was at first stunned by Sam's refusal; however, it was readily apparent that he did not remain stunned long, as the color of his face turned a deep red. The intern shouted, "Well, we'll just see about that!" He stalked off.

What happened to make those two people behave as they did? Talk about it. In instances when the care of a patient is involved, why is the word of the doctor law? Outside the area of patient care, what happens to the doctor's authority? Why? Do you know any other situations similar to this? Tell the group about your experiences. Are there people who have authority over you in one situation and not in another? What happens when people overstep their authority? What happens when a policeman invades a private home without a warrant? How can misunderstandings like the one in the story be prevented? What could the intern have done differently? What could the orderly have done differently?

Act the scene out the way you think it should have happened. Do it several times so that everyone has a chance to add his solution to the problem. Can there be more than one right way to solve a communication problem? See if your group can act out similar incidents from your own lives.

THE UNWORDS: WORD SUBSTITUTES

1 hour or more   *1 person or a group*

Do this and you will discover some ways your students' world speaks to them without words.

Does a traffic signal tell you something? What? What does the line down the middle of the road tell you? Does your teacher's face tell you anything about what he or she feels? What does a toddler do when he wants his mother to pick him up? Does she get the message? Why? Do the pictures in advertisements send you any messages beside the ones printed? What? What kind of message does the bell at a railroad crossing send you? Our world is loaded with unwords. See how many you can find. Start with where you are now. What do you do when the bell rings? How many unwords can you find at school?

If you have a group, make an unword dictionary. If you are working alone, find some pictures to illustrate your unwords and display some of them on the bulletin board.

STEERING COMMITTEE: STRUCTURE YOUR PRODUCTIONS

variable time   *3 to 5 people*

To prepare yourself for the organizational tasks of an activity classroom, do this.

If the activities of your class have to be scheduled in order for people to use materials that are too scarce to go around and if you need to schedule activities that require the attention of the whole class, plan a steering committee. If you would like to serve on it or would like to nominate someone who would be a good person to serve on it, give your name or your friend's name to the teacher. Ask the teacher to call a meeting of all those whose names he receives, and you can elect a chairman who can conduct an election of permanent members or members who will serve until the class decides they want another election.

After the members have been elected, you should meet to discuss your responsibilities: How will you find out about the activities that need to be scheduled? Will you have a sign-up sheet? What will you do if two groups or individuals disagree over who should have a certain time or certain piece of equipment? Who will decide, and on what basis? Will it be "first come, first served" or will you consider who has the greatest need? What could your group do to prevent such disagreements from happening? How far in advance should your schedule be made? For how long a time should any one group be able to keep equipment?

Tell your log about your problems and successes. Make suggestions that will help you in your own classroom.

INSIDE-OUT: GETTING READY TO PLAY A ROLE
15 minutes   *a group member*

To be more able to help sudents prepare for role-playing and be convincing in the roles they will play, do this activity.

Participate in a group performing a skit. Before you play your role, think about these questions: How will you find out what you need to know in order to play the person realistically? If it is a person in a book, should you research the book? How could you prepare to play a public figure or a person in history? What are the ways you might find out about your character? Use all of these ways and make a list of them.

Will you want to know what your character is like in his mind as well as how he looks? How can you find this out? Is it useful to know how other people feel about him? How can you find this out? If the character is one from your own imagination, talk to your imagination until you find out all that a story or play would tell you. How does a person like the one you have discovered in your investigation look and talk and behave?

Now do you feel comfortable and sure about what your character is like? Can you imagine that you are the character? Why is it best to think that you are the character rather than that you are you playing the character?

After your role-playing, tell your log if you were able to get inside the character. Did the person you were playing seem real to you? Why? How did you feel about the experience?

READY, SET, GO!: REHEARSING AND PREPARING

15 minutes   *a group*

To help students prepare for their performances in the classroom, prepare yourself for your skit by doing this.

Talk or think about these questions: Are you scared at the prospect of putting on a skit? Are you afraid you might forget what you are supposed to do or say? What if you were going to recite the ABC's? Would you forget even the alphabet if you were scared? How is that different from your part in the skit? If you knew your part as well as you know the ABC's, would it make you more confident of your memory?

Are you afraid your performance might not be convincing? When real people talk to each other, what makes them convincing? How do they know what to say next? Does it come from listening to what the other person says? How do people look when they are listening in a real conversation? Should an actor be listening to what the other actors say, or should they just be waiting for their cues if they want to be realistic?

Are you afraid you will make a mistake? What would happen if you did? Would the audience forgive you if you did not giggle or act silly about your mistake? If you are really listening to the others in the skit perhaps you will not worry as much about the audience.

Are you afraid that you will not be understood? You must speak much more loudly when you speak to several people who are not near you than you do when you speak to those who are close to you. Try to think as you speak that you are really talking to someone at the other end of the hall. Be sure you get a deep breath so that you will have enough breath for the last words in your sentences.

Would high school students have the same fears you have? Might they have any other fears? How could you help them relax before a performance? What happens before a ball game? What do players do, especially before a basketball game? Can you invent some warm-up exercises to use before a performance? What about dancing? What are some of the warm-up exercises you learned in kindergarten? Try shaking your hands, then your arms, to music. Try shaking your feet and then your head.

Perform a skit. Be sure to tell your log how you prepared for it and how you felt during the performance.

SKITTING: YOUR SKIT IDEA

1 hour   *a group*

This activity will give you ways of helping students to choose skit ideas which suit their needs and interests.

Find a group of people who would like to perform a skit. To find a skit which will fit the needs of your group, discuss these questions: How does the number of people affect the kind of skit you can perform? How many people could possibly be involved in the performance of a radio show skit? A television commercial? A dialogue between characters from history or a book? Could your group do a crowd scene from a play? Could you find scenes from your own experiences to use for your skit? Could you act out a family problem? Have you heard of an interesting event from a friend? What is happening in the news? Could your group act out a scene from the news? Would you like to interview a celebrity? Could you use scenes and stories from your favorite novel or drama as the basis for a skit? What about your favorite song or poem?

Is it necessary to include only what is in the literary work, or can you change and add to the ideas? Can you add characters or take them out? Could you change the setting to fit your classroom's restrictions? Could you change the outcome of the story? Would you like to read from the story or poem? Could you pantomime to a background of music or reading?

Decide upon a subject for your skit and how you will deal with it. Decide whether or not you will act it out as it comes to you or rehearse it first. Will you have a script? Will you read or memorize? Will you have props and a set? Will you perform for an audience or just for yourselves?

When you have made all these decisions, perform your skit. Record your feelings about your performance in your log and make suggestions which you could use with high school students who are trying to prepare a skit.

TRY TAPE!: TAPING YOUR SKIT

variable time   *a group*

If you do this, you may have a better understanding of the problems, joys, advantages and disadvantages of using tape in oral language activities.

Find a group to perform a skit. You may want to use a skit idea from another activity. Locate a tape recorder. Make sure you have tape for it. You may want to buy your own so that you can save it. Reserve the recorder for the times that you will need it. Be sure that it has a microphone and an extension cord if you need one. Check it to be sure everything works. Everyone in your group should know how to operate the recorder with confidence. Take as much time as you need to become familiar with it.

Whether or not it is necessary to have a script, it can be very useful— even if you decide not to follow it all the time. You may find it useful and fun to rearrange the parts of your script or leave them out or add to them. You will enjoy making up your own sound effects too. Record a short segment then replay it to see if it sounds the way you wanted it to. Erase whatever part you didn't like and do it over. Different members may want to try out different parts to see whose voice sounds most convincing as those characters.

Some people like to record the sound part of their skits and then perform the actions to the sounds of their own voices. Some groups like to pretend that their recorded skits are radio programs.

Present your recorded skit for the class.

AFTERWARD: DEBRIEFING YOUR SKIT

15 minutes   *a group*

To be more able to guide students in thinking about and talking about their experiences, do this activity.

After your group has performed a skit, meet to discuss these questions: How did you feel when you played the role? Did you become the character? Did you feel what you said? Did you say what you felt? Did the other characters respond to your character as you thought they should? How did you feel about the other characters? How was playing the role like living the story? How was it not like living the story? Did you forget the audience? How did you feel about the audience? Did you think they approved of your performance? Were you afraid they would be critical? Were they? Did you look at the audience? Why or why not? Did you giggle? Did you ever want to? Why or why not? If you made a mistake, how did you feel about it? Why? After you had finished, how did you feel? Were you proud? Relieved? How did you feel about the story? About the characters? About the author? Would you change anything about your performance? If so, what? Did members of the audience make any comments afterward? How did the comments make you feel?

Comment about your reactions to the skit and the debriefing in your log. Did talking about the experience and your feelings about it change your feelings in any way? If so, how?

THE SECRET SCENE: KEEPING SECRETS IN IMPROVISATIONS
30 minutes   *3 to 4 people*

If you do this activity you will be able to help students acquire poise, confidence, and appropriate words to say in difficult or embarrassing situations.

Form a group to do improvisations. Agree in advance that one of you will not know something that all the others will know. The aim will be for him to get you to say something that will tell him what you know that he does not. Then plan a scene where each of you plays a character. Decide which character does not know the secret, and do not let the person playing the character know the secret. Discuss for several minutes in advance who the characters are, what their relationship to each other is and what is going to happen in the scene—everything but the secret, which all of you know but one.

Then begin your scene and see how long it is before the character player guesses the secret. You may want to plant clues for him if he does not guess for several minutes. Your aim should be to work with the situation in as natural a way as possible and make the revelation of the secret to the person as much as you can as it would be in real life in a conversation where each of us is continually finding out things he did not know.

You may want to try this activity with two persons unaware of the secret. Another way to manage the situation is to have improvisation going for several minutes before some of the characters join it. They should not be able to hear what is happening before they enter the scene, just as happens in real life.

After the improvisation discuss how the person feels who comes into a group which already has information that he does not. How long does it take him to get comfortable? When does he get comfortable? How important is sharing everything with others? How do we build trust in others?

FAST TALK: EXTEMPORANEOUS SPEAKING
variable times   *4 to 15 people*

Practice extemporaneous speaking so that you may experience the problems and feelings you will need to consider in planning extemporaneous speaking activities for your students.

Form a group to practice extemporaneous speaking. Pull your desks or chairs into a circle. Without showing the person next to you, write three topics that you would like either to talk about or hear about in a short speech. Draw straws or ask for volunteers to find someone to take the first turn. The person to speak first takes the paper with the three topics on it from the person on his right. He chooses one of the three to talk about. He is allowed three minutes to prepare what he will say and three minutes to talk. (You will find it useful to elect a timekeeper.) When his three minute preparation time is finished he hands his topic paper to the person on his left, and that person goes to the hall to prepare while the first speaker is talking. This continues with each speaker so that one person is in the hall while the other is speaking until the last person speaks.

When you have each spoken, discuss your experience. Were you satisfied with your topic? Why or why not? Did you have any problems thinking of what to say? Did you think of more to say when your talk was over? Did you listen to what other people had to say and show interest? Do you remember what they said? Did others seem interested in what you said? How do you feel about what you said? Would you do anything differently? Were you relieved when your turn was over? Why? Would you like to try this again? Why or why not?

HAVE A PUNNY DAY: PLAY WITH PUNS
30 minutes   *3 to 6 people*

To find ways that students may discover the joys of manipulating words, do this activity.

Find a group to talk about puns: What happens to the sounds of words when you make puns? You may want to find some puns written by famous authors and see what they have done to words to make puns. Shakespeare uses many puns. How do you feel when you hear or read puns? Why? Are puns sometimes silly? Are they easy to make up? Why do so many people use puns?

Start with the word "pun." Can you put your hot dog in a pun? Can you opun the window? If you do what will hapun? Will you be punished? How many punny funnies can your group invent? Do you know any "knock-knock" jokes? Are they puns? Look for puns in the newspaper and in magazines. Do you hear puns in conversations?

With your group make up a punny story. You might want to start, "Once upun a time . . . "

LAUGH TOGETHER: WHAT IS FUNNY?

1 hour some out of class   *3 to 6 people*

To help students enjoy and consciously examine language in their lives, investigate the ways language is used to make people laugh.

Form a group to talk about and share jokes and cartoons. Begin by finding some examples of what makes you laugh. At home each of you should listen for jokes or comments that seem funny to you. Write them down. Look through newspapers and magazines to collect a variety of jokes and cartoons which appeal to you. Bring your examples to class, and talk with your group about your discoveries.

Work together to see if you can sort your funny choices into several categories. Here are some questions which may help you: Do different jokes make you feel different ways? Is all laughter the same? Why or why not? Does the way the jokes make you feel have anything to do with the reason you laugh? Try to decide why each selection makes you feel like laughing. Could you sort them according to the ways they make you feel? How do puns make you feel? Why do some people groan when they hear them? Are some jokes deliberately absurd? Find some examples from your selections. Are some misstatements or overstatements? Find examples. Do some show situations that you recognize from your own life? Why do they seem funny to you? Are some very silly? Do you laugh even though they are obviously silly? Why? Can you categorize jokes and cartoons according to their subjects? Do you have any animal jokes? Political cartoons? Spaceman jokes? Jokes about marriage?

When you are satisfied with the way you have sorted your cartoons and jokes, choose your favorite ones and present them to the class. You may find that some are very effectively dramatized as short skits. Others may simply be read or recited. You may choose to present some comments on why the jokes are funny and why you chose them, or you may let your audience make their own judgments.

GADABOUTS: YOUR OWN TALK SHOW
2 hours   *3 to 10 people*

Try this activity to become familiar with a technique for classroom speaking activities.

Form a group to stage your own talk show like ones you have seen on television. If you have a video-tape recorder you may want to use it. If not, perform your talk show live for the class. Meet as a group to make plans. Here are some questions which may help you: What talk shows have you seen on television? Is one person the host or hostess? What kind of personality does the host or hostess have? Does he need to know how to encourage his guests to talk if they are shy or shut them up if they talk too much? How does he do that? Does he ever give the commercials or prepare you for the commercials? How does he talk to the audience? Does he ever make you feel that you are in the same room? If so, how does he make you feel that way? Who in your group would be a good host or hostess? Could you have auditions?

What other people are necessary for your talk show? Will you need a cameraman? Who would like to find out how to operate a video-tape machine? Would a director be useful to see that the right events happen at the right times? What will you do about commercials? How many guests should you have? Does that depend upon the time you plan to spend? What kinds of people are usually guests on talk shows? Should you have a script writer to find or write funny or witty ideas for the host or hostess?

Although a talk show is impromptu, you may want to try a little of it first to see how it works, especially if you are going to perform it live for the class. Perform your talk show or record it on tape to show the class.

BLACKS MEET WHITES: TALKING OVER ISSUES
25 minutes   *6, 8, or 10 people*

To be able to help students talk over racial differences in point of view and apply language skills to the solving of social problems, use this activity.

Form a group of two teams with 3, 4, or 5 black people and 3, 4, or 5 white people. Choose a topic from current news events which most or all of you feel strongly about. Ask the black people to decide how they think whites would feel about the topic and the whites to decide how they think the blacks would feel about it. Ask the blacks to play the parts of the whites and the whites to play the parts of the blacks. Some people make themselves white or black masks to wear when they do this.

When you have heard how the other group thinks you think, tell them what you really think and see how your ideas were different. Did hearing the other group say what they thought you thought change your opinions? If so, how? In what ways were you wrong about what you thought the other group thought?

Write your conclusions about this activity in your log. Did you make any discoveries about your own feelings? About the feelings of others?

INVESTMENT IN THE FUTURE: JOB INTERVIEWS
2 hours 2 or 3 sessions   *2 people*

When you have completed this activity you will be more able to help students acquire the verbal skills which will help them get jobs.

Find a partner. Work together to make a list of jobs your students might want to apply for. Be realistic. Remember that they will not be college or even high school graduates. From your list select four jobs which might be appropriate for the various potentials within your classes. Act out interviews for these jobs. Take turns being either the applicant or the hiring official.

To help you plan your role playing, you may find it useful to make a list of questions an employer would want to ask. Perhaps you might like to conduct some research on what questions interviewers ask. Could you consult your school's guidance office? Could you get a sample application to fill out? How could you find out more about the requirements of the four jobs you have chosen? Could you construct a written interview, leaving spaces for the answers?

How can you make your interview scenes as realistic as possible? Should you dress for the interviews in any special way? What could you tell your students about wearing certain kinds of dress? Would you use special language? Why? How will the hiring official react to your language? The interviewing partner may add some unexpected questions if you want to give yourselves practice in answering questions you did not know would be asked.

What questions might the prospective employee have a right to ask the employer? When you go into the interviewer's office, and he asks you to sit down, do you reply? How? How do you shake hands if the interviewer extends his hand? Practice shaking hands. What kind of a handshake feels confident and polite? Would it be a good idea to tell the interviewer how you heard of the position? How would that help your cause? Have you carefully thought of all the things that would make you a good employee? Sometimes the most important things are not what you know or can do but the kind of person you are.

If you are reliable, hard working, prompt and cheerful, how can you find a way to tell the employer you have these qualities? If there is someone else who could say these things about you, you may want to refer to them. What kind of person would know these things about you? Your minister? Your doctor? Your teacher? Use all of them. Of course, you will want to ask them if it is all right to use their names if you do so.

As you repeat the activity, you may want to add some items you may not have used in the first interview. How could you help students prepare for a job interview?

Design and write one or more activities to help students prepare for job interviews.

MEET THE WORLD: RINGING DOORBELLS

2 hours   *3 to 8 people*

To be able to help students relate their language activities to their life experiences, experiment with the ways people react to your persuasive efforts in real life situations.

Form a group and agree to try these experiments. First you will each need to get ten dimes for a dollar at a bank or store. Each of you should choose a block, perhaps near your school, where you will ring doorbells and give away your dimes. When you have given away all of your dimes, come back and discuss what happened. How many doors did you try before you had given away ten dimes? Did anyone shut the door in your face? Why? How did you get people to leave their doors open and listen to you? Were people reluctant to take the dimes? Why? How did most people react? Why? How easy is it to convince people that they should trust you? What stories did you tell people? What stories worked best? Why?

Now try the situation in reverse. See if you can collect a dollar's worth of dimes by borrowing them from people. For this you may prefer to try your friends rather than to ring doorbells. When you have collected ten dimes, be sure to return them, and explain what you were doing. Return to your group and discuss the results of your experiment. How many people did you ask before you got ten dimes? What did you say to them? What problems did you have? Was it easier to give away the dimes or to borrow them? Why? What differences did you discover in people? What are the best ways to get people to trust you?

Write your conclusions about this activity in your log.

GUESS WHAT!: A WORD MEANING QUIZ GAME

50 minutes   *10 to 30 people*

Be better prepared to plan games for your classroom by knowing how it feels to participate in them. Do this.

Arrange for a large group or the whole class to participate in this game. To be in the quiz game you will need to look up five words from your studies to be sure you know their meanings well. Then, on one side of a card write the words you have chosen and one question about the meaning of each word. Be sure to put your name at the top of the card so that you won't be asked your own questions later on. Try to make up questions that cannot be answered unless the person asked really understands the meaning of the word. On the back of the card write correct responses.

Form two teams. You may want to line up into two lines. Choose someone to be a quizmaster and someone to be scorekeeper. The quizmaster collects the cards and asks the questions, alternating from one line to the other and giving each person only one chance to answer a question correctly. The scorekeeper decides whether the answer is accepted and scores one point for each correct answer. The person answering gives the reason for his answer by giving the meaning of the word.

After the quiz tell your log about the experience. Did you learn any new words or new meanings for old words? Was it a good way to spend your time? Would this game be helpful to high school students? Why or why not?

TWENTY QUESTIONS: FOLLOWING THE CLUES

20 minutes   *5 people*

To help your students play games which can improve their abilities to think and talk extemporaneously, try playing language games. Do this.

Find four other people to participate in this game with you. There will be two two-person teams. The fifth person will be the moderator. He is a very important person in the game. He chooses the name of a person, place or thing and writes it on a piece of paper which he keeps without showing it to the two teams until one of them has guessed what he has written.

Each team is allowed to ask twenty questions, taking turns, until one team guesses the correct word. Whichever team guesses the word first, wins that round of the game. You may ask any questions except, "What is it?" and "How do you spell it?" After each round choose a different person to be the moderator.

When you have played the game for twenty minutes, tell your log about the experience. Did you discover certain questions which gave you the most information? Are there some words which work better than others for getting clear answers? In what ways might this game be useful for high school students?

THE SOMETHING STORY: A STORY ROUND

40 minutes in class some time out of class   *8 to 15 people*

Here is an activity to try which will prepare you to inspire high school students to think creatively and enjoy telling stories.

Collect some strange objects . . . a family picture from long ago, strange music, a skull, a dead animal, an African drum.

You are going to make up a group story about one of these things. First decide which object you will use by taking a vote. Someone should volunteer to begin the story. After that, each person around the circle adds a line or a sentence. See if you can keep the story going until you have a climax and a logical conclusion. Either record your group story on a tape recorder as you make it up or choose one member of your group to write the story. If you have someone write the story, each member will need to repeat his part of the story for the writer.

Either play your tape for the whole class or choose a member of your group to read your story to the class.

STORYTIME: TELLING STORIES TO CHILDREN

variable time   *3 to 8 people*

To experience some problems and successes which high school students might encounter in an activity to improve their language ability by telling stories to younger children, do this activity.

Your teacher may be able to help you arrange to visit a school where you can borrow a group of children during class hours to use as an audience for story telling. Or, you may make plans and share problems as a group but find your own audience of children individually outside of class time. In either case you may find it wise for your first story-telling experience to begin with only a small group of children—from one to three children. With a small group you will find it possible to stop to answer questions and make explanations when this seems necessary. Later, you will be able to anticipate these questions and explanations so that you can include them in your story-telling or simplify your story-telling so that they are not necessary.

Before your story-telling experience, meet with your group to share ideas and discuss these questions: What age will your children be? What do children of that age like to hear about? What stories might be appropriate? Will the children understand the words? Can you put the story in easier words? What will you do when you meet the children? Will you introduce yourself? Will you ask their names? How will you capture their interest at the start? Do you have pictures to show them? How will you make them feel comfortable and at ease? Will they sit in a circle? On the floor?

How long will it take to tell the story? Should you time it? What will you do if you talk faster than you have planned and run out of things to say? Could you plan an extra time-filler just in case? How do you know you won't forget? Will you memorize your story? Would some notes be helpful? How will you keep the children interested in what you are saying? Will you use gestures and pantomime? Will you involve the children in acting out parts or responding with actions or words? What will you do if the children don't like your story? Could you have a different one ready to tell? What will you do if the children want to tell you a story instead? Will you listen? Will you practice your story telling? Would a mirror help? Try a tape recorder.

Tell your story to children. Tell your log how you feel about the experience. Do you want to do it again? Why or why not? What suggestions can you make for high school students who are planning to tell stories to younger students?

SPEAKING AND USAGE

Since the Greeks, teachers and laymen alike have believed that being able to speak and write well depended upon a knowledge of grammar, the supposed rules that manufacture meaningful utterances out of words. They have continued to believe this although many people in all times have spoken and written supremely well without any such knowledge, and many who have had such knowledge have spoken and written without either grace or power.

Some theorists held that grammar disciplined the mind. Doing unpleasant or difficult grammar exercises would inculcate a submissive attitude that would enhance learning. Foreign languages seemed easier to teach to students accustomed to think of language learning in terms proposed by grammar, probably because foreign language teaching was for so long approached by this same circuitous route of grammar teaching. Some saw grammar as an approach to learning literature. Others thought grammar teaching would ensure that a body of correct English would be perpetuated from generation to generation. And teachers were sometimes reluctant to surrender grammar exercises since these were a convenient way to concoct grades. Minority groups defended teaching grammar, lest failure to learn it would deny their children an opportunity for social mobility.

Few learning theorists today consider these or other reasons credible arguments for teaching traditional grammar, the more recent structural, transformational grammars or other kinds of formal grammars in English classrooms if the aim is to produce more effective speakers and writers. Traditional grammar is irrelevant to the way people speak. It focuses on formal written English and ignores spoken English, of which writing is only a dialect. Hence, much grammar that has been taught has failed to show how language really works, and students are often bored or confused by it. As for the belief that grammar preserved the language, anyone who reads the great literature of the past knows that it was not written in one language but in many dialects of English. It might be nice to speak the language of Chaucer, Shakespeare and Wordsworth, but this hope was long ago defeated by the fact that these worthies did not themselves speak the same kind of English.

Fashionable research in the fifties and sixties found grants to conduct exhaustive investigations about whether teaching grammar to students improved their use of language. These accumulated to indicate small, if any, connection between learning and knowing traditional grammar and using language with proficiency. Knowledge of parts of speech and other cornerstones of traditional teaching were found not to be associated with the ability either to interpret literature or to write effectively.

Denial of benefits previously claimed for teaching traditional grammar is now enshrined in the literature, and time-wasting teaching of traditional grammar is slowly being erased from English classes. But the past clings stubbornly. This half century of language research, which invalidated most of the thinking that went into past philosophies about grammar teaching, has not been internalized by English teachers. Even college entrance examinations had abandoned requiring knowledge of traditional grammar for some time before many English teachers were willing to believe that they had done so. To cease teaching traditional grammar in the English classroom may seem like a revolutionary idea, but to some, finding it in the English classroom is like finding astrology in the physics lab or alchemy in the chemistry lab.

Despite the fact that most people have "had" grammar, they know surprisingly little about how the language really works. Fortunately, they do not need this knowledge in order to speak and write English effectively. The proof of this is that many of them do speak and write well without this knowledge. And many who have this knowledge do both ineffectively. But many laymen have strong opinions about grammar and the necessity for teaching it. If such a person has opinions about how a bridge should be built or a brain operation performed, he will observe, for the most part, a becoming modesty about asserting them. But when he is equally uninformed about linguistic science, he holds and defends strong opinions about it. Most of his information is mythology, distorted at best and actually false at worst, and cannot be the basis for the creation of objectives for the teaching of language in the schools.

The controversy over what can be achieved by grammar teaching has largely been diverted into a new question about what grammar should be taught, if any is. A student who deals with language with less ability than his situation calls for often has not realized its power and explored its possibilities. Traditional grammar does not help him do this. However, just because the study of traditional grammar has been shown to have no bearing on any skill of language use and just because English teachers no longer feel responsible for helping the foreign language teacher do his work, they are not ready to abandon the study of language or to think it has no relevance in helping students to produce and receive an ever larger variety of effective usages of English. Understanding the language system in an inductive way may have such relevance. The characteristic difference between proficient and inadequate users of language is not only the lack of an acceptable dialect but a poverty of structures and vocabulary. Having control of many structures and ways of combining them, often discovered through linguistic investigations, allows the student to develop habits of precise connections and emphasis.

The child's growing maturity of ideas should be accompanied by growing expertness in finding adequate expression of those ideas. Only by conversation can the child learn to ask questions which will help him discover how his environment works and get control over it. And only by this process will his usage grow the flexibility to meet his needs. Language is primarily a set of behavior patterns for handling meaning in speaking. Grammar taught in a humanistic classroom identifies the way meaning gets into words as they are grouped with other words. And meaning is not a single but a multiple relation between the utterance, its parts, relevant features of the environment, and cultural, physical and personal patterns between speakers in the settings of human society.

The child is more linguistically mature than teachers have been accustomed to think, and his grammatical patterns are the interpreters of his experience: plurals, gender, verbs, and adjectives define the kinds of experiences he can have with the things they describe. He early gains mastery of a complex system of communication, but during the rest of his life he will polish, refine and expand his control over linguistic patterns by learning to read, write and manipulate linguistic conventions in a variety of usages. He will gain the ability to use structures that differ in complexity, making precise distinctions, modifying ideas, handling emphasis through subordination, controlling unity through transitions and arrangement, providing for expression of cause and effect, and making tentative propositions.

These arenas of growth the activity cards related to language explore. They provide experience in assembling ideas into sentences, reducing wordiness, simplifying conclusions, condensing by embedding, and expanding ideas by adding sophisticated structures. Activities pursue linguistic assumptions in discriminating between prescribing and describing—considering the latter a more important process for the humanistic curriculum. Grammatical description, classification, definitions of elements and structures, and rules for generating utterances appear in the humanistic curriculum as matters of observable performance in writing, reading and speaking, in generating and producing language.

Grammar is an important study in everything from poetry to science, where language is the source of equipment for scientific progress. All areas of knowledge are grammatical categories. An age of scientific growth is an age of scientific neologisms, a fact apparent from comparison of dictionaries of thirty years ago with those today. Science is a language which mimics the world. Scientists see a projected language in the cosmos. A change in language changes what they believe about the cosmos. Time and matter concepts depend on the language through which they are developed. The facts of astronomy have always been there, but until man could conceive a light year and name it, he could not talk successfully about space. Not by chance is the largest technological university also a center for the study of linguistics.

Humanistic methods of studying language are those of the scientist: observation and discovery, formulating and testing hypotheses. Activity cards do not give definitions. They create situations whereby students may engage in processes that result in definitions, made whenever they are needed. Definitions are developed as generalizations about observed phenomena. Like any other scientific enterprise, language study cultivates open-mindedness, detachment, critical inquiry, disagreements, and alternative points of view. There is not much concern for developing a body of information but for developing ways to explore use of language and attitudes toward that exploration. There is not search for final and irrevocable answers but for ways to ask interesting and useful questions. Humanistic language study is not an act of obedience but of inquiry. Its object is not a stockpile of information but the investigation of a process in action. Assertions about it must be verifiable. Gathering data about language use is the same order of activity as that of scientists in a laboratory and deserves the respect accorded such workers. Students investigate the way language works in experience; they look at structures, regularities and signals that make up language; assess varieties and choices the speaker has, and project the results of a variety of choices; hence any generalization must be tested, retested and modified. The process whereby a student does this must become part of the response he makes to language if he is to be its student throughout his life.

Humanistic activities are designed to provide excitement, challenge, amusement, uncertainty and adventure in language exploration. Whatever facts are learned are likely to be on their way to obsolescence. The student is a creature of a changing linguistic culture, and he will have a different set of linguistic needs tomorrow from those he has in the present. No one can predict what language need he will have in the future except to say that they will be different from those he has today. For this uncertain future humanistic language study prepares the student.

The activity teacher needs a philosophy for dealing with the concept of "correctness" in use of language by students. There are two sets of facts about language. One is the form of language, its phonology, morphology, and syntax. The second set of facts concerns the attitude of the speakers of the language toward various linguistic forms. Some speakers insist upon the terms "right" and "wrong" as appropriate ways to describe language. But many of the greatest speakers ignore the right rules and have always done so.

Language is the primary vehicle of man's culture, and cultural norms are reflected in language patterns. By verbal signals, man declares himself as an individual, explores his environment, defines and organizes the web of his human relationships, and gains full access to the human world. Because a language system whether it belongs to one person, a subculture, or a whole culture, embodies a set of assumptions about the nature of reality, speakers and listeners are bound to their own unconsciously entertained backgrounds.

Each individual has a language community or a set of language communities. His language defines his culture, his geographical region, his ethnic group, his social class and his unique experience as a human being. And each man is affected in some degree by linguistic prejudice, linguistic chauvinism, which assumes the inherent superiority of his particular language, dialect or idiolect. When a student is made to feel that he has no right to this feeling, that his dialect or idiolect is inferior, his individuality is damaged, and he is weakened psycholinguistically. His ability to use language in situations where he knows this prejudice is operating is crippled.

The teacher, too, is a product of social class attitudes toward language. If he is lower middle class and has the hopes, fears, and orientations of that class, he may insist on "correct" usage as a method of emphasizing his identity with that class and its acceptance of him into its system. Behavior characteristics of the lower class such as "incorrect grammar" are a threat. Using the ideas of "correct" and "proper," he may attempt to change the orientation of his student since the student's usage signifies the student's identity in that student's own class in-group.

Direct conflict ensues, because both teacher and student recognize such efforts try to change the total orientation of the student. The student defends himself by forgetting, misbehavior, indifference, or "laziness." Because the events in his life have often been inexplicable, illogical, and uninterpreted verbally, the lower-class child rejects abstractions, tends to need concrete experience as a basis for learning, and does not readily generalize verbally from experience. Words have failed to achieve the aims of the disadvantaged, so he is often suspicious of words. He does not lack culture but is a participant in a different culture, based on non-verbal as well as verbal signals. His school curriculum is outdated and irrelevant if it is based on the belief that he cannot communicate. He does communicate within his own social milieu. It is the school and perhaps the teacher that does not communicate with him. If such a child enters school and is told that his language is wrong, because it is at odds with school usage, he is disadvantaged by the school, not by his home background.

"Good grammar" ranks with obedience, industry, neatness and other middle class folkways, which the middle class has invented and propagated because they have enabled that class to impose its will successfully on its world. But, in the lower-class world, these virtues and folkways have not paid off and have been rejected by the minority culture, which has had to invent its own systems of survival. At one time teacher efforts to indoctrinate students with these virtues were successful because they were tickets to a middle class to which everyone wanted to belong. However, great numbers of the lower class and the young have rejected this ambition, the former because the door has for so long been subtly but firmly shut in their faces, and the latter because of the apparent bankruptcy of middle-class values.

How then shall the humanistic teacher behave? Teacher attitudes should embody interest and curiosity about the intention and form of every student communication. Reproach should never be implied or spoken about his language. The humanistic teacher never tells the student which language is best but instead creates a situation where the student may make an informed choice for himself. Occasions are created where students may see the results of differences in speaking and writing, and students observe and report these results, deciding what language will help them achieve their own objectives in similar situations. Students can design ways to behave with linguistic adequacy in situations they forecast as well as in their present experiences.

The teacher of linguistics is no longer custodian of a correctional institution or a guardian of usage. The study of language is not designed to antidote toxic usages. The activity teacher becomes a guide and colleague to those who are finding out about language. He shows them where to look and how to draw conclusions about what they see. He is not a watchman but an explorer, an adventurer in ideas. He is concerned with all language, not with imposing a special language for the classroom which is neither heard nor used outside of it. He does not believe in linguistic original sin, and his aim is not linguistic purity but linguistic flexibility. The most important thing about teaching language is not to keep it from being incorrect but to help the student produce and receive a larger quantity of language more effectively.

A student should not be cautioned to avoid saying "ain't" because it is wrong. Through experience he should discover he might be unwise to choose to use this locution at certain times. People he will have to deal with if he wishes to succeed in life will be those who say "isn't," and they are prejudiced against those who say "ain't." "Ain't" can be understood to mean what its user wants it to mean. Unfortunately, to some listeners it means also something its user probably does not want it to mean. It may cause users of "isn't" to feel that users of "ain't" are not effective in positions of trust or dignity, and, insofar as they control who gets such positions, they will discriminate against users of "ain't." This is simply a quite understandable truth, as statements about the rightness or wrongness of "ain't" may not be. The "isn't" users are in charge of most of the prizes in our world, and the "ain't" users are not. All this is to indicate that teachers of language must teach language in terms of what people really do when they use language, and no statement about language is complete unless it takes account of feelings people have about the way language is used on various occasions.

Most statements about usage are not statements about the English language but about social prejudice. When speakers make linguistic choices, they are making social rather than grammatical choices. Learning about saying "ain't" is learning not about grammar but about the power structure of society. It is a rule of etiquette, not grammar. If English teachers make students think that "ain't" is unacceptable in the classroom, they are interpreting the attitude of English teachers, not the structure of English. A sentence containing "ain't" may be perfectly organized. The speaker has simply chosen a word that has unfortunate social consequences among many middle-class people.

Correct usage is a prestige dialect, used by only a small part of America's population. Rules have helped a rising middle class as well as large numbers of diverse immigrants to regularize their use of English. Personal insecurities that cause many to cling to these standards are stimulated by the upwardly mobile character of American society, which encourages those who move to higher socio-economic levels to adopt rigid standards of English usage as a reflection of social class. School texts and teachers represent the fantasies and prejudices of the power class in language as in all else.

But these fantasies are important, since rhetoric is the process of producing effects on receivers of language. If rhetoric is successful, it achieves its intended effects without getting others that are not intended. Language has effects that are non-intellectual, conveying attitudes and feelings. "Him and me done it" makes perfect sense, but when it is used in situations where it has bad effects, giving the listener bad feelings about the speaker, it becomes bad English. It is bad because it limits the situations in which the speaker can take part with confidence and be sure of the respect of others. A speaker needs to say "he and I" when he is with those who will discriminate against him if he does not do so. There are even some people who do not like sentences that end with prepositions because they have read some of the eighteenth century grammarians who thought that because Latin did not do so, English should not. Perhaps, for awhile, speakers need to humor even prejudices like these. English teachers can demonstrate, however, and students can begin to learn that a listener's responsibility is not to make corrections but to show appreciation and enjoyment of whatever a speaker says that is good, learning to accept and relish a variety of usages.

Language is a social institution with the same counteracting tendencies as other institutions toward adaptability and stability. It is founded in man's social nature and used for the satisfaction of his social wants. While individuals are the agents of the formation and modifications of words and meanings, the community alone makes and changes language. As long as marks of social and educational status in society are used, some of these will be linguistic. Language superiorities are myths, but much of society's adjustment is adjustment to its myths. No dialect has any inherent superiority. Its selection was the result of socio-economic differences. Superiority may be found in the growth of certain specialized vocabularies, the existence of a great literature, the social prestige of those who use it and the territory over which it has spread. But, teachers need to help students make realistic evaluations of current language myths dominant in their society and see how much these myths are observed by others, for the most important function of language, students learn, is to be useful to them now.

Words not only express ideas but shape them, and language is not just an instrument but an environment. It has much to do with the philosophical and political conditioning of a society. Dangerous misconceptions and prejudices take root in language and undermine human values. Skin color, for instance, is tied to plus and minus attitudes, and "black" and "white," as defined in our culture, are loaded terms. Detailed in dictionaries are many synonyms for blackness, most of them unpleasant. Since thinking is subvocal speech, an enormous trap of racial prejudgement works on anyone who is born to speak the English language. The speaker of English denigrates black and uplifts white in ordinary speech. Since the English language enforces cultural bias, teachers of language need to be aware of this enforcement and help their students become aware of it. Students do not realize that they have been conditioned since childhood by the power of words to demean or ennoble. Awareness cannot change what is, but it can invent ways to keep the bias from doing damage.

Synonyms for white almost all have favorable connotations. No less evil than the meanings for black are those for yellow. Of course, "black," "white" and "yellow" are not very useful terms for describing races, since skin color varies widely. But these terms have become symbolic. Negative language infects the language of other peoples too. Westerners are not alone in imparting prejudice by color words. In Chinese "white" means bloodlessness, mourning, coldness, weakness, or insensitivity, while "yellow" means sunshine, openness, and beauty. The word "black" in many African languages has connotations of strength, certainty, and integrity, while "white" is associated with paleness, anemia, and untrustworthiness. Cultures are self-serving in their language. Earth dwellers have a choice of making their world into a neighborhood or a crematorium, and language is one of the factors in that option. The right words do not automatically produce the right actions, but they can be part of the process. Teachers and students can do their part to create neighborhoods by reducing word-induced prejudice.

A teacher who wants to break through his own and his students' linguistic barriers and isolation will find ways to demonstrate that he knows no language is inherently inferior. But the teacher is right who assumes that lower-class dialect patterns in business and society cause negative reactions and affect job getting, job relations, and self and status images in minority groups. A non-standard dialect may deny employment to its speaker. Even though it is not that speaker, but his bigoted and intolerant employer from the majority culture who needs to be educated, the employer is in control, and what he decides happens.

In the world's history riots and killings have enforced the virtues of various dialects, but our culture merely sentences speakers of nonstandard usages to economic death by job discrimination. Effective speakers find they must defer to their listeners' inability to adjust to dialect differences by speaking in ways that will not stimulate prejudice and limit their own linguistic effectiveness. Thus they manage situations in which prejudiced listeners might make decisions unfavorable to them., Minority speakers must do this just as they wear the clothing, acquire the eating habits, and accept other aspects of the life-style of the majority culture if they want to gain access to the advantages controlled by the members of the majority culture, advantages which they find desirable for the comfort and well-being of their own life-style. They compromise their dialect just as they compromise their other idiosyncratic life styles in order to have access to advantages of the majority life styles.

This attitude may itself be a reflection of prejudice, but it seems to have some consonance with the realities of our lives. Until there is some redistribution of the power patterns of our society, prejudice will probably reflect these realities in the lives of our students. However, if they are to believe in language as power, they must find it out for themselves, and if their experience tells them that they do not want the language of the majority culture as part of their language equipment, respect must be shown for this decision and their right to make it. The returns are not all in, and they may be right in thinking that times have changed enough that their minority dialect will not disadvantage them.

To become proficient in using a dialect other than his native one, a speaker must go through several processes. Of course, the Black child is bidialectal from the time he ventures into the majority culture to go to school, but to become proficient in using the second dialect he must have some training along with interaction with others who speak the majority dialect. And because language growth comes from need for using language, change in usage comes only when the user has enough oral language experience to become aware that others speak differently and to want to reconstruct the grammar of his native speech. If he comes from a culture where he hears one form, he will use that form until he consistently hears other forms. If he is to speak an alternative dialect well, he must hear it as he is socially integrated with those who naturally use the dialect.

The activity teacher realizes also that one of the important facts about language learning for the Black is that for two-thirds of his life in this country, he was forbidden to learn to read and write. Also, ghetto children are deprived of basic experiences white children have; hence they lack linguistic elements of these experiences. When Blacks were first brought to this country, slave owners mixed tribes, and Black people from various linguistic regions of Africa had to use a language they could all speak; hence they adopted the pidgin they had learned in Africa. So, even yet, some American children from Black minority groups speak their language in ways that vary from standard dialect.

To survive, the urban Black functions in two worlds, the world of the Black ghetto where he lives and the world of the white industrial complex where he works. The language of the white world is far different from his own colorful, melliflous, inventive, Black dialect. Denied contact with the larger society, part of the way he maintains his identity is to develop a language with its own vocabulary. Rapping in his language is part of his survival scheme in his hostile world, a customary response of an out-group member. Specialized language is a natural and traditional refuge of those who are suspicious of others. It is a protective coloration, in which words have meanings not known to the majority. Some express the very opposite meaning from that attributed by the majority dialect.

Twenty million speakers use this Black dialect. It is a creation of personal pride, and justly so. For instance, a vocabulary of at least six hundred colorful slang terms has been developed, many of them understood only within the Black culture itself. It requires considerable temerity as well as willful blindness on the part of the majority culture to call such inventiveness linguistic deprivation. In fact, the Black vocabulary has had a profound effect on the majority language, particularly in the language of musicians and the language of youth. Those who do not speak standard English do not have a limited linguistic development; they have a different development.

The Black dialect has rules just as sophisticated as those of the majority dialect. These need to be identified by linguistic investigations carried on by both teachers and students in English classes. Sounds and structures characteristic of the Black dialect, such as special handling of vowel sounds, verb endings, and plural forms, should be identified and corresponding usages of the majority dialect introduced orally as alternative choices where students themselves decide they want to use these majority variants. Minority speakers can identify ethnic, regional, or social class forms which constitute the grammatical signals diverging from the majority dialect through individual or group investigation, comparisons of data gathered from listening situations where students can see which features of speech are identified with certain groups. These listening situations are created in the activity cards, which enable the student to see the results on listeners when they hear certain dialects.

Teachers themselves must become familiar with characteristics of dialect usages of minority children. They will not adopt these patterns themselves but must be responsible for understanding easily what children are saying and what they mean. Plural and verb omission of the "s," or omission of the verb altogether, characterize the Black dialect. The subjunctive which has disappeared from standard English appears often in Black English. First syllables and endings are often dropped. The cluster "str" becomes "skr"; "ch" becomes "sh." Some of these variants come from African speech patterns and some from plantation English and slave creole of the seventeenth and eighteenth centuries. Teachers must do action research with their students until they discover and understand the differences.

Some direct conditioning of children to make verbal responses useful in their social and business lives may be accomplished by drill. But all drills must be sound drills, since usage must sound right before students will adopt it. Drill is a repair mechanism and must be preceded by understanding and desire on the part of the child for the drill. In an atmosphere of confidence and self-respect, students may or may not choose to use drills which establish an alternative in their speech repertoire. Drills should be fun, short, and invariably successful, if they are to accomplish change.

If adults in a language community speak an easily predictable, simple rhetoric, it does not stimulate speech flexibility in children of that community, flexibility which would enable them to learn to communicate with out-groups. It limits the ability of its users to organize meaning. A group that uses more elaborate verbal symbols produces in its children linguistic flexibility that allows the child to internalize social structures of many kinds. The user of less flexible rhetoric possesses a smaller number of linguistic devices to solve problems. Because a child shapes his consciousness by speech, his communication will help enforce his received social patterns. Those who learn only a restricted rhetoric in their linguistic culture are handicapped, for to use language to advance their social purposes, they must use words to mean what others use them to mean. By words a child tests his ideas against the ideas of another, but many language habits reflect life inadequately. Stereotypes are another example of linguistic poverty. An adequate education in the use of language creates language habits that reflect more adequately the realities of life, producing evaluations closer to objective reality. Effective education for a minority culture means effective learning of language which will give access to the goods of the majority culture. And effective language education for children of the majority culture means, at least in part, seeing the uselessness of linguistic stereotypes.

Above all, any student who is to become proficient in language use must feel that he uses language well and can learn to use it even better. And the teacher must feel that all dialects are clothed with the right to be. To accept the way another speaks is to accept him; to reject the way he speaks is to reject him. To accept the way a child speaks is to increase his ability to respond to the world and recreate it in his words, to give him new ways to partake of the world, to make him more aware of what he can become and what the potentials of man are.

The assumption of the humanistic curriculum is that every child has a right to learn language in a climate of respect for any and all dialects which he feels are appropriate to his lifestyle, subject to the rights of other members of the group not to have to listen to language which offends their sense of decency and religious or other deeply held convictions. At the same time, the child has a right to know that other dialects are used by those who will be interacting with him, and they may be distracted and discriminate against him because of some of his usages. He must be encouraged then to choose whether to learn to use, on occasions of his own choice, dialects which are not native to him as part of his language of power. This opportunity for choice is presented with the same dispassion and lack of censure with which we teach cooking students to whip whites of eggs separately to make a cake lighter than it would be if eggs were put in the batter whole. An alternative dialect is not more right but more useful to get certain results, just as are the whipped whites of eggs.

In this country 108,000 Indians speak English as a second language. New York City has a Spanish-speaking population of one million. Texas educates half a million Spanish-speaking children. Some Maine communities have 90% French-speaking children. When a ghetto dweller moves to a distant city, he rejoins his speech community in a new setting and spends much of his time speaking to its members in their own dialect. If a minority speaker changes his dialect completely, he loses his own speech community identification. But he usually keeps his dialect because the people he lives with use it. He does not need to quit using his native dialect, but may choose to have a second dialect available to him when he speaks to those who are more interested in him if he speaks as they do. The day when all dialects have equal acceptance is not as far away as we assume. Speech communities are becoming more inclusive of a variety of dialects, since there is in this country a great increase in mobility, both geographical and social.

Activities

KNOTTY WORDS: IS LANGUAGE LOGICAL?

15 minutes   *1 person*

If you do this activity, you may discover ways to help students internalize appropriate language usage.

Consider these questions: What does "untie" mean—take away the tie? Then what does "unloose" mean? Is an outlaw the opposite of an inlaw? If we say "later on," does that mean it is all right to say "early on?" Is the "lead" in the pencil lead? What are tin cans made of? Why do we use these expressions when they do not tell the truth? Would the truth sound funny? Have you ever heard the expression "in a few short weeks?" Can one week be shorter than another? What is meant? Do we know that what is said is not what is meant? How do we know? If a friend asks if he should open the window, and you say, "By all means," do you really mean that he should use any means—like an axe?

Is something that is better, better than that which is merely good? Is whatever is best the highest good? What if Jack has bad handwriting? If he improves, how will we describe his handwriting? But it will still not be good. Can it be better, then, without being good? What if Jack has two friends who write even worse than he does? If we were talking about the three of them, how would we describe this writing? But it still would not be good, would it? So good would be the most and not the least in such a situation.

You can play this game with other words. In January you can say that the weather tomorrow will be warmer, but will it be warm? And there will be one day in February that will be warmest, but it will probably not be warm. So "warm" can be warmer than "warmer" or even warmer than "warmest." If it is 80 degrees inside and 40 outside, we would say it is twice as warm inside as it is outside, and it is not even warm at all outside!

Is there any difference between what happens when your house burns down and when it burns up? What about downtown and uptown? What is the difference between flammable and inflammable? How many ways can you use the words "make up"? Combine "make up" with "train," "face," "mind," "friends," "story" and "mistake" to make sentences. How does it work in each? What is the difference between sit down and sit up? What about sit out, sit in, sit around? If we can sit still, can we sit loud? Which can we do, sit tight or sit loose? Can we undercome or overcome? Can we be overwhelmed or underwhelmed? Can we undergo or overgo? Can we outdo or indo? What can you do with shut—in, out, down, up?

Do you know most of the answers to these questions? What is the point of asking them? Did you know without thinking about it the rules for using and understanding these words and phrases? How did you learn about them? Did you ever memorize a list of rules for them? Is this the way you learned to use language? How could students learn rules of usage that they do not already have inside them?

In your log write your conclusions about how students may internalize rules for appropriate language usage. Could questions like these help them to gain confidence in their abilities to learn such rules? Could you plan activities in which they could learn by doing?

GETTING WORD WISE: WORDS OF FOREIGN ORIGIN

1 hour or more   *1 person*

To be able to interest students in the sounds and origins of words in our language, do this activity.

Find some words you suspect came from another language. Perhaps you could keep a pencil and paper near you as you read and list interesting words to look up later. Check out your suspicions in a dictionary which shows word origins. You may also want to use Mary S. Serjeantson's *History of Foreign Words in English,* which lists thousands of words that have been borrowed from other languages.

Think about these questions: Can you see any patterns in what you have discovered? Were there certain time periods in history when some languages contributed heavily to English? Can you find historical reasons for this? What kinds of words did we borrow from each language? Which ones gave us verbs? Which ones gave us nouns? What kinds of verbs and nouns did they give us? What languages contributed names of cities? Of plants, animals, nautical terms, household words, scientific terms, clothing, cooking terms, surnames? Tell your log what you have discovered.

Advertise your words. Make a picture, cartoon, or advertisement for each word. Put these up on the bulletin board or in the room. You might put up a new one every day for this week. Be sure to include what language the words came from and when they entered our language.

TREASURE HUNT: WHAT CAN YOU FIND IN A DICTIONARY?

several hours   *4 to 8 people*

To be more able to help your students use language effectively, do this activity.

Form a group to investigate the functions of dictionaries. Begin by discussing these questions: What kinds of dictionaries are there? Make a list. Are these different kinds of dictionaries used for different purposes? What are they? If you are interested in the etymology of a word, what dictionary would you choose? If you wanted one with pictures to interest a ten-year-old, what dictionary would you choose? If you wanted one to carry with you so that you could look up word spellings on the spot, which one would you choose? What dictionary would you choose for your home? Why? Which dictionary tells you about the standard and non-standard usage of words? Which dictionary is apt to show you how a word was used by famous authors?

Get several different dictionaries, and bring them to class for a comparison. You may want to move your group to the school library where you will be able to use several kinds of dictionaries. Sit together at a table in the library or with your desks in a circle. Each of you should have a dictionary to examine. Give your dictionaries these tests, comparing your discoveries:

Check to see how the entries are arranged. How are the words arranged? How do you know to pronounce the words? Is it the same with other dictionaries? Are other systems of pronounciation used? What does your dictionary tell you about spelling? Look up the word "enclose" under both "i" and "e." Which is the preferred spelling? How do you know? Look up a variety of words. How do you know when a word can be abbreviated? How do your dictionaries divide words into syllables? Do all the dictionaries use the same marks? Look up "made up." Is it listed as two words in all the dictionaries or is it hyphenated in some? Look up the word "making." Which dictionaries give you compound words that are formed with "making"? Which compounds are two words and which are one? Does your dictionary have pictures, diagrams and maps? What information do they give? Does your dictionary give the inflected forms of nouns and verbs? Does it list the parts of speech of words? Does it tell you if a verb may be transitive or intransitive? Does it give synonyms and antonyms? What does your dictionary tell you about derivatives? What abbreviations and symbols are used in your dictionary? Are others used in other dictionaries? Find out what they all mean. What about prefixes and suffixes in your dictionary? Look up the prefix "mal-" in the *Funk and Wagnall's Standard College Dictionary*. Why are

33 words listed in this entry? Does your dictionary indicate how words are used? What is a colloquialism? Compare meanings. Are slang words included in your dictionary? What is a dialect? Does your dictionary indicate levels of usage? Look up the words "ain't," "corn," "drop" and "adorable"; and compare the labels that are given for each word.

How can you get high school students to discover what dictionaries can do for them? Each of you should make an activity card to help a student use his dictionary more effectively. Concentrate on just one aspect of what the dictionary can do for him, like helping him with syllabication or with the inflected forms of nouns and verbs or satisfying his curiosity about the literary allusions he finds in his reading.

MEANING HUNT: WHAT IS GRAMMAR?

45 minutes *a group*

To be more able to help students relate their language studies to their street conversations, do this.

Discuss these questions: What would you think if you saw a word all alone—for instance, "eggs." What are the possible ways this word can work? Does it work at all unless you add other words to it?

Now add some other words to it—if you have a group, each person should add his own words to it. What happens to the word you started with? Does it do more work, say more, mean more? Now take those words away and add others. See how many ways you can make that one word work just by changing the other words around it. What is your word doing in each different case?

What general statement would you make about words when they are alone and when they are with others? That's what grammar is—the way words affect other words. Try the same thing with other words. Are there some words that go with others all the time? Which words tell you that other words are following? Are some like traffic cops who show where other words go?

Tell your logs your conclusions about what grammar is and how words tell about each other.

NEW WORLD: INVENT YOUR OWN LANGUAGE

2 hours or more *4 to 15 people*

Here is an activity which will prepare you to help students discover how language is structured.

Form a group and plan to invent your own language, which only your group will be able to understand. Here are some questions which may help you with your plans: Will you want to use the word order of the English language for your new language? Have you ever studied a foreign language? What other ways of arranging the words in sentences might you use? Using the usual English words, experiment with different word arrangements. What do they do to the meanings of sentences? Could you make up a new language which other speakers of English could not understand, merely by changing the system which governs the arrangement of words?

Can you invent a language which substitutes words you have made up for ordinary English words? Would you use the same English endings for your words, like -ed, -en, -ing, -ly, -er, and -est? What about -ion, -ate, -ent, and -are? Would you keep usual prefixes, like un-, up-, in-, and im-? What would you do with "a" and "the"? How will you show tense changes in words which have internal changes in the English language, like gone and went, run and ran, did and done, and have and has? Would you like to regularize such words in your new language?

Will you use the English alphabet? Will the same letters represent the same sounds? What letters and sounds do other languages have that ours does not? Will you have a written language, or will yours be only a spoken language? Will all the words in your new language be spelled as they sound?

How will you remember the rules of your new language? Will you need a dictionary and a grammar book? Practice talking in your new language. Practice until you can carry on a 10 minute conversation without reverting to the use of English.

Tape record a conversation in your new language, and play it for the class. Explain to the class how your language works.

WORD BUILDING: HOW WORDS ARE MADE
1 hour   *2 people*

To be able to help students satisfy their curiosity about how words are made and to help them with spelling, do this.

Make up your own words. Invent silly roots and add prefixes and suffixes to them. Here are some common prefixes to help you: in-, ir-, im-, un-, il-, semi-, de-, super-, ad-, anti-, be-, bi-, dis-, epi-, ex-, for-, inter-, mal-, mis-. Can you find others? Here are some common suffixes: -ly, -ful, -ize, -acy, -age, -ance, -ence, -ancy, -ency, -ary, -ate, -dom, -ee,

-en, -er, -ery, -ess, -et, -fold, -hood, -ic, -ice, -ify, -ing, -ism, -ist, -ity. How many more can you think of?

After you have made a list of twenty or thirty words, decide what each of your words means. Are some of your words nouns, verbs, adverbs? How can you tell the difference? Use your words in sentences to each other.

Make a chart for the bulletin board showing how your words were made, what they mean and why you decided on that meaning, and how they can be used in sentences.

WORDS THAT SOUND LIKE THEY MEAN: A SOUND POEM
1 hour   *a group*

To help students enjoy the sounds of their language and discover how sounds are used to support meaning, do this.

Read Edgar Allen Poe's "The Bells" aloud to yourself. How has the author used the sounds of words to make you feel the meaning of the poem? Together make a list of all the words you know that imitate sounds. In some of the words you have listed is the basic sound repeated twice, as in click-click, cuckoo, and quack-quack? Do you have some words in which the second is changed slightly as in bow-wow, zig-zag, and fiddle-faddle? Did you think of any words in which the last part rhymes with the first, like hoity-toity, walkie-talkie, and killer-diller?

How many of the words you found were slang expressions? How many of the slang expressions do you think will become parts of our language in years to come? Why?

Make a poem, using as many of these sound words as you can. You may want to make a group poem, with each person adding a line or a verse, or you may decide that you each want to make a separate poem. You may want to make your poem funny or silly, or you may want to try a descriptive or serious poem.

IT IS AS IT DOES: WORDS THAT WORK IN DIFFERENT WAYS
15 minutes   *1 person*

To be able to help students distinguish between nouns and verbs as words which function in different ways, do this activity.

Read these sentences aloud to yourself:

Do you have a *slice* of ham?	I will *drive.*
I will *slice* the ham.	I will go for a *drive.* (Which of
Are you expecting a	these is the most natural for
telephone *call?*	you to say? Why?)
He will *call* later.	It is *Spring.*
The *pass* is free.	The *spring* is bent.
Don't *pass* that house.	*Spring* lightly over the fence.
Climb the mountain *pass.*	Get *up* and go *up* stairs.

If you said the italicized words without the sentences, the same words would have the same sounds; and you would have no way of knowing whether they were nouns or verbs. How does the relationship of the italicized words to the other words in the sentence tell you what it means? Does your voice know the difference when you read the sentences? You might want to read them into a tape recorder and then listen. Listen to what your voice tells you about these words:

Call the *control* tower.	I *object!*
How do you *control* it?	What is the *object* of this?
He lacks self-*control.*	He has *transfer* orders.
The baby is *content.*	*Transfer* these apples to that box.
What is the *content*	I got a *transfer* of my grades.
of the mixture?	
Read the *content* analysis.	

Are some of these words used in other ways than as nouns or verbs? How can you tell? How could students draw conclusions about words that seem alike but can mean differently? Make a list of conclusions that students might be able to form about words like these, and tell your log what questions you might ask to help students find their own conclusions.

SNEAKY WORDS: FINDING ADJECTIVES AND NOUN PHRASES
30 minutes   *1 person*

To be able to help students distinguish an ordinary adjective and noun from a noun phrase, do this activity.

How do you say race horse? Is it the same way you say stone wall? What does your voice do in each case? In which case does the adjective become part of the noun? How do you know?

How about blackberry? What other signal do we have here that shows it is all part of the noun? Do you say the two parts of the word more like race horse or stone wall? When stone wall becomes a man's name—Stonewall Jackson—which way is it said?

Can you draw a conclusion about when a word is used as an adjective and when it is part of a noun? Try to see what the use of "drinking" is in these sentences: *The drinking water remained fresh. Drinking water from canteens is wise.* How does drinking work in each? Can the sound tell you the difference? What does it tell you?

See if you can find some examples of your own to put in your log. Tell your log what success you have had finding the adjectives and noun phrases.

PORTMANTEAU: BLENDING WORDS
40 minutes   *3 to 6 people*

To be able to help students examine the ways words are formed in our language, do this activity.

In your group read Lewis Carroll's poem "Jabberwocky." Think and talk about the strange words in the poem. Do the words have denotative meanings? What words are pleasing to you? Why? How do the sounds make you feel about the words? Do the sounds give you clues to the meanings? Do you like or dislike "slithy"? Why? How do you think Lewis Carroll arrived at that word? If he combined two words to make it, which two words did he combine and what does the new word mean? Is the new meaning a combination of the meanings of the words from which this one was made? What do you think a Jabberwock is? Should you be cautious around a Jabberwock? Why? What is "frumious"?

What is a portmanteau word? Look up the term and discuss it in your group. Can you make up new words by combining parts of other words which have meaning to you? Make a list of blended words you have invented and give meanings for them.

Make a poem or paragraph using your words. Post it in the room and see if your classmates can discover what you mean.

THE GOOD AND BAD OF IT: SAYING THE RIGHT THING
35 minutes   *4 to 5 people*

To find ways of helping students discover that good usage is speaking appropriately, do this activity.

Talk about these questions: If you were on the field, had the ball and your captain yelled, "Who has the ball?" would you say, "It is I" or "It's me"? Would you be using correct language? Are there some ways of speaking that are more correct than others? What does "correct" mean? Does it describe something that is always the same, or something that is appropriate to some particular time and place? Could a way of speaking be correct in one situation and not in another? Why? Find examples from your own experiences to support your opinions.

Did anyone ever tell you that what you said was "bad grammar"? What did you say? What did your critic want you to say? Why did he want you to say it his way? Did you change? Try each way on someone in the group and see what effect each way of speaking has on another person. Can you purposely talk in a certain way to get other people to think about you what you want them to? Might different ways of speaking make others decide you are a certain kind of person? If so, how?

Role-play some scenes in which you show the effects of appropriate and inappropriate language in various situations. Be grade school children who say "ain't" in school. What happens? Show them on the playground using the same word with each other. What did they learn about language from their first experience? Find other situations from your own experiences. How do you speak to your minister, your mother, your boss, your friends, your little brother? What would happen if you spoke the wrong way to the wrong person?

Make several such scenes into a skit, and perform the skit for your class or for another group.

WITH YOUR EYES OPEN: WATCHING THE TELEVISION PEOPLE
TALK

1 hour   *2 to 5 people*

This activity may help you to interest students in critically analyzing the uses of language in their environments.

Form a group and agree that each of you will watch a television show to discover how language is used in it. You should plan ahead of time what programs you will each watch. Would you find out more if you each watched a different program? Take notes as you watch so that you can discuss what you have seen when you return to class. Here are some questions which may help you know what to look for:

Did all the characters or participants talk alike? How does a sports announcer or newscaster talk? How is that different from the way a character in a play talks? Do characters in old movies talk differently from characters in modern shows? How? Has our everyday talk changed also? Do you hear any words that were not considered proper on television five years ago? Do you notice any pronounciations that are different from your own? How were they different? Were there any words used that you would not use? If so, what were they? What would you have said? How did the characters talk to each other? Does a master of ceremonies talk differently when he is introducing an act or guest than when he is telling a joke? In what way? What is the tone of your show? Is it formal, business-like, narrative, conversational, familiar? How does this affect the way the persons on it speak?

Share your discoveries with your group, and write your conclusions in your log.

THE YOU KNOW AND I MEAN PEOPLE: LANGUAGE FILLERS
1 class period   *1 person*

To be able to guide your students to a clearer perception of their own speaking habits, study language fillers.

Be an eavesdropper in class today. Listen to the sounds people make when they are trying to put their words into order to express a new idea. Which people clear their throats? What can you tell about the people in your class by these mechanisms for taking up time until they are ready to say something? Which people say "You know" and which ones say "I mean"? Are they a different group from the ones who say "Well" and "ah"? In what ways are they different or the same? Why do some people make noises like "uh-hu"? Are there special gestures which go along with these language fillers? What do the gestures tell you? Do some individuals jingle keys, wad tissues or handkerchiefs, pick at the buttons or lint on their clothing, tap pencils, rub their chins, or flex their fingers? Why do they do these things? Are they sending any messages to those around them by these actions and other language fillers?

Make a list of all the people in your class and during one class period watch to see what each person does and says. What are the characteristic fillers each person uses? What do they tell you about him?

Record your discoveries in your log.

NEW LIFE FOR OLD SAYINGS: CHARADES ON CLICHES
30 to 40 minutes   *6 to 12 people*

To make students more sensitive to the overuse of stock phrases and sayings in oral and written communication, here is a game that also builds oral language skills. Try it with your group.

Divide your group into two teams. Set some rules before you start. How many and how few words will you allow for each cliche that is to be acted out? How much time will each person have to act out his cliche? Elect one person to be the timekeeper and referee. The person who acts out the cliche is not allowed to talk while he is performing. You may want to set a penalty for those who forget and talk.

Arrange your chairs so that the two teams are facing each other. It helps to have two cups, hats or other containers to put slips of paper in after cliches have been written. Each team writes as many cliches on slips of paper as there are members in the opposite team. These are then put into the container for the other team and given to the timekeeper, who holds it out to the member of the opposite team whose turn it is to act next. The person whose turn is next draws the slip of paper, reads the words and gives it to the timekeeper to hold. Allow the person who is to act out the cliche one or two minutes to compose his thoughts and plan his actions before the timing begins. You may want to draw straws or cards to see who begins first. Each team scores when they correctly guess the cliche which is acted out by their member.

When each of you has had a chance to act out a cliche, you may want to pull your chairs into a circle and discuss your game. Which cliches were the easiest to guess? Why? Which were the easiest to act out? Which ones were the most familiar? How did you feel when you were the one acting? How did you feel when you were watching? How well were you able to think under pressure? Why?

GIVING VOICE: USING YOUR VOICE EFFECTIVELY

2 hours   *1 person and a helper*

You will be able to help students use their voices with more confidence and effectiveness if you do this activity.

Make a tape of a speaker who feels strongly about what he is saying. Or you may use a recording of an actor speaking lines in a play.

What methods does he use to get his vocal activity to match his feeling about what he is saying? Note pitch, loudness, variation in tone, vocal color effects like quavers, changes in any of these. Does his clear enunciation make it easy for us to listen to his ideas instead of being distracted by having to try to understand his words? Does his voice have any distracting qualities such as nasality, sibilation, twang, stridency, shrillness or intrusive dialect? What is the effect of these? On the communcation of his ideas? On the attention or sympathy of the listener? What vocal characteristics would have made it more acceptable to you?

Make a transcript of the speech or parts of it and see if you can deliver it effectively. Use a tape. Try it several times and see if you can improve. What causes the improvement? What vocal characteristics are different as you improve?

Now construct a small, one-minute speech on a subject you feel strongly about (perhaps how you should be allowed to use the family car or have one of your own, or not be grounded for late hours). Deliver it on tape and listen to the result. Could you alter some of the vocal characteristics and make it more effective? Try it. Get another student to listen to your delivery and help you improve it. Record in your log your conclusions about the use of vocal control in effective speech making. Would this be true in individual conversation as well? Would it be less true there than when you are talking to several people at once? Why? Record your consideration of these questions in your log.

BEGINNING: HELPING A CHILD LEARN LANGUAGE
time out of class
two weeks   *1 person*

Here is a way you can help someone learn to use language and see how the process of language learning works at its beginning.

Do you have a small brother or sister? A neice or nephew? Do you know neighborhood children? You can help them learn about language. Teach them how to imitate the sounds of machines and animals. Whenever you see an animal, imitate it until the small one can do it too. Keep saying the word for the name of the animal at the same time. Can you make a game of it? Have you ever played "What animal am I?" You can use pictures of animals from magazines or books too. Do you like to read or tell stories? This is a great help for children who are trying to learn about words.

If the child is very small, get him to point and repeat when you say, "Where are your toes?" "Your hair?" "Your bed?" "The door?" Get the child to point and ask the names of objects, and tell him the ones he does not know. Show the child that every object and action can be translated into words. As the child plays, describe what she is doing aloud: "You are dropping stones in the wagon; you are putting your doll in too." Then you can change the way you say it . . . "Put some stones in the wagon." When bedtime comes the day's activities can be repeated: "Remember when Jimmy put the stones in the wagon?" and so forth. All this is before the child even learns to talk. Sometimes the child will learn to speak with one or two-word remarks. Expand these for him into sentences by saying what you think he means.

Keep a record in your log of the child's responses. After two weeks tell the class about your experience and how you feel about it.

CRACK THE WORD BARRIER: USE HARD AND SOFT WORDS
25 minutes   *1 person*

If you would like your students to be more persuasive when they talk and at the same time to be able to resist the persuasive talk of others, finding out about hard and soft words can help you.

If someone says the word "chair" to you, do you understand what he means? Why? What kind of picture does that word bring to your mind? Do you feel any emotion when you think of "chair"? Why or why not? How is "chair" different from "lazy"? What kind of picture does "lazy" bring to your mind? How does the word make you feel? Why? Are there other words that make you feel good or bad when you hear them? List five words that make you feel some kind of emotion when you hear them.

If someone were talking to you and used a lot of words in his conversation which made you feel bad, how would you probably feel about what he was telling you? Imagine a friend is describing someone to you that you have never met. Your friend says, "She's skinny." What kind of picture do you have of the girl being described? If, instead, your friend says, "She's slender," what kind of a picture do you get? In this case "skinny" is a hard word and "slender" is a soft one. Here is a list of words containing soft and hard word pairs. Like "skinny" and "slender" they could be used interchangeably but would create very different ideas in the mind of the person who hears them. See if you can match them up and tell which is the soft word and which is the hard one. Check with the dictionary if you need to.

Husky	Determined
Stubborn	Courageous
Blunder	Fat
Gabby	Error
Thrifty	Talkative
Plain	Stingy
Foolhardy	Ugly

Now find five examples of how hard and soft words are used by advertisers to sell products. Look at billboards, TV commercials, magazine and newspaper ads, even the fronts of packages in the supermarket. See what manufacturers say about their own products and about their rivals.

Put these examples in your log. If you have clippings, paste them in. Now you can look back to that page when you need to help students "sell" their ideas or listen objectively to persuasive talk.

THE SONG YOUR WORDS SING: WHY DOES IT SOUND AS IT DOES?
1 hour   *1 person*

To be able to help students with their speaking problems and to aid them in pursuing their curiosity about language, do this.

Find out how and why our language has the sounds it does. What are the consonants? Sound aloud to yourself the sounds that correspond with each letter of the alphabet that is not a vowel. Is the sound made the same way you pronounce the letter? Where in your mouth was each of the sounds made? Try to describe how your mouth made each one. Make a chart for your log. Are some duplicates? Which ones? Which letters make more than one sound? Are there some sounds in our language which combine letters? What are they?

Where in your mouth do the vowels sound? Do they always make the same sounds when they are in words? What are the rules about the sounds vowels make in words? When do you hear the schwa sound?

Close your eyes and listen to the people around you talking. Do you hear all of the individual letter sounds distinctly? Do you hear all of the individual words separately? Why? Is it necessary to hear all of the sounds to understand the words or to hear all of the words to understand the meaning of what is said? Why? Does a sentence also sing a song which tells you meaning? How can you tell when someone is asking a question? Giving a command? Listening with your eyes shut, can you tell which voices are tired, impatient, cross, happy?

In your log write your conclusions about the sounds of our language.

WHO'S A SKUNK?: PLAY A GAME OF METAPHOR
40 minutes   *1 person*

If you would like to show your students how people substitute exciting, interesting, or funny words for ordinary dull ones, do this activity.

What are a skunk, pig, rat or mouse? Do these words mean anything more than they mean as animals? Can you think of some other words that stand for different types of people or things? Make a list of these words along the right hand edge of a piece of paper. In a second column across from the first, write the things these words have come to stand for. Pick out five of these words and use them in sentences. Now write the same sentences without using the words in the right hand column.

What is the difference between the sentences? Which ones do you like best? Why? Metaphors are one kind of comparison. Which group of your sentences contain metaphors? What is being compared with what?

Sometimes a metaphor gets used so much for something that it really comes to mean that thing. It gets put in the dictionary and people forget that it ever meant something else. Do you know any words that are becoming like that?

Sometimes, when a metaphor gets used over and over, it's not interesting or exciting or funny any more because we are so used to it that we don't even think about it. Are any of the words on your list like that? Do you use any when you talk? Listen to yourself and your friends talk during one class period and see how many you can find.

Tell your log about your discoveries.

WORD CHOOSING: LITTLE OR ELEGANT WORDS
15 minutes   *1 person*

Discover a way to help students sharpen their abilities to make effective word choices by doing this activity.

Do you like big words or little ones? Which are you most comfortable with? Which would you use if you wanted to be clearly understood? Which would you use if you wanted your conversation to be most interesting? Which would you use to make a formal address? Why? Which would you expect to have the most powerful effect? Why? Match some little words to the big ones given here:

extinguish a fire   dismount from the horse   ascend the stairs
__ __ a fire   __ __ the horse   __ __ the stairs

When you filled in the blanks, you used a combination of a little verb and what part of speech? What are some of the other little verbs that can be combined with prepositions? Make a list for your log. Some of these little word phrases have many meanings. List some of those meanings in your log also. How can you help students discover these word alternatives?

WHERE DO YOU PUT "THE"?: YOUR BUILT-IN SYSTEM
10 minutes *1 person*

Play this little game to better understand how your built-in language sense works for you or your students.

Try these phrases, putting "the" where you consider it appropriate:

go to __ college	found at __ home
go to __ university	found at __ house
go to __ church	catch __ typhoid
go to __ hospital	catch __ measles
go to __ town	catch __ flu
go to __ city	catch __ cold (What does work here?)

Are you reasonably sure which ones are the places to put "the"? Do you know the rules for knowing which words to use "the" with? Then how do you know how to do them? Do we speak English because we know rules or is there some other reason? Do we learn to speak satisfactorily by learning more rules or by some other system? Can you think of some factors that greatly affect how people speak? Write about them in your log. How can students learn to speak more effectively? What could students learn from an exercise like this one? How could you put the factors you have just listed to work for you to cause changes in your students' speaking habits?

I LIKE GIRLS: INFLECTIONS IN ENGLISH
45 minutes *1 person*

Do this to discover a way to interest students in analyzing inflections and how they use inflections.

Suppose that "Do ruffite gorpun" means "I like girls." Would it mean the same thing if you said "Gorpun ruffite do"? Or would that mean

"Girls like me"? Do you know any languages in which the words do not need to be put in a definite order to have meaning? What if "Do ruffite gorpun" and "Gorpun ruffite do" both mean "I like girls;" but "Dooy ruffite gorp," "Ruffite gorp dooy," and "Gorp ruffite Dooy" all mean "Girls like me"?

Could you change the meaning of an English verb in the same way you might change ruffite in this make-believe language by saying: ruffiteo (I like), ruffiteas (you, singular, like), ruffiteat (he likes), ruffiteamus (we like), ruffiteatis (you, plural, like), ruffiteant (they like)?

Does English have inflections? What are they? Are the plural forms of nouns given in your dictionary? Are the inflections in English always the same? What is the plural form of "mother-in-law"? Of "duplex"? What is the past tense of "ricochet"? Look in your dictionary. If more than one form is given, which is preferred? Can you find the principal parts of the verb "dive" in your dictionary? Try the verb "open." Are all the principal parts given in your dictionary? Can you find them in another dictionary? Where would you tell a student to look for them? What is the singular form of the word "media"? Is "alumnus" singular or plural? Does it refer to a man or a woman? Are there any inflections in our language for sex? What about pronouns? How are pronouns different from our other words in their inflections? Why are they different?

How could you plan an activity which would interest students in finding out about the accepted forms of these words so that they could use them more effectively? Based upon what you have discovered, write an activity card for a high school student.

HEAR, HEAR: HOW CLEARLY DO YOU SPEAK?

throughout one day   *1 person*

To be able to alert students to their unconscious speech habits, become more aware of what you say and hear. Do this activity.

Do you ever mistake what people say? Why? Do others mistake what you say? How do you account for this? Say the sentence, "We'll own cars." Could you sound as if you were saying anything else? How can you make it clear? Where do the pauses go? Try this one "That's tough." What does it sound like? Is the pause needed? Try "Sun's raise meet." Try "assist her."

See if you can understand what is meant by these sentences. You may have to say them out loud before you know what they mean: "Waddle I do?" "We watched a harr movie on teel vision." "Dad says dough way farm." "He's got a ming." "Did you use the lawner mat?" "You cheed me out of my turn." "She was there a mindigo." "He sleft." "Iswashed my hair." "I ham sennum." "Isgot here." "We had poorhouse steat." "Can't cheer me?"

What can you or your students do to help people understand you? Are there times when you could separate your words more clearly?

Try it for one day. Whenever and wherever you talk, remind yourself to listen to how your words must sound to someone else. Make your words as clear as you can. At the end of the day tell your log about how you felt and about how you feel now that you have done it.

DIALECTS: BE A COLLECTOR

several hours   *1 person or a group*

To be able to encourage the mutual acceptance of dialect differences in the classroom, become informed about dialects.

When you are tired, do you say you are "all in," "beat out," "bushed,""done out," "done up," "fagged out," "give out," "killed," "perished," "petered out," "played out," "tuckered out," "used up," or "worn out"? Do you know any people who use some of these expressions that you do not? Do you "catch a cold," "get a cold," or "take a cold"? Do you say "idear" instead of "idea,""warsh" instead of "wash," or "greazy" instead of "greasy," "thoid" instead of "third"? Your use of these words can be traced to the part of the country you came from and the social background of your family or your education. What can you tell about people by the words they use? What do you know about the dialect of your area?

Where can you find out more about the dialect areas of the United States and about the other influences that contribute to personal dialects? Ask your teacher or librarian. Find out as much as you can about dialects. Make a collection of local terms and classify them according to source: family, friends, reading, and so on.

Write a newsletter article or make a report for your class in which you tell about your discoveries.

SOUND PUZZLES: A USAGE HELP GAME

several hours   *2 people*

To discover a way of helping students acquire new sounds for their dialects, do this activity.

Pretend that you and your partner speak non-standard dialects, and practice helping each other. You will need a space where you can work jig saw puzzles and perhaps leave them undisturbed for a day or two. You will need to buy or bring two jig saw puzzles from home. Decide what kind of dialect problem you have. How do you pronounce the x in axe? If it sounds like sk you need to pronounce it like ks. Have your partner print it on the backs of some of your puzzle pieces. Then before you can put those pieces in place you must pronounce the word correctly. Do you use the word "be" when other speakers would use "have"? Ask your partner to print the word "have" on the backs of more of your puzzle pieces. Before you can put those pieces in place you must use the word "have" correctly in a sentence. Do you get confused about when to add an "s" sound on plural words? Have your partner print an "s" on some of the pieces. When you want to put those pieces in place, you need to use a plural in sentences in the standard way. Do you get confused about when to make verbs singular and plural? Do you sometimes say "He go." and "They goes"? Have your partner print "go" and "goes" on the backs of some pieces. You will need to use them in sentences in the standard way before you can put the pieces in the puzzle. Do the same with other troublesome verbs.

Now you program a puzzle for your partner. Perhaps you would like to do some research to discover the most common usage problems of nonstandard dialects.

Make your programmed puzzles available to anyone in the class who would like to experiment with them. Be sure to place a sheet of instructions in the boxes with the puzzles.

A USAGE PROBLEM: HOW CAN YOU HELP?

1½ hours   *1 person*

If you would like to be able to help students who need to acquire new or second usage patterns, do this.

Begin by finding out what the most common usage problems are. Talk to some high school teachers. Talk to some students to find out what they would like to change, if anything. Listen to some students who speak non-standard dialects and see what you think needs to be improved. Find a dictionary which gives usage levels. What does it say about the usages you have noticed?

Find or imagine one particular student with a usage problem. What are his special needs? Does he say "he do," "It don't belong," "I be," "nobody don't," and "They okay"? How did he learn to talk that way in the first place? Try to help him by planning situations in which he can learn a new or second dialect in the same way he learned the first one—by listening to and talking to people who talk that way. Can you arrange for him to work and talk in class with someone who speaks a standard dialect? Can you program a tape for him to listen to which has the standard versions of sentences and conversation he needs to use? Can he role-play situations in which he needs to use a standard dialect?

Plan a program for your student's usage needs. Include all the details. Be sure you make a tape for him to listen to. Play your tape or parts of it for the class, and explain your program.

THE USAGE SCENE: WHAT SHOULD YOU SAY?

1 hour   *4 to 5 people*

If you do this activity you will be more able to help students analyze their usage needs and choose appropriate ways to meet their needs.

Discuss these questions: Do you use these words when you talk—*have went, ain't, couldn't never, seen* for *saw, done* for *did, learn* for *teach, that there, him and me, is* for *are, them* for *those?* How do you feel when other people use those words? What do you think about people who use those words? What do they think you think about them? Pretend that one of you is a high school student whose dialect includes some or all of the above word usages. Act out some scenes which might happen to him. Here are some suggestions:

You want to borrow money to buy a car, and you go to the bank to borrow money.

You try to get a date with a beautiful girl who speaks a standard dialect.

You apply for a job in a department store. You want to be a salesman, but the personnel officer wants you to work in the stock room

You are asked to prepare a talk on the weekly Bible lesson for your youth group at church.

You are trying to convince the guidance counselor that if you are allowed to be on the basketball team, you will be able to keep up your grades.

Try these scenes, and invent some of your own. Each time let a different group member be the student. Be sure he uses the nonstandard dialect in his own speaking. The other group members should play parts of other people in the scenes and show how these people react to the student. To show what the characters are thinking about each other, have a group member stand behind each character and tell his thoughts. You may also want to try the scenes with the same characters, but with the student speaking a standard dialect to see if the result is different.

Present your favorite scene for the class. Afterward, write about your role playing in your log. When you were the student how did you feel about yourself? About the other person or persons? What discoveries could high school students make about themselves and their dialects by role playing? Could students who speak standard dialects become more accepting of those who do not?

SPEAKING AND READING

Students today are less print-oriented than many of their teachers, most of whom have learned efficiently through reading. But schools and the tasks they give students depend strongly on reading. So students must read. However, the way to teach reading may not be to teach it directly but to teach readiness for reading, a preparation often used only in the early grades. The chief ingredient in reading readiness for secondary school students is the language experience of abundant good talk. Speaking is a prerequisite and concomitant of all language learning, and reading is no exception.

Experience, not listening to the teacher or reading assigned content, is the initial part of a good learning design. Experience has primacy over verbalization. Movement, handling, manipulating, and reacting to objects and events may, of necessity, be limited in the English classroom, but talking with peers can be the experience raw material which forms a background for reading. Such interaction provides perceptions and concepts that may be enlarged and tested by reading. This reading readiness experience expands and supplements other kinds of experience, not readily available in the limited confines of the classroom.

Another kind of oral language experience can supplement discussion. Enlarged viewpoints and trials of new roles emerge from feeling and responding in role-playing and debriefing discussion. Acting out is based on inferences drawn from meaning cues a reader finds in his reading. And one who enacts a piece of literature, either in skit or play form, must recall what is in the text: facts, events and actions. He must return to the text to check or recheck these facts.

The student should use another speaking experience, oral reading, to present ideas, prove points and display answers to questions. A student who wants to read orally for these purposes should use phrasing that clarifies ideas and interprets the writer's meaning. He should also read aloud in groups the writing he and his classmates do. Another kind of oral reading is choral speaking. This democratic activity deemphasizes leading roles. Excellent or confident performers furnish a standard without operating as stars; and voice, diction, breath control, pitch quality and duration appear in a context where each makes sense. In a group there is comfort for the inept or shy. The diction deviate hears and changes without embarrassment. The importance of knowing words and saying them clearly becomes naturally apparent.

Most reading programs rely on a reading and testing pattern which does not apply corrective measures for deficiencies discovered by tests. The comprehension check in a test is a meager facility at best and leads to small understanding, compared with the check a student can make of his ideas when he talks with others who have also read the materials. Unlike the traditional read and test pattern, discussion, and acting out the meanings of what has been read develops awareness of inferences upon which alternative interpretations are based. Students who discuss reading materials or develop roles from what they have read gain insight into a variety of ways of looking at ideas. And more important than being able to answer questions is the ability to formulate them. From discussion the presence of questions inherent in any situation becomes apparent. In the interaction of reading and discussion and role playing, students constantly produce and receive a growing range of written and oral language styles, vocabularies, and sentence structures. They speak, listen, read, and move in response to language and receive constant feedback from their language experiences through interactive speaking with others. This design for growth in reading proficiency is the most economical plan for obtaining feedback to students from their ideas and far surpasses the effectiveness of machines, which only teach and test and lack the complicated and sensitive responsiveness of human interaction.

Giving practice in vocabulary and word appreciation skills, oral language activity also helps the student appreciate the aesthetics of literature. Intensity of pleasure in literary performance depends as much on the reader's perception of the skill it manifests as upon the presence of that skill itself. A student should learn to respond to arrangement as well as content of words. The grammatical texture of sentences employing felicitous use of words should be examined, for grammar shows how words affect other words. Such examination reveals ways writers play games with sentence structures and disentangle the interlaced ambiguities of syntax. Students should play with sentences they find in their reading, seeing how parts fit together and which can be or perhaps can but should not be shifted from one place to another. They should see the ambiguity or nonsense that results from stringing words together in ways that violate the order principles of the English sentence. However, they should discern the purposeful inversions characteristic of poetic diction. These searches for meaning uncover the grammatical fact that a word in itself has too many meanings, so it has none until it combines with other words. That is grammar and that is literature.

Awareness of the student's need for producing and receiving a large variety of words underlies the customary emphasis on vocabulary building. However, growth in vocabulary appears within the context of that very reception and production of language and not in isolated dictionary exercises. Dictionaries must be subjects of fascinated interest, pleasant language companions, not the source of dull searches for what students do not really care to know. Only about two hundred years ago man learned to make them. Before that time dictionaries were statements from someone who said he knew what was right to someone who was expected to agree that he himself did not know. Then dictionaries appeared that described language in terms of what people were actually doing with it, and the science of lexicography was born. Unfortunately, many speakers of English, even some teachers of English, still expect dictionaries to perform pre-scientific activities of pre-lexicographic dictionary makers and tell them what is right instead of what is happening. Multiple meanings of words in dictionaries should remind students and teachers that meanings must be sought not in the words themselves but in the people who use them. The specific referent of a word in a dictionary must bow to the meanings of speakers who use it.

Content area teachers often depend too much on reading to develop percepts which come only from experience. In content areas students are sometimes expected to read about ideas with which they have had little or no experience and in which they have little or no interest. Hence many students do not "get" their assignments. If an experiential groundwork were laid in student discussion and interaction whenever actual experience is unavailable, assignments in reading content would be more effective. When a problem is located through student examination and interaction, a group is able to apportion out duties of collecting information so that the task is less onerous. This process leads directly to reading in a setting of purpose. From reading in a context of purposeful searching, there is a return to discussion where gathered information may be evaluated and verified. New searches may be instituted to supplement original ones. Other kinds of information gathering, such as interviewing, supplement reading and provide oral language experience.

Minority children may need extra help in reading. If they speak a dialect which differs markedly from the standard writing dialect, they may have to translate print into sound and then into their own dialect before they get meaning. This process, of course, slows reading speed. The fastest way to help such a student may involve speeding this mediating process so that it will eventually be telescoped. The step which may be eliminated or speeded by practice is the gap between the sound of his dialect and the sound of the standard writing dialect. Pattern practice in which the student uses and hears the sounds of standard English will help more than intensive practice in reading. At least it deserves a try if the minority group student has reached the secondary school with reading problems after being exposed to remedial and developmental procedures in grade school, as many students have been who still have reading problems.

More use of the same reading improvement devices that have before failed such a student may produce more of the same poor reading skills. Practice in sound discrimination is a useful tool that may help where others have failed. But, pattern drills are only the most obvious and most mechanical of such aids. Group discussion with peers who speak standard dialect, choral reading and immersion in many oral language situations are more important practice situations. The speaker produces language most effectively when he believes he can speak well about something he wants to say to someone he is confident will listen with interest to his ideas. A speaker in this situation is led naturally to adapt his phonological, syntactical and lexical systems to a dialect which will make him understood by his listeners. During interaction, if it occurs where speakers of standard dialect predominate among his listeners, he will hear and eventually begin to adjust his speaking and eventually his reading to the dialect he needs.

Activities

DO TELL: TELLING ABOUT A BOOK I

15 to 20 minutes   *1 person*

If you want to help students talk to individuals or groups about books they have read, consider the problems they will have and the feelings they will experience by giving a book talk yourself.

Choose a book to tell about. If it is one you have read in the past and you are not reading it especially for this activity, review it carefully. Arrange an audience for your book talk. Talk to the steering committee or find a listener from the help bank. Think about what your audience would like to know about your book: What would you like to know about a book before you read it? What could someone tell you about a book that would make you want to read it? Are there some people who might not like the book even if you did? It is only fair not to direct the book to these people. Be sure to say just which kinds of people would like the book. Can you tell about the book without giving away the plot?

Give your book talk. Tell your log how your audience responded to your talk. Does anyone you told about your book want to read it? Why or why not? Is there anything you will do differently the next time you tell someone about a book? Could you interest high school students in reading a book? How? What suggestions could you give to a high school student who is planning to give a book talk? What can a listener do to make talking about a book easier for one who is speaking? If your students tell you about their books, how will you respond?

SMART WORDS: TELLING ABOUT A BOOK II

30 Minutes   *1 person*

To help your students give successful, convincing book talks and feel good about their presentations, prepare yourself to guide their decisions about word choices.

If you are planning to give a book talk, consider these questions in deciding what you will say: When people talk about cars, do they use special kinds of words? What are some of the words people use when they talk about sports or music? When you are giving a report or talk in front of a group, how do you try to use special language? Why do you use special language? What questions might you ask to lead a student to discover his need to use special language when he gives a talk?

If your students want to know what words could help them, here is a list they might find helpful in telling about what their author says: *points out, declares, indicates, argues, asserts, observes, alleges, maintains, contends, claims, describes, asks.* Look them up in a dictionary to be certain you understand all their meanings and uses yourself. Try to use them in your book talk.

In planning your talk use a thesarus to help you find words which may add variety to your book talk. Look on the reference shelf in the library for other sources of interesting word alternatives. Write down the titles of these books so that you can refer students to them. Make your own list of useful word choices which could help students. Write it in your log.

Give your book talk.

BOOK GROUP: COMPARING BOOKS

variable time   *3 to 6 people*

Discuss books with a group to discover how you may help students with their book discussion groups.

Form a group. Each should have a book he wants to share. It is helpful if you bring a copy of your book to the discussion. If you have not read a book lately, read one or review an old favorite. There is no one right or best way to share books. One good way is for each person to choose his favorite passage and read it to the group, explaining why it is his favorite and what its significance is to the story. After you have done this, you may want to compare certain kinds of passages from the books. You may become interested in the ways authors show the personalities of characters or in scenes which describe dramatic action. Some of the best scenes to share are humorous ones. You might present some readings of similar scenes where the same or even opposite situations occur. You might want to prepare questions for each other about different books.

Depending upon what your books have in common and the interests of your members, you will need to set your own goals for what you hope to accomplish as a group and how much time you want to spend doing it. If you would like a product to present to the teacher, you need to decide that also. If you need help in making these decisions, you may want to review earlier activities in this book.

When your group has accomplished what it intended, write in your log about the experience. Did your discussions proceed smoothly? Why or why not? Did you do what you planned to do? Did you enjoy hearing about other people's books? Why or why not? What advice could you give to a group of students planning a book discussion? Could you think of another way your group might have talked about books?

ENDINGS: DO YOU LIKE THEM HAPPY OR SAD?

40 minutes   *3 to 5 people*

Try this approach to discussing reading with a group, and you may discover ways students may resolve unpleasant feelings about endings and respond actively to literature.

Find a group and discuss these questions in your group: What books or plays have you studied which have unhappy endings or which don't seem to give answers to questions they set up? How do you feel about them? Are there answers to the questions we meet in life? Which kinds of real-life questions have easy answers? Are there many different kinds of answers? Can you think of a question where the fact that there is no answer is an answer? Is there a range of answers, none of them wholly wrong and none wholly right for everyone?

If you kept these questions in mind as you read or watched a play, would it call for more active thinking or less active thinking on your part? Why? Would it be more interesting to you? Why? Is it as comfortable? Why?

Compile a list of suggestions for people who have trouble with sad endings. Make them into an activity card. Use your own suggestions. Each person should report back to the group about how they worked for him.

PRESENTING ALL SIDES: A PANEL BOOK DISCUSSION
1 hour   *4 to 8 people*

For helping students accept and deal with varying points of view about stories and ideas in their reading, become skillful yourself at dealing with other viewpoints. Do this.

For this activity you need a group to read the same work. You may choose a book, essay, poem, or play; but you will either need to find copies for everyone or read the work aloud in the group. As you read, look for the author's opinions, attitudes and values. Do you agree with him or not agree? Why? Are there some items that some of you hold one opinion about and others another? Elect one member of the group to keep a record of your group's agreements and disagreements about the author's viewpoint. Choose the unsettled ones as a focus for your panel presentation. When you are planning your panel discussion, you can look back at these ideas. Each person who is going to be in the panel needs to have clearly in mind (or on paper) at least three positive points in favor of his opinions. These are his reasons why the listeners should be convinced that his way of seeing the situation is best or makes the most sense. Choose a chairman to preside over your discussion.

Invite an audience from the class to hear you present all sides of each issue. You may want to report this discussion by a newsletter article to the class.

THE WAR SCORE: LITERATURE OF WAR
1 hour or more   *a group*

To be able to help students examine the effects of social attitudes and world events upon literature, investigate the subject with a group.

Consider this problem. In this country we very often classify our literature in time according to what war it was associated with. Why do we do this? What effect does a war have on literature?

To find the answers to these questions, do some detective work on literature of past and present times. Look for examples of literature written during different wars in our history. What about diaries, letters, and poems? Can you find examples of any that were written by people involved in wars? What kinds of picture do they show of wars? What about novels? Were their authors really involved in the wars? Did their authors have some special ax to grind? Were the novels written during the wars or afterward? Do they show the wars as glamorous, cruel, or matter-of-fact? Can you find any examples of newspaper or magazine articles written during wartime? In what ways do you think they are realistic or not realistic? Try to find some information about the newspapers in this country before and during the Spanish-American War. What kind of literature is likely to come before a war? What kinds of things do people have to be feeling before they will get into a war? What kinds of songs come out of wars? Can you name some from the Revolutionary War? The Civil War?

Choose one particular war in our history and make a war-literature collage, using both words and pictures to show the different kinds of literature produced by people who get involved in the feelings of war. See if you can show by your arrangement of the pictures and words which kinds of literature or even which particular works were important to the times—for instance, *Uncle Tom's Cabin,* "John Brown's Body," and "Dixie" in Civil War times.

If you are working alone, you might get help from the help bank on art work.

SPEAK IT: DRAMATIZING A CONVERSATION

1 hour   *2 to 5 people*

Here is a way students can make the books they've been reading seem more real and interesting. Try it.

Are there some scenes in the material you are reading which are presented as conversation? Find a partner or two—however many you need—and cast the conversation as a little play. Decide whether or not you will need a narrator to read some of the non-conversational material. But some may be left out altogether. Or you may act descriptions of how characters behave as they speak.

Read your conversation. Record in your log new ways you see the story and its events when you have done this for some scenes.

READING PRETTY: READING A POEM ALOUD

20 to 30 minutes   *1 person*

When you have finished this activity, you will be able to advise and help students who are planning to read poetry aloud.

Listen to recordings of poetry readings. You may get them from the public library or from your teacher's collection. Read the poem silently with the recording. What does the reader do when he reaches the end of a line and there is no punctuation? Does the reading of a sentence of poetry sound more like a sentence of prose than of poetry? Why does the reader try to make it sound like conversation? Does the reader pay attention to any special kind of words? What parts of speech are stressed? What happens to the rhythmic pattern? When you prepare your reading, what are you going to do about choosing pauses? Be sure to determine what mood the poet is trying to convey. If you can make yourself feel this mood, what effect will it have on your reading?

Choose a short poem, which you have practiced, and read it aloud to the class.

GO MODERN: PUTTING A CLASSIC PLAY IN MODERN FORM

several hours   *a group*

If you want to help students relate classic literature to their own lives and enjoy doing it, this may help you find ways.

Could you make your classic play into a play of our own times with people we could identify with? If you were producing it today, could you make it into a musical? Do you have some records that would fit the ideas and the mood of the play? Is your classic a serious one that deals with serious problems? Could you modernize it and still maintain the serious tone of the play?

Consider ways a modern play is different from a classic. Perhaps you will want to go back and review other activity cards on drama. Will your modern version be planned for filming, television, or the stage? What will you leave out? What will you add or change? Besides the setting, will you also change the way the characters talk? Will their attitudes and values be different? How? How can you show these things in the script? In the acting? For extra help with acting look for cards on acting under speaking.

Rehearse your production. Then put it on before the class or record it on video tape.

PEP UP YOUR ACTING: FIND THE STAGE ACTION IN THE WORDS
variable time *a group*

To help students convert what they have read into actions on stage, discover the actions in the words yourself.

Join or form a group to perform a play or a scene from a play. Since Shakespeare includes few stage directions in his plays, you might find it useful to try acting a scene from one of his plays. After you have decided who will play each part and have chosen a director, read the scene aloud together. You may want to have each person read his part. It helps to have copies you can write on; but if you do not, take some notes about your part. Look for verbs that tell you what the character is doing. If Juliet says, "Come hither, Nurse," what is she probably doing as she says it? When Cassius says, "But, soft, I pray you," does he whisper? What might he do with his hands? Can you tell what one character is doing from what another says? What is Macbeth telling about himself when he talks about his "hangman's hands"? How can the words used to describe a character tell you about how he feels and about how he acts? What does Hamlet's mother tell you about his actions when she tells him to stop looking "for thy noble father in the dust"? Are there descriptive words like "grizzled" or "bold" which give you clues about how a character behaves? If someone is described as "innocent," how can you act out "innocent"? From the scene you are reading choose several such words and practice expressing those qualities with your actions or posture.

Use what you have discovered about expressing words in actions to help put your scene into motion. Present it for the class.

WHY RECITE?: HAVE A READER'S THEATER

several hours *3 to 30 people*

To become familiar with a way of teaching literature dramatically that is easier for students than activities which require memorization, do this.

Plan a presentation which is read rather than recited. Discuss these possibilities: Do you want to write your own script and pretend that you are performing an old radio show? Would it be a soap opera with a name like "Bill's Other Love," or would it be a more serious show? Have you ever seen readings from the Bible performed? Have you studied a play or poem you think would be effective in this form?

Do you want to wear any special clothes? Some people wear robes. Would a musical background help? Does anyone you know play drums or a guitar? Do you want anything else to be happening in the background? Will you plan for a backdrop or a pantomine performance to accompany your reading? Will you read on stage? Will you want a narrator to introduce your reading and provide transition? Are there some parts, like the refrain in some poems, that might sound better read in unison?

Find someone to type copies of the reading for each participant. Find or make attractive folders to put your papers in while you are reading. Rehearse your reading.

Invite your class or another class to watch your performance.

AN EAR FOR READING: READING ALOUD

10 minutes   *1 person*

This activity will prepare you to help students read aloud.

Join a group that is reading aloud or arrange to participate in a reader's theater. When you are reading lines in a reader's theater, what are you doing when you are not talking and someone else is? What is the best thing you could do? Do you listen to what the other speaker is saying or do you keep looking at your own next lines? How can you make yourself listen? Which would make your next reading better, looking at your next lines or listening to him? Why?

The next time you read aloud try listening to the other reader. Think about what his words really mean. How does that character feel? Then, don't just read your lines because they are what comes next, but read them because they are a response to what came before.

Afterward, tell your log how you felt before, during, and after the reading.

STRAIGHT TO THE SOURCE: INTERVIEWING A BOOK CHARACTER

1 hour   *1 or 2 people*

If you do this you will be more prepared to help students use their imaginations to visualize and sympathize with the characters in their books.

Plan to stage an interview with a character from your reading. You may want to find a partner to play the part of either the interviewer or the character, or you may want to tape your interview and play both parts yourself. Here are some questions which may be helpful: Does your character have an unusual or interesting personality? How much does the book tell you about him? What might your audience like to find out about him? What might you logically make up about him? How would he talk? Would he have a dialect or use special words? Will you describe him for the audience? Will he be dressed for the part? Will you refer to information in the book in asking questions? If your character comes from the past, will he be brought into a modern setting or will you put yourself into his setting? What interesting events have happened to him that you could ask about? Does he know any famous opinions that should be brought out? How did he see other characters in the book? One useful question might be, "How did you feel when you did so and so?"

You might decide to pretend that you are interviewing the character on television or radio. If you have a partner, work together to plan the questions. Be sure you have both had a chance to read the book so that you will not be embarrassed by any inconsistencies.

Perform your interview. Interviews work well on sound or video tape also.

ACT IT OUT: CHARADES ABOUT BOOK CHARACTERS
1 hour   *4 to 10 people*

Play this game with your classmates to discover how students would feel and react to this method of bringing their book characters to life.

Make a list of the books you have all read lately. This will prevent someone's using a character from a book that not everyone in the group has read. Choose a person—it can be someone from the help bank—to be in charge of drawing names for turns and keeping score. You will also need a watch. Any person who takes ten minutes without the group guessing his character tells the name of his character and sits down. Names should be put on slips of paper and drawn from a hat or box.

Each person in the group writes several names of characters he would like to act out on small slips of paper. When his name is called, he gives the one he will act out to the scorekeeper. The idea is to communicate the character's name to the group without talking or making a sound. When someone guesses it, the person acting out the character gets one point and the first person to guess the name gets one point. If ten minutes go by with no right guesses, no one gets any points. ·

This game gets harder as it goes along because a particular character can only be used once and all the easy ones get used up.

Let the person who gets the highest score be the scorekeeper the next time.

MAKING A BREAKING: READING ABOUT A FAMILY BREAK UP
1½ hours   *1 person or a group*

To be able to help students work out their feelings about book situations concerning family problems, explore the subject with a group.

Form a group and discuss these questions: What kinds of things cause families to break up? What are the causes in your book? Are these like any you have heard of in real life? What attempts do people in the book make to prevent the breaking up of the family? What more could they have done? What would you have done if you had been one of the characters?

Is it best for a family whose members bring each other unhappiness to break up? Are there other ways to solve the problem? What solution is offered in the book? Does it seem like a solution that might happen in real life? Do you think that it would have solved the problems as the writer states them? Do you have another solution that you wish the author had written into his book?

Discuss these questions as a group or think about them as an individual. Decide upon one or more solutions that you think could have been tried in the book.

If you are working as a group, improvise your solutions in a scene. Think about how the characters would think, feel, react in the new situation you have planned. If you are working alone, try writing a different ending to the story, using your own solution.

KNOWING IS NOW KNOWING: UNCERTAINTY IN LITERATURE
1½ hours   *2 people*

To be more able to deal with the uncomfortable feelings some students may have about the uncertainty in literature, do this.

Choose a book you have read in the past or find one to read which shows a character whose fate is unresolved. The character may not be presented as wholly good or bad.

Look in the help bank or choose a partner from the class. You need someone who will be a good listener—maybe you can agree to listen to him next time if he listens to you this time. It would help if he has read the story, but it isn't necessary. You can explain it to him.

Answer these questions, not in your log or in your mind but aloud to your listening partner: Does your author have any reasons for wanting to leave you in uncertainty? What could they be? Is it possible that the writer is saying that both sides or several sides of the question have values that need to be respected? How do you know that he wants you to feel this way? What clues reveal how the writer feels? Which writer tells you the truth, one who lets you know who is good and who is bad or one who tells you that good and bad are present in every person? Would everyone agree about what is good and what is bad? Ask your partner for his opinions.

Pretend that you are the author of the book. Let your partner interview you about your reasons for writing as you did. In planning your interview consider these questions: What is the function of uncertainty in our lives? Are there some things which never yield definite answers? What are some of them? What things do we never get certain knowledge about? Are these usually the important or the unimportant things? Would the writer know this? What is the writer trying to show when he deals in questions and uncertainties rather than definite answers and certain outcomes?

Record your interview on tape or present it before the class.

GOING PLACES: IMPROVISE A SCENE FROM GEOGRAPHY
45 to 90 minutes   *a group*

To see how you can plan activities which help students relate language skills to their reading in other subjects, do this.

Form a group or work on this project with your already established group. Find a junior or senior high school geography book, and plan to use some part of it as a basis for an improvised scene.

Imagine that one or two members of your group are planning to visit as tourists the place described in the book. What might happen to them there? Would their plane land in the capitol city? What sights would they want to see? Would they hire a native guide? How would they feel about the customs of the place? Would the clothing be different? Would the travelers be conspicuous? What would be their means of transportation? Would they go shopping? What money would they use? How would they make themselves understood? Perhaps you want to act out a shopping scene in which they try to communicate by sign language or a scene in a restaurant where they eat the local foods. Perhaps it would be interesting to act out a scene in which they discover the local customs or comment on the sights. You may want to supplement the information in the geography book by doing some research in the library.

Improvise the scene. Be sure you show how the inhabitants react to the tourists as well as how the tourists react to them. You may even want to do several scenes in a time sequence as the travelers continue their trip. Afterward, tell your log what you think about the place the tourists visited. Would you like to visit the country? Why or why not?

BACK IN TIME: IMPROVISE A SCENE FROM SOCIAL STUDIES
45 minutes   *a group*

To enable your students to relate their language activities to their social studies reading, find ways they can act out or improvise scenes from history. Try this activity.

With your group, plan to act out or improvise historical happenings. You may want to act out a scene like the first meeting of the Continental Congress or the surrender of General Lee. You may decide to bring historical figures back to life and interview them in a present setting. In either case, consider these questions: What are the facts of the lives or events in your scene? What kind of people were the historical characters? Were they dedicated? Did they have children? What was at stake for them? How would they have felt in that situation? Why did they do what they did? Were they ambitious? Frightened? Foolish? Were they philosophers? If so, what did they philosophize about? What did they do for recreation? What events had come before and would come after the one in your scene? How do those events affect the scene? How do you feel about the characters? Does all the tradition about a famous character like Abe Lincoln help or hinder you in trying to imagine how he would act in real life? If you need more information than is available in the text book, do some research in the library.

Improvise or act out your scene. Tell your log afterward how you feel about the event or person in your scene.

DIFFERENCE OF OPINION: WRITERS WHO DISAGREE
1 hour   *2 people*

To help students talk about differences of opinion in what they read as well as in their own experience, discover for yourself the advantages of a debate between authors.

Choose men whose ideas about war, human relations or even personal subjects like religion or politics are in opposition. You may have a friend who has read the same books or who has read one while you have read the other. Perhaps each of you is an expert on the views of his author. Your authors may have lived in different times and places, but what would they have to say if they could debate the subject they disagree on? What arguments would each one make for his viewpoint?

Plan a debate between your two authors. Act out the debate. Tell your log about arguments that were used and what they revealed about the two authors. What do you think of those two authors now?

MEETING THE CHALLENGE: AN INTERVIEW WITH AN AUTHOR
30 minutes   *1 person*

Doing this activity will provide you with a tool for helping students become interested in authors and for satisfying their interest.

Choose an author from your own reading to investigate. If you could interview your author, what would you ask him? Make a list of questions you would ask him about the book you have read that he has written. Tell what was in your book that made you enquire. Post these questions on the bulletin board and challenge anyone who has read the book to suggest ways the writer might reply to any or all of them.

What kinds of answers did you get? Were they a help to you in understanding the author? Did they help in any way in understanding the book? Tell your log about the results of your challenge.

WORD EXPERT: OPENING THE CLASS WITH A SPECIAL WORD
one week, 15 minutes per day   *1 person*

Become a word scholar if you want to be able to interest your students in expanding their vocabularies.

Every day for a week open the class with some word that you think your classmates would like to learn or know more about. You may want to ask them for suggestions about specific words or about the kinds of words they want to learn.

After you have chosen each word and know its meaning, make up a sentence in which the meaning of the word is clear. At the beginning of each class write the word on the board and read the sentence aloud. You will also need to have the dictionary meaning of the word written so that you can answer the questions of people who are not satisfied with relying on the sentence for the meaning of the word.

You might want to ask your classmates to also try to use the word in a sentence—just to make sure that they got the meaning that you meant for them to get from your sentence.

You will probably need to spend only 5 minutes or less telling your word to the class, but you will need more time each day for looking up words and writing good sentences.

Record in your log the words and sentences you use. Tell about the responses you get from the class.

WORD ART: MAKE A WORD COLLAGE

1 to 1½ hours   *1 person*

Try this way of remembering words so that you can use it with your students.

Find a word with many meanings. It can be a new word to you or one that you already know some of the meanings for. Make a collage of pictures of the many meanings of the word. Try to find at least one picture from magazines or the newspaper to show each different meaning. You may want to use several pictures for some meanings.

You will need something to paste your pictures onto. That depends on how many pictures you have, how large they are and what you can find. You will also need to write or print the word somewhere on the collage—as large as you can. You might also decide to do some other writing, like writing the meanings under the pictures, but that is up to you.

Plan your arrangement of pictures before you paste them on. You may not want to use all of them. You may want to put similar meanings near each other. You may decide you need more or different pictures. You may want to use the opposite of the word to make contrasts.

Tell your log about any problems you had and how you solved them. Tell it also how you feel about the collage you made and the word. What advice would you give to someone else about how to make a word collage?

BRIGHTEN YOUR TALK:
TURN A READING WORD INTO A SPEAKING WORD

35 minutes   *1 person*

To help students add reading words to their speaking vocabularies, try this with words from your own reading.

As you read today, whether you read the newspaper, a novel or some other kind of literature, look for unusual words or words you do not understand. Keep a notebook or piece of paper nearby to write these words on. At the end of the day choose 10 words from the list that you would like to add to your spoken vocabulary. Look them up in the dictionary. When you understand their meanings and pronunciations, think of situations which might occur in your life in which you could use these words. Try to think of three different ways you might be able to use each word. Write sentences in your log, showing how you might be able to use each word. Whom would you be saying these sentences to? What would the purpose of your communication be? The next day use each of your words as many times as you can.

Afterward tell your log about how you used the words. Were the people you used them with surprised? Did you feel comfortable using the words? Did you have any unusual replies? How many times did you use each word? Which words were the easiest and which were the hardest to use in conversation? Why? Which word is your favorite? Why?

FANTASMA: A BIG PRODUCTION

variable time several hours   *3 to 5 people*

If various groups in your class are making skits and doing scenes from the same play or story and you would like to see them all put together, do this.

Form a group; you may want to include the steering committee in your group. You will need one or two people to visit each of the different groups to find out exactly what they are doing. If these groups have scripts or written plans, it will help you if you can get copies of these.

As soon as you have this information, you need to find ways of putting it all together into one production—or at least so that each skit is in an order which makes sense. Ask yourselves these questions: Is there one idea that all or some of the skits have in common? Do they have anything in common? Characters? Type of presentation? Mood? Setting? Is there anything your group can do to bring out the common elements? Do you want to follow the chronological order of the original story or would some other arrangement work better? Would some kind of narration presented between skits by your group help? Could you use a moderator or master of ceremonies? Who would do it? What would he say? Could some members of your committee write the words and another member act as moderator?

Are you going to present the whole thing on video tape? Before the class? Before another class? On sound tape?

As you plan your production, be sure to let groups involved know what you are planning. They will request changes and give suggestions.

After the production has been recorded and viewed, the committee should make a short written report for the purpose of giving advice and helpful hints to the next people who do this activity.

PLANNING AHEAD: MAKING A READING UNIT

several hours   *3 to 8 people*

To prepare yourself to make clear, sequential, thorough plans for language study related to reading, do this activity.

Form a group. Imagine that you are teachers meeting at the end of the year to plan next year's units of study for the seventh grade at your school. Begin your plans by discussing what theme you will use as a basis for the reading selections of your first unit. Could you use sports, poverty, personal values, heroes or war as themes? What possibilities can you list? Choose one about which you feel certain you can find literary works of all kinds. What sub-themes or topics can you develop within the theme you have chosen? Check the card catalog in your library for books dealing with your theme. Where can you find a list of the current paperback books available? Where can you find out about records, tapes, film-strips, slides and films? Where can you find out about magazine articles? About poetry? About short stories? Each of you may want to take the responsibility for surveying the prospects in one genre or medium.

How long will your unit be? Will it be a 3 week, 6 week, or 9 week unit? How long will it take seventh grade students to read each selection? Which ones support the theme and sub-themes you have chosen? How can you find out? What are your objectives for the unit? What do you want the students to know or be able to do when they have finished it? How will you know if they have arrived at the objectives? How will you evaluate what they have done? How will they work? Will they have discussion groups? What will they discuss? Will you need to set specific assignments and questions for discussion? Will there be a schedule to show when they should have each assignment or amount of work finished? Will there be projects to complete? What suggestions for projects can you make to go with your unit? Can you include all these items in your unit plan: a theme, objectives, a list of materials and sources, a sequential plan of how and when the materials are to be used by students, activities, questions, projects, products, feedback by the students, methods of evaluation?

Write your plan. Then type it in a form that a seventh grade student could understand and follow.

CHAPTER VI

The Student Writes

Writing is a dialect, a special manifestation of language, and most students who can be taught to speak can be taught to write things down in order with some degree of conviction and polish. The goal of teaching writing in the humanistic curriculum is to help students put themselves down on paper, study themselves as revealed, and use further writing to develop themselves. With constantly more complex experiences in growing up, the learner needs to communicate with ever more mature expression. He wants to be understood; to express his feelings, knowledge, interests and moods; to organize his thoughts; to enjoy his writing; and to master the mechanics he needs to make his writing acceptable to his readers. He may be unaware that through writing he can also enhance his own creativity and develop a personal style.

Many students see no writing in their homes except an occasional grocery list or a form to be filled out. The only writing they themselves do is writing they are made to do for or at school. They draw the quite natural conclusion that writing is something only people in school think is important. And, since things the school considers important are often rather unimportant in their lives, such students classify writing as something they do to get through school but which will not really matter either now or later in their lives.

Because many students write little after they leave school, the alternative of spoken composition in English class should be chosen frequently. Some writings can be taped. Some ideas develop as effectively on film as they do on paper. Efforts in story and drama should often be acted. There is nothing sacred about pen and paper, but because students need to practice organizing their thoughts and setting thoughts to words, looking at them on paper is one useful way to learn to manipulate ideas.

GENERATING STUDENT WRITING

What is the process of writing? Where does it start? Some have suggested that it begins with finding the matter, that it finds its genesis in itself. Proponents of this view sequence writing assignments from description through narration to explanation and expressions of supported opinion. Lists of methods of development—defining, comparing and contrasting, finding cause and effect—make the purpose of writing to do these things. In this approach, each is explained and dissected as method; for instance, description is explained as a method of writing about an object by ordering details from top to bottom, inside to outside, around, or in some other prescribed pattern. The humanistic activity curriculum could adapt to any of the approaches usually outlined in textbooks. Though these materials exist in abundance and constitute the major thrust of the teaching of writing in composition courses in high school and even college, they have not produced large numbers of good or even willing writers among either students or their teachers.

Many student writing experiences are negative ones, arising in a context of fear or tension. The "essay" test, sometimes considered superior to the "objective" test (when both often depend upon evaluation of non-typical student behavior and are equally invalid), is such a negative context for student writing. Students taking essay tests identify the process and purpose of writing with being judged critically. Such a writer tries to write exactly what he has been told is right. Punishment, in the form of a low grade, awaits his deviation from this expectation, and he identifies writing with feelings of apprehension and uneasiness.

Written work is sometimes used as drill to impress upon memory spelling or other usage patterns. Here writing is associated not only with lack of achievement but with boredom. And in some classrooms writing is used as punishment for infractions of behavior rules, a custom which says something about how teachers themselves feel about writing. The activity curriculum uses such approaches only within activities designed to encourage students to write for joy as they would sing, to write for rage as they would scream, to write for sorrow as they would cry, to integrate writing into their human experience, placing it alongside their other expressions of human emotion, using it to express their human feelings.

If the student lacks experience or has not investigated experience in terms that cause him to write about it, he will be unable to write about it effectively just because he knows the rhetoric of using cause and effect, comparing or contrasting. Teaching formal skills and provision of assignments from textbooks which do not reflect his experience do not forward a learner's writing growth. Activity cards must prescribe experience and ask questions which persuade the student to analyze experience. Lack of this debriefing experience usually means that his writing will be insignificant both as process and as product.

The function of humanistic teachers of writing is to mobilize experiences for the student, helping him discover his need and desire to write to fulfill his own purposes. And the occasion of experience is not an activity of spelling, punctuation or syntaxing; it is a process of writing something for a reader. The time to teach writing is not when a theme is due, once a week or thereabouts, and the teacher's function is not to assign writing but to help students decide when they need to write, what purpose they have in writing and who their readers will be. The activity teacher also helps students discover mutual interests so that one student perceives his need to write for another student or group of classmates.

Writing should not take place until students conceive ideas important enough to make them feel those ideas must be written down. The teacher creates by means of activities an experience which talks to the student of his need to write. The time to teach description is when a student needs to describe. For instance, he should feel the teacher is interested enough in the things in his life that he would like to describe some of them in detail for that teacher. And more effective than long lists of ways to observe and record detail are questions about detail, written by the teacher or other reader in the margins of the student's descriptive essay.

The time to teach narrative is when the student has a story he wants to tell. Again, features of narrative style are best taught by marginal comments of the teacher . . . "Could you have started your story with this detail to get the interest of the reader?" or "There seems to be something missing here. Did anything else happen?"

The time to teach the character sketch is when the student has observed a character in life experience or in reading that he wants to tell about, that is worthy of being recorded and analyzed. Likewise, the time to teach cause and effect is when the student has found an effect he wishes to ascribe to a cause. And the time to teach students to write explanations or instructions is when they need or want to give explanations to others. The time for writing reasons is when the student wants to convince another of his viewpoint. To assume that all students should be taught the same one of these methods during the same class period is to make assumptions about the sameness of students and their needs which the humanistic curriculum does not make.

The humanistic curriculum in writing encourages the student to choose the content of his own work. Rather than assign writing, the teacher generates it by prewriting activities, by encouraging spirited response to reading, lively group activities, individual reports to groups, interpretive or controversial reading, and consideration of varying viewpoints about ways to handle problems of current interest to students.

Group work is a theater of ideas which often demands recording of those ideas, and raw materials generated from group work prepare the learner to write in a multitude of contexts. From group activities the student writes notices for a bulletin board or a newsletter. More experienced writers serve as an editorial board to collect and edit materials for the newsletter and bulletin board. The log, a first try at recording experiences and generalizations, becomes a fruitful source of formal writing materials. Students should reread their logs to discover changes in how they feel and think and what they know now that they did not know when they first began to write. They may find ideas they want to pursue further or research in depth. They may find ideas they would like to tell others.

If the student is reluctant to write in his log, the teacher may write in the log a number of comments and questions, a kind of friendly letter, perhaps, to tell the student how the teacher feels when a student does not write in his log! Students who write in logs materials which they are not ready to share can tape the pages together to indicate their desire for privacy. These might be called "mono-log." The rest, of course, is "dialog," which the teacher should answer in the margins. The teacher will not have time to read all that students write. And even if there is time to read all of it, there is not time to respond. But the teacher who gets into the habit of spending spare moments with student logs will find it an interesting way into the thoughts of students and will find students writing better as their writing gets a response.

Students who do little other writing often write on walls and write notes to classmates. If the teacher is going to teach writing successfully to these students, use should be made of already established habits which meet their own needs. Often, these habits of natural writing are discouraged or even punished. Instead, let there be as many occasions as the teacher can invent and as many as will arouse student response for students to write notes to each other. A strategically placed message board can be the repository of notes from students to students and from teacher to students. Logs should record whether the student feels he is getting from his notes results that he considers appropriate.

A grafitti sheet, covering one section of a classroom wall, can record public messages students feel like leaving there. Students might discuss the purpose of such writing and what kinds of writing go on it. Most writing is means to express strong feelings of the writer, not designed to reach any particular audience. Usually graffitti are anonymous.

Students should write letters to secure information or to express their feelings to public figures, admired sports or entertainment personalities or anyone for whom they have a message. Their logs should record whether these letters get desired results. Sometimes the spacing and parts of a letter are taught to students, to the neglect of the real purposes of letters— to inform, amuse, enquire, convince, or show respect or concern. A study of the purposes for writing a letter and a log entry on whether the letter gets results lead to a study of rhetoric appropriate to serve a letter writer's purpose. Without such study, student letters tend to be like the small boy's letter home from camp—"How-are-you-I-am-find-I-caught-a-frong." This writer must have rhetorical experience in giving the details of events which have affected him. A canned assignment he gets when he returns to English class—to tell in a theme what happened on his vacation—will do little to teach him this rhetoric.

Activities

AS IT HAPPENS: BE A REPORTER

1½ to 2 hours   *1 person*

Prepare yourself to help students write about news events for their classmates by being a reporter for your class newsletter.

If you are going to be a reporter, you need to think and question about news and how it is reported. When you report news, will you tell what happened, or will you tell how you feel about what happened? Is there a difference? What is the difference?

Where in newspapers do you find stories about how people feel about events? What other differences can you find between news and editorials? What does an editorial leave out? What does a news story leave out? Which is more likely to use emotion-producing words? Why?

What is a "feature story"? How does it differ from an editorial or news story? Is the subject different? How soon after something happens does a feature story tell about it? Is this different from the way a news story is reported? How? Does a feature story begin with the result and tell how it came about or with the cause and then tell the results?

Report on a meeting or event for your bulletin board. It may be a youth group or political event or any event that would interest the class. Report it as a news story first, only telling what happened. Then try reporting on the same event as an editorial item, giving your opinions and feelings.

Post your two versions of the news side by side. Could you do the same event as a feature story? How would you do it? Tell your log. Tell your log also what you have discovered about reporting news.

BE PRINT PEOPLE: NEWSLETTER I

variable time   *4 to 10 people*

Use this activity as opportunity to learn about details of printing a class newsletter so that you may provide similar outlets for your students' writing.

Organize a group from your class to print a newsletter. Decide how you will solve these questions. You will need to consult your teacher about some of them.

How will you print your paper? Does your school have a mimeograph machine you can use? Are there any other kinds of copiers available to you? Will paper, stencils and other materials be furnished or will you need to pay for them? Where will you get the money?

You will need a stencil or master copy. Can anyone in your group type? Would someone agree to learn? Would you need two people to type? What typewriter could you use?

What kinds of things would you put in your newsletter? Would you use news from the whole school? Are other people in your class interested in writing articles? Would you accept articles from other classes? Would you turn down articles if you did not think they were appropriate? How would you decide?

How often will you print your newsletter? Whenever you have enough news? How much is enough? How many pages do you want? How will you arrange news in your paper? Will you have special pages for different things?

How and to whom will you distribute your newsletter? Will you want to sell copies? Would you like to give away copies to class members and sell some to other people? How much would each copy cost? If you do that, how many copies will you need to print of each issue? How many copies can you make from one master? If you do sell copies, what will you do with the money you make?

Who will gather the news and how? Will you have an artist to draw illustrations and cartoons? Will you have advertisers? How would you get them? Will you have classified ads? Will someone proofread the articles? Who? Will you have an editor in charge of putting the whole thing together?

Use these questions as your guide in planning your first issue. After that you will have more ideas of your own. You will need to make your newsletter fit the special needs of your class and your group.

INVITE GUESTS TO VISIT YOUR CLASS: NEWSLETTER II

30 to 50 minutes *a group*

To use guest visits both as an opportunity for social writing and an inspiration for responsive writing in your classroom, prepare yourself by doing this activity.

If your class or group has an activity that other students in school, other teachers or administrators would enjoy, invite them to visit the class. You should talk this over with the teacher and other students first to make sure that it does not interfere with their plans.

You will need to give written invitations to your guests. The invitations should be written on plain paper and be placed in envelopes. Be sure to mention the time and day. You may want to ask them to reply as to whether they will come. The usual way to do this is to place RSVP on the invitation. This is French—"respondez s'il vous plait." Please respond. If you are worried about other details of form, your teacher can help you or tell you where to look for answers to your questions.

Guests should be greeted at the door and a seat found for them. If they need books or other things to help them understand what is happening, be sure these are provided.

After the visit think about these questions: What did the visitors do or see in your class? What comments did they make? Did they all arrive on time? How did the class react to them? How long did they stay? What was said afterward by class members? As a group, plan a society page for your class newsletter, with each member of the group contributing an article about the event. Each of you should choose a different aspect of what happened—preparations, exhibits or activities planned, comments or reactions of women as opposed to those of men, comments and reactions of specific individuals, your internal reaction, comments of class members during or after the event, a historical review of other such events which have taken place or not taken place at your school, suggestions for the next time or perhaps a different slant of your own. Remember to find details to support your impressions of what happened.

WRITE ABOUT SPORTS: NEWSLETTER III

variable time out of class   *1 person*

Write about something you enjoy, to see how you can relate the interests of students to their writing activities.

After each sports event you attend this season, go home and write an entry in your log about what happened and how you felt about it. It will be your own private record of the sports season.

At the end of the season write a summary of your school or community's sports activities for the class newsletter—or you may want to keep the class posted with weekly sports bulletins.

REPORT AN EXPERIENCE: NEWSLETTER IV

1 to 2 hours   *1 person*

To prepare yourself to guide students in finding experiences to write about and in putting their experiences into words, do this activity.

Between now and the next class meeting do something you have never done before. Here are some possibilities, but you may think of better ones: visit a museum or public building you have never been in before, attend a religious revival or a service of a religion other than your own, visit a mental hospital, go to a dog show, see a foreign film, or visit a court room. During your experience take notes to help you write about it later. Make observations of your own reactions, feelings and sensory perceptions. Was it a large building? Did it echo? Were there many people? How did you feel about the people? What were the sights, sounds and smells of the place? What events took place while you were there? Did you have any new feelings about what you saw as you thought about the experience afterwards?

Write about your experience for the newsletter. You may take any kind of tone you feel appropriate for your writing. If you write in a serious tone, how will that affect the words you choose? What words might you use for an ironic or a comic tone? How would the tone you chose change the way your reader felt about your experience?

FASHION REPORTER: NEWSLETTER V

variable time out of class   *1 person*

Do this to learn how to plan an activity that will help students relate their interests and personal experiences to the use of writing.

Plan to write a fashion article for your class newsletter. Are there fashion shows where you live? Does your school have them? Look for advertisements and fashion news in the woman's section of your newspaper. Attend a fashion show. Where else could you find news about fashions? What could a thirteen-year-old tell you about fashions? What could the sales lady in your town's largest department store tell you about fashions? What would a woman tell you about fashions? What would her husband tell you? What could you find out if you watched the people walking on the street downtown and counted the numbers of people wearing different styles of clothing?

Collect information about fashions that you think would be interesting to your class, and write an article for the class newsletter based on what you have learned about fashions.

SUPER SNOOPER: NEWSLETTER VI

1 hour   *1 person*

To be able to involve your students in writing and provide them with interesting topics for writing, learn about interviewing by doing it.

Choose someone to interview—a classmate, teacher, businessman, or some person in the community with an interesting hobby or occupation. Make an appointment for your interview. Write out the questions you are going to ask, leaving space to note the person's answers. What would your classmates like to know about him? Look in *U.S. News and World Report* to see what the reporters for that magazine think is important to know about a person. What kind of language will you want to use with the person you are going to interview? What will you wear?

Write your interview like one in *U.S. News and World Report*. Be sure to use lead headings as the *Report* does. Submit your interview to the class newsletter.

DEAR ABBY . . . : NEWSLETTER VII

2 hours   *1 person or a group*

Here is a way students can practice writing, use their imaginations and have fun at the same time. Try it.

If you have a writing group, choose one member to be Abby. Each one of you should then try to think of a situation which requires her (or his) advice. Write a letter to dear Abby as though you were the person in need of help. Sometimes it is interesting to be very serious over the problem and sometimes it is fun to get silly and see how outlandish you can make the problem.

It is Abby's job to write answers. Afterward you might all discuss the answers to see if you agree with them. You might try to see how real and believable you can make both the letters and the answers. Let everyone have a turn as Abby.

If you are working alone, you might try writing your own Dear Abby column, answers and all.

In either case, share the fun with the rest of the class by writing a Dear Abby column to put in the class newsletter or on the bulletin board.

COMIC STRIPS AND CARTOONS: NEWSLETTER VIII

1½ to 2½ hours   *2 to 6 people*

To interest students who do not like to write in participating in writing activities, you may find it useful to know how to plan a comic strip or cartoon activity.

Organize a small group and plan to do this activity. First you will each need to collect cartoons and comic strips from magazines, comic books, and newspapers at home, and bring a variety of each type to class. Cut the caption off one cartoon and paste it on a separate piece of paper. Paste the picture without the caption on a different piece of paper. Each of you should give his caption page to one member of the group and the picture to another. You should each have one caption page and one picture page which have been given to you by other group members. Make up a caption to go with the picture, and either draw or describe in writing a picture to go with the caption you have. Compare your products. How was your caption or picture different from the original? Which do you like best? Why? Which was easiest to invent, a picture or a caption? Why?

Now try the same process with a comic strip. Cut the word bubbles out, and paste the comic strip on one piece of paper and the words on another. Give them to other group members as you did before. Is it easier or harder to find words and pictures to go with comic strips? Why? Can you decide how a character looks from what he says? Can you decide what he would say from how he looks? How are your versions different from the originals? Did you put your own words into the characters' mouths? Which is more true-to-life, yours or the original? Which do you think other people would enjoy most? Why?

Now that you have experimented with the words and pictures of cartoons and comic strips, work together to make your own comic strip. Choose a scene from literature to use as your story. Stories from *Canterbury Tales* are interesting to try. Read the story or scene you have decided to use aloud in your group so that you are all sure of the details. You may decide to draw your pictures or ask for an art helper from the help bank to help you, or you may choose to cut out magazine pictures to illustrate your ideas. Plan to have at least five frames, and don't forget word bubbles. If it seems necessary to your story, you may want to include some narration at the beginning and end of your comic strip.

Is your story clear to someone who does not know it? Can your reader follow ideas from one frame to the next without getting lost? How can you make this easier? Are the pictures simple enough that they do not confuse the reader? How can you show a change of scene?

Share your comic strip with the class by submitting it to the newsletter or posting it on the bulletin board. You can copy your cartoon onto a ditto master if you paper clip it to the ditto master and trace over the pictures and words by pressing hard with a ballpoint pen.

ECOLOGY EVENT: EXAMINE THE EVIDENCE

several hours   *1 person or a group*

Try this activity to discover how you may structure writing experiences which involve the thoughts, bodies and emotions of students.

Discover some facts about the state of your local environment, and write a report about it. You may want to visit a river to examine evidence about pollution of water or you may want to investigate air pollution. Here are some questions which may help you plan your investigation:

Does your newspaper or television weatherman report daily on the amount of pollution in the air? Where does this information come from? What could you find out from the city sewage or sanitation department about the amount of garbage, sewage, chemicals and trash emptied into local streams? Could the conservation department give you information? What does it do to animals? Fish? People? What are the sources of pollution? How much of the poisonous material in water is put there by individuals? By private industry? By the city? Are some materials more harmful than others? Which ones? If you visit various factories in your city, what can you discover about their pollution or non-pollution of the environment? What color is the smoke that comes out of the smokestack? What chemicals are probably being put into the atmosphere if the smoke is yellow? Black? Brown? White? Which is most harmful? Why? Why isn't anything done about pollution? What can be done about it? If you wrote some letters to find out, would they be answered? Try it. What would a member of the city council tell you? What would a factory manager tell you? What would the head of the local Urban Affairs Department tell you?

Collect and examine the evidence. Each of you may want to write a different person and report on a different aspect of the pollution problem. You may want to consider how pollution in your local area compares with that in other areas of the country or the world. You may want to investigate radiation pollution or people pollution or even noise pollution.

Choose your own method of presenting your reports. You may decide to make a bulletin board display with charts and pictures; you may wish to combine your discoveries into one report given on tape or as a panel discussion to the class; you may wish to submit a series of articles to the newsletter or simply read your reports to each other in the group.

WRITE WITH YOUR EARS: HOW IS
WRITING DIFFERENT FROM CONVERSATION?

50 to 60 minutes   *1 person or a group*

To take advantage of classroom conversations as an exercise to build writing skill, do this.

Come to class early. Have a piece of paper out and write all the bits of conversation you hear as people come into class. Or set up a tape recorder and play back conversations so you can write them. If you have a group, you will probably all hear different things.

Spend a few minutes reading what you have written. Would it make good sense to a reader? Why or why not? Take some parts of it that seem to fit together to make into a piece of writing. Make this a conversation which could be read comfortably or a descriptive paragraph.

Think about these questions or talk about them as a group: How does your second piece of writing differ from what you wrote originally? How does the sentence structure differ? Did you change any of the slang or grammar? Did you take out any repetition? Did you take out any "fillers" like "you know," "I mean" or "uh, er"? Or did you just not write down these in the beginning when you heard them because you automatically knew that they were not useful in writing?

Why can we use such a different dialect for our speaking than we need to use for our writing? Would our writing be improved sometimes by being more like our speaking? How shall we decide what makes good writing out of good speaking? Did you ever read a writer who had such a sensitive use of written language that you could hear in your mind the characters saying what the author said they said? What does an author do to make this happen? Perhaps you could find some examples to discuss in your group.

If you are working alone, discuss an example from your reading in your log. In either case put the writings you have done for this activity in your log and give your opinions about how to make conversation sound good when you are writing it.

BE AN EAVESDROPPER: CAN'T YOU HEAR THEM TALKING?
1 hour   *1 person*

To be more able to generate writing activities for your students based upon their reactions to people and events in their own lives, write your own imaginative response to such a situation.

Did you ever overhear a conversation and make up your mind from what you heard what kind of person was speaking even if you did not know the person? Try overhearing in your mind two people talking about an issue that they either agree on or disagree on.

Decide what kind of person each one is. Then create a dialog in which each one talks in the character you have given him. Be sure that each one says only those things that fit his character. Will his character and his viewpoint always be the same? Will the words that tell his viewpoint be enough to reveal his character, or will he need to say things in a certain way beyond just saying his viewpoint for the reader to know what kind of person he is? When in doubt close your eyes and see if you can picture him talking just that way.

Try to see how many ways you can reveal his character in a page of conversation.

Just as the proof of the pudding is in the eating, the test of your writing is in the reading. Give your writing to someone else to read and see if he gets the picture of your character as you meant it to be. Better still, give it to several people to read. Maybe there is even someone in your class who has put his name in the help bank as a proofreader or writing helper or listener. Be sure you talk to these people afterward about their impressions of your character. By listening to what they say, you can learn how to make your ideas clear to them.

TEAM OBSERVATION: WHAT DO YOU SEE?

1 hour   *3 people*

To help students become more conscious of individual differences which affect their perception and writing, do this.

Find two people and form a team. Choose a person or a group in the class whom you will observe for 10 minutes. You will find more to observe if you choose someone who is actively speaking or moving. You should have watches or there should be a clock in the room which you can all see. Agree upon the exact time you will start and stop your observation. Choose different vantage places in the room where you can watch your subject and where you will be able to take notes without being conspicuous. For ten minutes write everything you can about how the individual looks, sounds and acts. When the 10 minutes is over, meet to compare and discuss your observations. Here are some questions you may find helpful:

How are your accounts the same or different? What differences were caused by the fact that you could hear or see different details from your spot in the room? Which account tells most about the person or group? Why? Which account is most complimentary to the person or group? Why? Do differences in the details you noticed show differences in what is important to you? Did you report only what you saw and heard, or did you also tell how you felt about what you saw and heard? Is it possible to tell about what you see and hear without being influenced by what you feel? Why or why not? List the ways your three reports differed the most. Can you decide where the truth lies in each of these instances, or do you still disagree?

Write a report about your observation experience, telling about the ways you disagreed, why you disagreed, what you think now, and how you have settled or not settled the matter.

As a variation of this activity, you may want to observe a spectator at an athletic event, a student in the chemistry lab, students or teachers in the cafeteria, people at a school dance or students in a card game in the student lounge.

WHO IS BEHIND THE WORDS?:
KNOWING MORE ABOUT AN AUTHOR

1½ hours   *1 person or a group*

Some students become attached to a favorite author. To be more able to use that feeling as an inspiration for student writing, do this.

Plan to write a report about your favorite author. Where can you find out about authors? The library is probably the place to start. Have a visit with the librarian and ask her to point out the place where you can find biographical material. You should record in your log where you look and how you use the books so that you can use them another time.

In even a short biographical sketch you can often find items that remind you of things you have read in the writing of the author. See how many things in the author's life, the places he lived, and the people he knew are related in some way to the writing he did. Be cautious. You can't be sure how much these things influenced him, but you can see possibilities.

If other students are reading the same book you are reading, you will want to share your information with them. You might do this in a small group, in a class report, in a bulletin board news story or in the class newsletter. You can also form an "authors" discussion group, with each member of the group working on a different author and then reporting back to the group about what he has found.

In any case, put the information in your log. Can you find any statements by the writer himself about how much or how little he was influenced in his writing by the things that happened in his life? Are these statements more or less reliable interpretations of the influences on his life than those made by people who have studied his life? Why?

Are there parts of the writer's writing you understand better because you know facts about his life? What aspects of his life made him a one of a kind sort of person, unique in his ability to convey certain kinds of impressions to his reader? Are there some experiences of his life that made it impossible for him to write in certain ways or about certain kinds of things?

SWIFT SWITCH: EXCHANGING AUTHORS

45 minutes   *1 person*

Do this activity to discover a way students can learn to write comparatively and imaginatively while they are talking about writers and reading experiences they enjoyed.

Think about two stories you have read and enjoyed. Consider what would happen to your stories if each author had written the other story instead of the one he did write. What changes would have been made in plot, setting, character? Would sentences and words have been different too? How? Find examples of possible changes and justify them.

Write in your log your conclusions about the way each author has a style of his own. Remember to put in examples that will help you recognize these things in other books you read.

GO AHEAD, NO ONE'S WATCHING: DOING YOUR THING WITH POETRY

25 minutes   *1 person*

To be more skillful in helping students to enjoy poetry, do this.

If you were just as good at making poems as you are at making prose, and you wanted to write about something unreasonable or illogical, would you write about it in poetry or prose? Why? Do you know of some poems that are illogical? What could you put in a poem which you would hesitate to put in a piece of prose? Are there some things you keep stuffed down in the bottom of your imagination—special angels and monsters—who roam around, roar, growl, and sing that you could bring out into your thinking and use in a poem?

Try it! You don't have to show it to anyone if you don't want to. How did you feel about this kind of poetry experience? Tell your log.

DIAMONDS ARE FOR WRITING: DIAMOND POEMS

30 to 50 minutes   *1 person*

Here is a way to help students improve their skill at writing poetry and enjoy what they are doing. These poems are fun to share too.

Make a diamond shaped poem. How could the words be arranged so they look like a diamond? In order to have a middle line longer than those on either side how many lines could you use?

How would you make ideas fit into the diamond shape? Could you make the ideas in the bottom half of the diamond contrast with the top half? Think of two opposite ideas for the top and bottom and let the fourth, or middle line, be a transition between the two halves.

Try this recipe for building the lines of your own diamond poem:

a word—	subject noun
words—	adjectives
words—	participles (ing or ed words)
words—	nouns related to subjects
words—	participles
words—	adjectives
a word—	noun

After you have written your first diamond poem, you may want to make some changes of your own in the recipe, or even make a ladder poem or a triangle poem or a circle poem. Could you find ways to make the words and meaning fit the shape? Try it; it's fun. You might even organize a contest among your classmates to see who can find the most original shape for a poem—and make the meaning fit the shape, of course. That's part of the game.

Put your poem or poems on the bulletin board or in the newsletter so that everyone can enjoy them.

MAKE A MOVE:
CAPTURE YOUR SPORTS ACTIVITY IN A MOVEMENT POEM
40 minutes   *1 person*

If you have participated in sports, use your experience to prepare yourself to help students use their experiences as a source of writing ideas.

Feelings are very important in poetry. How do you feel when you are participating in your sport? What kind of movements do you make in your sport? How does it feel to be moving in that particular way?

Are you part of a team? How does it feel to be part of a team? How do you feel about the other members? The opponents? The spectators? How do you feel about yourself before you play? While you play? After you play? What are the different movements you make and the feelings that go with them? Do you ever feel frightened? When? Do you ever feel important? What are you doing when you feel that way? Do you ever feel elated or angry? What are you doing when you feel that way?

How does it feel to do those things? What words can you use to describe your movements and your feelings? Think of all the action words you can find that seem to describe what you do in your sport. List them. List all the feeling words that seem to describe the way you feel when you move. Do some of those words seem better than others? See if you can pick some action words and some feeling words that go with them that seem to fit best. What other kinds of words could you add to these to make them make more sense?

Try some different combinations of these words together and see if you like what they say. Your poem doesn't have to tell a story or have some kind of special message that you write into it. It already has a message about feeling and moving.

Try reading your poem aloud to yourself and listening to the sounds of the words. It doesn't need to rhyme. It will probably sound better if it doesn't. But listen to the words to see if they seem to follow one another as if they belong there. If you don't like the way the words sound together, find different ones.

Is there any way you can use words to show movement instead of just telling about it? What does it do when you repeat some words over and over? What is the difference between "I ran fast" and "I ran faster, faster, faster"? Could you arrange the words on the page some way that would show movement? How? Experiment a little.

Write a sports movement poem and put it in your log or post it on the bulletin board. In fact, try several.

THE WORLD FROM WHERE YOU ARE: DESIGN A POEM
50 minutes   *1 person*

If you want to arrange activities which will lead your students to enjoy poetry and feel good about their abilities to write it, try this and see how you feel about it.

Arm yourself with writing tools—paper and a pen or pencil—and find some scissors and paste.

Look around the room, out the window, or out the door, wherever you can see from your seat. Make a list of words—between twenty and thirty—of what you see. Cut the words apart. Now start to arrange them into designs, but don't paste them yet; just enjoy them.

Try making different things out of them: ladders, stair steps, pyramids, circles, spirals, designs, symbols, figures. See if you like certain designs better than others and if you like the way certain words fit in the designs. Maybe you like several different arrangements. Every time you make an arrangement of words read what you have written. Can you make the meaning fit the design? You might want to make more words so that you can repeat some or add to the meaning.

When you are satisfied with one or several word designs, paste them in place.

You have created poetry—your own—not like any poetry that anyone else ever wrote before. Put it in your log or post it on the bulletin board.

PLAYING IT COOL: WRITE YOUR OWN PLAY
2 hours   *1 person or a group*

If you do this activity, you will be more able to help students write their own plays.

What would you like to write about? Try to sum up your idea in a sentence. What kind of characters will you need? How many? What story will you tell? Which would get your message across best, a comedy or a tragedy? What setting would help your story most? How will you choose a setting that is practical for your classroom? How will you show it to the audience?

How will you find good names for your characters? Where is the longest list of names you could find quickly? What problems do the characters have to overcome?

What are the divisions of a play? Even if these are not used in a short play, are there divisions when new characters come onstage or the scene changes? In a short play how many scene changes is it best to have? Choose your setting. What form should your first writing take? Some people write a summary of the story first and then break it into short parts. Then write the conversation for each scene. Sometimes it is fun just to try out the scene and improvise the conversation with a partner or your group before you write it.

What will you have to accomplish in each scene? Can you keep the story moving in the direction you want it to go? How will you end the play? You might try several endings and let your listeners choose an ending they like best. Or you could leave the ending unwritten and start a contest among your listeners for the best written ending.

If you have a group, put on your play now. If you are working alone, try to find an acting group to put on your play. Perhaps you could even "sell" it to a group. You might need to revise it to fit their special needs, just as professional writers do.

WRITING EASY: PICTURES AND PARAGRAPHS

50 minutes   *1 person*

Try this activity to discover how you can involve students who feel unsure of their abilities to write.

Find a large magazine picture that seems to express a strong idea for you. What is the idea? Put the idea into words. Write just one clear sentence that says it. Now add all the details the artist or photographer has used to show you his idea and influence you about it. Put only one detail in each sentence.

List the sentences in some kind of order: from one side to the other, from least to most important, or in another way. Select a particularly telling and vivid detail for a final sentence. You have a picture and a paragraph!

Try using your paragraph as an oral "speech" to someone in the class, explaining your picture. Show your picture and paragraph in your folder.

BE GOOD TO YOURSELF: NO TROUBLE ON ESSAYS
20 to 30 minutes   *1 person*

To be able to help students write essays painlessly and clearly, try this activity yourself.

When you are just talking, do you manage to explain things? Do you usually say what you mean? Do you ever persuade others to your line of thinking? Do you ever win arguments? How do you do these things? Could you do in writing the same things you do in talking? Try it.

Think of an issue that you have a strong opinion about. Think of it as a question like, "Should the voting age be lowered to 16?" Find a blank page in your log to write your essay. Now follow this simple guide, writing your sentences in paragraph form: At the beginning of the paragraph make a one-sentence statement that answers the issue question. List some sentences after the beginning statement that tell why it is true or tell interesting things about it. This is the long part of your essay. At the end of the essay put your beginning idea into different words to remind your reader what it was and to take into consideration everything else you have said.

To know if you have succeeded in making your ideas clear and convincing try your writing on a real reader. Give your essay to a friend to read. If your writing is messy or has spelling errors, you may want to copy it so that these things will not get in the way of the meaning for your friend.

LOG LOVELIES: USING YOUR LOG MATERIALS FOR WRITING
1 hour   *1 person*

Try this to see how you may be able to help students who do not know how to begin their writing.

Choose one of the longer entries in your log. Find a word that describes most of the ideas in the sentences. This should be a key word you use in a topic sentence introducing the rest of the sentences. After you have written a topic sentence which tells the important thing you are going to say, cut all the sentences that don't fit the topic sentence.

Next arrange your sentences in some sort of order—maybe according to the time when things happened or from most important to least important or from least important to most.

Now find someone to help you. Look in the help bank or choose a work partner. Read your paragraph aloud to him. Is your paragraph just a list? Should it be more than that if it is going to be interesting?

What words could you add at the beginnings of the sentences to make the paragraph easier to understand? What about "first," "later," "then"? Are there others? You might hunt through some of your reading in textbooks in science or history for additional words you can use to tie sentences together.

Could you make a list of rules for writing a good paragraph and put them in your log? Just list what you have done here.

CLEAR THE LOG FOG: TALKING TO YOUR LOG ABOUT YOUR BOOK
15 minutes   *1 person*

If you do this, you will be more able to help students write in their logs about their reading.

Choose a book to write about in your log. See if you can find some ways that your book talks about life. Does it show life as you know and understand and experience it? As you write about this question, be sure you use the people and incidents in the book to prove that the book really says what you say it says. Do not make any general statements that are not backed by examples from the book because you will need facts to be able to recall the story when you read your log later.

How important are the experiences being told about in the book? Would such things matter now to many people? Were these things important in the past? Will they be in the future? How important is it that a book be for all people in all times?

Try talking about the language in the book. How long are the sentences? What kinds of verbs and adjectives does the author use? How does he use them in sentences? How do these words make you feel when you read them? Is that how the writer wanted you to feel? Remember to give as many examples as you can.

Write in your log. Sometimes it helps to think of what you would say to a person if he were sitting in front of you and you were just talking to him. Then write those same words down.

WALK, SEE, WRITE, COMPARE: TEAM WRITING

1 hour   *2 people*

To be more able to guide your students in working together to discover descriptive details and examine the feelings which influence descriptions, try this activity with someone from your class.

Find a partner to work with. You will each need a notebook and pen or pencil for taking notes. With these in hand take a walk together. As you walk think about what you see and feel. Write down your impressions. Begin where you are: You are going to walk to the door, and go out. Will you walk side by side or will one walk ahead? How do you feel about the way you are walking? Look at the room you are leaving. How do you feel about leaving it? How does your partner feel about leaving it? What are your impressions of the room? What are your partner's impressions? Are they different? Why? Who will open the door? What kind of a door is it? Do you like the door? Do you want to get through it quickly or do you want to linger? How do you feel about what is on the other side of it? Do you see in your mind what is on the other side? Now that you are outside the door, how do you feel about the door? About the room? Your partner? The hallway? The people in the hallway? The walk you intend to take? What do you see in the hallway? What is important about the hallway to you? To your partner? What do you think about as you walk down the hallway? As you approach the corner? What do you expect to find around the corner? How do you feel about it? What do you find? Do you feel about it as you thought you would? Go outside. Does it feel different to be outside? How is it different from being inside? Is it cold or warm, cloudy or sunny? How do you feel about the weather? Does the building seem different from the outside? In what ways? Does it seem smaller or larger? Do you walk the same outside as you did inside? Why? Do the other people outside talk and walk like the people inside did? What is the same and what is different? Walk around the building. Would you rather walk around the building or through the building? Why? What do you find as you walk around the building? What do you feel as you walk around it? How are your feelings different from your partner's? Do you feel the same on the shady side of the building as on the sunny side? Why?

When you return to your room, read your notes together, and organize them into a two-page description of your walk. You may want to work together to tell about each part of your walk, you may want to contrast your views of what you saw and felt by alternating paragraphs telling about each item, or each of you may want to write a separate description and join your descriptions by prefacing them with a paragraph about what you were doing and by adding a transitional paragraph between them.

Read your description either to the class or a writing group so that they may share what you have learned, or display it where others may read it.

TELLING TOMBSTONES: WRITING EPITAPHS

1½ to 2 hours   *1 person or a group*

To involve students in writing you may find epitaphs useful. Gain experience in writing them by doing this.

Find a group or work alone. Have you ever seen tombstones that tell something about the person who is buried there? Visit an old cemetery together or separately, and find some examples. Read aloud in your group some selections from *Spoon River Anthology* by Edgar Lee Masters. Are the epitaphs in the *Anthology* like the ones in the cemetery? Why or why not? Which do you prefer? Why?

Write some epitaphs of your own; try some for people you know, famous people who are living or dead, imaginary people or yourself. Find some magazine pictures of people and write epitaphs for them.

Make slides of the pictures and have a slide show. Read your epitaphs as you show the pictures, or use a tape which you have programmed with your epitaphs. You may wish to use musical backgrounds. If you do not have the equipment or money for making slides, you may prefer to make a collage or bulletin board display from your epitaphs and pictures.

MINUTE MESSAGES: A FUNNY BUTTON COMPANY

30 to 60 minutes   *2 to 5 people*

Try this activity to discover how you may interest non-writing students in writing.

Find some people to work with, and form a funny button company. You will need construction paper, scissors, straight pins and black pens. Cut shapes from colored construction paper and use straight pins to pin them to clothing. Write messages of two or three words on each one. Remember that a "funny button" needs to be readable at a glance. Print with large, black, simple letters. Collecting words to say on your "funny buttons" may not be easy. Can you experiment with words that rhyme? You can't be too silly. Look at signs, posters, billboards and poems to find "catchy" phrases. Listen to slang words and jingles in television. Play with the words, putting them together in different ways.

What does a "funny button" tell about the person who wears it? What does he want it to tell? Why does he wear it? What could you say that starts "I'm . . . " or "Stop . . . " or "Go . . . " or "Be . . . "?

Advertise your "funny buttons" for sale at 1¢ or 2¢ each. Wear them in class to show your handiwork.

FAN LETTER:
WRITE TO A HERO

45 minutes   *1 person*

If you do this, you will be more able to plan letter writing activities for students which meet their personal needs.

Write a fan letter to someone you admire, or pretend that you are a high school student and write a letter to someone you might admire if you were in high school. Why does someone write a fan letter? Does he hope to get something back—a letter or an autographed picture? Is there satisfaction in the thought of the great person reading one's letter? How do you want your great person to feel about you and your letter when he reads it? If you want to make him feel good, what can you say—that you watch all his shows and save all his pictures, that you buy his buttons, stickers, and rings, that you voted for him, that you read his book and admired it? Would he like to hear about why you admire him or his ideas? How will he feel about you if you misspell a word or use non-standard grammatical forms? If you want him to send you something in return, did you include your address?

Write your letter as neatly as possible and mail it. Wait for a reply. Tell your log whether or not you received a reply and how you feel about it. Did you get what you expected? Have your feelings about your hero changed in any way? If so, how?

TAKE A WRITING TRIP: WRITING YOUR THOUGHTS

50 minutes *1 person*

Do this to practice writing from your own thoughts so that you may help students discover the value of their thoughts as a source of writing material.

Go off by yourself for fifteen minutes and write everything you think about. You are always thinking about something—even if it is something silly. Don't worry about whether it is silly or not, just write down as much of what you think as you can. Of course, since thoughts are much faster than the speed at which you write, you may miss some things, and your ideas may seem disconnected. You can fix that later if you like. The most important thing is to be completely honest with yourself and not to change what you really are thinking into what you think you ought to be thinking. Just keep writing until your fifteen minutes is up.

Afterward you can organize it if you want to, and fill the gaps. Sometimes it is good to put what you have written away for a whole day and come back to it with a fresh mind. When you reread it, you may want to add things and to take some things out. You may want to look for some unifying idea in what you have written. You may want to try the experiment again to see if you can improve your concentration or accuracy in recording your thoughts.

After you are satisfied with what you have written, you may want to share it with others by putting it in your log or by reading it in your work group.

MIND THE MUSIC: TUNING IN YOUR CREATIVE IDEAS

1 week *3 to 8 people*

If you do this activity, you will be more able to handle the classroom logistics of using music to inspire creative writing.

Find a group and agree to experiment with the use of music in setting a mood and providing ideas for your own creative writing efforts. After your group has decided to try this, you will need to make some decisions. What kind of music would be most inspiring for creative writing? How can you find out? Do you have some records at home you would like to try? Would you play the same song or songs over or use a variety of different ones? What would work best? Would you play the music the whole time you are writing, part of the time, or only before you write?

How can your group listen to music at school without disturbing other people? Will you use a record player or a tape recorder? Is there a secluded corner where you can play the music? Headphones?

Will you read your writings aloud to each other when you have finished them? Will you discuss your writings? Will you write in a particular genre like stories or poems, or will you write anything the music makes you think of? How will you know when you have succeeded in writing more creatively? Will you share your writings with the rest of the class? How?

Whether or not you decide to share your writings with the class, tell your log how you feel about the experience. Did you accomplish what you wanted to? Why or why not?

WORM'S EYE: WRITING FROM YOUR IMAGINATION
30 minutes					*1 person*

Do this to better understand how students may be guided to write creatively as a result of an unusual situation suggestion.

Try writing a short paper. Imagine that you are level with the grass. What do you see? Are there bugs, worms, roots on the ground? How do they look if you are very, very small? How does a grain of sand look? What does a blade of grass look like? A spider web? Are some very ordinary creatures frightening? Are colors the same? How much of the world can you see?

If you are a worm, will you crawl back into your hole? How will it feel? Do you like the sunshine above, or do you like the darkness of your hole? Why? Is the ground wet or dry or don't you care? What do you eat? What do you do if you meet another worm? Do you wonder what lies beyond the next clump of grass? Is a foot a long distance for you to travel? What do you think when you see a flower? Do you think it is pretty, do you want to smell it, or do you want to eat it? What do you do if it has insecticide on it?

Suppose the world were under water and we had gills like fish. Suppose all the world's problems were solved and no one had to do anything but sit around and be happy . . . What "suppose" situations can you think of that could inspire students to write?

Write a paragraph about the worm or another "suppose" situation. Tell your log how you feel about "supposing." In your log list some situations that students might enjoy writing about.

MANAGING STUDENT WRITING

Experiences, then, in the activity curriculum provide structures for writing experience. Structure begins with experience itself, either outside the classroom or within it, perhaps from one of the activities involved in receiving language. This experience is debriefed, through questions, which the student answers from the activity cards, either individually or in concert with his group. The debriefing leads to written log records, which analyze and generalize from experience.

Each student has a unique and special experience of life to bring to his writing, an experience which activity cards help him discover and investigate. In his formal writing he shows this experience to others in ways interesting to them, making himself accessible to others by producing language, just as he does when he speaks.

Students with difficult experiences of life develop through their writing ways to perceive the world, not as a jungle, but as a place of infinite opportunity to impose their pride of self by defining it in language. Black writers, among them the electrically successful Melvin van Peebles, have found this pattern of success. The gifted child will be a gifted writer about his experience, but the teacher of the gifted must rarely expect conformity in response. Brainstorming is useful for such learners. Their ideas often pour out in quantity. Later they can sort and separate. All kinds of students gain skills in mobilizing materials of experience into written expression as they talk with their peers and as their talk in and to their logs becomes writing. Let activity teachers stimulate each by valuing the individuality of each response.

Students find thoughts coming to them as they write, emerging in their logs, when they feel free of the need to impose planning rules on what they write. Actors and oral interpreters know that concentration on rules of expression inhibits their ability to read lines well. Their skill in performing is based on thinking of ideas as they say them. So it is for student writers. Their writing tends to be more spirited and effective if, as they write, they think of their ideas rather than of their writing design. This is not to say that proofreading and revision may not improve a final product, but that product must be created from focus on ideas, not mechanics.

So students in a humanistic curriculum use writing as a way of finding out what they think as well as communicating or recording what they have thought. New ideas continually appear as students process experience into writing. As processing takes place, they learn to write effectively and like to write, treasuring the experience of writing for its feedback into their thoughts. They write their ideas to see what those ideas mean, to find out what they really think. They conceive their ideas by expressing them. Such students write, not only what they know, but what they want to find out.

Writing itself becomes their way of knowing, clarifying, arranging and relating their ideas.

Group, individual and class discussion should explore the importance of writing, its purpose, choice of topics, central ideas, necessary sentence structures to express kinds of ideas and the usefulness or uselessness of plans and outlines. The writer's need for general statements, definitions of key terms, and examples and details should be investigated. Poor student writing often begins with a randomly selected detail, continues with an unstructured list and ends only when enough words have been written to fulfill the assignment. When spontaneous writing does not meet the needs of the writer, he must work out carefully what he wants to say, plan his organization and select details appropriate to his intention, discriminating between detail and generalization. However, if he uses properly prepared activity cards, he will be accustomed to collect and develop generalizations from details of his activity experiences. These activities provide practice in perceiving the pattern of detail that emerges as a generalization.

Various methods of developing an idea become part of the student writer's equipment as he develops a need for them and uses them. For instance, after he has repeatedly related events and told how these events changed him, he is ready to analyze just how he writes about cause and effect. Teacher comment reinforces this perception. Such comments begin, "Was . . . the reason you changed your mind about . . . ?" or "How did you feel about . . . before this happened?"

Comment directs the student's attention to his ability to make his reader understand how he feels and why he feels this way, so he sees that his writing has power. When the teacher follows his descriptive comment with the further comment that the student's writing has caused him as reader to feel or think in response to what has been said, the writer, in addition to feeling that he has the competence to write, knows that he has the power to affect others by his writing. The more specific the comment the teacher makes, describing precisely some writing behavior of the student, the more powerful will be the reinforcement to repeat that specific writing behavior because the student knows what he did was effective. This powerful stimulus, a strong resource for affecting the writing of students, the teacher-reader has at his fingertips.

Students should constantly seek help from the teacher and from each other in their writing. They can exchange writing in the process of seeking help. In helping each other they teach themselves. Teachers should help students in every way—telling them how to spell words, how to get an idea into a sentence, doing for students whatever will help them. Writing should be shared, not a lonely occasion, unless the student wants it to be so and writes best when he does it alone. The student writer should get all kinds of help, short of having another set pen to paper for him, and there may be times when effective help includes having a helper write a sentence or two for him. Helpers can be fellow students, teachers or others of a student's choice. Approval, not opprobrium, should attach to giving and receiving help in writing. In the help bank diverse kinds of help can be listed for writers who want assistance in planning, sentence structure or spelling.

Good writing, like other good use of language, grows from practice in oral language, so students should often read their work aloud to themselves, to others, or to the tape recorder, to which they then listen. The writer should, in fact, write with his ear, hearing what he says as he writes. As he listens to his own writing voice, the writer becomes reader as well as writer, and he grows a concern for his readers, their comfort and understanding. Listening to his writing voice helps the student writer spell and punctuate, since intonation and sound key letters, combinations of letters and pauses. And the writer who hears his own work learns the value of reduction, as he strikes the balance between prolixity and brevity which constitutes economical effectiveness.

But clarity and organization do not constitute style. A writer's style emerges from the total effect of the writing. The student who hears his writing learns to know what sounds like him, like what he wants to say in design as well as content. Unconscious selection becomes conscious choice, and arrangement of linguistic elements appearing with enough frequency becomes his characteristic style.

If students are to believe writing is a good thing to do, students should see teachers writing and should read teacher writing. Students should always leave large margins on their papers where teachers may write replies. And teachers should write when students do formal writing and exchange their writing with students for mutual discussion.

Activities

YOUR CHOICE: SELECTING WRITING MATERIAL

20 minutes   *1 person*

Use this activity to help you select materials for your writing so that you may be better prepared to help students select writing materials.

You are going to write. What are you going to write about? Does it matter what you are going to write about? Why? Who will read what you write? Do you want to choose a subject that will interest your audience?

Why will your audience read it? What will they expect your writing to do for them? Do you want to write to fulfill a need of another person or a group? Does the newsletter need an article? Does a group need a skit or play? Does a friend expect a letter? Will the reader you choose affect the materials you will use? How?

Decide upon an audience, even if it is your log. Write a note to yourself telling what your audience wants or needs from your writing. Decide upon a reader. Look into your own feelings and experiences for material because they are what you know best. What did you do today? What did you feel today? What did you see, and whom did you meet? You may want to make a list, writing down as much as you can remember. Which of these events and feelings would be most interesting to your audience? Which would best fit the reader you have chosen? Would you use your feelings more for a poem or for a skit? For which could you use information about people you met and talked to?

Choose the information you will use, and write. Did you think of new ideas to write about as you worked?

THE SOFT CENTER PROBLEM:
HOW SHALL WE ESTABLISH A TRUTH?

1½ hours   *1 person*

To improve your ability to help students solve writing problems logically, do this activity.

If you ate five pieces of candy out of a box and all of them were soft centers, would you be justified in thinking all the pieces would have soft centers? How many would you have to eat before you would be reasonably able to say all were soft?

If the label on the box said they all had soft centers and you found one hard center, would you think the rest would all be soft centers and not hard centers? Or would you decide they were mixed? Why? How many times must you collect examples before you can say that something is generally true? Do you ever make general statements when you have really investigated only a few instances?

Another way of getting at what is the truth is to establish that one thing is the cause of another. Do we ever find we have made mistakes about what causes something? How do you make sure about cause and effect? When one thing happens after another, does that mean that the first caused the second? What more do we have to know beside the time when they happened?

Is the truth of anything easy to find? Why or why not? Is thinking logically harder than playing ball or dancing? Why? Does each have its rules? What are rules both have in common?

Set a writing-thinking problem for yourself. What is something you would like to know the truth about? What rules can you think of that might work for finding the truth in this case? Can you collect examples and make a generalization? Can you find a cause and effect that is true? Write out your problem in your log and tell your conclusions about it. Show how you came to those conclusions. Check your conclusions against the questions on the first part of this card. How well have you established the truth?

STRAIGHT THINKING: SAYING WHAT YOU MEAN
1 hour   *2 to 5 people*

To help your students see the need for consistency, planning and forethought in their writing, try this activity with your group.

With your group discuss this situation from literature: What problems was Daniel Defoe having with his thinking-writing process when he told about Robinson Crusoe running to the shore, throwing off his clothes, plunging into the surf and swimming to the wreck where he climbed on deck and filled his pockets with biscuits? What had Defoe failed to do that would have kept him from describing how a man with no clothes on filled his pockets with biscuits? What kind of thinking and planning would have prevented this problem? What kind of thinking can any of us use to be sure that what we are writing creates a good picture in the mind of our audience?

Have you found inconsistencies or careless writing in your reading? What do they make you think about the writer? Bring examples to the next class meeting to share with the members of your group. You can notice such illogical happenings on television also. If you do, make a note of them and tell the group.

Work together to collect your examples and use them as the basis of a bulletin board display showing mistakes to avoid. Include suggestions about what the writers could have done to avoid their problems.

THINK NEAT!: WRITING IS ORDER FOR THOUGHTS
50 minutes   *1 person or a group*

Help your students write clearly and effectively by discovering how you may guide them in the ordering and sorting of their thoughts.

Decide upon a writing project, and apply these questions and ideas to your writing activity: Do you like things to be neat and orderly? Does it make you feel good? When you put things in order, how do you do it? Do you have to throw out some things, change some things, make labels for others, sort things? Writers have to do this too!

Try this with your writing. What can you throw out? What do you need to classify? Where else do you need to have order to make a writing situation do what you want it to? Is there a certain order for letters in words? What happens if you get sloppy with that particular order when you are writing? What about the order of punctuation and of words in sentences? How do you decide which ideas to hook together in sentences and which ones to make most important? How do you sort out the ideas that are so unimportant to what you really want to say that they shouldn't be there at all? What ways do you know for getting rid of words you do not need? Do some ideas need more words than others? Are there some ideas that should be repeated? How can you repeat an idea without sounding repetitious? How do you know which ideas to put next to each other in a paragraph? What different ways could you arrange the ideas in a paragraph? Look in some books to see if you can find some different ways of putting ideas into paragraphs. List some of these ways in your log so that you can see them the next time you are writing. Does the kind of order you choose for your writing situation depend on the thing you are going to write about? In what way?

How do you know how much order and what kind of order to use in your writing? What order is there in nature? How do certain kinds of books make order? Dictionaries? Telephone books? Sports? Business? What does each of these different kinds of order do for the reader? Is order a trap or a way to be free? What kind of freedom does order provide? Freedom to do what? What are the bad things about order?

In your log tell about the ways you use order in writing. Have you discovered any new ways of using it or any new reasons for using it? The next time you are planning to write something, turn to this page in your log and review these ideas before you start. Tell your log if it helps you.

IDEA SORTING: MAKING CATEGORIES

2 hours   *2 people*

To be more able to help students acquire the ability to categorize and use categories in their writing, expand your own categorizing ability by doing this.

Find a partner, and make arrangements to do this project. Bring several old magazines from home. A wide variety is desirable. You will also need scissors, rubber cement and paper to mount pictures. Read the tables of contents of several different magazines. What categories are listed? Could you categorize the contents in any other ways? Are the advertisements listed in the tables of contents? Cut out a variety of ads and categorize them by sorting them into piles. See how many ways you can categorize them. Can you sort them by what they advertise? How many cigarette ads can you find in one magazine? How many soap ads? How many for automobiles? For coffee? For shampoo? For baby food? How many different products are advertised in one magazine? How are the ads different in different magazines? Could you sort them according to what magazine they came from? Could you have categories within categories? How would you show that by the arrangement of your piles of ads?

Use another magazine. How else might you sort the ads from this magazine? Is the product advertised always the central idea of the picture? Do ads usually have people and scenes in them? Could you sort them according to what the pictures show? Could you sort them according to the age, sex or interests of the people they are trying to persuade? Could you sort them by size, shape, color, the number of words on them, or the sales techniques used? Could you sort them according to where they occurred in the magazine? Could you sort them according to whether or not you like them or how you feel about them?

Paste examples of your categories on pieces of paper, being careful to label each paper according to the category you have made. Display your collection of categories either by putting your pages in a notebook in the project display area of the room or by displaying them on the walls. How many categories did you find? How many different systems for categorizing did you find? Tell your log about your discoveries.

PARAGRAPHING ALONG: BUILDING PARAGRAPHS

1 to 2 hours   *1 or 2 people*

To be able to help students write effective paragraphs, write one following the instructions in this activity.

Write your main sentence first. This will be the thing you want to talk about or prove. If you don't really know what your main sentence, or topic sentence, should be, find a partner and talk about your subject until you are able to express it clearly. Then try writing it. Indent five spaces.

On a piece of scrap paper list all the ideas you can think of about your main sentence. These may be reasons for or details to support your main sentence. Go back and read over each idea you have listed to make sure it tells about the main sentence. Now make these ideas into sentences. If two ideas or more seem to go together in some way, you may want to join them into one sentence. Some ideas may seem unimportant or out of place. You may want to leave those out.

Arrange your sentences into a paragraph in the way that makes the most sense to you. It helps to read the whole thing over to yourself each time you add a sentence. End the paragraph with a good closing sentence, one that says the same idea as the main sentence but refers to the details you have given to support it. Or you might use one good detail to close. Or you might close with a question to make the reader think about what you have said or to help him formulate his opinion.

Proofread your work carefully. Your partner can help you here. Check your spelling with him and with the dictionary. Try reading aloud to him as a way of proofreading. He can also tell whether your writing can be easily understood.

If your paragraph is to be stored in the folder or put in the weekly newsletter or on the bulletin board, you may want to copy it on a clean sheet of paper. Then it must be proofread again. Leave a wide margin like a picture frame on all sides so that the reader will be more comfortable as he reads.

PUTTING THINGS TOGETHER: HOW DOES A SENTENCE WORK?

1½ hours   *3 to 7 people*

To be able to help your students understand the values of sentence structure and make wise sentence pattern choices, do this.

Form a group and begin your discussion by considering this problem: If you had a bunch of words, how would you make a sentence out of them? Arrange these three words into a sentence that makes sense— hit, John, Bill. Give the same three words to every person in your group to arrange. Do you all put them together in the same way? How do you know which is right? Is there anything about the words that tells you in what order to put them?

Talk about it. How do you know which words go best in certain spots in the sentence? Can you change the meaning of a sentence by changing the order of the words? Write down some sentences you hear in talk around the room or find in the newspaper. Try rearranging the words of these sentences to see if you can change the meanings without changing anything but the order of the words. Which is more important, the words or the order in which they are said?

What do we call the word that belongs in the first spot in a sentence? Do we call it anything else? Where else in a sentence do you need to put a word before it makes sense? What do we call the word that goes in that spot? Can you find any more words that go in special spots in sentences? What are they? Where do they fit and where don't they fit?

Try these words: *Order and pattern some must have they sense make to are words if.* What is wrong with them that makes them nonsense? All the words are there that are necessary to make sense. What do you need to do to make sense of them?

What have you discovered about the importance of order in making sentences? Suppose you were trying to explain how our language works to a small child who is trying to learn to talk correctly or to someone from another country who is trying to learn to speak English. What helpful things could you tell him about the way our words get put together? How could you help him find the sense in our sentences? See if your group can make a list of guide rules for him to follow—a list that will help him understand the way English works.

JIG SAW SENTENCES: A GAME WITH SENTENCES

1½ hours   *3 to 6 people*

If you do this activity, you will be more able to help students become skillful sentence writers.

Talk about these questions as a group: Do writers vary in the lengths of sentences they use? Which writers do you know that use very long ones? Are there times when writers use short sentences? What difference does it make? Do long sentences make you feel any differently than short ones? How? Do most writers use both long and short sentences? Why? What kind of sentences do you use? Would you like to be able to use whatever kind of sentence fits your feelings and ideas best—short or long? You can learn from the professional writers how to use longer ones.

Select one of the longest sentences you can find. Each person should find one long sentence and write it on a piece of paper leaving spaces between the lines and words for cutting them apart.

Read your sentence aloud to the group while the group listens for pauses in your voice. Where you pause cut the sentence apart. After everyone has read his sentence and cut it apart, give your sentence to the person next to you so that everyone has a jumbled sentence to work on. Try to arrange the pieces in some way that makes sense other than the way the author did. Then write down your new sentence on another piece of paper and pass the jumbled sentence on to the next person. Pass the cut-up sentences around the circle until everyone has had a chance to rearrange each one.

Now take turns reading your revised versions of the sentences aloud to each other. Ask yourselves if the writer's way is better in any way than yours. Why or why not? What makes a sentence work well? Appoint one of your members to act as a secretary to write down your conclusions. Present your conclusions to the class either as a report or in the form of a debate in which you argue the virtues of long vs. short sentences.

WAYS OF SAYING: TRANSFORMATIONS

1 to 1½ hours   *3 to 6 people*

To help your students find various interesting and appropriate ways of stating their ideas, become familiar with the ways English sentences may be rearranged.

Find a group, and pretend you only know how to write sentences that are made like this: "Students work. They make projects. Groups are busy." How can you express these ideas in a more interesting and varied way? How many ways can you find to put these sentences together or rearrange them? What can you do with "Students who work . . . " or "Working students . . . " Where can you put "Making projects, the . . . " or "Projects are made by . . . "? How would "Busy groups" work? How could you use "Groups that are busy . . . "? Would it change the meaning? How does "Are groups busy" change the meaning? In what ways is each of the original sentences different from each other? What can you do with each one that you cannot do with the others? Can you make rules which tell you what you can and cannot do to each one to make it more interesting and useful without changing its meaning?

Working together formulate rules which tell how each of the three original sentences may be transformed. Test your rules by making up similar sentences and trying your rules out on your own sentences.

Write your rules in your logs and include examples of your own sentences showing how and why each rule works.

MIND FOOD: GROW SOME SENTENCES

1 hour   *1 person*

To be more able to help your students replace short inadequate sentences with longer and more effective ones, do this expanding exercise with your own writing.

Start by writing the shortest sentence you can. Will it have one word or two? Write a two-word sentence. How can you expand it? Make it bigger and longer by adding words and groups of words that make the meaning clearer. How many words can you add to the sentence before it sounds silly?

Turn to a page in your log. You had a message when you wrote the sentences on that page. Was the message always clear? Find some sentences from your log which could be made clearer by the addition of words to describe or explain what you were trying to say. Write the sentences on another piece of paper, allowing several lines between each sentence for recopying. If you have a three word sentence you want to expand, first add some words before the noun. What does this do to the sentence? Now add some describing words and try to use some possessives. Now add some words that can be added after the noun. Now find some words that can be added to verbs. Try these different kinds of additions with a variety of sentences. Are some of your added words more effective than others? Why?

Where did you place the words you added? In what spots can you put a "the" or "a"? Where can you put describing words? When you add a whole group of words to a sentence, how do you hook them onto the other words? Do you just stick them into the middle of the sentence, do you hook them onto the end or the front of the sentence, or do some groups of words sound best in special spots? If they do, how do you know which spot is best for those words? Will some groups of words fit in more than one spot in a sentence? Try moving some groups of words around in your sentences to see how many different ways you can say the same words. Does it change the meaning of the sentence when you move a group of words from one spot to another? When you move a group of words from one spot to another, what happens to the little words that sometimes act as hooks to hold the word groups to the sentences? Can you put word groups within other word groups? Show some examples in your log.

Write your conclusions about how sentences may be expanded in your log. Could high school students expand sentences? How could they practice and enjoy expanding sentences so that they would write clearer and more interesting sentences? Tell your log your suggestions for sentence-expanding activities for high school students.

JOINERS: USING WORDS THAT LINK IDEAS

40 minutes   *3 to 6 people*

To be able to guide your students in their use of transitional and conjunctive words, do this.

Meet as a group. Turn to any page in your logs, and examine your writing. Count the number of sentences on one page. How many simple sentences have you used? How many times have you joined sentences together with "and," "but," "for," or "so"? You have made choices— to join or not to join. Why did you choose as you did? Have other people made the same choices you have? Compare your answers to these questions.

Look at your logs again. How many sentences did you begin with "and," "but," "for" or "so". Why? In Faulkner's "A Rose for Emily," five out of eleven paragraphs begin with "so" or "and." Have you been told not to begin with these words? Why? Are there times when these words are used to start sentences, when the sentence should just continue? Find some examples to support your answer. How can you tell when they should start a new sentence? Could you join some of your sentences with them effectively? Could you use them to start some sentences? Experiment with some sentences from your log. You may want to try "but" first. Why is a sentence which starts with "but" less likely to be the continuance of a sentence and the start of a new one than one which starts with "and" or "so"? Compare your results. How do you feel about starting a sentence with these words?

In your log did you use another kind of transitional word or phrase? How many times did you use words like these: "furthermore," "however," "nevertheless," "moreover," "in addition," "all-in-all," "finally," and "on the other hand"? Do you feel comfortable using these words? Why or why not? What authors do you know who use words like these? What can these words do for your writing? When might you want to use them and when might you not want to use them? Why?

Tell your log your conclusions and include examples of sentences from your own writing. Would you like to be more flexible in your use of joining words? Are there any new ways of joining ideas that you would like to try?

CALORIE COUNT YOUR SENTENCES: REDUCTION
50 minutes   *2 people*

If you want to help students cut the extra words out of their sentences for clearer, more concise writing, practice reducing sentences by doing this activity.

Find a partner and examine your own writing in your logs. Turn to any page, and look at the first sentence. If there any way you could express the same ideas with fewer words? Check each "the" and "a" to see if it is really necessary. What about words like "which", "that" and "who"? Look at your descriptive clauses to see if you could not replace them with a shorter phrase, an appositive or descriptive word. When you have shortened your sentence as much as you can, tell it to your partner and see if he can think of any other ways to make it shorter, but still express the same ideas. See if you can help your partner shorten his sentence. Are there any "filler" words like "I mean" and "really" that don't mean anything in your writing, but have crept into it from your spoken dialect? When neither of you can shorten the sentence any more, try the second one on the page. Continue with each sentence on your page until you have each completed one page from your logs. Rewrite the page as it would be with the corrections you have made. Compare your before and after pages. Do they both say the same things? Which do you like best? Why? Which is easier to read? Which is easier to understand? Why?

Choose an author who writes very concisely, and find a page of his writing to examine as you have examined the writing in your logs. You might want to use Stephen Crane's "Open Boat." How many extra words can you find? What can you remove without changing the meaning of what he has said? Are his sentences different from yours? If so, how?

What conclusions can you draw from this exercise? Tell your log. If you formed the habit of reducing sentences as you wrote them, would you be a better writer? Would high school students be better writers? If they saw that it would improve their writing would they want to do it? Why or why not? Could they do it? How?

UP, NOT DOWN: POSITIVE AND NEGATIVE DESCRIPTIONS

30 minutes   *2 people*

To help your students find effective rhetoric for their descriptions, do this.

Find a partner and play this description game: One of you should name an object, and briefly describe what it is. The other person matches the first statement by saying what it is not. Try to make this second statement about what the object is not, something that a person might mistake for it if he did not know. Take turns making the first and second statement until you have a collection of positive and negative descriptions. Choose items to describe which would interest others. Try to find descriptions that might help people understand something they would not know about otherwise.

Choose the best of your descriptions to use for a newsletter story or to post on the bulletin board. Tell your logs your opinions of describing something by telling what it is not as well as what it is.

READING AN OBJECT: DESCRIPTION

30 minutes   *1 person or a group*

To be more able to help students describe objects with sensitive and truthful detail, do this.

Consider these questions: Can you read a page of print? Where do you start? How do you move your eyes? What do you do when you cannot understand? Can you read an object the same way? How could you read a building? Where would you start? How would you read it until you knew you were finished? What would you know about it when you had "read" it that you did not know before? How would you test yourself to see if you had read it well?

Write a description of an object so that other people can read the object on the paper just as you read the object by looking at it. How did you choose your starting point? Are there other possibilities for starting points? Why is the one you chose best? What if you were writing this description for a certain kind of reader? What reasons might other people have for wanting to know about the object? Does it depend on who they are and how they might want to use the object?

Now write a second description of the object to suit the needs of a particular person because you want him to know about the object for a special reason. Think about your reasons. Do you want him to be convinced of some truth about it? Do you want him to have convictions about it? Do you want him to use it? When you have finished your second description, think about how it differs from the first one. Which details did you choose to emphasize? Did you leave out any? Why? Did you try to read the object through the other person's eyes and tell him the things that would make him believe what you wanted him to believe about it? Did you stick to the truth? Is it the truth when you select the truths or parts of the truths you will tell? What does this exercise tell you about the problems of an advertising writer? If the cigarette advertisement writer tells you that cigarette smoking will make you feel like one of the group and will make you feel comfortable, is he telling you the truth if he does not also tell you that there is a good chance it can also kill you?

Go back and read your last description. Tell your log about your conclusions. How really truthful was it compared to your first one? How justified are we in telling only part of the truth to get people to do things we want them to do? Do you want others to do this to you? Should you do it to others? Is it all right to do it as long as it won't really hurt anyone?

SEEING A BEING: DESCRIBING PEOPLE IN A NEW WAY
35 minutes   *1 person*

To be able to help students write about people with insight, become a perceptive observer of people yourself.

Choose a person you would like to write a descriptive sketch about. How do you think of him? What way do you use first to describe him? Is it a way of describing his "outside"? How could you describe his "inside" better? Try looking at what he owns. What personal property could you use to give a clue to what kind of person he is? Try a pocketbook, a car, a workshop. What does he say about current affairs to reveal the kind of person he is? Could you ask him any questions that might reveal what kind of person he is? What would his answers to questions about sex, religion, politics, war, drugs, taxes, integration or the high cost of living tell you? Make a list of questions to ask him, and then ask them.

What could your person's favorite television show tell you? The foods he likes? The friends he chooses? The newspapers and books he reads? How does he walk into a room? Is his voice loud or soft? What can these bits of information tell you about the "inside" man?

Write your character sketch. Do you feel differently about the person now that you have written about him? If so, how? Tell your log.

GOOD THINGS COME IN PAIRS: MAKING COMPARISONS
1 hour   *1 person*

If you do this, you will be more able to plan activities to help students use comparisons in their writing.

Fill in the blanks in this phrase: As ____ as ____. Do it over and over until you have several. Try filling in this one: A ____ is like a ____. Make a list of these also. Now try a more direct comparison: A ____ is a ____. Make as many of these as you can think of in five minutes. Can you think of any other ways of comparing ideas? Look at some poems to see how poets make comparisons. How can you make comparisons work for you?

Look at your comparisons now, and ask yourself this: Are two items that are compared ever completely alike? As you look at your list, find the ones that are alike in the most ways. Then list the ways that the two items compared are alike. Make some original comparisons: Can you find some items which are really very much alike in some ways although they seem very different? Try taking them from some area of your life that you are most familiar with and that you have strong feelings about.

Put some of your favorite comparisons on the bulletin board or see if you can arrange them into a poem. Or, since comparisons can sometimes be very funny, you might want to make a collection of funny ones to share with the class.

LOOK AROUND YOU: SEEING LIKENESSES
25 minutes   *1 person*

If you want to help students discriminate likenesses and differences for more perceptive descriptive writing, become more alert to likenesses and differences by doing this activity.

Did you ever notice that objects which seem very much different are often very much alike too? And objects that are very much alike still have differences? Try this activity. Choose an object from one side of the room and then choose any object from the opposite side of the room. Find the likenesses—you know one already. You found them both in the room! Tell your log about as many others as you can. Now find the differences. Start with the fact that they were on opposite sides of the room. What are others? Make long lists.

Can you divide the likenesses and differences into categories or classifications? For instance, the first kind of likenesses and differences mentioned above was about the *place* where each was found. Time might be another category—or materials that the items are made from. What are others? See if you can construct a paragraph telling all the likenesses. Write a second paragraph describing the differences between the objects you described in the first paragraph. Join your two paragraphs by writing a sentence for the beginning of the second paragraph which ties your two paragraphs together.

Submit your two paragraphs as an article for the class newsletter.

WORDY GOODIES: FINDING SPECIAL WAYS TO SAY THINGS
25 to 30 minutes   *3 to 6 people*

If you do this you will be more able to help students find ways to make their writing more interesting and effective.

Find a group and discuss these questions: Why do we want what writers of literature have to say written down instead of just being said and forgotten like what most of us say? What makes the thoughts of literary writers special?

Is it always just the original ideas they have or is there something else? Is that something else what really makes them writers and not psychologists or historians or something else? Look for some of the things that make their writings special. Consider the way they often compare things that they want us to understand to things that are familiar to us so that we can see how they feel about a new idea. Sometimes they even say something is something that it really is not just to show how much like it the thing is. Do you ever do this?

Did you ever talk about someone who was a "big cheese" or a "big wheel"? What did you mean? What were the characteristics of the cheese or wheel you wanted to show that the person had? Which is the best comparison? What makes a good comparison? How many ways does a wheel describe importance? A cheese?

Try judging how good a comparison is by counting the ways it describes the things the writer wants to describe about his subject. How well does the expression "mouth of the river" work? How well does "foot of the mountain" work? Find some others used in common speech and judge their effectiveness.

for a whole day. Can you find any certain kind of people who use more of these than other people?

Look at a book that has lots of different kinds of writing in it and see if you can find one kind that has more of these than others. Why is this? Why would a writer who wanted to use few words want to use many of these comparisons? What value would they have for him? Why would a writer who wants to get his readers to feel strongly about a subject use them? What kind of speechmakers would use many of these? If it is near election time, you might listen and test your theory.

Tell your logs what you find out.

INVENT A WORD: USING WORDS TO KNOW THE WORLD

several hours   *3 to 5 people*

When you have finished this activity, you will be more able to help your students learn to make wise and effective word choices for their writing.

Our perceptions are based on the language we have to name the things in them and describe them. How could we know a wave from the rest of the water if we had no word for it? How would we know the quality of the difference between blue and red if we had no names for them? Would we see the world differently if we had different words to describe it or how we feel about it? Would we enjoy a sunset more if we had more or better words to describe it? Could we solve a problem better if we had better words for talking about it?

Form a committee to improve upon the English language. Each member will need a small notebook to carry with him every day for one week. Every time you feel something that you can't find words to express, invent a word to express it: and write it down in your notebook along with the definition. The committee should meet each day to share these new words and to consider whether they should be included in your improved language.

Compile a dictionary of these new words. At the end of a week present your dictionary to the class.

PUT YOUR FINGER ON IT: GETTING STARTED SOLVING YOUR WORD WORRIES

15 minutes   *1 person*

To be able to help students recognize the need to improve their writing vocabularies and to set goals for meeting their needs, examine your own vocabulary needs.

Make a list of all those you hear people use during a noon hour or even

Think about these questions: Would it help you to be able to use more words? When do you feel a lack of words? Do you have problems having words for all your thoughts when you speak? In what kinds of speaking situations do you have needs that are not met by your store of words? Do you have enough words when you are writing? Do you know enough words when you are reading your subject assignments? Which textbook is the hardest to understand? Which teacher uses words you don't know?

In your log summarize your word needs. Now that you know where your word storehouse needs to be filled, decide upon activities that you think will help you and do them. Tell your log what you have decided and why.

THE WORD BAG:
BUILDING YOUR WORD STORE I

10 minutes a day *1 person*

To discover effective ways of helping students build vocabulary, work on your own word needs.

List and define your own vocabulary needs. Which one would you like to work on first? Perhaps you could take each subject field and learn one useful word for each. Perhaps you want to concentrate on words that will help you with some other area of using language. Every day, put a word in your log from your reading or listening in each area you want to build.

This activity won't be enough to help you learn the word so that you can really use it, though. You will need to do something more to make the word really yours. What do you do when you learn a new song? You practice it, don't you? Try practicing your words. Find a way to use each new one in a sentence in your talking within a few hours after you put it in your log.

Another way to learn new words is to learn all the words associated with any new experience you have. That is the way you learned to talk when you were a baby, and it is a good way. Ask what everything is called. Don't be afraid to show that you don't know. Most people like to explain to others, and they don't expect you to know everything.

At the end of each week that you work on your word store, tell your log about your experiences with words, and what new ones you have really learned to use. Do you think you have learned everything you need to know to solve your word worries? If you want to go on building your word store in more and different ways or if you were not satisfied with the way this word building activity worked out for you, try "Happy Hints: Building Your Word Store II."

HAPPY HINTS:
BUILDING YOUR WORD STORE II

10 minutes a day   *1 person*

If you try these vocabulary building ideas for yourself, you will be more able to help students apply them to their word study activities.

Does a word usually have many meanings or just one? One way to get your word store to grow is to learn new meanings for words you already know one meaning for. Which is easier to remember, something you know a lot about or something you know only a little about?

Use your answer to decide how much you need to know about a word you want to remember. What are all the different facts you could know about a word in addition to its meaning? Where would you find all these facts?

When you were little, did you first learn words from seeing them or from hearing them? Is this a good way? Why? Try doing what little children do. When there is a word you want to work on, recite it to yourself or make a little rhyme out of it. Say the word, or the rhyme, to yourself between classes all day.

Another good way to learn a word is to learn the opposite of the word. Where will you find these opposites? Try listing pairs of opposites in your log.

Which is your own largest word store—the one you use for reading, speaking, listening, or writing? Are there some words you can use in one of those experiences you cannot use in another? Which has the most words in it and which has the least? Could you transfer words from one of your word stores where you have more words to another where you have fewer words? How could you do this? How could you make words you are able to read or listen to and understand useful in your speaking or writing word store? Perhaps the best way is to practice by speaking and writing the words you find in your reading and listening.

At the end of each week that you work on word building be sure to let your log know how you are doing with these methods of taking possession of new words. Have you really used them in your talking, listening, reading, and writing? Where and how? Have they become a habit? Can you use them without thinking about them any more? Are you satisfied?

When will you finish adding new words to your store? Will you always discover words you do not understand in your listening and reading? Will there always be some situations in which your word store fails you?

GRAB A WORD:
HAVE YOU FOUND A HARD WORD YOU WANT TO LEARN?
15 minutes *1 person*

Try this word building exercise yourself if you want to be able to show students more ways of remembering new words.

You may need to experiment with different ways of remembering words to see which works best for you.

Compare the sounds in the word with the letters that represent them. Are the letters in your word the ones you would expect to find? Are there any silent letters or strange combinations of them? Does your word have more than one part? What is the root? You will usually find the root in the middle of the word, and if there are prefixes or endings, they will be attached to it. The dictionary will help with finding the root since it divides the word into syllables and tells what each syllable stands for.

Try to find a word that rhymes with your word and is spelled the same in the parts that are hard to learn and remember. Some people like to make sentences out of their hard words. They make up a silly sentence in which every word begins with a letter of the word. Of course, the words have to be in the same order as the letters of the word.

In your log tell what you have done with your word. Divide it into parts and / or write your silly sentence so that you can check back if you forget. Leave some space on this page of your log. At the end of one week come back to this page and tell your log how well you remember the word and how many times you have used it.

BECAUSE . . . . : WHY SPELL ONE WAY?
25 to 35 minutes *2 to 6 people*

If you do this activity, you will be more prepared to answer students' questions about the importance of spelling and to interest them in improving their spelling.

Discuss these questions: What are some of the disadvantages of having to spell just one way? Can you be inventive in spelling, or must you always spell words the way everyone else does? Are there people in our society who make a living out of making interesting spellings of words? Find some examples of advertisements that use spellings that are combinations and inventive ways to make new words. What words are combined to make "Bisquick"? Why? What is "Quink"? What words are combined in it? Slur the word "advertising" and you get "overteasing." What is the connection?

When is standardized spelling useful? Why? Try this little exercise: Each of you should find a paragraph in a textbook and copy it onto a piece of paper neatly. When you copy it, misspell several words. Give your paragraph to the person next to you so that each one of you has one to read. Read the paragraphs and discuss your reactions. What happened when you came to the misspelled words? Were there delays in your reading? What happened to your concentration on the idea you were reading? What would happen to your readers if they read words in your writing that were spelled differently? Which is more important— to use an appropriate word you want to use but cannot spell, or to use one that does not fit as well that you do know how to spell? How can you solve this problem?

Does everyone in your group agree about the usefulness of standard spelling? Do you agree about how important it is, or do your opinions differ? State your opinion in your log, and tell your reasons for this opinion.

THE MORE THE MERRIER: SPELLING TOGETHER

variable time   *a group*

To find ways that you may help students work together to give mutual support in solving spelling problems, work with a group from your class.

Find a group to experiment with methods of improving spelling. Talk about your spelling problems and what you could do to solve them. You may want to make a list of words that you all think it would be good to learn. There are some here which may help you by producing suggestions for memory tricks and for games to play. You might agree to proofread each other's writing papers.

Set goals for your group and make a plan to reach them. Don't be afraid to try a different solution if one doesn't work.

Try out your solutions. Talk about them, and write about them in your logs. Does the same solution work for everyone? What was best for you? Why? How does it make you feel to work on spelling with a group? Does it help you improve your spelling? Why or why not?

SPICE UP SPELLING: INVENT MEMORY JOGGERS

1 hour *1 person or a group*

If you want to help students improve their spelling, some tricky little sentences or devices will remind them how to spell especially difficult words. Try this.

If you are studying spelling in a group, you might make these memory joggers for each other or share the ones you have discovered for yourself.

Here's one for "dessert"—that nice food at the end of dinner. Remember that we always want more dessert, and there's more than one "s" in it! Try your hand at inventing ways to remember how to spell "their," "embarrassment" or any other words you have trouble with. You might remember that the abbreviation for "Wednesday" is "Wed." so don't forget the "d" when you write the whole word.

Most people have their own private memory joggers for special words. Ask some different people—don't forget parents and teachers—about their ways of remembering difficult words. Make your own collection of memory joggers.

If you have a group, put your collection in a theme cover and make your own little booklet out of it—a speller's guide. If you are working alone, try posting your favorite joggers on the bulleting board—maybe one each day for a week.

Tell your log if you think your spelling has been improved by the memory joggers.

DOUBLE-DIPPED WORDS: SPELLING "TWO-T" WORDS

15 minutes *1 person*

To help students who get confused about whether to put one "t" or two in some words, do this.

Here are two lists of words. See if you can see how they are different:

writing	fitting
exciting	sitting
biting	knitting

Are there differences in sounds between the two lists? How do the vowels sound in the first list? In the second list? Are there differences in spelling that seem to coincide with the differences in sound? Find ten or a dozen more words that fit this sound-spelling pattern. List them in your log. From what you have learned about these words can you make a rule that will help you with spelling problems in the future?

Write your rule in your log, and try sharing it with a friend, or even the whole class.

SPELL-A-PICTURE: SPELLING WORD PICTURES

20 minutes   *1 person*

If you do this activity, you may discover a way to make words so interesting that students can't forget them.

You may have special spelling words to use for this or just some words you want to be able to spell.

Make a picture, but instead of using lines to draw, use the letters of the words you have chosen. You can use the letters right side up or upside down. You can make them large or small. You can either write them or print them, but do not do both on the same picture. You must keep the letters in order, but you can use the same word over. Do not draw any lines.

Share your finished picture with the class. You may want to display it in the project corner or on the bulletin board.

SPELLING AUTHORITY: USING THE DICTIONARY

25 minutes   *1 person*

To help students use the dictionary to solve their spelling problems, do this.

Look up the word "enclose" under both "i" and "e" in your dictionary. Which is the preferred spelling? How do you know? Try several other dictionaries. Do they all give you the same information? Which dictionary would you recommend to a student? Why? Look up the word "color" in your dictionary. What does "Also esp. Brit." mean? Where does it appear in the dictionary you are using? In another dictionary? Look up the word "adviser." Are two spellings of the word given in your dictionary? If so, is there any explanation of the two spellings?

How do you know when a word can be abbreviated? Look up the abbreviation "mag." in the *Thorndike-Barnhart High School Dictionary.* Compare the entry with entries in other dictionaries.

Summarize your discoveries in your log, and make suggestions for using the dictionary as a spelling aid in high school.

PLEASE PUNCTUATE: PLACING PERIODS AND CAPITALS

30 to 40 minutes   *2 people*

If you want to be more able to help your students use periods and capitals sensibly in their writing, do this activity.

Find a partner, and each of you copy five sentences from a book or your log, leaving out all punctuation and capitalization. Give your sentences to your partner and ask him to read them aloud. Talk about what happened. Did you get confused, and go on past pauses that were necessary for clearness? What did you do then? What happened to your concentration on the ideas that you were reading when you had to go back? If you were to think of punctuation as a message to the reader, what would it say? Make a list of all the punctuation marks you know, and the messages each delivers. You can find lists in old grammar books and lists of rules about them. The rules are real messages from writer to reader. Write rules for the messages in your logs.

When you are writing or proofreading what you have written, return to this page in your logs and read these materials aloud. It will often become apparent to you just what messages you want to give your reader about pauses and matters other than words to make his reading easier and focus his attention on your ideas.

Can you think of some sentences where the meaning might be changed completely by punctuation or the lack of it? Try this sentence— or sentences: "I knew I would have to butcher my mother wanted to do her meat canning." Of course you can see from this little example what would happen if you make a mistake, and how easy it is to find many period places. You are an expert—all native speakers of English are— on the voice pauses that tell you where to put the periods and capitals. Even inside sentences you can find the meaning through pauses. Try this sentence: "He gave her dog biscuits." Who got what? How do you know? What if it was the other way around? Who would get what? What does the pause tell you? Is there any difference between these two sentences? "At the age of thirty five men had chosen their careers." "At the age of thirty-five men had chosen their careers." How is the hyphen important to the meaning? What rule can you put in your logs about one time when you need hyphens? Is this true of other numbers? Which ones?

What conclusions can you draw about the pauses in speaking and writing? Would high school students draw these same conclusions? Would it help them to improve their writing? How? Tell your logs.

BACK TO THE BARNYARD:
WHERE DID THE STRANGE PLURALS COME FROM?

25 minutes *1 person*

If you would like to help your students feel more comfortable with irregular plural forms and interested in finding out about them, do this to learn more about them yourself.

A long time ago there were several ways to form the plurals of words in our language. Now there is just the "s" sound even though it is sometimes spelled "es." The plurals of English words have become more simple with time. Can you guess why this change happened?

If you could not read and write, which would you be able to remember best, just one ending or several? Which would you remember, the special endings of the words you spoke most often or the ones for the words you spoke least often? In early England the peasant who could not read could remember the word for oxen that pulled his plow and this lasted. And mice did too. Why? How about feet? And teeth? And geese? And lice? Did the peasant use books? So he just added an "s" to this one.

These peasants cleaned a lot of useless endings off our words and made our language easier to learn.

Make a list of all the words you can think of that have strange plurals. Perhaps some of them came from languages other than English. Can you tell which ones came from England? Are all of these words as important in our lives today as they were in the lives of the peasants? Then why haven't they lost their funny plurals? Why don't we say oxes? How is it written in our books? When something is written in a book, is it harder to change? Why do you think this is so?

In your log write your list of strange plurals and your conclusions about these questions.

DID YOU EVER VERB A WORD?: FIND OUT ABOUT VERBS
45 minutes   *1 person or a group*

If you would like to help your students discover ways to make their sentences interesting and varied, do this activity.

Do you know how to find a verb? When do you need verbs? Can you make a sentence without a verb? Is there a special name for a sentence without a verb? When is that kind of sentence useful? Is there any other kind of sentence without a verb? Find some examples in your reading. Do you use them in your writing?

Are you sure you can find verbs? Could you pick out the verbs from a list of words? How can you be sure a verb is a verb? Can you find the verb in this sentence? "These cars do not platform at Scarsdale." Is this word usually a verb? Is it all right to use it as a verb? Why? Here's another sentence: "The cigarette travels the smoke." Is travel used as a verb in other sentences? Is there a difference between this use and others?

Make a sentence using travel as a verb. Does it work the same way as the sentence about the smoke? How is it different? Did your sentence say something about where you traveled? Find the verb in this one:

"Airlines jet to France in a hurry." What is the verb here? Is it usually a verb?

Does a speaker have a right to use a word any way he likes to use it? What effect does the use of a word in a strange way have on listeners? What effect does that have on a person's right to use it? Are the verbs in the sentences you just read any different from those in these sentences:"The boats dock in the river." "The boats anchor in the harbor." How are the two sets of sentences alike? How are they different?

Can you verb a word that isn't usually used as verb? Try it. Write a few sentences with verbed words in your logs. Try to make them sentences you might use. When would you use them? Tell your log what you have decided about language correctness and using words in unusual ways.

THE CASE OF CASE: WHO OR WHOM?

variable time   *1 person*

To prepare yourself to deal with student problems about "who" and "whom," do this activity.

Consider these questions: Where in a sentence do you usually hear or use the word "who"? Does "whom" ever appear in the "who" spot in a sentence? When you are speaking, how do you know if you are saying it right? In this case does the proper usage sound right to you? Is it easier to figure out the right usage when you are speaking or when you are writing? Why? If some other word is really the word before the verb and the "who" word belongs after the verb, traditionalists believe it should be "whom." However, for most people the word in the subject position takes the subject form.

Which is easier to pronounce, "who" or "whom"? To say the longer and harder to pronounce word takes physical and mental effort at odds with most speech situations, which are spontaneous. Sometimes people get so confused by the "who" and "whom" problem that they say "whom" when they should say "who." Many people try to avoid using either word because they do not feel certain about them. How many people do you know who use "who" and "whom" correctly? Study the rules on the correct usage of the words in a grammar book. Then become a "who" watcher. Listen for the use of "who" and "whom" by all the people you talk to during one day. How many used "whom" correctly? How many used it incorrectly? How many did not use it at all?

What conclusions can you draw for your log about the use of "who" and "whom"? How important is it to correct the misuse of these words by high school students? Why?

STREET TALK: SHOULD YOU WRITE IT?

1½ hours   *a group*

To be able to help students adapt their verbal patterns to the medium of written rather than spoken language, do this activity.

Find a group, and discuss these questions: Is slang as useful in writing as it is in speaking? Why is it so useful in speaking? Why was it invented? Would it have been invented if an equally effective way existed to say the words without slang? Has it any limitations in writing usefulness? Is slang precise or does it have some uncertainties in meaning? What do the uncertainties add to the meaning? Does this work as well in writing? Which needs to be more precise, writing or speaking? Why? Which changes more rapidly, slang or standard language? Which will live longer, writing or speaking? Why? Are the same conclusions true about non-standard dialects in writing? Why? What happens to your reader if you write in a non-standard dialect?

Are there ever good reasons for using slang or a non-standard dialect in writing? Find some selections by modern writers who use street talk in their writing. Read several of these selections aloud in your group. Why does the writer use the words he does? Are his word choices effective? Why? Can you form any conclusions about the advantages and disadvantages of using street talk in writing? When is it useful? When might it interfere with the purpose of the writing? How can you help students to be aware of these choices?

Prepare a report for the class in which you discuss the advantages and disadvantages of street talk in writing and give examples to support your conclusions.

AT THE SOUND OF THE TONE . . . : EXPRESSING TONE OF VOICE IN WRITING

1 hour   *1 person or a group*

To be able to help your students express strong feelings in writing effectively, find out how writers do it.

Find a passage in your reading in which a writer describes strong feelings. If you have a group, discuss these questions. If you are working alone, think about them:

How does the writer show strong feelings? What punctuation does he use? Is it any different from the punctuation he might use if he were writing a weather report? Why? Where does he use strong verbs and adjectives? Does he repeat words? Which words? Why? Is there likely to be conversation used in this passage? Why? Which words express movement? What does movement have to do with the feeling of emotion? What shows you that the writer is building to strong feeling by piling up emotion? Does he use numbers of people or events to achieve the effect? Does he use color? What other devices can you find that the writer uses to create tone?

Try your hand at creating tone. Decide first what you would like to describe, a scene or an event. Decide what tone you want to convey. Often this can be expressed in one word—sadness, warmth, loneliness, peace, and so forth. Then use all the devices that you have found to create your desired tone.

NUGGETS TO NOTE: WHY BOTHER WITH FOOTNOTES?
1½ hours   *1 person*

If you would like to be able to help your students understand the value of footnotes and use them appropriately, do this.

Do you have a book that contains footnotes? Where do you find them on a page? Are there other places where footnotes can be put? Try looking in some magazines to find the answer, especially journals or technical magazines. What kinds of information do you find in footnotes? Make a list of all the different kinds of information you can find in footnotes. Do some footnotes give you help with understanding or reading what is written and others tell you about where the words came from before they were written in the selection?

Why do people need both kinds of footnotes? Where are you most likely to find these different kinds? Think of some examples from your own writing experiences of times when you could use these two kinds of footnotes. Write them in your log as a reminder for the next time you need them.

Are there any facts about footnotes that seem to be always the same? Do some parts of footnotes always come in the same places? Why would it be useful to always know just where in the footnote to find each item of information? What does the punctuation tell you? In your log write some sample footnotes showing the positions of the different items that you usually find in the two kinds of footnotes. If you were writing a paper that needed footnotes, would you follow these same patterns? Why?

Just to see what it feels like, think of an idea that you could write a paragraph about and use a footnote. Write your paragraph and its footnote in your log or submit it to the newsletter.

AFTERTHOUGHT: ARE YOU SATISFIED WITH YOUR WRITING

35 to 45 minutes   *1 person*

If you want to help your students evaluate their writing objectively, feel good about themselves and what they have written, and make appropriate judgements about future writing, examine your own writing.

Evaluate something you have written. You probably have good reasons why you are satisfied with your writing. What are some of them? What did you do well? What makes you choose to write in one way instead of another? Are you satisfied that you said just what you wanted to say? Did you have a reader? Did your reader react as you wanted him to? Is there anything you would like to add? Where would such a statement belong? How do you decide where to put each idea? Why are some ways of saying it and some places to put it better than others?

Are you satisfied that you always said what you meant? What can keep you from saying just what you mean? What can you do about that problem? Did you ever test yourself by saying, "If I do this, what are all the ways someone could understand what I say?" How can you make your reader read it the way you want him to understand it? Can you make it impossible for him to misunderstand what you mean? Try what you have written out on as many people as you can to see if they misunderstand or if they ask questions. Did this help you to know what you need to change or add?

Tell your log how you feel about your evaluation. Did it help you to improve your writing? Did you discover anything that you want to use the next time you write? How did you feel about your writing after you had evaluated it? Did you like it more or less? Why? Were you more or less satisfied when you had finished? How did you feel when people criticized something you had written? How can you talk to students so that you can help them to improve their writing without making them feel bad about themselves or what they have written? What could someone say to you that would help you without hurting you? Are some ways of saying it better than others? What are they? Can you give examples? Is criticism easier to accept from some people than others? Why?

FINE FIXING: DO YOU WANT TO REWRITE?

25 minutes   *1 person*

To be more able to help students who need to rewrite their papers, find a paper that you have written but are not satisfied with and rewrite it.

Ask yourself these questions before you begin: Why have you decided to rewrite this particular paper? Make a list of the things you know you want to do differently. Do you know some things you did not know when you started to write? Should you have chosen a different subject? Should you have chosen a more effective form for saying what you want to say? Did you try to say too many different things? Did you start out to say one thing and end up saying something else? Did your sentences turn out too long or too short? Are you unhappy with the words you chose? Did you explain ideas so that they could be clearly understood? Do your examples show what you want them to show?

Look at your list. How will you make these changes? If there are some things you don't know how to fix, see if you can find cards to help you with them. Let this list be your plan of action and be patient with yourself. Remember that for some ideas—especially beautiful ideas— there aren't any short-cuts.

Be proud of your finished writing. Make it look as attractive as you can. Invite others to read it by writing it in ink and leaving wide margins. Post it on the bulletin board, or place it in your folder for the teacher to read. Tell your log how you felt about rewriting. Did you like the paper more or less when you had rewritten it? How did you feel before you started? How might a high school student feel about a paper that needed to be rewritten? Would he be discouraged? How could you help him not to be discouraged? Would he feel that he had been a failure as a writer? How could you help him not to feel that way? How could you keep him from feeling bored with the task of rewriting what he had already said before?

PROOF POSITIVE: BEING A PROOFREADER

30 minutes   *1 person*

If you would like to help your students find ways of proofreading for each other, this will provide you with both experience as a proofreader and ideas you can use.

Proofread a paper for another member of the class or register in the help bank as a proofreader. To prepare for this task consider these questions: What should you do when you proofread? Should you look for spelling mistakes? Should you check to make sure that everything makes sense? How do you do that? Would it help to read aloud? Should you check to make sure that punctuation and capitals are where they need to be?

What other things could you look for to help people improve their writing? Take a look at the verbs to see if they could be more descriptive and more active. See if the nouns and modifiers could be more detailed and descriptive. Do they bring a picture to your mind? What could you change to make them do that? Are there any useless words in the writing? Could you eliminate them and still make sense out of the sentences? Try it.

As a helper, how can you help people to see these things in their writing without making them feel discouraged or angry? What kinds of words can you use when you talk to them to make them feel good about what they have done but still want to improve it?

Tell your log how you feel about being a proofreader. What reactions did you get from the people you helped? Would you do anything differently? If so, what? What suggestions can you make for someone who is planning to be a proofreader?

SUIT YOURSELF:
PROOFREAD YOUR OWN PAPER

30 minutes   *1 person*

If you do this, you may discover how students may use this method of helping themselves finish their papers.

Let the tape recorder help you proofread. Read your writing into the tape recorder after you have written it. You may find some things you want to change as you read. Be sure you know how to operate the stop button so you can stop the tape while you make changes. Now play the tape back and listen as you reread what you wrote. Do you get other ideas for changes? Repeat this as often as you like to hear your language. You may find words and phrases that do not sound just right. Sometimes, you may realize you have even left out words or word endings. If you have had problems with subject and verb agreement, you may find it easier to write correctly when you can hear the sentences. When you practice being the reader yourself, maybe you will find punctuation that makes it easier for the reader.

Do you find there are differences between what we say when we are talking and what we say when we are expressing the same ideas in writing? You may make a comment about the conclusions you reach about this subject in your log.

RESPONDING TO STUDENT WRITING

Generating and managing student writing are important duties of the English teacher. The teacher of the humanistic curriculum finds another of his functions is responding to student writing, not evaluating or judging it. In teaching writing, more than in teaching any other language art, it is tempting to focus on product rather than process as a basis for seeing what is accomplished. Perhaps this is because writing has been a method, the most common method, of testing areas of scholastic achievement. This temptation must be resisted.

In evaluating student writing, teachers often locate whatever the student has done wrong and call it to the student's attention. A humanistic curriculum, on the other hand, emphasizes not what is wrong but what is right. The teacher-reader searches for what is good, not what is bad. The futility of close marking and revision is indicated by the fact that, although many teachers do a great deal of it, students continue to make the same mistakes that have been marked on previous papers and even by previous teachers. The same weaknesses persist. Instead of calling attention to bad things, teachers should reinforce good writing as specifically, strongly, and precisely as possible.

Only reader reactions helpful to the writer at his present stage of progress and accomplishment will be revealed by the teacher. Teacher comments will be made in ways that can be accepted by the student, for he will not respect his own writing and ability to write unless others do so. A teacher who wants honest writing must not threaten the student's confidence or pride but must accept all efforts with respect and benevolence. The sad little shortcuts of teacher comment which used to cover student papers with such menacing unintelligibilities as "awk," "misp" and "dang" will not be used by the activity teacher. The humanistic teacher will replace the traditional list of such abbreviations with a repertoire of rhetoric for comment on student papers . . . "What did you decide about . . . ?" "Could you help your reader to know you did not mean . . . ?" "How could you help your reader to see how this idea relates to your main idea?" "Did you mean . . . ?" "What would happen if . . . ?" "What would have been the result for your reader if you mentioned this in an earlier paragraph?" "I have been wondering what you meant by . . . " "Does this contradict . . . ?" The teacher will find innumerable gentle, precise, suggestive ways to direct student thought to alternatives whose advantages he might not have considered.

Letter, or worse, number grades do little to help a student learn to write. They are emotionally charged messages about the teacher's measure of the student. They destroy rather than enhance growth, eliminate, not strengthen, the weak. The grade, if grade there must be, should not be based on how much to "take off" but on how much value has been built into the work. Teacher comment directed to the value of what the student has done replaces fear in the student's thought with a sense of his need to build. A humanistic teacher reacts to student writing, but keeps correcting and grading to whatever minimum is possible in his school situation.

As the activity teacher reads student writing with interest, curiosity, and excitement, his comments show these attitudes. He expresses respect for ideas as well as design and style. Often there is little on a student's returned English paper to show that the teacher has been affected by what the student was thinking when he wrote. Even when a grade is given for "content," as it is called, there is rarely anything on the paper to show that the student's idea has been reckoned with by the teacher and that the teacher is paying it the respect of a response. If students write papers teachers find dull, let them accept responsibility for helping students to do writing that is exciting to read by responding when they do so.

The humanistic teacher uses the margins of the paper for comments on ideas of the writer, methods he has used to support his ideas, and remarks on felicities of expression, work, and structure, along with occasional pleas for clarification. Comments build on successes of the writer. By comment offered on the uniqueness, universality, significance, or implications of the writers' thought, comment recognizing both content and structure appreciatively, the teacher responds to ideas students express. He talks frequently with students in conference about their ideas and their writing structures. Emphasis is on the teacher's positive intellectual and emotional reactions. He has respect for the writer as a human being of dignity, important ideas, purposes, feelings and potentialities. He is interested in the writer's unique view of the world, his desire to understand it and make statements about it. He has curiosity about further development of the writer's ideas and alternatives. He questions assumptions underlying assertions the student has made. He inquires into clarifications of statements and offers comment on the effectiveness of the writer's ideas. And he makes clear that his are questions any writer who expects to be taken seriously will arouse in the mind of a friendly reader.

Students write just as they speak when they trust their audience. Their volubility is a measure of their teacher's plausibility in building their confidence. If the student writer finds he has said something that commands admiring attention from others, he wants to repeat this activity because it makes him feel mastery. The specific response of the teacher helps students write better. It communicates not only good feeling but precise information students need. It strengthens ability as well as motivation and interest. The teacher of writing must know, then, what good writing is and how to verbalize his recognition of it in order to cause repetition of the writer's often randomly selected, effective structures.

The teacher in the activity curriculum changes the monologue of writing to a dialogue between reader and writer. His job is to be an interested reader, sensitive to his students' wish to communicate something to one who will respond appreciatively. Students seize writing opportunities when they know that response is valued. They enjoy the lonely task of the writer when they look forward to having an interested reader. Students who enjoy writing welcome opportunities to write, and a teacher can provide this motivation of student satisfaction by his display of interest and appreciation. Compositions then become conscious efforts to communicate ideas students consider important to respected readers.

Correctness in using standard writing dialect is a problem for many students. The activity teacher attaches greater importance to fluency than to correctness because ability to use standard writing dialect comes to those who do not naturally use that dialect only after fluency is achieved. Emphasis on correctness before fluency is achieved results too often in paralysis both of ability and willingness to write. A free flow of ideas should be encouraged, even though it produces grammatical anarchy. No complaint or criticism should shadow the student's sense that he can master writing and continually enhance his skills. Communication—useful and valuable communication—takes place at all levels of language and in all standards of English. The teacher for whom correctness is a primary aim often helps the student write things that yield small satisfaction to the writer and are of little or no interest to anyone else. No one was ever corrected into becoming a good writer when that correction was directed only to mechanics.

How marking should take place is a matter teachers and students should solve together, and students often know best what can be done to help them. All should discuss how and whether nonstandard usage spoils communication and how the teacher can help students write well. Some may want the teacher to make marginal notes of all nonstandard usage. Others may want such notes used only at certain times, if at all. They may want collections of their nonstandard usages made for special study. Some students may want help from other students, not the teacher, on this phase of their work. The student writer's prime obligation, like that of other writers, is to be clear and coherent and only secondarily to be grammatically fashionable. And students want to learn and can learn to use words well when they have something they want to say to someone they want to reach or move. The activity teacher must be that someone. Let no student in an activity classroom find writing a clash between himself, dutiful, indifferent, or rebellious about what he thinks his writing can or cannot communicate, and a teacher who thinks his own primary function is to teach correctness.

Spelling, for instance, is important only because of the way it affects the reader. To tell students that spelling has any inherent virtue besides this is to mislead him and to exaggerate and denigrate at the same time the importance of standard spelling. Spelling conventionally is a courtesy to the reader that keeps him from being distracted from the idea of the writer to the fact that he must translate the way a word works for the writer into the way it works for him as reader.

Time and effort expended on teaching spelling often far outweigh results attained. Teaching of and from general lists, lists of demons, personal needs lists, curriculum lists, context situations, phonic rules and games often brings honor to those who already know how to spell and dismay to those who do not. Traditional spelling bees give the most practice to those who remain in the game longest and thus need practice least and leave those watching who most need learning exercise.

Attitudes and habits must be changed if poor spellers are to be affected. Ordinarily, even poor spellers spell most of their words right. They miss just those whose letters do not match their sound. Words which are regular can be taught in linguistic sets. Others must simply be learned as irregularities. Students can help each other with these in two-person drills. Some can invent mnemonics to help themselves. But testing as teaching in spelling will probably help no one. Spelling can be tested only in typical writing behavior. For the student, the dictionary should be a treasured source of information, not a source of punishment or boredom. Teachers must not force students to do dictionary exercises that cause them to dislike the dictionary.

Teachers and students together can analyze reasons for using or not using speech or writing characteristics peculiar to individual students. The teacher may explain the advantages of standard usage where they exist, but sometimes, if the supposed advantage is exposed to rhetorical analysis, it may be found that standard usage is really not adequate to convey the feelings and ideas of the writer. Students remain the final authority of whether they want to use particular locutions.

Teacher and student should explore possible alternatives if there is a likelihood the present structure of a student's writing may be misunderstood. The writing either does what the writer intends effectively, or there are usages which would make it more effective. Just as the writer needs to be led to consider the effect of alternate ways of presenting ideas to his reader, the same issue appears in making grammatical or punctuation changes. When a writer sees the effect an alternative makes on his reader, he can see why he should consider or reject changes. This is realistic correctness.

Correctness has value if it produces clarity or economy. But measuring the success or failure of a piece of writing by the willingness or the ability of the writer to conform to arbitrary standards of correctness places undue emphasis on one of the least important requirements of good writing. The humanistic teacher makes it plain to the student that, although the student writer often may want to conform to standard English to avoid distracting his reader's attention from his intended meaning, standard usage alone will not make writing effective. The writer should be reassured that his teacher is more concerned with the total effectiveness of his writing than with making the writer conform to usage standards.

Usage improvement often comes without special attention being paid to it when the writer writes for an interested audience. Above all, the teacher does not reject the basic meaning tool of the user of language, his native dialect, in which he has a heavy emotional investment. The teacher must show the writer how to increase his stock of meaning tools by rules that can be introduced when they are really needed and can be discovered by rhetorical investigation. If the rule improves the work, it helps the reader get the meaning more effectively. That is the sole test. And when the writer does use effective rhetoric and improves his linguistic manipulations, the teacher notes attentively these evidences of progress. The double purpose of writing is to discover the truth and to communicate it effectively, and grammar and syntax are the servants, not the masters, of this attempt. Well-organized writing that has nothing to say, even if it says that nothing grammatically, is not the objective of the activity curriculum.

Teachers should encourage students to read each others' writing, providing wherever possible some sort of publication of the writing of students in bulletin board displays or newsletters. Students whose writing has been treated to teacher appreciation learn to react similarly to the writing of their fellow students, using a rhetoric that has been used to them to support the writing experience of their classmates by comments on each others' work. This process starts with sharing parts of logs, reading these or more formal writings in small groups, using a rhetoric of positive comment and interested questions.

The humanistic teacher knows that writers who have no daring never find that anarchy may be as creative as order. Language is variable, changing, living. One who uses it well is bound to make changes in it to suit his purposes. However, language must also be traditional. That men understand each other at all depends on centuries of agreements and conventions which, beginning as inventions, hardened into useful habits that help us understand each other. And, if throwing away a convention makes the language less able to express all it can express, then the writer is less free than before he discarded the convention.

Because writers, then, write well only when they want to communicate something they want to say to someone they want to say it to, a sound relationship between teacher and student and between students themselves is the basis of good student writing. The student writer should feel toward his teacher the way any good writer feels toward his favorite editor. From activities suggested in this chapter, the prospective teacher can derive suggestions for making activity cards appropriate to his own classes as he does the activities during his own preparation.

Activities

LOGGING: PRACTICE YOUR GOOD RESPONSES

2 weeks   *2 people*

To be more able to respond wisely to student writing, do this.

Find a partner—someone you would like to have read your log and someone whose log you would like to read. Agree that for one week your partner will play the part of a teacher and you will be the student. During the second week you will reverse the situation. During the first week you should both work on projects with other people as you normally would, but rather than giving your log to the teacher to read, give it to your partner. Before you begin, you may want to discuss with your partner what kind of comments you would like him to make. During the second week, you make comments in his log. At the end of each week, meet to discuss these questions:

Do you feel any differently about your partner, now that you have been reading his log or writing to him? In what way? Why? Which comments did you like best? Why? Which comments made you want to write more? Did any comments make you angry? Why? How does it feel to write comments in someone else's log? Why? How do you decide what to write? Were you ever misunderstood? Why? What did you do about it? How much time does it take to read a log and write comments in it? Did you get better at doing it? How? If you are the log writer, would you rather find many comments written in your log or few? Why? How did you feel if no comments were written? If you were criticized? If you were praised? Why? Which is more important, what you say or how you say it? Why?

When you have finished your log sharing and are ready to let the teacher read your dialogue, include in your log a summary of your conclusions about these questions and any other discoveries you have made as a result of this activity.

DIA-LOGUE: QUESTION YOUR TEACHER

variable time *1 person*

If you want to prepare yourself to find good responses to student writing, do this.

Talk to your teacher about your responses to his comments in your log. Ask him how he feels about what you have written and how you have responded to his comments. Do you feel frustrated if he doesn't seem interested in an idea you thought was great? How do you feel if he comments on your sloppy handwriting, but doesn't say anything about a new idea you have used? What can you do about it? What happens if you make a joke and he takes it seriously? How do you feel about yourself when you make a foolish mistake in your writing? How do you feel when you do something creative and intelligent and the teacher appreciates it? What is the best thing he said to you in your log? Did you let him know that you felt good about what he said? If you didn't, try it.

Did you do or say anything to try to make your writing more clear and attractive for him to read? What did you do? Did you feel that you succeeded? Did you feel that you were rewarded for your efforts? Why or why not? Which causes the strongest feelings in you, a good comment or a bad one? If there were comments which made you feel bad, did you tell your teacher how they could have been changed to make you feel less bad? If you want your teacher to tell you his reaction to an idea you are talking about, do you ever just ask him? How do you think your teacher feels when you say bad things or nothing at all? Why don't you ask him? How do you think he feels about your successes? Do you tell him about those? Do you ask him to tell you how he feels? Do you respond to what your teacher says, or do you only expect him to respond to what you say? Try to find ways you can respond to what he says. Can you tell him which comments he made that you liked best, and why? Can you think about his ideas and tell him about your conclusions or reactions? Can you respond to his ideas with ideas in a similar vein?

Apply as many of these questions as seem appropriate to your situation to your dia-logue with your teacher. As you continue your dia-logue with your teacher, practice putting yourself in the teacher's place and make your own conclusions about how teachers and students can best respond to each other in logs. What can the teacher do to let the student know it is all right to express his feelings and ask questions? Is criticism ever necessary? If so, how much and when? How can the teacher best phrase questions and comments so that they do not harm the student's enjoyment of his writing or his feelings about himself? What things is it best not to talk about? If a teacher does not write clear sentences or spell correctly, what kinds of responses should he expect?

MULTI-LOGUE: A LOG GROUP

6 days   *5 people*

To practice the skills you will need to deal with and respond to a variety
of student logs and writings, do this.

Find a group of five people, and agree to share your logs. Choose a
project you will work on as a group—a project which requires log writing
every day. At the end of each day choose one member whose responsibility it will be to take the logs home, comment on them, and return
them to you the next time you meet. Discuss your feelings about the
experience of being the log reader and about having your log read. You
may want to discuss these feelings each time you meet, or you may
prefer to save your comments until the sixth day. You will not be able
to write to the reader in your log the next day because someone else
will be reading it, but if you feel it is necessary, you can write your
replies to his comments in a note and give it to him. However you
arrange your discussion, here are some questions which may be useful:

When you were the reader, how long did it take you to read the logs?
Did you mind spending the time? Which was easier to do, read the logs
or write the comments? Why? Did you find yourself saying the same
words over and over in your comments? Could you change that? Do you
need to? How much did you write? Did you try to keep the person you
were responding to clearly in mind as you wrote in his log? How did you
do that? When you were the person who had written the log, were you
anxious to get your log back so you could see what had been written in
it? Why? Which were your favorite kinds of comments? Why? Did anyone
write "That's good" or "very good" in your log? How could they have
written to tell you more about what was good? Did you feel bad about
anything that was written in your log? How could that bad feeling have
been avoided? When you read the comments in your log, how did you
feel about the person who made them? Did you remember how you felt
when you were the one writing the comments? In what ways was it
different, being the reader and being the writer?

Use the conclusions you draw as a result of your discussion to formulate your own set of "dos" and "don'ts" for responding to others'
writing. Write your "dos" and "don'ts" in your log.

MONO-LOGUE: WRITING JUST FOR YOU

25 minutes   *1 person*

To be able to help students use writing as a tool for solving personal
problems and clarifying emotional thinking, do this on a day when you
are feeling angry, confused or disappointed.

Think about these questions: Are there some problems in math that you can do in your head and others that you need a pencil and paper to solve? Why is there a difference? Is there a difference in the kinds of problems you can solve by these two methods? Which is harder? How does it help to write the problem out? Have you ever written out a problem that was not a math problem so that you could solve it? What form would you use to solve a life problem? Would you state the problem and then the possible solutions? Would you write the arguments for and against each solution? Or, would you just write it all at once until you got your feelings out of your system? There are many who use both methods. Writing lets you get it all down in order of some kind, whether it is the order of logic or the order of your feelings.

Do you feel that you can live with the problem more comfortably, now that you have written about it? If there is any part of what you have written that you do not want read, just fold the paper and tape it together into a mono-logue instead of a dia-logue.

FINDING THE WAY:
SAYING GOOD THINGS

1 hour   *a group*

To be more able to use the rhetoric of positive reinforcement in helping students improve their writing, do this.

Form a group and examine the rhetoric teachers have traditionally used for commenting about student writing. Each of you should look for old papers on which teachers have used traditional markings and for textbooks which give lists of abbreviations which teachers use for marking papers. Compare the abbreviations you have found. Do all teachers use the same marks or abbreviations to convey the same meanings? If a student were going to know the meanings of all the possible marks teachers might put on his papers, how many symbols and abbreviations would he need to memorize? Do you know them all? Working together make a list of positive comments teachers might make on student papers to replace each of the symbols and abbreviations. On a paper make two columns, one showing the traditional marks or abbreviations and another showing comments which might be used by an activity teacher. List two or three good comments which might replace each traditional criticism.

Consider these questions: How can you turn comments about what is wrong with student writing into comments about what is right with it? How can you show by your comment what the student could do to make his paper better without telling him that it is bad? Could you ever say "The way you used that word is very interesting. Most people use it in a different way."? Would the student be interested enough in using the word the way most people do to ask you about it? When a student has a problem with a lack of punctuation, would it help to say something good about the punctuation he does use rather than criticizing him for not using it? What might happen if you searched out the good aspects of his paper? If you found just one comma, could you say "I like what you did here. I felt comfortable when you made me pause here"? Would he want you to feel comfortable more often when you read his papers? These are comments you make to help students realize how they can better manage the structure of their writing so that is is clearer to the reader. You need also to respond to the ideas in student papers by showing interest and curiosity. Such comments might begin with "I would like to know more about . . . ," "I'm curious about . . . ," "How did you . . . ?" or "What do you think about . . . ?" Talk about how the activity teacher uses these comments on real papers. If you have old papers you have written in the past, share them with the group. Give them to other members so that they can respond to them with positive comments rather than traditional ones. How do you feel if you get your paper back with lots of good comments on it? Is it better not to say anything if you can't say something good?

So that others may see and use your ideas, make a list of traditional and humanistic comments into a chart to be posted in your room. Make it on a large piece of cardboard or posterboard so that it may be easily seen and read. You may also find it helpful to include an explanation of how positive comments may be used to point out the good rather than the bad.

BEFORE AND AFTER: QUESTIONING STRATEGIES

1 to 1½ hours   *a group*

To be more able to ask questions which will cause learning in your students, do this.

Find a group to act out some learning situations in which good questioning strategies may be used. Suppose a student working with a group in your class upsets the plans of other group members several times by not doing his out-of-class work, and other group members have to do his work to get their projects finished. What can you say to him that might change his behavior? What do parents and teachers usually say to young people in such situations? Act out a traditional scene which begins with the teacher making a statement like one of these: "John, you never . . . ," "When are you ever going to . . . ?" "You always . . . ," "Haven't I told you . . . ?" Do these scenes make the adult feel better? How do they make the young person feel? Do they cause him to change his behavior? Did such upbraiding cause you to change in the way adults wanted you to change when you were a child? How did you feel if you were the student in this scene? Did you want to do what the person in authority wanted you to do? Why or why not?

Now picture the same student with the same behavior problem, but replace the traditional teacher with the activity teacher. Can you make your statements descriptive and non-judging? You might start your talk with one of these phrases: "John, I see that . . . ," "Your group leader told me that . . . ," "How do you feel about . . . ? Why?" followed by "What could you do about it?" Try several such scenes. See if you can lead the student to make judgments for himself of how he feels and what his problem is and what he can do about it. When the student decides to do something about his behavior, show in your role playing how the activity teacher gives him positive reinforcement for his decision by showing approval. How can you show approval? Try it in your role playing, and then ask the person who was the student to tell you what made him feel best. Make up some situations of your own to act out.

Present a before and after sequence to the class and explain the reasons for the activity approach.

STARTING WITH PEOPLE: GENTLE CHANGING

variable time   *1 person*

Here is an experiment that will help you get people to change in ways you want.

Make a plan to bring about a change. Find a page in your log for writing down your ideas about making changes. List some of the changes you would like to make in people you know. Examine your list. Would all the changes you have listed be good for the people you would like to change? Why or why not? Who else would these changes benefit? How? Would some of these changes be impossible for you to do anything about? Why? Which changes could you bring about? How?

Sometimes big changes are made up of many little changes, each one leading you a little closer to where you want to be. Pick out two or three of the changes you have listed and see how many little changes you can break them into.

What person in your life would you like most to change and how would you like to change him? What will he do or say—how will he behave when this change has happened? How will you know when it has happened? What good thing would this change do for you, for him, and for other people? Break this change into the smallest, easiest little changes you can. List these little changes in your log. Choose one of these small changes to begin your plan.

What can you do to make this change happen? Write every answer you can find in your log. These questions may be useful: Why do people do old things instead of new things even when they know the new things work better? Could you arrange a situation to reward the person for changing as you want him to? If so, how? Is there anything that might be making the thing you want him to do seem unpleasant or unattractive to him? If so, what could you do about helping him want to change? What hidden goals does your person have? How can you show him that if he makes the change you want he will also get what he wants? Can you create an atmosphere that makes change seem safe and inviting? How? Is there anything he does now that is like the thing you want him to do? Is there anything you could praise him for?

Make your plan and try it out on the person you want to change. Record the results in your log. What worked and what didn't? Why? You may want to make several entries about the results and space them a few weeks apart, depending upon what kind of change you want to make. A big change might require time and patience.

WATCH YOUR WORDS: REINFORCING OTHERS

1 day   *1 person*

To be more able to reinforce your students with positive responses, build your store of positive rhetoric by using it in your own life.

For one day watch and listen to yourself talking with others. Try to turn your negative or critical thoughts into positive comments and reactions. If you are thinking "I wish he'd be quiet so I could read," would you normally say "Be quiet, please, I'm trying to read" or frown and say as little as possible? Could you say "It's so nice of you to realize I am trying to read" or "I'm glad you don't mind that I am reading while you are trying to talk"? If a friend shows you a new book, painting, or article of clothing he's bought and you hate it, how can you reply? Can you say that it's interesting or unusual? If you can't find anything good to say about it, can you describe it to him? Could you say "What a bright dress!" or "I see your new hat has lots of flowers on it"?

Whenever you hear yourself thinking critical thoughts, try to find something positive to say.

Tell your log how you felt about changing your critical thoughts to positive ones. Did you ever forget? If so, when? When you made the positive comments, how did the other people react? How did you feel about what you had said? How did you feel about the other person after you had said it? How did you feel when you said something critical? Did other people say what they thought would make you feel good when you said what you thought would make them feel good?

THE WORD PILL:
ARE YOU FEELING UPSET TODAY?

30 minutes   *1 person*

If you would like to help your students learn to use writing as a means of working out unpleasant feelings, experiment with writing as a release when your feelings hurt.

On a day when you've been fighting with your best friend or just have the blahs, do this: Tell your log just how you feel. Tell it when you started to feel that way, what made you feel that way, what you have been doing since you felt that way, and what kind of things happen to you when you feel that way. Imagine what could happen to make you feel good again. What could you do to make yourself feel good again?

Make a plan for doing it if you can. If it is someone else's fault you feel this way, is there anything you could do about it? Could you just go and tell him how you feel? What would happen if you did? Would that be worse than going on feeling this way? If you decide to tell the other person, remember to tell him how *you* feel. Don't tell him what he has done or how he is and feels because you can't be sure if he does feel that way.

If you want to tear this page out of the log and not turn it in, that's all right. There is only one requirement. If you are going to tear it out, you have to fill both sides with writing. If you run out of ideas, just write words—any words that you want to, but be sure each one is a different word.

REVERSING: GIVING THE TEACHER AN ASSIGNMENT

15 to 30 minutes   *1 person or a group*

If you would like to see how teacher-student feedback can work both directions, do this.

Ask your teacher if he or she will agree to accept a writing assignment from you. There will not always be time, but perhaps your teacher likes to write and would like to do some once in awhile. Choose a writing card for your teacher or make one. What would you like the teacher to tell you about?

Read your teacher's writing with the outlook of an activity teacher. Try to find something good you can say to your teacher about it. Write your conclusions about comment-writing in your log.

IV

ACCOUNTABILITY

CHAPTER VII

Generating Reports

Traditional testing and grading do not generate adequate reports for the humanistic activity curriculum. These methods of evaluating the activities of a student in an English class involve such widely varied components and such inconstant manipulation as to make the whole process of doubtful validity and reliability. Sometimes, one ability is given more weight, sometimes another, varying with the caprice or convictions of the teacher and the control of the school administration. Traditional grading in English is based on a wide range of objective and subjective factors: skills; information about all sorts of things, varying from the lives of writers to the structure of sentences; language habits learned as a result of membership in ethnic or socio-economic class; creative talent in writing or speaking; or combinations of these and other factors. It involves the teacher in many hours of putting red marks on papers, perhaps for each "error," counting these, and subtracting them from a previously determined value to find the "grade." Teachers who use the activity curriculum will still find that, in most school systems, students must have grades: so they will need to find ways to work with students to see that the process of arriving at and administering grades does as little harm as possible to learning and reflects as nearly as possible some kind of honest answer to the enquiry that is being made by parents and community by the requirement that there be grades.

TESTING

Testing is sometimes the most important factor in determining the grades of students. But test construction poses dilemmas virtually unsolvable except by compromises that render the test unreliable or invalid. And the record of decisions based on test results looks less and less attractive. At one time, for instance, college entrance opportunities were strongly affected by test results, but recent reliance by colleges on the student profile uses test results only minimally. Testing services have had to confess that in spite of efforts by the best experts, results of some years of college entrance examinations have been positively misleading. Hence, school authorities have less and less faith in decisions they make about students on the basis of objective testing.

A test of language proficiency must test not only what a student can do but what he will do in language situations. It requires a sampling of items inaccessible in the ordinary classroom to get at typical behavior as opposed to behavior elicited by the test itself. In the field of language, test behavior gives little indication of typical behavior, which cannot be extrapolated from test behavior. This is readily apparent when results of spelling tests are compared with the use of those same words in student writing. Use of language is more strongly related to will and conviction than it is to factual learning about language and is profoundly affected by habits and life style. Hence, choosing items for a test of language proficiency is a matter not solved by most tests given in classrooms. Some good work has been done by testing services in constructing items in which students may choose effective passages of writing or may improve passages, but these are not in wide use, and they have many flaws.

In some classrooms even skill exercises are used as tests. Sometimes they are the only measures used. But a skill exercise samples the means or the process of learning, not the outcome of learning, the behavior change. A good sample would have to examine skills and understandings in their actual use, not just review the activities that were designed to cause students to gain skills and understandings. A game is not awarded to a football team on the basis of excellence in performing warm-up exercises.

When exercises are used for tests or when items are used in a multiple choice situation, simple choices are forced. Some students, seeing shadings and implications in crude and blandly-worded test choices, may even fail to finish such a test as they agonize over impossible alternatives. Answers reduced to two-value orientations lead students to believe important choices can be made by simplistic logic. Such learning is intellectually, morally and socially dangerous.

Other student misconceptions are encouraged when test items themselves are assumed by students to be the most valuable objectives of learning because the reward system is based on the proper handling of these items. The grade is the reward, a message from the teacher that the test items define what is important about the learning. In addition, some tests reject language behavior quite acceptable in many circumstances. Too, tests do not reveal that language may be "correct" but tedious or odious, sins as great, certainly, as those of "incorrectness." Testing also may develop student tensions and negative attitudes toward learning. They can be counterproductive of good feelings about the attractiveness of ideas and the process of dealing with them. Whatever does not make students have good feelings about learning or whatever acts to prevent learning has no place in the activity classrooms. Traditional testing and grading occupy class time and preparation for activities irrelevant to learning, since the accumulation of facts to get a test grade focuses on quick-vanishing materials, often not very important in the first place.

The pretense of objectivity in testing is a dangerous and dishonest illusion. Test items have been chosen through the human judgment of those who have decided what students should know and how this should be measured. Even when the statistical paraphernalia of sampling procedures and item analysis have been used, they mitigate but do not prevent objectivity. Long lists of authorities appear as guarantees of standardized tests. Does this mean that their decisions are valid? How do they qualify to select samples of what teachers and students they have never seen have been teaching and learning? There might be some logic to their expert choices if there were some body of knowledge that all could agree constituted "English," but there is not such a body. And even if tests are made by teachers of students tested, selection of items is subjective. The plea of the tester, "Testing is not good, admittedly, and test scores are not perfect judgments, but they are the best we have. They are better than subjective reports," has been accepted too long by those who are awed by plausible statistical manipulations.

Objective tests are not the best ways we have of judging learning. They are subjective, and there are better ways of being subjective than by abdicating by commitment what is maintained in fact, subjectivity. Honestly faced and responsibly used, the subjectivity of student and teacher, working together in an atmosphere of mutual trust, search and discovery to evaluate what has happened to the student can be a value, not a disvalue. It is better for teachers to use subjectivity responsibly and professionally, engaging the student himself in evaluation. All too often, the objectivity myth obscures what is happening in evaluation, and the good things that can be done, even in a fairly rigid situation, when extensive avenues of student input—goal setting, product evaluation and self-report—are used.

The activity curriculum accumulates a test of learning through visible products in logs, folders, self-reports and pupil-teacher conferences. These enable teachers and students alike to know how the student uses language and progresses in that use. These artifacts of the teaching-learning process yield a multivaluing experience. Using every available structure for student input, the teacher can find in these evidences whatever judgment he must make, bringing to bear upon that judgment the best professional balance he can develop.

Activities

WHAT IS A TEST?: LOOK AROUND YOU

40 to 60 minutes   *1 person*

To be more able to design effective and realistic testing-learning situations in the classroom, do this.

Think about these questions: What is a test? How many times a day do you test? Do you test the meat to see if it is cooked? Do you test the oil in your car or the air in the tires? Do you test ice to see how solidly it is frozen, or paint to see if it is wet? Be your own shadow for one day and write down every situation in which you test something. Now imagine that you could not test in each of those situations. What would have happened to you? Why is testing important?

What is the difference between the kind of test you've been thinking about and the tests you take in school? When you test the meat to see if it is cooked, you know what you want to find out so that you can make a decision about what to do, based on that information. How is a school test different? Why? Does a school test need to be different? Could a school test be designed to test the state of a student's thoughts or feelings so that a decision could be made about what to do next?

Suppose a high school teacher assigns some reading to his class and then gives a test to discover if his students have thought and felt about this reading what he wants them to think and feel about it. If he gives them an essay test, will he find out what their thoughts and feelings are, or will he find out what they think he wants them to say? Will he find out which students were most deeply moved by what they read, or will he discover which ones are the most skillful writers? Will he find out which ones will remember that story for the next twenty years, or which ones can spell well? Has he found out how he can improve his next literature lesson, or has he discovered that most students write poorly on tests because they are frightened or trying not to make mistakes?

What happens if he gives a multiple choice or matching test? How long will students remember the main character's name if they did not enjoy the reading? Will they enjoy the next reading assignment more or less as a result of the test? When they read the next assignment, will they be looking forward to the test at the end of it? Will that make them read with greater pleasure or concentration, or will it make them concentrate less upon the author's ideas and more upon the main character's name?

How could a test provide the teacher with helpful information about the students' feelings and thoughts without defeating the purposes of learning? How do you know when the meat is cooked? You smell it, you look at it; you may even touch or poke it. What can you tell about the insides of students by listening to them, by watching them, by talking to them and asking them questions?

Discuss your conclusions about these questions in your log. Be sure to give reasons for your opinions.

ARE TESTS USEFUL?: FIND OUT I

several hours   *2 to 6 people*

To be more able to make wise choices concerning tests and their use in your class, and to talk intelligently to parents and administrators about your choices, do this activity.

Find a group to investigate the value of tests in determining the college enrollment and employment status of high school graduates. Agree that each of you will write a letter to or talk to at least one hiring official and one college admissions official or counselor. You will need to write letters and plan interviews. Then allow two weeks for arranging the interviews and receiving the answers to letters.

Try to find out what kinds of tests are given for admission to the college you choose, and what the admission requirements are. What methods besides tests are used to evaluate a young person's potential for success in college? If tests are given, how much weight do they carry? Is there any body of information or degree of verbal skill which is considered prerequisite? If so, what is it? Is it possible for students in some colleges to be admitted without taking any tests or being evaluated in any way by college officials?

What do employers want most to know about job applicants? What do they expect from grades as an indication of success? Does it vary according to the kind of work? If so, how? Do employers give tests? If so, what do they test? How important are grades to employers? How important are interviews? What is evaluated in an interview? What traits do they want to find in a prospective employee? Are these traits taught or tested in school? Could these traits be taught or tested in school? Why or why not?

When you have collected this information, meet to discuss your discoveries. For which vocations are grades considered most important? At which colleges are they considered most important? What would colleges and employers like to know about the people who come to them? What can tests tell about people? What can't they tell? How useful are other methods of evaluation?

Plan a report to the class telling about your conclusions. Present your report in the form of a panel discussion in which each member of your group has a chance to tell about the information he discovered and the conclusions he has reached.

WHY TEST?: FIND OUT II

several hours   *2 to 6 people*

To be more able to judge the value of tests in classroom situations, do this.

Form a group to ask teachers about why they use tests. Each one of you should plan to talk to at least 3 people who are teachers—try to find some who teach in high school, junior high school and elementary school as well as college. But before you start asking questions, think about what you want to find out; and how you can get such information without asking questions that would be difficult or threatening to answer: Could you ask teachers about specific tests they give, and what the tests tell them? Could you ask them why they decided to give that test and not a different one, and why they chose the particular form of test they did choose? Is one more highly recommended than another? Is one easier to administer or grade? Does the teacher want a specific kind of information? Which test does the teacher consider most fair as a basis for grades? Why? Does the teacher choose one kind of test because he believes that by taking it the student also learns something? Why? Which kind of test does he think is a more reliable indication of a student's ability, the student's performance on an "objective" test which measures memory or his performance on an essay test which measures his ability to express his ideas clearly? Why? Does the teacher think ability is the only thing which should be measured? If attitudes are to be measured also, how do you grade them and how do you know how much weight to give them? Does the teacher make adjustments for able students who do very little and for slow students who work hard? If so, how?

Does the teacher ever plan tests with a number of simple questions whose answers anyone could guess so that the grades will not be too low? Is this a good policy? Why? Does he ever plan tests with a few hard questions that are nearly impossible to answer so that the scores will not be too high? If so, why? Does he ever use tests or quizzes to "settle the class down" or to punish or frighten students for not doing homework? If so, what are the results? For the teacher? For the students? Does he ever use tests as an incentive to get students to study? How do students study for tests? How much do they remember? Why do teachers complain year after year that the students have forgotten everything they were taught the year before?

After you have gathered your information about why teachers use tests, discuss what you have learned with the other members of your group. What information do teachers hope to get from a test? Do they want to find out how well they have taught, explained, demonstrated, or helped students to discover principles? Do they want to find out what the needs of each student are so that they may help him learn what he needs to know and do to live successfully? Do they want to find out how well they have taught him what he needs to know so that they may find a better or more appropriate way of teaching him next time if that is necessary? Do they want to discover the ways in which they might not have helped him so that parents and school can help the teachers to help students?

Report your discoveries and conclusions to the class in the form of an article for the newsletter.

ASK A STUDENT: FIND OUT III

2 hours   *2 to 6 people*

To be able to deal more effectively with the question of tests, investigate the attitudes and behavior of those who take tests.

Form a group, and talk to the members of your class about tests. You should each interview several of your classmates about tests they have taken throughout their school careers. Here are some questions you may want to think about and discuss as you decide what questions you will ask your classmates. You may want to decide upon one set of questions to ask:

Do you like to take tests? Why or why not? Is there any way you would rather be graded? Why or why not? What kind of test would you prefer to take? Why? How do you feel before, during, and after a test? Does the way you feel about the instructor affect the way you feel about the test? If so, how? Do you usually worry about tests? In what way? How do you prepare for tests? Do you have any systems of your own for remembering facts, taking notes, or organizing materials? Do you always read all of the assigned material? How much and what do you memorize? Do you ever talk to other students about what to expect? Do you compare notes? Do you try to figure out how well other people in the class will do so that you know how much to study? Do you try to find out what they are studying so that you will have studied the same material? Have you ever studied with another person or a group, asking each other questions and sharing information? If so, how helpful was it, and how did you feel about the other person? When the tests are difficult and you have trouble with them, how do you feel about the other people in the class? Do you ever think that tests are unjust? Why? Could you have improved them? If so, how? Did you ever feel that you had not been given an opportunity to demonstrate what you know? If you could go back to any course or class you have taken in the past and change the tests, what would you change and how would you change it? Have tests helped you to remember what you studied, or have you forgotten most of the materials covered on the tests you have taken? How have tests made you feel about the subjects you were tested for? Did you ever take a course or have a class that had no tests? How did you feel about it? Why?

After you have decided what questions you will ask, take a survey to discover how your classmates feel about tests and what tests do or have done for them. Discuss the answers with your group. Were there any answers that everyone agreed on? Were there some areas of great difference? What were they? What caused the similarities and differences? What students liked tests and did well at them, and what students did not? How did that affect their answers? What conclusions can you draw about the effects of testing upon students' attitudes and behavior?

Present an oral or written report to the class telling about your findings and explaining your conclusions. Explain why you have come to these conclusions.

RIGHT IS RIGHT: WHERE IS OBJECTIVITY?

1½ hours   *2 people*

To be more able to deal intelligently with the subjective elements of test making and test taking, do this activity.

Find a partner, and agree that you will both read the same short story. Read the story separately without discussing your reactions. Separately, still without talking to each other, write down your ideas about the story—whether you think it is a well written story or not, the main idea or ideas, the author's purpose, style or anything else you find interesting or important about it. On the basis of your conclusions about the story, make up a test for your partner. Include ten multiple choice questions, and either ten fill-in-the-blanks questions or matching questions, ten true-false questions, and two essay questions. Trade tests and work them. You may choose to grade them or not.

Discuss your tests: Did you both ask the same questions on the "objective" part of the test? In what ways were your questions the same or different? Did you ever disagree about the facts or main ideas? If so, why? Were any of the questions ambiguous? In what ways? Did you make any incorrect answers because you did not understand the questions? If you thought different items were important in planning your tests, was one of you wrong? Were your decisions about what to include in your tests and how to phrase your questions objective? Why or why not? How can a question be objective when the information it is based on is subjective? Is a true-false question less objective than a multiple choice question? Why or why not? Is it possible for one item to be either more or less objective than another? What about the essay questions: are they less objective? What is the difference between the essay questions and the others? Is making one kind of question a less objective process than making another? How is the process of grading the two kinds of answers different? Who has decided which answers will be right or wrong in either case?

What conclusions do you draw about objectivity? Tell your log about your conclusions and why you have reached them.

TEAM TESTING: HOW CAN YOU MEASURE LEARNING?
several hours *6 or 8 people*

If you want to be able to deal more comfortably and confidently with testing and measuring needs in your teaching situation, do this activity.

Find a group of 6 or 8 people, and form two teams. Your task is for each team to design a test for the other team which will objectively measure what they have learned in this course. Meeting as one group, decide when you will give your tests to each other and how much time the tests should be designed to fill, but the material or learning to be tested as well as the methods of testing and grading should be decided by each team as it plans the test for the other team. When you meet as separate teams to make your plans, discuss these questions:

If you are going to design a test, what do you want to test? What are the objectives of the course? What do the people in the other team think they should have learned? What do you think they should have learned? Why? It may be helpful to make a list. How can you find out whether or not they have learned to do or know what you have listed? How can you know how long they will remember it, or if they will be able to apply the learning to situations in the future? If your test is to be objective, how will you know that it is? What does "objective" mean? Find out. What means will you use to give your test? Are there any means you could use other than pencil and paper to measure what you want to measure? What will you know when you have administered the test? Will you have statistics—numbers of right and wrong responses, percentages of questions answered as you expect them to be answered, degrees of rightness and wrongness, letter grades? What will the statistics tell you? What will the statistics or symbols represent in terms of what the other team knows or can do or will be able to do in the future? Who will decide which responses are good and right and which ones are not? Are there some items on the list of what was to be learned that cannot be tested? Why? Is there any way to measure those items? What could you find out if you gave the other team members a teaching or working task and watched them do it? Could you consider that a test? Why or why not? Would it be objective? Why or why not? Can you test attitudes? How do attitudes show in behavior? How do enthusiastic, interested people behave? Could you make a list of those ways of behaving, and design a test to see if the other team members demonstrate that behavior?

After you are satisfied with your tests, plan a report to the teacher showing the results of what you have learned. Choose whatever system of reporting seems most appropriate to you—checklists, letter grades, descriptive comments, or conferences. Which grading system was most satisfactory to everyone? Why? Which testing system was most objective? Why? Which produced the most useful information? Tell your logs your conclusions about testing.

GRADING

Reports to the administration, parents and community are a serious responsibility of the classroom teacher, and these reports must be made in ways those who receive them can understand and in terms meaningful to them. Making records of student achievement for those who use such records—administrators, parents and others who need to know about students and schools—is a legitimate demand on teachers. These persons have a right to understand what is going on in classrooms. This does not mean that limited ideas of such persons about what they want need to be accepted as the last word. They can learn, as can teachers and students, to want ways of reporting that tell them more than they originally knew they wanted to know. They can learn how sterile and meaningless are grade systems they previously thought they liked. They can learn to value a child and his learning without knowing how many students are better or worse than this child. Hence, teachers need to press for anecdotal or even judgmental scales reports rather than traditional grades. Their arguments should center on the fact that grades are inadequate records for the purposes of any that profess to need them. Then students, teachers, parents and the community should busy themselves developing better ways of reporting.

Grades are a convenient shorthand for communication between parents and their children's teachers. But it is an inadequate communication, which tells too little and is susceptible to divergent interpretations. The kind of message that is sent may well not be the kind of message that is received. The symbols may give different messages to sender and receiver.

It would be useless to pretend that a kind of report other than grades would take less or even the same amount of teacher time. Reporting in other ways will take more time. But it will save the emotional burden of grades which has been heretofore detailed. Teachers are too often burdened not only with time-consuming tasks but with discomfort-producing tasks of making students do what students do not want to do and telling students and parents things that make those people uncomfortable. Also, teachers are, after all, professionals, entrusted with important duties which must not be slighted. And time which once was used in "averaging" grades and marking papers in traditional school settings can, in the activity curriculum, be applied to writing fuller reports for parents or in consulting with them. Scales which allow a range of responses from the teacher may be used to shorten some reports. The rhetoric of such scales should describe what the school has done for the child and what he has done for himself in the school setting. Reporting to parents and others is part of the accountability that is being demanded of schools, and if proper accounting takes more time, this will need to be part of the responsibility schools and teachers must assume.

Just as traditional testing fails to measure learning, grading is an inadequate way of reporting learning. It can even be misleading. The A B C D F system, a judgement record, not a description, should be abandoned because it is often harmful and sometimes used to get students to do things that have little connection with real learning. Three elements go into most grade-making. The first is how well a student does in relation to what other students do. This is usually decided by a teacher who averages lists of grades he has given on tests, reports, projects or recitation. The second measure has to do with how well the student does in relation to how well he can do, judged by what the teacher knows of the student's mental rating and the general achievement potential established by his past record. This measurement fails to take into consideration emotional and interest factors, which may affect the student's learning products. These are at least as important as the student's mental rating and are equally out of the student's control. The third facet is how well the student does in relation to an arbitrary standard, what the teacher thinks could have been done or what others in another class or at another time may have done. It cannot be glossed over that all these measurements are subjective. The important thing is that subjectivity be made the servant, not the unseen, concealed or denied master of evaluation.

Justification of the traditional grading system by the need to generate properly useful student records is a false issue. Traditional grades are inadequate for purposes to which they have been put by school authorities and those outside of schools, and they should be used only transitionally, while fuller methods of assessing and reporting achievement are developed and become accepted. A parent, for instance, needs to know much more than a grade tells him. He needs analysis, not shorthand. Parents need to know in what ways their children achieve, where their strong points are, which the school is helping them to maximize, and where the school wants to help the child to improve more effectively than it now is doing. If failures are noted, they should be stated as failures of the school to help the child in certain respects, and the report should note precisely what the school is doing to correct its failure.

The administration needs descriptive data on which to base decisions about curricular change. One example of the inadequacy of grades to guide curricular decisions is the now bankrupt system called laning. In the beginning tests were used to guide decisions about grouping students. Additional subjective factors were added to the decision-making process until grade records and objective tests were used less than simple teacher recommendations. Finally, the whole sorry system of laning fell into disrepute and is now being abandoned. There is correlation between grade records and further grade records in academics, but there seems to be small correlation between high grades and vocational success. Hence, grade records mislead employers who depend on them for predictions about which prospective employees will be most useful to them. Far from being a help to such employers, furnishing grade records allows them to continue to be misled into believing that such records are reliable predictors of employee achievement.

Colleges are increasingly unwilling to use grades as the determining factor in college entrance, just as they have become disillusioned by testing. They now use the student profile, which relies equally on written references and interviews. These multiple indices, in addition to open enrollment, which depends on none of these, reduce the importance of the school record. Emphasis on alternatives to college training, which are either open or dependent on a demonstration of skill or aptitude, are also elements in reducing the importance of grade records as indices to future success in academics or training.

But in schools that use grades, the teacher must be responsible for decisions about grades that are presented to the administration. However, much of the pain and damage of this school requirement can be mitigated by encouraging as much student input into the decision-making process as the teacher can structure. The activity curriculum assumes that students working with teachers are able to set up goals. Further, when students and teachers set goals, they are competent to decide the grades to be attached to accomplishment of these goals.

Equipped with the log and the folder of student products, which might include anything from bulletin board advertisements of a book read to a filmed essay, the teacher has enough materials to determine a grade, justify his class activity or perform whatever other professional reporting duty he has. Conferences between students and teachers and careful attention to student products enables the teacher to construct a set of standards which meet the need to assign grades to satisfy school authorities and parents.

In student-teacher conferences there should be a continual process of reevaluating decisions about goals and grades. This growing body of decisions should be recorded in logs. Teachers may want to make excerpts from past logs into a booklet on grades and goals for future classes. From the folder and log, teacher and students together can judge the growing ability of the student to read, listen, speak and write language. In conference, teachers and students should work to balance elements that go into grades: how well the student does in relation to what other students are doing, how well he does in relation to what he can do, and how well he does in relation to standards that can be agreed on between students and teachers. Because of their exchanges in group activities, students will usually be sharply aware of the range of achievement of students in the class, and if part of the grade must depend on what the student is doing in relation to what others are doing, the student's own judgment about this factor is at least as important as the teacher's and can usually be depended on not to be too far from what the teacher also would choose. This process of grade-making can often be a readiness or need analysis, pointing to the next step in student learning.

Activities

GROUP GRADING: COMPARE YOUR EVALUATIONS
1 to 2 hours   *4 to 8 people*

If you do this, you will be more able to assess the objectivity of grading systems.

The problem of this activity is to discover ways in which members of your group are the same or different in their grading of the same papers. To do this you will need one or more student papers to grade. For instance, you might decide to use three, each from a different source or each representing a different level of maturity. Your own teacher may be able to help you get these, or you may know a teacher who can provide papers. You might borrow a paper from a classmate. Since each of you will need to arrive at his own grade for the paper or papers, it would be helpful to make copies of the works to be graded so that you could each write on your copy and so that the process where each one of you reads and then gives the paper to the next person will be shorter. If you cannot make copies, you may want to take notes on a separate piece of paper as you read.

Be sure you have your system for deciding upon a grade clearly in mind because you will discuss it later. What should a paper be like to merit an "A," a "B" and so on? Which aspects are most important? Do some aspects weigh more heavily than others? Do you add or subtract points? Do you figure out percentages? How much does your decision depend upon whether you like or don't like an idea, the handwriting, the grammar or spelling or the tone?

Decide what grade you will give each paper without discussing it with anyone in the group. When you have made your decisions, take turns telling the group what grade you have given and why. Did you all consider the same aspects of writing to be the most important? What were the criteria that different group members used? Did some members interpret the writing differently than others? Did some concentrate on different details? How did these differences affect the grades? Do the grades show anything about why the group members arrived at the grades? Would it be more useful to a student to know what the teacher thought was important than to know the grade the teacher chose as a result of what he thought was important? Why or why not?

By what authority is one person's opinion about what is important in a paper better than another person's opinion? Is there one best way of writing? Can you think of some famous writers who might not have fared well in traditional composition classes? Why could this happen?

In your logs write your conclusions about the possibilities of obtaining objective grades for student writing.

WHAT IS A RECORD?: GETTING THE INFORMATION
1 week   *a group*

To be more able to keep useful classroom records, do this.

Grade books are often called "record books." Is a grade a record? What is a record? What do you do when you record? Is recording different from judging? What is judging? What does a judge do? Can you record without judging? Can you judge without a record? When do you keep records? Do you have a checking account? Do you pay taxes? Do you make notes of what happens in classes? Do you record the gasoline mileage of your car? Find some examples of record-keeping in your own life and note them in your log. What do you do as you record to make the information more useful? For what do you use the information? When you need to make a judgment, how does the information you recorded help you?

Does a grade tell information so that a judgment can be made? Does it tell the judgment the teacher has made as a result of his information? Might it do both? When? If a collection of grades made by many teachers is called a "permanent record," what is it a record of? Is it a record of what happened to a student in classrooms and how he changed as a result?

If you were going to start a singing group in high school, would you make a judgment about prospective members of your group on the basis of their grades in singing class or would you hold auditions? Why? Does a student who receives an "A" in a literature class necessarily enjoy reading literature? Of what is his "A" a record?

If you looked at Sam's report card, and instead of an "A" you saw "Sam sings well," would you know more or less about Sam? If you read "Lucille enjoys the music," "Mark has a good sense of rhythm," "Mary is eager to come to class," "Jim has memorized all the lyrics," how would you know which students were better or worse than the others? Is it important to know which ones are better or worse? Why? What would you know about the students instead? How might that information be useful?

For one week keep a record of the work and attitudes of the other people in your group. This means that each member of the group will be keeping records of you, and you will be keeping records of each of them. You will need to look at each other's papers frequently and talk about your reactions to class work. Can you make records without comparing one person to another? How can you describe the way another person acts and feels? Is everything he does and feels important? Of what do you want to keep a record? What would another person want to know about his work or behavior in this class? What are his important characteristics as demonstrated in this class? What is he learning to do? Is he satisfied with what he is doing and learning? Who might be interested in using your records to make future judgments? Would the person you are keeping the records about find them useful? How?

At the end of the week give your records to the people you made them for. No person should feel that he needs to give or show his records to the teacher unless he wants to. Tell your log about how you felt when you were keeping the records of other people and how you felt when you read the ones that had been kept on you. What judgments might you make about the experience?

HOW DO YOU KNOW YOU'RE GOOD?: GRADES AND PEOPLE I

1 to 2 hours   *3 to 8 people*

To be more able to deal with the individual and social problems which may arise in a classroom as a result of the grading system, do this.

Form a group to improvise some scenes in which students and teachers react to grades. Begin by trying to put yourselves inside of a character you might play: What does an "A" student think about when he does his homework? Is he planning how to get the grade he wants? What are the tactics he might use to get what he wants? Does he worry about his grades? Does he feel pressured by his parents, teachers or friends to keep up his grades? What might happen to him if he didn't? What does he think would happen to him if he didn't? How much does his sense of worth as a person depend upon his high grades? What does he think and feel about people who make low grades? Does he envy them? Look down on them? What could be his reasons for either of these feelings? Invent such a person. Give him a name, a family, a teacher, friends, a life style and personal interests. Is he popular with the other students? Why or why not? Do the teachers like him? Why or why not?

What kind of teacher does he have? What kind of teacher would get along well with him and what kind of teacher might make him feel uncomfortable or worried? How would he feel about a teacher who said, "I never give "A's"? or one who said, "If you come to every class and do the assigned work, you'll get an "A"? If the teacher said, "Only one person in this class will get an "A," what would he do to see that he was that one? Would he lend his notes to a fellow student who had missed a class? How would the teacher feel about him? Would he be called on to recite several times a class, or not at all? If he came into class late, how would the teacher treat him?

How do his classmates feel about him? Do they avoid him? Call him a "teacher's pet"? Idolize him? Try to get him to do their homework for them? Try to sit next to him so they can look at his papers? Is he a leader in social activities and group work, or is he a "loner"?

Invent a teacher and a class. Act out one or several scenes in this character's school life showing how the label of "A" student affects his feelings of worth and his relationships with others. You might try showing the first day of school. What seat does he choose in the classroom? Who sits next to him? What comments does the teacher make as he takes roll? What does the "A" student think as he listens to the teacher introducing his subject? Could you use another speaker to stand behind the character and tell his thoughts? You might try report card day when the student is either satisfied or dissatisfied with his grade. You might see what happens when he asks a girl for a date. What kind of girl does he choose? Why? Does she think he will be too smart for her, or do his grades make him seem glamorous? You may have better ideas of your own for scenes you would like to act out. Try different group members in various roles.

Afterward, write in your log about the role playing. How did grades affect your character's life? What would he do if grades were abolished at his school? Would he be relieved, or would he feel cheated? What did grades do for him? Did they do what they were supposed to do? What were they supposed to do?

UNDERDOG: GRADES AND PEOPLE II

1 to 2 hours *3 to 8 people*

If you do this, you will be more able to deal with the feelings of students who receive low grades.

Form a group to improvise some scenes from the life of a "slow" student. Invent a character. Give him a name, a family, friends, classes at school, hobbies, and perhaps a girl friend. Is he involved in sports? Does he like to watch television? How does he feel about himself? If he gets low grades, does that mean he is bad? If he is bad, are the teachers who give him the grades good? Or if he is good, are they bad? What do grades say to him and to the world about the person he is? If he tries to get good grades and he fails, what must he think about himself? Would it be safer not to try?

Does the "slow" label follow your character when he goes to a new class? What do teachers expect from him? How do they show what they expect? How does he live up to their expectations? Do his classmates also show that they expect him to live up to his "slow" label? How? Do his teachers use threats and bribery to get him to do the work because they expect him not to? Does he believe that he is too "slow" to do it or understand it by himself? Do teachers ever say that he is hopeless and give up on him? Do they try to ignore him? Does he try to sit in the back of the room and slouch in his seat so the teacher won't notice him? Why? Do teachers ever force him to do "make-up work" because he is behind in his work? Do they use extra work and bad grades as penalties for not understanding the lessons or for behavior problems? How do these tactics work? Why do teachers use them? What does happen to the student as a result of these tactics?

Does the student turn to other activities as a source of his sense of worth as a person? What activities might these be? Do his parents care about his grades? What do they think the grades say about their child's worth as a person? Do they feel their own sense of worth threatened by his low grades? How might this make them behave toward him? What do they say to him? Do they make him do his homework before he can go out? Do they help him do it? Do they think his teachers are unfair? Do they tell him that grades are not important? How are their own memories of school likely to affect their attitudes toward their child's grades? When a teacher asks for a conference with them, do they refuse to go because they are embarrassed or too busy? Are they apologetic when they see the teacher? Do they feel that they have failed in some way? Do they see the school and the teacher as good, right and wisely all-knowing and themselves as bad and in some vague and incorrectable way, failures? Or, are they belligerent?

What do the other students think about the "slow" student? Is he a hero? Is he included in their activities? Why or why not?

Act out some scenes showing how your character feels about himself and his grades. You might want to try a conference with the teacher, a discussion about his grades with his parents or his announcement to his friends that he is going to quit school. What situations can you construct? Act out several scenes and try several different roles.

Write in your log about how you could help "slow" students in your classroom to get rid of their label and find their individual sense of worth.

TEACHER'S TASK: GRADES AND PEOPLE III

1 to 2 hours   *3 to 8 people*

This activity will help you to anticipate and prepare for the problems you may face as a grade-giver.

Form a group to improvise some scenes in the life of a teacher involving grade-giving. Begin by considering the grade problem: You have 30 students, and you must rate them according to "A," "B," "C," "D," and "F" grades. What are the usual customs concerning grade-giving at your school? Can you find an experienced teacher who will tell you? If your distribution of grades does not approach a normal distribution curve, will you be called down to the office to explain why they do not? If you give too many "A's" will the other teachers think that you are compromising objectivity for popularity with the students? Will you receive an irate telephone call from a parent if you give a low grade to a student who usually gets "A's"? If you give a high grade to a "poor" student, will other teachers disapprove because "it might go to his head" or delude him with unrealistic expectations? Will you check the permanent records in the office about questionable grades to be sure you do not have these problems, or will you trust your own records to support your judgments in case you are required to explain your grades?

Invent a teacher to use as the subject of your role-playing. How does he or she solve the grade problem? What system does he use for recording grades, points, percentages, satisfactory or unsatisfactory performances? How does he average grades? Does he grade on the curve, use percentages or adjust grades according to estimates of how hard the student has worked? Does he give grades for class behavior? Does he give extra credit for extra work? Does he set goals, and does he evaluate on the basis of his goals? Does he ask students to set goals? What does he say when he needs to explain his reasons for grading on one aspect of a student's work and not another? Can he explain why one is more important to him than the other?

You may want to act out some scenes in which your teacher explains to students how and why they will be graded, when he talks to a student who wants to get his grade raised, when he talks to a parent about why he gave the grade he did, or when he talks to other teachers in the faculty lounge about his philosophy of grading. Does he always stick to the facts, showing how his judgment is based upon the performance of students, or does he sometimes use diversionary tactics? Does he bring in past school records or home life as reasons? Does he use manners, dress or dialect as reasons for grades? Does he justify his decisions with statements about sex like, "Girls are not good at . . . " and "You can't expect a boy to be as good at . . . "? Do teachers ever reinforce each other in such ways of thinking? Why?

When you have improvised several scenes from the life of your character and you have each had a chance to play the part of the teacher, tell your log about how grades look from a teacher's point of view. Are there pressures which may interfere with objectivity and fairness? If so, what are they? What can a teacher do about them?

A SCHOOL REPORT: GRADES AND PEOPLE IV

1 to 1½ hours   *3 to 8 people*

If you would like to make grades more useful and more truthful, do this activity.

Make a report card from the school to the parent, telling the parent how the school has failed to teach, rather than how the student has failed to learn. With your group, read and think about the activity "Underdog: Grades and People II." Invent your own "slow" student. Plan a report card for him in which the school says what it has not been able to do for him and what it will do to improve the situation. You might begin some of your reported comments with "We have failed to help Jim enjoy . . . We will try to improve this situation by . . . " or "We have not been able to interest Jim in . . . In the future we will try . . . " or "We have failed to . . . for Jim so that he will be able to . . . but we still . . . to help him."

After you have written your report, you may want to consider how parents would feel who received such a report. Would their attitudes toward the school and their child change? In what ways? How would the student feel about himself and about school? Would this kind of report be more or less difficult for teachers and schools to make? Why? Would it be more or less threatening to teachers and administrators? Why? Would it help teachers and administrators in any way? If so, what are they? Would schools and students benefit from lessening blame, fear and hostility?

Discuss your conclusions as a group and prepare a report about what you have discovered for the class. Post your report card on the bulletin board, and explain it either in an oral report to the class or in a written report to be posted next to the report card.

CHAPTER VIII

Evaluation

Students, teachers, administrators, parents and the community rightly hold the school curriculum responsible for developing end products which are proposed by the curriculum as goals. For purposes of organization, this book has categorized activities of the English curriculum as reading, listening, speaking and writing; yet in many activities each of these is inextricably involved with others, an admission of their interdependence and their inability to exist in any natural situation except in combination with some or all the rest. They are learned by means of each other. The activity curriculum commits itself to supply experiences which causes students to produce and receive the widest possible variety of all kinds of language. It must equal or surpass other methods of achieving aims, or it does not deserve to survive. And it should be judged on whether it helps "poor" students as well as "good" ones.

Let no teacher believe that the activity curriculum is more appropriate for poor students than good ones or more suited to junior than to senior high school. It is a method, not a set of materials, and is appropriate to any materials that the teacher may have in his program of studies, from teaching haiku and simple narrative in seventh grade to teaching the Greek plays or Shakespeare to senior high students. It is adapted to use with all kinds of materials and all kinds of students because it is based on the students' own reactions to materials. The rhetoric of activity cards, whether for younger or older students, should always be simple, evocative, and appealing, as well as clear and precise. It directs the student to involve himself with materials but to be concerned with the total nature of his involvement as well as the simple mental involvement he may have had in other systems.

ACCOUNTABILITY TO ADMINISTRATORS AND PARENTS

Finding out whether a curriculum works is not a simple matter of administering a set of tests. Because the effective English curriculum is what happens to the student as a result of the language experiences provided by the school, the total process of self and teacher evaluation of pupil progress, testing, grading and relating objectives to end products should be used to judge the curriculum and its results. The teacher who uses humanistic activities must be accountable to himself, to his students, to his administration and to his community, and they will, in many ways, call him to account, as they have a right to do.

The activity curriculum will be an innovation in most schools, and teacher will is the main factor in starting and making effective innovations. But, large scale changes which survive must be compatible with systems in which they are to occur, as those systems are now organized, within buildings as they are now arranged, with materials now available. The changes the humanistic activity curriculum proposes can occur without chaos in any of these settings. Any innovative teacher who wants to change must be willing to make some small, daily movement toward things that will make a difference. He works for change practically and relentlessly and feels obligated to be as honest and inventive as his own capacity allows, responsibly determined to do whatever he can do with whatever resources he can mobilize at the moment to change whatever he can change as soon as possible. And he must be willing, even eager, to have what he does evaluated and to evaluate it himself.

Frequently, if new ideas are competently handled, the school administration will be the best supporter the teacher has in seeking change.

Remedies for school curriculum problems are known to school administrative officers: promotion of active tries, promotion of those who innovate, budget provision for innovation, in-service training for decision makers, close relationships between universities and schools which want to innovate, involvement of the total community in schools, facilitation of change by removal of clutters of red tape and institutionalization of proved change. Some teachers in every school system innovate, but unless those teachers convince their administrations of the value of their innovations, new ideas tend to fade away, and old ways dominate. By evaluative processes the activity teacher must enlist the help of the administrator.

Because the activity curriculum is flexible, and changes can be as pervasive or minimal as the innovator finds comfortable, the teacher should enlist the support of the administrator in the plan to use and evaluate it. It can be used by one teacher alone without disturbing others who want to pursue more traditional methods. It can even be introduced by a one-day experiment without disturbing the pattern of the school. But the teacher who uses this new pattern of action must be prepared to evaluate and report his evaluation to administrators and the community. Teachers have a right to be judged according to their own goals as well as those of the administration. But they must know their own goals and be able to show that what they are doing has a reasonable chance of achieving the goals.

Many parts of society have a right to have expectations about what the curriculum will do for the children it serves. These expectations are occupational, social, political, religious, ideological, and aesthetic. Local objectives of this kind can be taken into account when activities are designed, but priority belongs to the needs of each individual student, needs which are the ultimate arbiters of choice and the source of final determination of the activities suitable for him. Each activity must face this marketplace of community desires and student need. It is to be hoped that these will often coincide. In the activity curriculum, students and teachers together can work to reconcile needs on the scene.

But conflicts occur. Some parts of the community think that their values will be served if children learn to be good. Others want children to know the truth. But many do not agree on what goodness and truth are and how they are to be expressed. The core of definitions and enforcements of these values has become fragmented, and many students simply do not accept being told what to believe, either by the school or the community. They must have experiences from which they can generalize what they are to believe and what values they are to cherish.

Talk about "open" classrooms and "freedom" often rouses threatened feelings in parents. They fear that structure will be abolished in such situations, and students will not learn. Parents should be shown how the activity classroom works to free all that is best in their children, and parents who feel uncomfortable about change should be shown how control, supposed to be a feature of traditional classrooms, is maintained in the activity classroom. They must see their children led to make choices of activities that help them learn. The best way to make such a demonstration is to involve parents during a back-to-school experience or during parent study meetings in using an activity board, whose pockets have been filled with activities that will help them understand the activity system. They can role-play and discuss just as their children do. It would be virtually impossible to explain the activity curriculum by means of a lecture.

The curriculum of the public school often bears the advancing front of a changing social order. In interprets the common denominators of the prevailing culture, and when the consensus of the old begins to break down, it predicts new patterns of organization. This is a heavy load for curriculum makers to bear. At times of rapid change parents can be especially useful in many phases of curriculum making, not to censor, but to advise on positive things like making more realistic objectives, things they want their children to do and be as a result of their schooling.

The activity curriculum can help parents understand that living and growing are the most important forms of learning. They can be shown that the activity classroom provides a real form of living that helps students grow. Reflecting the student's culture, it teaches him how to use language to investigate his thinking, express himself and get along with his age mates; how he can read and write effectively; how language interacts with conscience and morality; how he can see values work as he uses them in making choices and does not have to accept them on faith from preachments that make him skeptical and cynical. When the teacher can educate the administrator and the parents about these real curricular purposes and the way the humanistic activity curriculum operates to fulfill them, these groups will be effective supporters for all that the teacher hopes to achieve.

Activities

PAST THE SCHOOL ROOM: SPREADING GOOD WILL

variable time   *4 to 6 people*

Try this to see how activities you do in one classroom can spread to the community outside.

Form a group of people to become the publicity committee for you class. Discuss these questions: How do people in the community and outside your classroom know what is happening or has happened there? How can you be sure that people in your class will say good things about it? Do they all know the good things that are happening? How could you keep the class members informed? Do they all want to say good things? How could you improve class morale? Are there people at home who also read materials class members write? How can you make sure class members have good materials to take home?

Are there display cases in your school where you could show the projects your class makes? Are there bulletin boards in the school where you could post items about the good happenings in your room? Do you have a class newsletter? Could you start one? How?

Could you have an open house so that students from other classes could view your work and ask questions about what you have done? Could your class members bring visitors?

Which of these things would be useful and practical for your class? Perhaps you have other ideas about ways of spreading good will.

Try these ideas with your class activities. Report in your logs the results. What are the reactions of class members? Of outsiders?

WHAT'S YOUR BAG:
DIFFERENT CAN BE GOOD

45 minutes   *4 to 6 people*

This may help you discover how different kinds of teachers, including you, may all fit well into the scheme of things in public education.

Form a group of several people and discuss these questions: How many different teachers have you had in your life? Were many of them alike in some way? How? How were they different? What different ways did they manage their classes? What different ways did they use to capture the attention of their classes? What different ways did they arrange furniture in their classrooms? What was the most pleasant classroom you ever experienced as a student? Why?

Each of you in his mind picture the teacher you remember most vividly, whether you liked him or not. Tell the group about your teacher. What kind of person was he? How did he talk to students? How did he make you feel? Why do you remember him so well? How did the other students feel about him? How did the other teachers feel about him? Do you feel the same about him now as you did then? Why or why not? What did you learn from him? Did you learn anything besides the lessons in the books? Why or why not?

After you have heard about each person's teacher, talk about what kind of teacher you want to be. Make a list of qualities you think a perfect teacher ought to have. Would you be able to fit your own personality to that list?

Write your list and your conclusions about different styles of teaching in your log.

BACK-TO-SCHOOL-NIGHTS: TEACHER AND PARENTS, PART I
variable time   *6 to 8 people*

This may help you to deal with the expectations parents have about teachers and schools.

Form a group of people to create a drama about back-to-school-night as parents and teachers expect it to be. How many scenes will you need? Will you want to show parents as they are getting ready to come, or will you begin as they enter the school gym, cafeteria, or auditorium? Who will they meet when they enter? Where will the teachers be? Where will the principal be? Will there be a guest speaker? Will there be a piano for the musical entertainment? What kind of entertainment will it be? Will a group of children from the school sing, or will the director of music lead the PTA in a few well-known songs?

When the principal addresses the parents, what does he say? What does the guest speaker say? Is there a speech by an academically talented student? How is the back-to-school-night structured? Do bells ring so parents can move from one class to another? If so, how often? For how long? Are there coffee and cookies afterward in the gym? How can you show these different scenes? What do teachers say to parents in the rooms? How do parents react? How do they feel about the event, the teachers, the school? What questions do they ask? After the teacher has finished his talk, do parents introduce themselves? What do they say to him? Are some parents aggressive and others shy? How do they behave? What do parents say to each other about work they see displayed in the room? How do they talk about their children?

What has this back-to-school-night done for parents, for teachers, for children?

Plan your drama. You may want to write a script and memorize your lines. If you are going to show different scenes, consider how you will show the change of scenes, but keep your production as simple as possible. You will need also to decide upon a spot in the room where you can best present your drama. Practice it until you feel confident about it, and perform it for the class. Afterward, write in your log and ask other class members to write in theirs about their reactions.

BACK-TO-SCHOOL-NIGHT: TEACHER AND PARENTS, PART II

2 to 3 hours   *4 to 8 people*

This will give you some ideas for dealing with parents and for gaining their support for the activity program.

Form a group of people in your class to work on what a teacher can plan for back-to-school-night. Create an imaginary teacher. Decide what your teacher teaches, what kind of students he has, where the school is located, and what kind of school it is.

Consider these questions: What grade are the students? Are they laned? What kind of work do their parents do? What are their parents likely to consider most important in life? What textbooks are supposed to be used? What subjects are supposed to be covered? How can these requirements be fulfilled within the activity program? What does the teacher think it is important for the students to learn? How does he use activities to teach them these things? How can the teacher show parents that students can learn all these things using an activity program?

Suppose your teacher decides to show parents on back-to-school-night how students learn from activities by asking them to try some activities from the activity board themselves. Find or make some cards a teacher could use on that night for the parents. How long should the activities take? What kinds of materials should they require? How many people should they require? What subjects should they cover? Which cards will show the parents that their children are learning what parents consider important?

Before the parents get cards, what will the teacher say to them about how to use the cards? About the purpose of having cards rather than usual lessons? How will the teacher make the experience comfortable for parents? Will parents have questions or criticisms? What will they ask? How will the teacher answer them? After parents have worked the cards, how will the teacher debrief them? How can he be sure parents will leave feeling the way he wants them to feel about activity learning? How can the teacher make the parents feel that they and what they say are important? How can the teacher enlist the active support of the parents? What can they do at home to help their young people?

Will the room be decorated in a way to make the parents feel welcome and at home? Will there always be someone to help them and answer questions? Will there be coffee or refreshments afterward?

Write your plan for back-to-school-night. Be sure to include what preparations the teacher and class need to make before the event, how much time everything will take, what the teacher will say at the beginning and ending, what kinds of questions might be asked and what the answers could be, and what goes on the cards for parents. You might want to divide this work so that different group members have different tasks. Put your finished plan on display in the room where other class members can read it.

THE ROAD TO SUCCESS: ATMOSPHERE FOR CHANGING

1 hour   *4 to 6 people*

Here is something you can do to discover what an administrator or a teacher can do to make the climate of his school a good one for learning and changing.

If you have been working with a group on some other project or activity, try this with your group. Discuss these questions: What makes a group of people who are working together work successfully? Why do some groups of people do good work and lots of it? How do they need to feel before that can happen?

The teachers in a school are a group of people who work together. By looking at what happens in your group, you may discover what happens in a school. Does everyone in your group know what his responsibilities to the group are? How can it be arranged so that everyone does know? Perhaps there are those in the group who do not behave in ways that help the group get on with their business. How do you deal with such group members? What are possible ways to deal with them? What would be your goal in whatever method you use to deal with them?

How is leadership distributed? Is there a way of getting the person most able to do something to take leadership of that particular activity and so pass leadership around, with different people taking it at different times? Do some people seem too bossy? Are others too quiet? How could you all encourage quiet ones to be more active and bossy ones to be encouragers of others rather than dominators?

Does everyone in the group take an interest in the work of others and offer praise of what is good about it? How can your group talk about these things until they are able to operate them better? Can you share your feelings that group activities are not going well when you feel they are not? If not, why not? Do you want to find ways of sharing your feelings of uneasiness? How would sharing them help resolve them? What are the problems you have in finding ways to share them? If your group does not always find ways to share their ideas, what gets in their way?

How can barriers be dissolved? Could the group decide on ways? When your group makes a mistake, how do you handle it? Do you blame one person or just go ahead and get back on the right road? Is it necessary to blame one person or just go ahead and get back on the right road? Does blaming someone sometimes get in the way of solving a problem? How?

Do you always let anyone talk out his feelings if he wants to? Do you shut him off? Is it possible to shut someone off so that he never talks out the problems he is having? Have you ever felt so uncomfortable about your problems that you did not say anything about them at all? Did that help them go away?

Working as a group, compose a list of all the things a group can do to create a climate in which people can think and work well. Also write a statement about how these things produce changes in a school. Post your list and statement on the bulletin board.

TEACHER EVALUATION: MEETING THE SITUATION
45 minutes   *6 to 10 people*

This game may help you participate in a teacher-principal conference for evaluating your worth as a teacher.

Follow the chain of accountability. A teacher is accountable to his principal. The principal is accountable to the superintendent and school board, and they are accountable to parents and community. Divide the people in your group into these categories. Decide upon one to be the teacher, one to be the principal, one to be the superintendent, and if you have enough people, some to be the school board and others to be the parents.

Each group or person should, without consulting the others, (the parents and the school board should consult among themselves) decide upon two things he or they think the ideal teacher should be like and what the children should learn. These should be made into two lists of at least five items each. Remember to make your lists fit the role you are playing.

Meet as a group but arrange your chairs in a line, not in a circle. Arrange them so that parents are on one end, then the school board, superintendent, principal, teacher. Parents give their list of criteria to the school board. They talk about the list and may mark out items or add them. The school board adds its list and hands both to the superintendent. They talk about the lists and may mark out or add to them. The superintendent adds his list and hands it to the principal. They talk about the lists and mark out or add to them.

All other group members form a circle around the principal and teacher. The principal asks the teacher how he rates himself on each of the items on the list and compares his own answer with the teacher's. Together they decide whether he is good, bad, or average at each thing on the lists. The principal puts his mark next to each item and gives the lists back to the superintendent, who gives it to the school board. The superintendent advises the school board whether or not they should hire the teacher next year. They vote. The parents decide whether or not to elect the school board next year. They vote.

If your group decides to, you can try the game again, using different people in the roles.

Meet either as one large group or as two small groups to discuss your feelings about this experience. Did you feel that your group was treated fairly? Why or why not? Did you feel that your group had as much to say as they should? Why or why not? How could you have improved what happened? How did you feel about other people in the different groups? If you could, would you change places with any of them? Why? Are you satisfied with the way things turned out? Why or why not? After you have discussed these questions, write your answers in your logs.

FORMULATING AND USING OBJECTIVES

Teachers are turning away from reliance upon textbooks and curriculum guides as learning designs for students' day to day activities. These learning packages were often cramped and unimaginative. Their prescriptions relied excessively upon reading and factual content tests, with occasional writing exercises and few oral language or listening experiences. They paid slight attention to what changes were to be made in students as a result of what they were asked to do.

Questions stimulated by the failure of schools to help some children caused professional school people to cast about for better ways to design learning experiences. A look at what they were doing convinced some teachers they needed to know what they wanted students to be like as a result of what they were having students do, and the behavior objective was born. This was a statement of exactly what kind of behavior teachers expected the student to exhibit as a result of the learning activities he performed. When specified behavior seemed too vague, "performance" objectives were required, in order to state the objective more specifically.

Teachers of the humanities, especially English teachers, however, saw that many of the aims they wished to achieve could not be stated in these terms; they needed what they called humanistic goals in order to include intangibles like appreciations, whose appearance was not immediately apparent. But more and more school corporations are demanding that all teachers use performance objectives in order to budget the cost of educating students, and English teachers will probably have to accede to the demand for some sort of behavior objectives for what they do. They will either have to make objectives for themselves, or they will find that someone else has defined objectives for them.

Formation of objectives for teaching English has usually moved from very broad objectives for whole subject matter areas to smaller units to be achieved in smaller time spans. The humanistic activity curriculum suggests another way of deriving objectives, an inductive method. Objectives should be built or emerge from promises and products on activity cards designed to involve students in what English is by definition: reading, listening, speaking and writing. The promise on the card is the objective: the product is the performance. To design activity cards with these specifications need not be unduly restrictive, but it does lend a disciplined shape and a justifiable pattern to the procedure.

Demand for accountability which has caused school professionals to feel their need for objectives has usually come from administrations and school boards. Yet the ultimate and immediate consumer of education is the student. The humanistic curriculum sees its greatest responsibility as accountability to this consumer. The promise each activity contains is a behavior objective, stated in student terms, in terms of something he may choose to do in order to accomplish an objective he considers important or attractive. It is often stated thus: "If you want to (be able to do or understand something) . . . , try this." At the end of the card the student has created a product which demonstrates to the student, the teacher or any other interested person that the objective has been reached: questions have led to the formation of a generalization recorded in the log, a skit is performed, or a piece of writing is created.

As the teacher constructs these cards, his learning designs, he gains skill in designing accountability—a goal and a product that shows whether that goal has been achieved. Thus a large fund of objectives and products are generated. When accountability is demanded by the school administration or a community, the teacher is prepared by this kind of thinking to accede to the demand without feeling that he must create some specious pattern that he doesn't really follow or believe in or even one that belies what he believes in. A teacher who follows the activity card pattern is aware at all times why he asks students to do whatever he does ask them to do and whether the learning designs he makes achieve their stated objectives. The consumers, the students, tell him by their work with the cards. Most important, he has kept faith with the basic commitment of the humanistic curriculum, to consider the desires and needs of the students first in designing learning. His real accountability is to them.

The fundamental defect of most behavior and other kind of objectives is that they are designed for professionals by other professionals who are talking to each other about students. They talk about the student as though he were an object to be manipulated; the activity card promises talk to the student as though he were precious and uniquely self-determining. Product behavior is something students design as they choose the activity and perform it. And as they begin to make cards for themselves, as they will, they further increase their input. As teachers make new cards and revise old ones, they redefine, develop and expand their objectives and promises. This process, while it meets the accountability demands of school systems, meets also the requirements of a humanistic activity curriculum, whose emphasis is on taking students into the decision-making process.

Activities

WHERE ARE YOU GOING?: HOW DO YOU KNOW?

variable time   *3 to 6 people*

If you would like to be able to explain your reasons for doing what you do in the classroom, this activity may help you.

Form a group, and make plans to ask teachers about their reasons for doing what they do in their classrooms. You will need to be more specific in your questions. Do they make plans before they teach? In their heads, or on paper? How complete are their plans? Do they have certain tasks they want students to accomplish? Try to get a list of some specific tasks. What are students learning to do or know when they do these tasks? Do teachers lecture to students? What do they lecture about? How do teachers know that students have learned to do or know what teachers want them to do or know? What would teachers like students to have learned as a result of their teaching?

Talk to high school teachers if possible. When you have gathered as much information as possible from a variety of teachers, meet again to discuss what you have learned: How many teachers were able or willing to answer all your questions? Why? Is there any difference between what teachers teach and test and what they want students to learn? Why? How many of the teacher's goals would enable students to listen, speak, read or write better? Why do you think the teachers chose the specific tasks they did instead of others? For instance, why does a teacher choose to teach through lecture instead of through group work? To what degree do you think teachers' choices were motivated by the need to fill time? To keep students busy and quiet? To make grade decisions easier? To follow tradition—because that is the way they were taught? Can these be necessary and important reasons for teaching in a particular way? What would you like your reasons to be? Can you make a list? What teaching methods would best suit the reasons you have chosen?

When you have discussed your conclusions, combine your ideas to write an article for the newsletter. In your article include what you think your own reasons should be and tell why.

WHO NEEDS OBJECTIVES?: WHAT CAN THEY DO FOR YOU?
2 hours *1 person*

To be able to use objectives effectively in your own planning, do this activity.

Think about these questions: Are there some activities in life you do just for the fun of doing them, like driving around in the car without a destination, just because you enjoy driving or want to see scenery? Do you have a reason for doing that too, just as you would have a reason for going to a particular place? How are the two reasons different? At what point do you find reward in each situation? In an activity card where do you find reward? Can you find reward in both the process and the product?

When is it important to have a clear idea of where you are going? In your own life how much do your expectations of rewards influence your decisions about what you will do? Give examples from your own experience. If you were driving toward a clearly known destination and you made a wrong turn, how would knowing the exact location and description of your objective help you to find the right route again? How does this same principle apply to activities for teaching?

Suppose you have been driving to a strange address. You have the address written on a piece of paper which is in your pocket. When you arrive, you check the address on the house against the one on the paper. If they match, you know you are at the right place. In an activity card which part would be the address in your pocket and which part would be the address of the house? Will you know by the performance of students if the objective was a good one? How?

Can performance or product also tell how well the student is doing his task of learning? If grades are necessary, how could performance objectives help you and your students make decisions about grades? Could objectives help you explain what you are doing in your class to parents or administrators? How? Can you think of other ways that objectives might help you plan and talk about what happens in your classroom?

What might arguments against performance objectives be? See if you can find out from teachers or from professional periodicals which contain articles about performance objectives.

In an article for the newsletter or bulletin board state the pro and con arguments about performance objectives, telling your opinions and your reasons for your opinions.

ENGLISH IS . . . : FINDING TEACHING GOALS

2 hours   *2 to 5 people*

To set realistic and worthwhile classroom goals, do this.

Research to find out what experts and teachers think education in English should accomplish. Can you find articles about the purposes of education in English in professional journals or magazines? Look in the card file to see if you can find books on the subject. What would the head of your English department be able to tell you? Do you know other English teachers who might also have ideas on the subject? Collect as much information as you can. You may want to divide the tasks in some way so that each of you is researching a different source.

Either meet several times as you collect your information or when you are finished to discuss these questions: Do all of the articles, books and persons agree about the goals of English education? In what ways do they differ? Can you find any similarities? Can you divide the goals into categories? What categories can you find? Are some general and others specific? Which are most enlightening? Do some deal with attitudes and others with skills? Do some deal with facts to be learned or memorized? Are some concerned about moral values? Do sources ever disagree about which facts, skills, attitudes or values are most important? How do they disagree? Which goals would be easiest to teach? Why? Which do you think are most important, and how do you think they could be taught?

Hold a debate or a panel discussion in which you defend your points of view.

WHERE IS THE OBJECTIVE?: LOOK AT THE HAPPENING
1 hour   *1 person*

To be able to find and write logical and relevant objectives, do this activity.

Write some objectives for what you do during one day. You got up this morning. Why? What was the "If you do this you will . . . ?" What was the reward? What was the activity that made it possible? You got dressed. Why? What was the objective of getting dressed? What was the product? Was there a need to get dressed? What was it? Make as complete a list as you can of your needs, objectives, actions and products for a day. Here is an example: I feel hungry (need), If I eat breakfast I won't feel hungry any more (objective), eating (activity), satisfaction (product or reward).

When you have written such a list, think about what you have written. The objective in the example above was a short-term one. Did you find any long term objectives? If so, what were they? Is it always as easy to find the objective? Why? Is there sometimes more than one objective? Why? Do more complicated activities have more complicated objectives? Do they still work in the same way? If you know the objective, can you foresee what the product will be? If you know the product, can you tell what the objective was? Can different people be involved in the same activity but have different objectives and products? Why?

If you are planning an activity card and you have an activity in mind, how can that help you to know the logical objective and product? If you have a product in mind, how can that help you to find the objective and activity? What can you do if all you have is an objective? How will finding these three basic parts of an activity card help you to know whether your activity is a good learning activity? Why is the need important? If the objective is not a result of a student's need, will it be a good activity for him? If you have an activity card with an objective and product, can you revise it to meet a student's need? How?

Make a chart for the bulletin board of your room showing the parts of an activity card and how one part grows out of another. Use your own examples.

THE CONSUMER: ASK STUDENTS

1 hour *2 people*

To be more able to plan activity cards which involve students, do this activity.

Find a partner, and discuss these questions: What do you want to be able to do better or know better as a result of this class? Are your answers different? Do you think that you want for yourself the same learnings that your teacher wants for you? Is the teacher right, or are you? Are both right? When a teacher wants you to learn something you think is silly or useless, do you learn it? How long do you remember it? In what ways does the teacher know more than you about what your needs are? In what ways do you know more about your needs?

Act out a teacher-student card-making session. One of you take the part of the teacher, and the other the student. The one who is the student should invent a need or use one that is true for him. This may be a bad feeling about some situation or a desire to know about a process or idea. Tell your need to the person who is the teacher. What is the objective which results from the need? Talk together to find an appropriate activity and product. Trade places. You may want to try this role-playing several times.

Each of you should write a card based upon one of the situations you acted out. Tell your log how you arrived at that activity. Do you think the card would help the student in the way that he needed help? Would you feel comfortable about giving it to one of your high school students? Why or why not?

SAYING YOUR OBJECTIVES: FINDING WORDS

45 minutes *1 person*

If you would like to state objectives more clearly and easily, do this activity.

Plan to write 10 objectives for activity cards. Since it is easier to write an objective with a particular need or activity in mind, find needs of your own, your classmates, or your prospective students or use exercises from an English textbook and find objectives for them. So that you will know how to write activity objectives, examine the ones at the beginnings of the activities in this book to see how they are made. Can you formulate rules which seem to be true for most of the activity objectives in this book? What are they? How many promises tell you to do something? How many tell you what your reward will be if you do? What kinds of sentence structure are the most common in activity objectives? What kinds of phrases are used most often? Can you make a list? Do certain words appear frequently in these objectives? Why? What are they? Can you think of better words which might be used without changing the meaning of the objectives? Experiment with some. Write five objectives which are used in this book in your log and substitute some words of your own for words that are commonly used in the objectives. Did you like the changes you made? Why or why not? How did these words work in the objectives?

How many verbs can you find in one objective? What is the purpose of the "to be able . . . "? What is the purpose of the "do . . . " part of the objective? In every objective there is another kind of verb which is the most important part. The "to" before it will help you find it. It is the one word which tells you what the activity is all about. What is the "to" verb in the objective for this activity? Some common ones are "to understand," "to respond," "to write," "to listen," "to read," and "to speak." How many more can you find in this book? Make a list of the most used verbs. When you need to write an objective, a look at your list will help you get started.

Try adding objects to the verbs on your list. For instance, "to write (a letter)" or "to listen (to a classmate)." Do this to several verbs. Where could you add qualifiers which would answer the questions, "Listen how?" or "Write how?" Add some qualifiers as in these examples, "to listen (more carefully) to a classmate" and "to write a letter (with more colorful detail)." You may also want to add words to give more information about the object of the verb, such as, "to listen more carefully to a classmate (give a speech)" or "to write a letter (to a friend) with more colorful detail." Add "If you do this you will be able . . . " at the beginning or " . . . , do this." at the end, and you have an objective. You can make variations of this formula to suit your needs. Try some variations of your own. Write 10 objectives.

Write your objectives in your log, and tell your log how you made them. Could you help a high school student to write an objective for an activity card he was writing? How could you make it simple, clear and easy for him? Tell your log.

CHANGING YOUR MIND: REVISING OBJECTIVES

30 minutes   *1 person or a group*

To be flexible in your goals and to keep up with the changing needs of your students, do this activity.

Did you set or write goals for yourself at the beginning of this course? Did you write activity cards earlier with objectives on them? Were the objectives reached? Have your needs or the needs of the person for whom the activity was planned changed? In what ways? Look at the objectives you had written earlier to see how you might revise them to fit the present situation. What were the needs then? What are they now? Would the same activities suit your present needs, or do you need new ones? Do you need to write completely new objectives, or can you just change the old ones?

In your log write at least five revised or rewritten objectives, and tell why these changes were necessary. Do you know more about writing objectives now than you did then? Do you like your new objectives more or less? Why? Were they easier or harder to write? Why? Were your ideas about what you wanted clearer the second time than the first? Why or why not?

TEACHER FEEDBACK TO STUDENTS

The activity curriculum, then, must be evaluated, and products of student learning, the basis for this evaluation, should be assessed by teachers and students, looking together at products and judging them according to goals that have been mutually agreed upon. The student must learn to tolerate, even seek and initiate, evaluation of his performance, sometimes against the record of others, but more especially against his own past performance. As the former is important to the society which invests in a school, for him, the latter is important to his own progress. Evaluative interaction with peers and teachers gives the learner insight into his own behavior and its changes. The most useful judgment, fianlly, of whether the learner has really been learning is his own.

Much official school language concerning evaluation is threatening. It speaks of penalty. Evaluative words and rhetoric must not have this implication if there is to be a productive climate for evaluation. Activity cards should provide such a wide range of activities for students that success of some kind for each learner is almost inevitable. The activity curriculum depends on positive reinforcement and teacher avoidance of negative reinforcement. If negative reinforcement appears, it should come only as a direct result of student, not teacher, behavior, in the form of a bad result of something the student does. No deliberate use of it is ever made by a humanistic teacher. The assumption of the activity curriculum is that imposed negative reinforcement leads to inactivity, inertia and paralysis. These appear frequently in other curricular arrangements. They may be observed by anyone who looks into the classrooms of schools. If their opposites—activity, varied and flexible responses, and alertness are expressed in the activity curriculum in greater proportion than in other curricular arrangements, then the feedback and products of the activity curriculum are accountable for the goals it proposes.

Educational evaluation too often takes place only at the end of something, which is then considered finished. Because evaluation in the activity curriculum manages feedback so that it is milked of every possible educational value and engenders a minimum of counterproductive results, evaluation begins as soon as the activity begins—with feedback from the process itself. It starts when the student reads and chooses his card, making an evaluative judgment. As he moves through the card, questions lead him to make further judgments, as he builds toward the product, which is the climax of his experience in the activity. The visible product itself is a feedback of experience, and the card may suggest ways the student may look at and judge his product. Frequently he shares this judgment with peers involved in the activity.

The product is finally shared with the teacher who has helped in log and conference to share the student's interim judgments about the way the activity was developing. Replacing the habit of looking for what is wrong with sensitivity to what has value and disregard for what is not good takes self-discipline. It requires self-control, at first, for a teacher who has himself been manipulated by negative correctional comment and has been accustomed to use this laborious and unrewarding system to break the syndrome of pointing out bad things. For awhile, depending on the past experience and orientation of the teacher, he may, against his will and real desire, be drawn back by ingrained habit to old ways. He may even be struck by pangs of conscience which make him wonder how the student will learn if he does not make right what seems wrong with his work. But breaking old habits will be speeded when the teacher observes the quick and satisfying results of devoting his attention to searching and finding values in what students do. As the teacher becomes attuned to this pleasant and natural activity, he will be rewarded by resulting improvement in student work and will be positively reinforced for using positive reinforcement.

Verbal feedback from the teacher should be rigorously chosen and carefully stated to point out exactly the behavior which the teacher wants repeated. Selecting particular behavior helpful to student learning and stating it precisely is an activity making strong intellectual demands on teacher ability to analyze. The student must be carefully watched to see what kind of statement produces best results. But the teacher can quickly accumulate a repertoire of positive rhetorical ploys, asking questions in positive ways as well as making descriptive, as opposed to judgmental comments. Often such descriptions will refer to the teacher's reaction or to reactions the teacher has observed in other class members to language behavior on the part of the student. Such rhetoric refers exactly to what has been said and done. And it is directed to something the student can repeat and improve by giving it greater attention at the same time as he feels good about what he has already done.

In the rhetorical ploy of gently suggested alternatives, the humanistic teacher may pay some attention to items that need to be improved in language behavior. He may enquire, "Would this valuable detail be more effective in some other spot?" "How would you advise another person using this activity to handle . . . ?" "What did you feel was your most effective point here?" "When I read this, I found myself wondering . . . " "Are there other ways this character in your improvisation could show his strong feelings?" The teacher may point out how he may have misunderstood some of the language that the student used. If the teacher can get the student to take the initiative in enlisting teacher aid to solve his language problems, it will be easier to point out alternatives, since the student who seeks aid is aware of his need for help. Seeking such help is easy for a student who knows he will feel good while he is being helped because everything he does that is good will be noticed.

This kind of evaluation builds bridges between present and future learnings, as new objectives emerge from needs discovered within the framework of an activity. The student sees where he was and traces the road he has covered. He sees where he is and decides whether that is where he wants to be. He looks at places in his use of language where growth can come and feels readiness for further experience. He assesses processes that must be extended to get him where he wants to go and makes plans for further learning as he adopts new goals.

When a student has a special need to learn an insight or practice, the teacher can make him an activity card designed for his special need. Always the activity teacher turns away from didactic telling to constructing learning experience which involves the student and provides him with properly designed insight or practice. As a teacher gains experience with many different kinds of student learning needs, he develops a flexible and responsive accumulation of cards to meet various needs. And he will develop his instinct to provide experience rather than tell students what they need to know. He will find his faith increasing that the bridge between what the student knows and what he needs to know can be best constructed out of that student's own experiences.

Because a teacher needs supportive behavior from the students just as they need his, he should teach students to reward him. Some students are as much in the habit of complaining and finding fault with teachers as teachers are with them. They need to develop new habits, too. A teacher who is rewarded by student approval should show his pleasure, telling the student who has rewarded and reinforced him, "When you . . . , it makes me feel . . . " Other rewards that students give teachers in their behavior are to show that they like the activities, to make changes in activity cards or invent new ones, to show their pleasure in working with each other or to see extra opportunities to work with activities. And, although every teacher needs to examine constantly what he has done in his teaching, whether he has done any counterproductive things, he especially needs to reward himself by thinking about his successes more than his failures.

Activities

BEING REINFORCED: AT THE RECEIVING END

1 to 2 hours   *a group*

To be able to respond graciously to student reinforcement and to find ways to make the activity curriculum make you feel happy too, try this activity.

Form a group and discuss these questions: Is it easy to be good to someone who is good to you? Is it easy to be good to someone who is critical and disapproving of you? How can you as teachers find ways to help students show you that they like you and what you are doing so that you can do it even better? What are the ways that students show their good feelings about teachers? Role-play some situations in which teachers respond to student reinforcement.

When a student brings you a gift, what should you do? How can you show the student that you value him and his gift? Should you wear it or display it so that he can see you are proud of it? How should you respond to birthday cards, Christmas cards, and valentines? To love notes? To students who stay after school every night because they like it in your room? What is the best way of talking to students who want to carry your books and tidy your room? How do you reply when a student compliments your clothes or hair? When he tells you how much he enjoys your class? When he invites you to his birthday party? How do you respond to students who want to tell you their life stories? What do you say when a group of students call you on the telephone during the summer to tell you how much they miss you or visit your home? How can you stop students from making the same kinds of judgment between you and other teachers they have that you yourself don't want to make between them as individuals?

As you talk about these questions, you may think of some of your own. For your role-playing choose situations you found most interesting in discussion. Try several different situations, making certain that everyone has a chance to play a teacher part.

Talk to your log about your role-playing. Which situations are most difficult to handle? Why? Did your group members respond as graciously as possible in each situation? Did any of the situations seem embarrassing? If so, why? How could you deal with such feelings? Does your idea of how teachers ought to talk to students ever interfere with your responses? If so, what do you do about it?

Index